The King's Messenger

The King's Messenger

Prince Bandar bin Sultan and America's Tangled Relationship with Saudi Arabia

David B. Ottaway

Walker & Company
New York

Published by Walker Publishing Company, Inc., New York

All papers used by Walker & Company are natural, recyclable products made
from wood grown in well-managed forests. The manufacturing processes conform to the
environmental regulations of the country of origin.

LIBRARY OF CONGRESS CATALOGING-IN-PUBLICATION DATA

Ottaway, David.
The king's messenger : Prince Bandar bin Sultan and America's tangled relationship with
Saudi Arabia / David B. Ottaway.—1st U.S. ed.
p. cm
Includes bibliographical references.
ISBN-13: 978-0-8027-1690-3 (hardcover)
ISBN-10: 0-8027-1690-3 (hardcover)
1. Bin Sultan, Bandar, Prince.   2. Ambassadors—Saudi Arabia—Biography.   3. Saudi
Arabia—Foreign relations—United States.   4. United States—Foreign relations—
Saudi Arabia.   I. Title
DS244.526.B55O88   2008
327.56073092—dc22
[B]
2008030319

Visit Walker & Company's Web site at www.walkerbooks.com

First U.S. edition 2008

1   3   5   7   9   10   8   6   4   2

Typeset by Westchester Book Group
Printed in the United States of America by Quebecor World Fairfield

To my wife, Marina

Contents

Author's Note

During thirty-five years at the *Washington Post*, I had occasion to write repeatedly about Saudi Arabia and its first royal ambassador to the United States, Prince Bandar bin Sultan. My initial article appeared in October 1972 while I was covering the annual conference of the Middle East Institute in Washington. At the time, few U.S. officials or Washington think tanks were paying much attention to the Saudis. The prevailing viewpoint was that they needed Uncle Sam's protection far more than the Americans needed Saudi oil. At the conference, Saudi oil minister Sheikh Ahmed Zaki Yamani made an intriguing offer to the Nixon administration: If the United States would assure Saudi oil duty-free access to the U.S. market, the kingdom would guarantee an uninterrupted flow of crude to meet the nation's needs. The proposal was rejected out of hand by both the Nixon White House and American oil companies. But for me the story triggered what was to become a career-long fascination with that distant kingdom so important to America because of its vast oil reserves and religious authority.

Over the following year, my *Post* colleague Ronald Koven and I wrote a series of articles about what we felt was a looming oil crisis, and we highlighted the implications of America's growing dependence on Arab, and particularly Saudi, oil. One of those implications came to light in the spring of 1973 when Yamani warned in an interview with us that unless Washington changed its policy toward Israel and the Palestinians, the Arabs were going to wield their oil weapon to force a change. Of course, no one in

Washington took him seriously. But when war broke out in October 1973 between Israel and its Arab neighbors, the Saudis led Arab producers in a boycott of the United States that caused enormous indignation and shock in the White House and Congress. Suddenly, Saudi Arabia was at the center of American attention, and suddenly the prevailing assumption changed: We needed them as much as they needed us.

In March 1978, the *Post*'s foreign editor, Peter Osnos, asked me to go with him on a visit to Riyadh, Saudi Arabia's capital, even though I was then covering Africa and based in Addis Ababa. At that time, Saudi visas for American reporters were a rarity, and the newspaper was seizing on a Saudi invitation to take a peek inside the hidden kingdom. Little did I realize at the time that our visas were part of a Saudi public relations campaign under way in Washington to convince Congress to sell sixty supermodern F-15 fighter jets to the Saudis over the vehement objections of the powerful pro-Israel lobby.

Three years later, in 1981, I became the *Post*'s bureau chief in Cairo, Egypt, from where I traveled to the kingdom repeatedly over the next four years. I wrote scores of stories about the four-hundred-billion-dollar construction boom occurring there as a result of the quadrupling of oil prices after the 1973 Arab boycott and about the social, political, and economic problems stemming from the making of a modern Saudi nation out of a medieval bedouin society. I had occasion to visit many obscure corners of the kingdom, but the trip that left the most lasting impression was to the largest plant ever built for the publication of the Koran in the Muslim world.

At the time of my visit, in 1984, the King Fahd Holy Koran Printing Complex was brand-new. It is located on the outskirts of the pilgrimage city Medina, which non-Muslims are strictly banned from entering. But my host, the late prime minister of Lebanon, Rafik Hariri, had decided to run the risk of official Saudi religious wrath anyway. His company, Oger Saudi, had built the plant. Hariri wanted me to get a sense of his accomplishments as well as the new Saudi ambition to spread its religious influence around the world. So he smuggled me into Medina on his private jet and took me in his limousine across the city, after ordering me to lie down on the backseat to avoid being seen.

As I learned during the visit, the kingdom's Wahhabi religious leaders were planning to take control of the Koran's translation into multiple languages as well as the accompanying commentary on its verses. They also planned to hand out free copies to the two million Muslims who come from around the world each year to fulfill their religious duty to visit Mecca at least once in a lifetime. I still remember being awestruck as we wandered through the sprawling ground floor of the plant, which was filled with hundreds of printing machines that would shortly begin churning out tens of millions of copies a year. Later, I realized that I had been given the rare opportunity for a non-Muslim to witness one source of the kingdom's enormous "soft power," its ability as custodian of Islam's most holy sites, in Mecca and Medina, to spread its puritanical brand of Islam to the four corners of the earth.

Starting in 1985, I was stationed in Washington for five years working as the newspaper's national security correspondent. In that role, I occasionally accompanied Secretary of State George Shultz on his visits to the Middle East and also reported on some of the secret machinations of Prince Bandar. The prince was regularly conducting clandestine missions for President Ronald Reagan and Central Intelligence Agency director William Casey in their crusade to bring down the Soviet "evil empire." As it turned out, Bandar was at the same time negotiating behind their backs with communist China—with which Saudi Arabia had never had diplomatic relations—for the supply of intermediate-range missiles built to carry nuclear warheads. When their arrival in the kingdom was finally discovered in early 1988, Israel and Saudi Arabia went to the brink of war before Washington intervened to diffuse the crisis. But Bandar's deceit shocked the Reagan administration and cast him in a new light as a Machiavellian schemer ready to dupe his American friends if called upon to do so by king and kingdom.

Over the years, I kept running into Bandar both in Washington and in Saudi Arabia. The more I came to know the prince and those dealing with him, the more I realized he was a highly controversial figure. On the one hand, he was widely hailed as the most effective ambassador—Arab or otherwise—Washington had seen in a long time. On the other hand, many U.S. officials found him devious and highly manipulative. One senior Clinton administration official found that Bandar's accounts of what Arab leaders had allegedly told him had to be checked and double-checked for accuracy. At the *Post*, where he delivered many backgrounders, reporters and editors became increasingly wary of his often potentially highly newsworthy leaks and versions of events. We found confirmation was sometimes hard to come by or altogether impossible. On several occasions, we discovered he was not above presenting his own personal policies as those of the kingdom.

In 1996, I had occasion to write a long profile of the prince. He had by that time virtually disappeared from the Washington diplomatic scene, and his behavior was a mystery. Over a period of several months, I interviewed him at his homes in McLean, Virginia, and Aspen, Colorado, and at the Saudi embassy, where he was rarely to be seen. I found him exhausted mentally and emotionally, but also very talkative about his adventure-filled life of secret statecraft on behalf of either Saudi Arabia's King Fahd bin Abdulaziz or one or another American president. On more than one occasion, Bandar had served two masters at once.

After 9/11, former *Post* managing editor Robert G. Kaiser and I wrote a series of articles, published in early 2002, examining the past, present, and future of the beleaguered U.S.-Saudi "special relationship." Bandar invited us to spend a Ramadan night with him at his McLean residence, where he proceeded to talk almost uninterrupted for eight hours, unloading his feelings about the catastrophe that had befallen both countries.

It was a strange and unforgettable interview that went on into the early hours of the morning. He repeatedly bemoaned the failure of Americans to understand his secretive kingdom, or even to want to look at it for what it was. The American attitude reminded him, he said, of *Invisible Man*, Ralph Ellison's devastating account of white America's refusal to acknowledge the realities of black America.

"You don't see me not because I don't exist, but because you choose not to see me," Bandar said. "This closed society [Saudi Arabia], if it's open at all to anybody, it's to Americans. Yes, there is almost institutional blindness."

What was it Americans were failing to see? Presumably, in his mind it was the thick skein of economic and political ties woven between the two countries ever since the first American oil wildcatters had set foot in the kingdom in the early 1930s. Presumably, too, it was all the favors Saudi Arabia had done over the years for Democratic and Republican presidents alike. But after 9/11, Americans were intent on understanding why and how Saudi Arabia had become a breeding ground for Islamic extremists such as those who had blown up buildings inside the United States filled with thousands of innocent civilians. My own editors wanted to know what impact Wahhabism was having on the Muslim community inside America, particularly after the Federal Bureau of Investigation and local law enforcement officials began investigating Saudi-financed mosques, religious centers, and charities across the country.

This led me to probe how the Saudi government had organized itself to export its faith abroad. I went back to the kingdom in the spring of 2004 to talk to its religious leaders and scholars and examine the various institutions, agencies, and means at the government's disposal for exporting Wahhabi Islam around the world. The trip gave me a fuller appreciation of the kingdom's fundamental commitment to the goal of turning what had once been a marginal Islamic sect into the Muslim world's dominant school of religious thought. It also became clear to me that the kingdom's impressive soft power was likely to remain a potential source of trouble, even conflict, for the United States and the West for years to come.

I returned again in the spring of 2006, this time to focus on the Saudi government's struggle to contain the blowback from the Wahhabi extremism it had engendered at home and abroad. By then, the kingdom's security forces were engaging in pitched battles with Saudi al-Qaeda militants—at times even in the streets of the capital, Riyadh. The government had undertaken a systematic purge of mosques, firing several thousand imams and sending hundreds of others to theological reeducation schools. The battle had spread from the streets and mosques into cyberspace. There, government Wahhabi scholars and clerics were infiltrating *jihadi* Web sites and teenage chat rooms to argue on behalf of moderation. The government had also begun scrubbing schoolbooks of Wahhabi teachings that emphasized hatred of Jews and Christians and a general distrust of other Muslim sects. The official religious establishment that for decades had encouraged the spread of militant Wahhabism was now desperately trying to propagate another, more moderate interpretation of the puritanical sect and ostracizing all "deviants" from the new official line.

By the time of my last visit, in January 2008, the Saudi government seemed to have gained the upper hand in its five-year-long struggle to find and break up al-Qaeda cells before they could strike. Riyadh was more relaxed, and there was an air of confidence that had not prevailed before. King Abdullah bin Abdulaziz, Fahd's half brother and the successor to the throne, had just entertained President George W. Bush on his first trip to the kingdom, taking the American leader from whom he had become estranged to his desert Al Janadriyah Farm outside Riyadh for informal talks, just as Bush had invited him down to his private ranch in Crawford, Texas, on two occasions. The one senior Saudi official absent for the occasion was the person who had been the living embodiment of the U.S.-Saudi relationship for nearly three decades: Prince Bandar bin Sultan. Though he was the king's top national security adviser, Bandar had declined to attend for reasons that will become clear in the course of this book.

Prologue

ON THE NIGHT OF SEPTEMBER 10, 2001, less than twelve hours before terrorist attacks on New York and Washington were to change the course of American history, the happiest man in Washington was Saudi Arabia's ambassador extraordinaire, Prince Bandar bin Sultan. His trademark cigar in hand, he was relaxing in the warm waters of the indoor pool at his sprawling home in the northern Virginia city of McLean, overlooking the Potomac River, the tension oozing out of his exhausted body after the worst crisis in U.S.-Saudi relations of his career.[1]

Bandar had delivered a letter containing an ultimatum to President George W. Bush from Crown Prince Abdullah, de facto ruler of the world's largest oil exporter, threatening use of the powerful Saudi oil weapon in ways promising to roil the American stock market not seen since the 1973 and 1979 energy crises. He had watched with enormous relief as Bush and a lethargic White House had jumped into action, producing within forty-eight hours the promise of a major new U.S. initiative to settle the Israeli-Palestinian deadlock.

Just before Bandar went to bed, the anxious crown prince called to check on whether there had been any surprises that would delay Bush from going public with the groundbreaking announcement that he favored the creation of a Palestinian state and the launch of negotiations to make it happen. It had the makings of becoming the crowning achievement of Bandar's long career in Washington. After checking with the White House, Bandar called back to assure Abdullah that all was well: Either the president himself or Secretary of State Colin Powell would make the historic announcement within the next few days.

Bandar went to bed that night relishing the accomplishment of yet another secret mission on behalf of the House of Saud, the kingdom's ruling family, to avert a rupture in the half-century-old "special relationship" with its most important Western ally. For more than two decades, he had served as the human linchpin and guardian of that often stressful bond.

When he woke shortly before nine the next morning, Bandar turned on CNN as was his daily habit and saw smoke billowing from the upper floors of the North Tower of the World Trade Center. Watching in stunned silence as the announcer confirmed that a passenger jet had crashed into the building, he saw another airliner plow into the South Tower. It was 9:03:11, the precise moment in history when the special relationship came crashing down together with the Twin Towers—and Bandar's career in Washington.

The news all that morning just kept getting worse. Four Boeing airliners hijacked in Boston, Washington, and Newark and turned into suicide missiles with hundreds of passengers aboard; thousands dead as the Twin Towers collapsed; the Pentagon ripped apart; all civil aviation suspended and the U.S. government in full flight.

About ten the following night, Bandar got the first word that there was a strong possibility that as many as fifteen of the hijackers who had seized the four aircraft were Saudi nationals. The news hit him like a thunderbolt. He couldn't believe it. His first thought was that while the names might be Saudi, the passports were probably stolen or faked to implicate the kingdom and cause a rift with the United States. However, not only did fifteen of the nineteen hijackers turn out to be Saudis, but their leader, Osama bin Laden, was a Saudi, albeit one stripped of his citizenship, disowned by his family, and banished from the kingdom.

"I said to myself, if I got the ten who hated America in Saudi Arabia the most, who hated Saudi Arabia the most, and hated Islam the most, and put them into a room and awarded them one million dollars for ideas who can do more damage or worse damage to Islam or Saudi Arabia, they could not have done a better job than what those people did."[2]

In the coming months, the American media would turn on Saudi Arabia with a vengeance, castigating its leaders and blaming its puritanical form of Islam, known as Wahhabism, for inspiring those responsible for the attacks. Suddenly, the kingdom loomed as a security threat to the United States both at home and abroad, a startling new image for a country that had been America's staunch partner throughout the Cold War and key ally during the 1991 Gulf War. Overnight, this old friend had morphed in the public mind into a new enemy. Scores of hearings in Congress and studies by Washington think tanks were devoted to pondering this question: "Saudi Arabia—Friend or Foe?"

A lot more than public perceptions were about to change, however. The bedrock of the relationship was also about to split asunder. Starting in 1945, the United States and Saudi Arabia had forged a close alliance based on a very simple quid pro quo: Saudi oil to satiate the voracious thirst of the American market in return for U.S. protection of the House of Saud from all foreign foes. The world's number-one oil producer and its number-one consumer worked hand in hand to assure each other's respective vital need was met.

This oil-for-security formula worked relatively well for half a century considering that the two countries were truly an odd couple in terms of their political systems, dominant faiths, and social customs—one a secretive monarchy, Islamic theocracy, and Sunni monoculture and the other a religiously pluralistic society, wide-open democracy, and Babel of cultures. Holding the alliance together was a delicate diplomatic task for both sides, requiring the downplaying of differences, secrecy, and often outright duplicity. Still, during times when an oil shortage loomed or prices soared, the Saudis more often than not increased production, often at the direct behest of a U.S. president. And whenever Egypt, Iran, Yemen, or Iraq threatened the kingdom, the Americans dutifully sent aircraft and even troops at the king's request.

Starting in 1978, Bandar was at the center of this odd-couple relationship, and he stayed there for most of the next three decades. He made sure the oil-for-security formula worked to the satisfaction of both sides. He facilitated a growing U.S. military presence inside the kingdom against the wishes of powerful Wahhabi clerics and even part of the royal family, and he kept Saudi Arabia the number-one source of foreign crude for the American market, overriding the objections of Saudi oil ministers to do so. He made himself the indispensable middleman between the Saudi royal court and the White House, rendering personal and political services to five U.S. presidents to keep the special relationship going against increasingly long odds. He was at once the king's exclusive messenger and the White House's errand boy; he ran secret missions on behalf of some presidents and manipulated oil prices to help others stay in office.

Today, the underlying oil-for-security equation in the U.S.-Saudi relationship no longer holds, but American public hostility toward the Saudi kingdom since 9/11 is not the primary reason. Other harsh new realities have imposed themselves. Saudi Arabia can no longer alone meet America's oil needs or calm world markets, while the United States can no longer shield the House of Saud from its new militant Islamic enemies; worse yet, America has become a major source of the insecurity threatening the Saudi royal family. These painful truths have placed in jeopardy the U.S.-Saudi relationship, whose future is full of questions.

Historians looking for dates marking the turning points may well choose April 9, 2003, and May 21, 2004. On the former, invading U.S. forces reached Baghdad and brought Saddam Hussein's brutal reign to an abrupt end. On the latter, Saudi oil minister Ali al-Naimi announced that the kingdom would pump two million more barrels of crude to force spiraling world prices down and defend the benchmark ceiling price of the Organization of the Petroleum Exporting Countries (OPEC), then set at twenty-eight dollars a barrel.

The overthrow of Saddam's government was an earth-shattering event for the entire Middle East, but for Saudi Arabia it proved especially traumatic, for it fundamentally altered the nature of security threats to the House of Saud. Suddenly, the kingdom had to cope on its northern border with a civil war between rival Muslim Sunni and Shiite sects that was setting off shock waves reaching deep inside the kingdom and all across the Middle East. The Sunni-Shiite rivalry for religious and political supremacy was as old as Islam, and Saudi Arabia was ruled by Wahhabi Sunnis who looked upon the Shiites as heretics and infidels. The worst possible Saudi nightmare imaginable was coming true: Iraq fragmented into three separate Sunni, Shiite, and Kurdish entities and its central government largely under Shiite control thanks to Saudi Arabia's old protector, the United States. In addition, the shift in power from the Sunni minority that had ruled under Saddam to the Shiite majority had emboldened Shiite Iran to challenge Saudi Arabia's claim to leadership of the Sunni-dominated Arab world.

THE SAUDIS HAD always feared they would be left alone to pay the price of U.S. military interventions in their region. Iraq loomed as just as much of a quagmire for them as it was becoming for the Americans, a new Lebanon of proxy wars among eternally feuding sectarian groups sucking in neighboring states and foreign powers struggling for power or simply survival. Indeed, King Abdullah in late 2006 put Washington on notice that Saudi Arabia would not stand by idly and watch fellow Sunnis in Iraq slaughtered by the new Shiite-dominated government and its Shiite militia allies.[3]

The U.S. invasion and occupation of Iraq rendered Saudi Arabia more insecure for another reason. Iraq's Shiites harbored long-standing grievances against the kingdom's Wahhabis, whose warriors had tried to raid and destroy their shrines in An Najaf and Karbalā in the early twentieth century. Shiite extremists in Iraq might well decide to come south in aid of their religiously suppressed brethren in the kingdom, just as hundreds of militant Saudi Wahhabis were going north to help al-Qaeda fan the flames of sectarian violence and kill Shiites in Iraq. While Shiites comprise no more than 10 percent of the kingdom's population, they are concentrated in its Eastern Province, where the world's largest oil reservoirs happen to be located. Thus, they have long been regarded by the Saudi royal family as a potential fifth column for Iranian-inspired subversive activities inside the kingdom.

The U.S. occupation of Iraq set off another kind of struggle as well. Starting in mid-2003, Saudi Wahhabi fanatics under the banner of al-Qaeda launched a determined campaign to bring the House of Saud down through attacks on oil facilities, government buildings, and living compounds for American and other foreign workers. The Saudi government soon discovered that some of the terrorists were Saudis who had joined the jihad, or holy war, against American occupiers and heretical Shiites in Iraq and were now returning home to turn their attention inward. The al-Saud family thus faced challenges from both Sunni and Shiite extremists thanks to the American presence in Iraq. Not since the 1979 Islamic Revolution in Iran had the House of Saud seemed in such peril, and Saudis had not forgotten the inability, or unwillingness, of the United States to help save the shah of Iran.

MAY 21, 2004, on the other hand, heralded the end of the prevailing U.S. assumption that the kingdom alone could be the decisive factor in determining the supply and price of oil in the world. On that day, Saudi oil minister al-Naimi made clear that his government was ready to pump an additional

2 million barrels of oil a day for a total of 10.5 million to calm the market and lower prices after the cost of a single barrel crossed the $40 mark.[4] Formerly, such a pronouncement by the chairman of the world's "central oil bank" would have been enough to cause speculators to blink and the price at least to dip. After all, al-Naimi was to the world of energy what Federal Reserve chairman Alan Greenspan had been for seventeen years to the world of finance—an oracle whose softly spoken words sent markets up or down. But al-Naimi's words had the opposite effect of what he had intended. The price of oil on the U.S. market went up immediately by $1.79 a barrel and continued its upward spiral, finally reaching around $55 in late October just before the U.S. presidential election. Clearly, Saudi clout over the world oil market had been seriously blunted. There were simply too many other variables in the changing world oil picture beyond Saudi control.

Faced with these new realities, U.S. and Saudi leaders began scrambling after 9/11 to find substitutes for the old oil-for-security formula that had so successfully bound the two countries together for more than half a century. Both readily embraced the "war on terrorism" as a new common cause upon which to build a fresh alliance. Yet this new form of cooperation, while vital to both countries, was hardly a replacement for the oil-for-security keystone of their old alliance. Indeed, the Saudis began turning elsewhere for new oil markets, partners, and investments. They struck multibillion-dollar deals with Chinese, Russian, and European companies to develop their gas fields at the expense of their traditional American partners. Saudi oil exports to China surged, while those to the United States declined, and the kingdom lost its place as the number-one source of foreign oil for the American market.

The Saudis also turned elsewhere in search of military allies to shield the kingdom against potential enemies like Iran. They ordered the U.S. Air Force to stop using Prince Sultan Air Base and turned to Britain and Europe for the purchase of new warplanes. And they moved noticeably closer to Muslim Pakistan, a nuclear power in its own right with a proven track record of sending troops to the kingdom when called upon to do so. If Iran did become a nuclear power and threatened the kingdom, Pakistan could well become its principal defender rather than the United States. And if Iran supported Saudi proxies in an attempted takeover of the kingdom, Muslim Pakistani soldiers would be far more acceptable than Christian American ones, whose chief concern might well be securing Saudi oil fields rather than saving the House of Saud.

Just how oil, arms, and Allah have served either to bind or split asunder the U.S.-Saudi special relationship is the central theme of this book and Prince Bandar bin Sultan its central character. His remarkable career in Washington encompassed both the high points and the tribulations of that relationship over the past three decades as its "special" nature became more and more concentrated in Bandar's personal dealings with the White House. The ups and downs in his career there often mirrored those taking place in the overall relationship. Bandar became a kind of barometer of the state of U.S.-Saudi affairs. His standing at the White House soared steadily during the Cold War years, when he dealt with first President Jimmy Carter and then President Ronald Reagan. It reached its zenith during George H. W. Bush's time in office, thanks largely to the first Gulf War, which bound the two countries together on the battlefield in a strong common cause. Thereafter, the prince's status in the Oval Office began slipping. His relations with Bill Clinton were noticeably cool, even distant much of the time. But this was also true of the overall U.S.-Saudi relationship, which, in Bandar's own words, was drifting along on "autopilot." Finally, Bandar's standing at the White House bottomed out during the second Bush presidency, and so, too, did the entire U.S.-Saudi relationship, as we shall see. But first it is important to understand the origins of how oil, arms, and Allah became intertwined in a very tangled U.S.-Saudi relationship.

CHAPTER 1

Oil, Arms, and Allah

An anonymous tipster called a reporter working for United Press International in New York City on the night of February 16, 1956, with the news that eighteen M-41 light reconnaissance tanks were being loaded onto a freighter at a pier in Brooklyn.[1] Destination: Saudi Arabia. At that time, there was no requirement for the president to notify Congress about arms sales abroad, and the process normally took place in total secrecy. The tanks were, thus, the first major item of military significance to come under scrutiny in the American press.

The next day, the Democratic chairman of the Senate Foreign Relations Committee, Walter George, called for a congressional probe into what the Eisenhower administration was up to. George wanted to know why tanks were being shipped to an Arab country while the State Department had held up Israel's request to purchase $50 million worth of American arms. The Israeli embassy in Washington asked the same question. Minnesota's Democratic senator Hubert Humphrey demanded a "full scale investigation" of every shipment, "from tanks to wheat," going to a Middle Eastern country. Jewish protesters began picketing the Brooklyn pier. Dwight Eisenhower, on vacation in Thomasville, Georgia, abruptly ordered the suspension of the tank shipment. The outraged Saudi ambassador to Washington, Sheikh Abdullah al-Khayyal, then demanded the delivery of the tanks for which the kingdom had already paid—$135,000 per tank. "It is the hope and expectation of Saudi Arabia that the United States will soon find a way of carrying out its commitment in the common interest of both countries," he said. The press weighed in too. A *Christian Science Monitor* editorial under the title "No Arms to Saudi Arabia" called for a moratorium on all arms exports to countries bordering Palestine. The *Washington Post* called it "The Tank Fiasco" and said shipping the tanks would "have sapped the American moral position" in the administration's effort to calm tensions between Israel and its Arab neighbors. "How could we have justified our refusal to sell arms to Israel if we had sent them to one of her adversaries?" the newspaper asked.

Eisenhower's order to suspend the shipment lasted less than twenty-four hours. On the night of February 18, the State Department issued a one-thousand-word statement offering its justification for going ahead with the deal. The tanks were defensive and no threat to peace in the Middle East. Israel would get the $110,000 in spare parts for airplanes and military vehicles it was seeking, and the United States would give "most careful scrutiny" to the Israeli request for $50 million in jet fighters and other major weapons. The reasons behind the decision were spelled out in a secret State Department document a few days later: "If the shipment were canceled, it would unquestionably provoke the Saudi Arabians to the point where our future relations would be seriously jeopardized; they would probably proceed to buy arms from the Soviets; the negotiations for renewal of the Dhahran airbase would be difficult, if not impossible; and vital U.S. resources [oil] could be lost."[2] The "tank battle" of 1956 was a harbinger of things to come, the first in a long line of confrontations over arms sales to Saudi Arabia between both Republican and Democratic administrations and pro-Israeli supporters in Congress that would tear at the fabric of the U.S.-Saudi relationship over the next fifty years.

Indeed, the controversy surrounding the tanks exposed all the explosive ingredients in what has long been called the U.S.-Saudi "special relationship": Saudi demands for American arms and security guarantees and U.S. maneuvering for access to Saudi oil and land bases. Just who first coined the phrase "special relationship" regarding Saudi Arabia and when remains something of a mystery. Prior to World War II, American oilmen who discovered the vast wealth that lies beneath the Saudi desert sands always had such a relationship with the kingdom's rulers. But the term came into vogue much later and has come to be used by historians and officials from both countries.*

As notable as the relationship itself is the fact that the same issues have bedeviled it from the beginning. Declassified government documents from the post–World War II period depict a long, painful process of both sides searching for the proper distance, or closeness, these two very odd bedfellows wanted to maintain. When the Saudis sought security guarantees and a formal alliance, the United States remained standoffish; when the Americans sought permanent facilities and open access to air bases, Saudi Arabia sought to keep its distance. (This tension grew much worse after the first Gulf War, in 1991. The U.S. Air Force, which had been given the run of Saudi facilities during the campaign to oust Saddam Hussein's army from Kuwait, stayed on for over a decade, until its presence became a highly contentious issue.)

The first U.S. military mission to visit the kingdom dates back to December 1943, at the height of World War II, about ten months after President Franklin Roosevelt proclaimed that "the defense of Saudi Arabia is vital to the defense of the United States" and that the kingdom was therefore eligible for military assistance.[4] The mission was led by Major General Ralph Royce, then commander of U.S. forces in the Middle East based in Cairo, Egypt. The mission was a major event because King Abdulaziz al-Saud, founder of modern-day Saudi Arabia, rarely allowed foreign military personnel into the kingdom.[5] The king received his American visitors in the Red Sea port of Jeddah in proper royal splendor, marking the occasion with a banquet at which ten sheep were slaughtered and roasted and their eyeballs handed out as a delicacy. It was an austere affair with no alcohol served and no smoking permitted. But the austerity was offset by generous royal gifts—camel hair robes dotted with gold knobs and gold daggers for each of the eleven members of the American delegation and a gold- and gem-covered saber, plus a wristwatch with the king's name inscribed on the face, for Royce. The American gift to the king seemed highly utilitarian by comparison: a radio transmitter and an offer of a plane ride, which was politely refused.[6] It would have been King Abdulaziz's first.

---

* The term may go back to testimony given at a 1973 hearing before the Senate Foreign Relations Committee by James Akins, who was about to become U.S. ambassador to the kingdom. Akins said he was against any kind of formal alliance with Saudi Arabia but favored giving the Saudis "everything they want under a special relationship without actually formalizing ties."[3]

Nothing immediately came of the visit. But the outlines of an oil-for-arms grand bargain began to emerge early the following year. In February 1944, Secretary of the Interior Harold Ickes announced plans for the construction by American oil companies operating in the kingdom of a twelve-hundred-mile pipeline across Saudi Arabia to the Mediterranean coast.[7] Then on March 7, Royce returned on a second visit bearing gifts of another kind on his DC-3 aircraft: three thousand pounds of rifles, ammunition, helmets, and, incongruously, blowtorches.[8] Royce made the delivery the next day after locating the wandering monarch and two thousand of his companions in a desert oasis ninety miles north of the Saudi capital, Riyadh. The American general described his small planeload of arms as a token of bigger deliveries to come under the American wartime lend-lease program made possible by Roosevelt's certification of Saudi Arabia as "vital" to U.S. interests. Just why this might be true was spelled out on October 27, 1944, by Secretary of War Henry Stimson in a letter to Acting Secretary of State Edward Stettinius Jr.: "The most important military interest in Saudi Arabia is oil and closely following this in importance is the right to construct airfields, the use of air space and the right to make aerial surveys in connection therewith."[9]

King Abdulaziz's first wish list for U.S. military assistance was long and varied—a mission to train a standing army and air force; air transport for the king and other high Saudi officials; training for Saudi pilots in the United States; uniforms for eleven thousand men; six C-47 transport aircraft; four bombers; the construction of a munitions plant and roads in the kingdom; radio communications equipment; and the training of doctors for the Saudi army.[10] None of this was immediately forthcoming. In fact, nothing really happened to move the United States toward becoming the kingdom's major arms supplier for the next six years. Even the historic first encounter between an American president and a Saudi king, aboard an American warship in Egypt's Great Bitter Lake in early February 1945, did not produce much of substance. Roosevelt and Abdulaziz, one in a wheelchair and the other walking with a cane (Roosevelt gifted his backup wheelchair to the king), laid the basis for the later development of a partnership. But they did not announce any agreements and reportedly did not even talk much about arms or oil.

The main topic of conversation was growing international pressure for the creation of a Jewish state in Palestine, which the king vehemently opposed and Roosevelt was contemplating whether to support.[11] Still, Abdulaziz's pro American proclivity was already evident in his strong preference for working with American oil companies at the calculated expense of the British, whom he distrusted because of their dominating presence in the Persian Gulf Arab states flanking the kingdom. In 1933, he had granted Standard Oil of California (SOCAL), the predecessor of today's Chevron, the right to prospect for oil in the kingdom. By the time of his meeting with Roosevelt, SOCAL had struck oil outside Dhahran, on the Persian Gulf in the Eastern Province, raising hopes for an oil bonanza. The king seemed to have no objection to American wartime plans to build the world's longest pipeline across his kingdom at a cost of $150 million. Amid the first talk in Washington of dwindling domestic oil supplies, Secretary of the Navy William Knox told Congress in March 1944 that the war had made the U.S. government extremely anxious about oil. He pronounced what was to become America's postwar oil policy, namely "to provide for acquisitions of oil resources outside the limits of the United States for the safety and security of this country."[12]

The Saudi view of the burgeoning partnership was spelled out a few years later by the king in a private conversation with U.S. Assistant Secretary of State George McGhee. The meeting took place in May 1950, but the substance of their conversation only became known twenty-eight years later, when the State Department allowed it to be declassified.[13] It is a remarkable document. Abdulaziz unburdened himself of his most intimate fears for the safety of the House of Saud. However, his primary concern was not the one haunting Washington at the time, namely communist expansionism. Rather, he feared an imminent attack by the forces of the Hashemite royal families ruling in Jordan and Iraq; they had a grudge to settle after being driven out of the holy cities of Mecca and Medina by the al-Sauds in the 1920s. To deal with the Hashemite threat, the king wanted to enter a formal military alliance with the United States and obtain arms urgently on a grant basis. The British had already offered such an alliance, but he didn't trust them because they were the main backers of his Hashemite enemies. That was why, he told McGhee, he had given an exclusive oil concession in the kingdom to American companies and not allowed their British counterparts to share in the prize. And he had allowed the United States to build and use the air base at Dhahran "to show that Saudi Arabia's security should be of vital concern to both countries."[14]

In effect, Abdulaziz was outlining the oil-for-security pact the two countries would eventually put in place as the keystone of their relationship. But at that point, McGhee didn't know quite what to say to pacify the anxious Saudi monarch. What he did tell him could hardly have pleased. "An old style treaty of alliance" with Saudi Arabia was "contrary to our traditions," but the United States was "deeply concerned with the security of Saudi Arabia and will take immediate action at any time that the integrity and independence of Saudi Arabia is threatened." At the same time, the United States already had numerous commitments to defend other countries against the rising communist menace and didn't have unlimited resources. The best the United States could offer was a "treaty of friendship" that could include a program of military aid and financing for Saudi arms purchases if the kingdom agreed to a long-term arrangement granting the U.S. Air Force the use of the Dhahran airfield.[15]

The struggle over U.S. access to this airfield throughout the 1950s foreshadowed another to come in the 1990s when the Pentagon would press to keep troops and aircraft in the kingdom. Built by American engineers during World War II, Dhahran gained an aura of strategic importance after the war because of its proximity to the Soviet Union—"in B-29 bomber range of Russian oil targets," as one press report put it.[16] The U.S. Air Force also coveted the airfield as the eastern anchor of the postwar chain of bases it was building across the Middle East. For the Saudis, the airfield was the only bargaining chip other than oil they possessed in their dealings with Washington for military aid. Contentious negotiations begun shortly after McGhee's encounter with Abdulaziz at first produced only a six-month extension for U.S. use of the field. "That way it [Saudi Arabia] can ask for more concessions when the next renewal comes up," surmised an Associated Press dispatch from Cairo on February 25, 1951. Four months later, on June 18, the two governments finally signed a longer-term agreement. The United States could continue using the Dhahran air base "for maintenance, repair and other technical services of U.S. government aircraft" for another five years in return for the provision of arms and military training so that Saudi Arabia "may maintain its internal security and its legitimate self-defense or participate in the defense of the area of which it is a part."[17]

Once again, though, few arms were forthcoming. The Saudis had to wait yet another four years to use access to the Dhahran air base to pressure Washington to fulfill its promises. In February 1955, King Saud bin Abdulaziz, who had taken over upon Abdulaziz's death two years earlier, signed an agreement with President Eisenhower during a state visit to Washington, amid great professions of everlasting friendship and cooperation. The terms were the same: another five years for the U.S. Air Force in Dhahran and another promise of U.S. military assistance and arms for the Saudis.[18] This time, some arms at least did begin to flow—the eighteen tanks that caused such a media commotion in February 1956. The same month, the Pentagon confirmed that it had also secretly turned over nine B-26 bombers to the Saudis two years earlier. And the media made a second discovery on its own in May of that year of another shipment of munitions and spare parts, raising more cries of perfidy from Israel's supporters in Congress.[19] Two years later, the Pentagon quietly transferred to the Saudi Royal Air Force sixteen F-86F Sabre fighter bombers from excess supplies in U.S. inventories in the wake of the Korean War.[20] U.S. willingness to provide top-of-the-line aircraft was fast becoming the litmus test of the relationship for the Saudis.

Access to the Dhahran airfield was the key for the United States. In 1961, a year before the current five-year extension was to expire, King Saud stunned U.S. diplomats by refusing to renegotiate the agreement. The 1,332 American airmen stationed at Dhahran and the ten U.S. Air Force transport aircraft housed there would have to leave when the access agreement expired in April of the following year.[21] The message was broadcast on Radio Mecca on March 16, 1961, after three days of negotiations had failed even to produce an agreement on a joint statement. The king a month later explained that his decision had been motivated by U.S. assistance to "the so-called Israel," which he saw as an affront to Arabs and Muslims.[22] But an internal State Department memorandum blamed the king's "precipitous action" on what it called "the shaky internal position of his recently formed government." It revealed that Saud had sent a message explaining that he had to abrogate the agreement "to quiet his opponents both inside and outside Saudi Arabia."[23] Principal among them was a group of liberal royals known as the Free Princes, led by Talal bin Abdulaziz, who was demanding political reforms and, having fled to Cairo to seek Egyptian protection, the removal of the Americans from Dhahran. The State Department memorandum did acknowledge, however, that "the very presence of United States military personnel in Saudi Arabia, even though unarmed, had long been a target of Saudi and Arab nationalists."[24] In fact, Crown Prince Faisal bin Abdulaziz in December 1960 had informally suggested that the United States "voluntarily" give up its right of access to the air base.[25]*

The Saudi decision to kick the U.S. military out of Dhahran came just as the kingdom was mobilizing its Islamic credentials to create a countervailing political force to Gamal Abdel Nasser, Egypt's populist socialist leader, who was seeking to rally the Arab world behind his leadership under the mantras of Arab nationalism and pan-Arabism. The kingdom had become the main refuge for thousands of Egyptians belonging to the Muslim Brotherhood who were fleeing Nasser's bloody crackdown on this militant Islamic movement. The Saudis never allowed the brotherhood to operate inside the kingdom as an organized group. But they did permit its members, far better educated than their own citizens, to take up newly established jobs in the ministries of education, justice, and religious affairs. They were allowed, too, to organize and staff a new religious university in Medina, which would become the main center for indoctrinating foreigners in what would become an explosive mixture of Saudi Wahhabi fundamentalist doctrines and brotherhood political activism. These Muslim Brothers and their followers would become the foot soldiers of the Saudi kingdom's religious war against the Arab world's Nasserites, communists, and socialists.

The tension between Nasser and the House of Saud reached a new height in 1962 with the onset of civil war in Yemen on Saudi Arabia's western border. Egypt committed arms and soldiers to rebel Yemeni socialist republicans, while the Saudis backed the Yemeni royalists in their struggle to stay in power, sending arms and volunteers. In May of that year, Nasser established the Arab Socialist Union as Egypt's ruling party, with socialism as its doctrine. The same month, in response, the Saudis and their political allies from across the Islamic world established the Muslim World League at a meeting in Mecca, officially raising the banner of pan-Islamism against Nasser's "narrow [Arab] nationalism."[27] Among the twenty-one signers of the league's initial declaration was the Egyptian Said Ramadan, a key Muslim Brotherhood figure married to the daughter of the movement's founder, Hassan al-Banna. Ramadan was also secretary-general of the World Muslim Congress and director-general of the Islamic Center in Geneva. He was to play a seminal

---

* The Saudis would make the same suggestion in the same informal way when they wanted the U.S. Air Force to leave the kingdom in early 2002. This time the message came in an interview Prince Bandar gave to the *Washington Post*.[26]

role in spreading Muslim Brotherhood influence worldwide. Because of their superior educational qualifications, the Egyptians would again serve as the mainstay of the new organization's bureaucracy.

The other body created by the Saudis to promote Islam as a basis for countering Nasser and his secular ideology was the Organisation of the Islamic Conference (OIC). During the hajj in 1961, King Saud had first proposed forming some kind of Islamic league, an idea his successor, King Faisal, took up with a proposal four years later to create an Islamic Alliance. But it took Nasser's defeat in the 1967 Arab-Israeli War and an attempt by a crazed Australian Christian to set fire to al-Aqsa Mosque in Jerusalem before anything finally happened. The attack, in August 1969, finally galvanized the whole Muslim world into heeding Faisal's call for an Islamic summit. The event took place the following month in Morocco amid demands for the launch of a religious crusade to liberate the mosque from Israeli control. The only concrete result, however, was the creation of the OIC and a decision to establish its headquarters in Saudi Arabia. The binding glue was to be "Islamic solidarity."[28] But from the start, the OIC was a cacophony of monarchs, emirs, and elected heads of state and government with widely different agendas, a body much less susceptible to Saudi influence than the Muslim World League.

The scholar Dilip Hiro credits King Faisal with providing the inspiration and energy in the timorous House of Saud for turning Islam into a driving force of Saudi foreign policy.[29] Faisal, in many ways the founder of the modern Saudi state, became king in 1964 and ruled until his assassination by a mentally deranged nephew in 1975. He had also served for years as the kingdom's prime minister and foreign minister, had traveled widely, and was arguably the most worldly of the al-Saud kings, having represented Saudi Arabia at the founding of the United Nations in 1945. The entire Faisal branch of the al-Saud family was widely regarded as the most liberal and pro-Western. But Faisal was also dedicated to promoting Islam as a powerful policy tool, a kind of early version of what U.S. political scientists would later call a nation's "soft power." It was this power that would become such a serious problem for the United States after 9/11.

President Eisenhower also thought about mobilizing Saudi religious power. In his diaries in 1956, he mused over whether King Saud could be "built up" to become a spiritual leader of the Arab world to "disrupt the aggressive plans that Nasser is evidently developing."[30] While admitting he did not know him, Eisenhower noted that the kingdom harbored the two most sacred sites in the Muslim world and that the Saudis were considered to be "the most deeply religious of all Arab groups." The president did try to enlist Saud's support for the so-called Eisenhower Doctrine, enunciated in 1957 in a bid to contain the spread of communism in the Middle East. But as a choice to champion the doctrine, or even run House of Saud affairs, Saud proved a disaster and was forced to hand over much of his power to Crown Prince Faisal the following year.

Numerous scholars have asserted that Eisenhower did more than muse about using Islam to counter first Nasser and then the Soviet Union, in its efforts to penetrate the Arab world. They assert that the Central Intelligence Agency was used to funnel money and support to the Muslim Brotherhood.[31] Other scholars have documented the State Department's use of Radio Jeddah in Saudi Arabia as part of its Cold War public diplomacy.[32] On at least one occasion, Eisenhower met with twenty-four Muslim scholars and politicians from across the Middle East after they attended a conference on Islamic culture at Princeton University. Among them was the Islamic militant Said Ramadan.[33] The National Security Archive, a private research group located at George Washington University, established that the conference was organized and partly paid for by the State Department and the CIA.[34] What remains unclear about the meeting with Eisenhower is whether his previous visitor stayed on. The log indicates it was Allen Dulles, director of the CIA.*

By the mid-1960s, Washington's attitude toward arms sales to Saudi Arabia had changed 180 degrees, as it had become public knowledge that the Soviet Union was providing Egypt with massive amounts of arms—jet fighters, bombers, tanks, destroyers, and even submarines. Nasser was not only gearing up for a hot war with Israel. He had unfolded the banner of Arab nationalism and launched a cold war against the monarchs of the Middle East, Saudi Arabia in particular. The arms sales competition in which the United States found itself was not just with the Soviet Union, however. In 1965, the United States had to engage in a vicious bidding war with its

---

* In an effort to get to the historical truth about CIA involvement with the Muslim Brotherhood, I applied under the Freedom of Information Act in 2004 for all agency records from the 1960–63 period regarding its contacts with the group. Despite the passage of more than forty years, my request was denied because, I was told, the documents I sought would "relate to information concerning intelligence sources and methods."

closest European allies, Britain and France, to win what was then regarded as a massive arms deal, involving not just aircraft but also a missile and radar defense system covering the entire Saudi kingdom.[35] The price tag was put at anywhere from $250 million to more than $500 million, and the centerpiece of the competition was which cutting-edge aircraft—the American Lockheed supersonic F-104G, or possibly the slightly less sophisticated Northrop F-5 Freedom Fighter; the British Electric Lightning; or the French Mirage—would become Saudi Arabia's main fighter jet.

The 1965 bidding war, which lasted most of that year, was the first of many to come in which the three Western governments acted as super-salesmen on behalf of their national arms manufacturers. In May, Defense Secretary Robert McNamara wrote to Saudi defense minister Prince Sultan bin Abdulaziz, urging him to buy American and select the F-5 over the F-104G because it would be easier for Saudi pilots to master. Britain sent its under-secretary of state, John Stonehouse, to lobby the Saudis, and France dispatched a senior Defense Ministry official to press its cause.[36] The personal involvement by McNamara was seen at the time as marking an "important shift" in U.S. arms sales policy. According to a May 31 *Washington Post* editorial, the American government had previously carefully avoided becoming a major arms supplier to either Israel or its Arab neighbors. The new approach deliberately promoted the sale of arms to both sides to gain influence with their leaders while seeking to maintain a balance in the overall Arab-Israeli military equation. In the end, the Americans and the British, after tripping over each other, shared the prize: The Saudis bought both the British Lightning and the American F-5. But they also bought U.S. Hawks antiaircraft missiles and signed up for the Pentagon to begin building a radar defense system.

The Saudi thirst for the latest in modern aircraft became unquenchable as it became ever more affordable due to the country's rising oil wealth. The amalgam of American companies working in the kingdom known as Arabian American Oil Company, or Aramco, had struck the world's mother lode of oil reservoirs at Ghawar in the Eastern Province in 1956, and exports had begun to soar. Production nearly tripled to 1.3 million barrels a day between 1950 and 1960 and would grow to 3.8 million barrels a day by the end of the next decade.[37] Government income from royalties paid by Aramco doubled between 1963 and 1970 to $1.2 billion in current dollars.[38] The latter year would prove to be a turning point in United States oil production: the last year it would be self-sufficient in oil, leaving U.S. policy makers ever more sensitive to the strategic value of Saudi oil fields.

After obtaining the F-5 Freedom Fighter, the Saudis by early 1973 were pressing Washington to sell them top-of-the-line F-4 Phantom jets, which were by then the backbone of the Israeli air force.[39] At that point, no Arab country had been allowed to purchase the F-4, but the Saudis were determined to get twenty-four to thirty of them. Israel was just as determined to block the sale, arguing that the Phantom posed a direct threat because the aircraft had the range to strike at the Israeli heartland from Tabuk, in north-western Saudi Arabia. Furthermore, the F-4 had strong political symbolism for the Israelis, for it demonstrated a U.S. tilt toward the Jewish state and against their Arab enemies. If the United States also sold it to Saudi Arabia, the F-4 could no longer have that symbolism. Suddenly, whether the United States would sell its most sophisticated aircraft had become a litmus test of which side it was on in the Arab-Israeli conflict. The outbreak of war between Israel and its Arab neighbors in October of 1973 put an abrupt end to the debate. Egypt's success in breaking through Israeli lines along the Suez Canal, plus the Saudi-led Arab oil boycott of the United States, changed Washington's attitude radically.

The Saudi decision to wield its oil weapon against America struck Washington like a lightning bolt. Few in the U.S. government or Congress had thought the Saudis would dare turn against their protectors. Yet the kingdom, for all its respect for the American role in creating Saudi Arabia's oil fortunes, was caught up in the wave of nationalistic fervor sweeping third world oil producers. Libya, Iran, and Iraq were moving fast to nationalize their industries, and Saudi Arabia was feeling the pressure. During 1972, the Saudis had negotiated for a 25 percent share in Aramco, softening the blow to its American owners just slightly by calling it "participation" rather than "nationalization." The year of the oil boycott, they insisted on a controlling 60 percent interest on the way to a complete takeover.

Other factors were doubtlessly at play. One may have been King Faisal's sense of personal betrayal by President Richard Nixon, who had sent Faisal a message on October 14 pledging U.S. neutrality in the war. "Our policy at this time is not one-sided," Nixon assured Faisal. "The U.S. is neither pro-Israel, nor pro-Arab: It is pro-peace."[40] But when Israeli forces were in trouble, Nixon quickly rushed aircraft and tons of munitions to Israel and then pledged major long-term assistance. Nixon asked Congress to approve $2.2 billion in arms for Israel on October 19, and the next day the Saudi government announced a total oil boycott of the United States "in view of the increase in support for Israel."[41] By then, Egypt's army had been routed by the Israelis.

This was the second time Faisal had personally witnessed the United States go back on a pledge to a Saudi king. Franklin Roosevelt had promised King Abdulaziz during their 1945 meeting that the U.S. government would take no decision about partitioning Palestine to establish a Jewish state "without full consultation with both Arabs and Jews" and in any case "no action . . . which might prove hostile to the Arab people."[42] Roosevelt died a few months later, and Harry Truman never bothered to consult Faisal. On the other hand, Nawaf Obaid, a Saudi security specialist, attributed Faisal's decision in 1973 to a totally different cause—the powerful influence of the kingdom's Wahhabi religious establishment, which was pressing for a show of Saudi support for Egypt to stave off another Arab defeat. Obaid concluded that "the primary motivation was to preempt internal dissent and satisfy the growing frustration of the Ulema [the kingdom's powerful religious leaders]."[43]

Whatever the reasons, Faisal's decision brought about a full-scale change in the Saudi attitude toward the United States. The king had been of a totally different mind during the two years leading up to the war, seeking a formal military guarantee from the United States. He even sent a message to Nixon in the summer of 1972 proposing that "Saudi Arabia would guarantee to the United States a supply of oil necessary for its needs at a price it could pay for an absolute security guarantee."[44] In October of that year, while attending a Washington conference, the Saudi oil minister, Sheikh Ahmed Zaki Yamani, made public the Saudi offer of a guaranteed Saudi supply of oil, asking in return that the United States allow Saudi Arabia to invest in the U.S. oil industry.[45] The Nixon administration turned down all these Saudi proposals.*

In April of 1973, Yamani was back in Washington, this time with a radically different message: The kingdom was ready to use its newfound oil clout if U.S. policy toward Israel did not change.[46] Nobody was listening,

---

* Twenty-five years later, the Saudis would become major investors in the domestic U.S. energy sector without any guaranteed oil supply, except to the refineries and gas stations they had bought up in the United States.

which in retrospect is surprising. Washington by then had begun to realize the United States was becoming addicted to Arab oil. Domestic production had peaked in 1970, and foreign oil had become increasingly indispensable to satisfy the voracious appetite of gas-guzzling American car owners. Months before war broke out between Egypt and Israel in October 1973, the United States experienced its first real oil crisis. By June, two thousand gas stations had closed across the country because there was no gasoline available; one headline read, "U.S. Oil Nightmare: Worldwide Shortage."[47]

America had quickly become dependent on Arab, and particularly Saudi, oil and was already importing 27 percent of its total consumption. James Akins, the top energy specialist at the State Department, was warning Congress that the demand for crude oil was such that each year the country was consuming an extra one million barrels a day. Officially, imports from the Arab world and Iran in 1972 were just 15 percent of the total. But the U.S. government had deliberately downplayed the percentage by not including Middle Eastern crude shipped to the Caribbean for refining and then labeled as Latin American oil imports. "When we're talking about our oil needs, we're talking about one country—Saudi Arabia," Representative John Culver, the Democratic chairman of the House Foreign Economic Policy Subcommittee, observed, to which the *Washington Post* added, "The implications of this stark fact are only now beginning to be taken into account by top U.S. officials."[48]

CHAPTER 2

Making of the Messenger

IN APRIL 1978, PRINCE BANDAR, then a twenty-nine-year-old pilot focused on becoming a top commander in the Saudi Royal Air Force, was on his way home from a visit to California and stopped overnight in Washington. He checked in to the fashionable downtown Madison Hotel, a favorite, high-priced haunt for visiting Saudis and a five-minute walk from the White House. There, he ran into his brother-in-law, Prince Turki al-Faisal, as he was crossing the hotel lobby on the way to his room.[1]

After explaining that he had been on an air force mission in California and was homeward bound, Bandar remembered, Turki said to him, "You know, you came to me from heaven. I need you."

Turki was leading the Saudi lobbying effort in Washington on the sale of sixty F-15 jet fighters to the kingdom, and he said he wanted to ask Bandar some questions about the issue. He took Bandar upstairs to a room filled with worried American advisers and public relations experts who began plying him with questions about the F-15 Eagle. Bandar knew the Saudis wanted the top-of-the-line jet fighters badly, but he had no idea about the controversy in Washington surrounding their sale to the Saudis. Why did Saudi Arabia need this particular aircraft? Where did it plan to base them? What did the Saudis plan to do with them? Turki, head of the General Intelligence Directorate but with no expertise in military affairs, had been unable to answer these questions. But Bandar, who was by then an F-5 squadron commander, could easily respond.

Saudi Arabia was a vast, oil-rich country and needed the F-15s to defend its resources and religious sites, he told the American advisers. The jets would be stationed in Dhahran, on the eastern gulf coast, to protect the oil fields; in Taif, on the west coast, to cover the holy sites in Mecca and Medina; and in Khamīs Mushayt, in the south, to deal with the threat from Marxist South Yemen. The prince had quickly figured out how to dodge the hot political question of whether the F-15 would constitute a threat to Israel. He had avoided discussing whether the jets would be stationed at Tabuk, the only air base within range of Israeli targets, a commitment that could have been seen as an infringement of Saudi sovereignty.

Bandar so impressed Turki and the American advisers that he was asked to stay on for a few days. The next day, Turki took Bandar to meet two key members of the Senate Armed Services Committee—Democratic senator John Glenn and Republican senator Barry Goldwater, both former pilots and favorable to the sale. Then it was on to two staunch opponents, Democratic senator Frank Church and Republican senator Jacob Javits. After two days of traipsing from one Senate office to another answering mostly hostile questions, Bandar had had enough. He found lobbying "boring work," and he wanted to go home. His wife, Haifa, was waiting for him in Paris.[2]

But Turki had other plans for the pilot prince.

He had called Crown Prince Fahd and asked that Bandar stay on. Fahd had agreed, and Turki passed on the royal order. But Bandar didn't believe him, or didn't want to, anyway. "I said, 'No, thank you. I've stayed two days just to help you as a friend and colleague.'"[3] So Bandar continued on to Paris to pick up his wife, staying overnight there. As he was headed for the airport the next morning, he received a direct phone call from the crown prince himself. Bandar thought at first there was some mistake, since he had never known Fahd to call a jet fighter pilot directly like that, particularly one traveling outside the country. Fahd ordered Bandar to go back to Washington, where he found orders were indeed awaiting him: Help organize the lobby campaign to win the F-15 vote and "report to the White House."[4]

Bandar had been to the White House only once before—as a tourist while training at Maxwell Air Force Base in Alabama in 1973. "I went to the White House, and Hamilton Jordan [Carter's future chief of staff] took me in to see President Carter," he said. "Suddenly, there I was sitting in the chief of staff's office, and they take me to the Oval Office. I left really in a daze."[5] Carter asked him to work closely with Jordan, and so began what would become a legendary diplomatic career.

NOTHING IN BANDAR's childhood or upbringing suggested he was destined to become a super-envoy in the service of king and kingdom. His memories of growing up were hardly pleasant. They centered mostly on his search for a place in the royal family and reflected a profound sense of alienation and loneliness.[6] His birth on March 2, 1949, near Taif, a mountain resort village, was the result of a fleeting liaison between one of the most powerful Saudis in contemporary times, Prince Sultan bin Abdulaziz, and a black-skinned, sixteen-year-old household servant, Khizaran, of Yemeni descent. He was not recognized officially by his father in his early youth. His royal family protector turned out to be his grandmother Princess Hussa, King Abdulaziz's favorite wife, who took him in and filled his searching young mind with Saudi family lore. She also interceded to convince Sultan to recognize him.

Bandar's early difficulty in bonding with his father is widely thought to have had a lasting impact on his psyche and to explain his prodigious drive to prove himself throughout his career, first as a fighter pilot and then as a diplomat. He readily admitted to suffering from the stigma of being a bastard child and living apart from the brood of thirty-two half brothers and sisters belonging to Sultan's official wives. It made him feel "a bit aloofish" because, he said, "you don't have anybody to fool around with on a daily basis."[7] He also wished he could live with his father, and he remembered fondly his mother's efforts to make him "a boy instead of being a mother's boy" by taking every occasion to get him included on hunting trips with Sultan or at his court just listening to him talk with others.

Bandar spent most of his preteen years in Riyadh before the oil boom and before that desert capital, almost hermetically sealed off from foreigners, had any modern buildings, sprawling marble palaces, or even macadam roads. He remembered making his own toys and playing barefoot in the city's dirt streets. "We didn't have electricity in every room in the house I grew up in."[8] He took no trips abroad for summer vacations, though he was once sent to work on a farm in England, while his half brothers enjoyed the French Riviera. His first encounter with television came during a visit to an American oil company compound in Dhahran.[9] Recounting his early child-hood, Bandar clearly relished its fairy-tale quality; he once likened himself to a "peasant prince," the Saudi commoner who had to struggle and grovel before finding a place in the House of Saud.

To the extent that Bandar thought about the larger world before going off at age seventeen for pilot training in England, it was about the struggle for national liberation under way in Algeria and the plight of the Pales-tinians. Both were pan-Arab causes that served as national ones for many Saudis, too. His earliest political memories involved weekly visits to the offices of the Algerian and Palestinian nationalist movements in Riyadh to make collective school donations.[10] But young Bandar could not under-stand why all Arabs were expected to show solidarity for these noble causes while at the same time they were so bitterly divided between sup-porters and opponents of Egypt's fiery leader, Nasser, over what consti-tuted politically correct pan-Arabism. Before leaving for England in 1966, Bandar, like many young Saudis, secretly admired Nasser because he be-lieved Egyptian propaganda that Nasser had single-handedly forced France, Britain, and Israel to withdraw their forces from the Suez Canal in 1956. He had no idea of President Eisenhower's pivotal role in their deci-sion to retreat.

Bandar ascribed his decision to become a fighter pilot partly to his early exposure to the stream of Saudi military officers who began visiting his fa-ther's home after Sultan became defense minister in 1963.[11] In the civil war that had broken out in neighboring Yemen the year before, the kingdom was backing the royalists against upstart republicans supported by Nasser. A wave of patriotism swept the royal family, and Bandar, then thirteen years old, was carried away, too. He also desperately wanted to prove his worth to himself and his father. He concluded that the only way he could do so was to become a fighter pilot, the most prestigious career for anyone in the royal family. "When you're flying an airplane, it doesn't matter who you are. An airplane doesn't know if you're Prince Bandar or not. Either you know what you're doing or you don't. If you know, you live; if you don't, you kill your-self. I was not wise enough and smart enough to think about the risk."[12] Ban-dar felt that success would show other Saudis that he had real talent and guts of his own, and that he was not dependent solely on being the defense minister's son. Of eight princes in his peer group who went into the military in the mid-1960s, Bandar was the only one who succeeded in obtaining his wings.*

Bandar's political awakening came shortly after he arrived at the British Royal Air Force College at Cranwell, England's elite pilot-training academy.[13] The occasion was the third Arab-Israeli War, which broke out on June 5, 1967, and exposed him to the wide gap between Arab rhetoric and battlefield reality. The next day, he and other Saudis there tuned in to the Voice of Cairo and were ecstatic to hear that the Arabs were winning and had already shot down three hundred Israeli aircraft. Bandar ran around the halls of the college boasting to the English cadets and teachers that "one more time the Arabs will show you." At that point, he still believed the Arabs had scored a major victory in 1956. That night, he watched the news on the BBC. "I got the shock of my life. I can't believe it. I saw things I didn't know. I didn't see. The Israeli army took over the Sinai, all of it!"[14] It also took over East Jerusalem, the West Bank, and the Golan Heights in just the six days the war lasted. Bandar locked himself in his room for two days, becoming more and more depressed at the news, which finally included Nasser's offer to resign.

Bandar graduated from Cranwell in 1969 and the following year began a series of training courses in the United States to become lead pilot for the U.S.-built F-5 Freedom Fighter aircraft, the first of which began arriving in Saudi Arabia in 1971, to become the Royal Air Force's main multipurpose jet fighter for the next decade. Bandar has never forgotten his first day in America as he made his way to Lackland Air Force Base, outside San Antonio, Texas. While changing planes at the airport in Dallas, he encountered a rowdy group of football players belonging to the Dallas Cowboys team. They were attracting a lot of attention as they passed through the terminal, and what caught the prince's eye in particular were their "magnificent" cheerleaders.[15] From that time onward, Bandar was an avid Dallas Cowboys fan, a devotion that remained unshaken even after he took up residence in Washington, hometown of the Redskins, the Texas team's main opponent in the National Football League.

---

* His half brother Khaled left the same year he did for England to attend Sandhurst Military Academy and become an army officer. Khaled would rise to become cocommander of the coalition forces with U.S. General H. Norman Schwarzkopf during the 1991 Gulf War and then assistant defense minister to his father.

For the next seven years, Bandar concentrated mind and energy on making himself the best F-5 fighter pilot in the Saudi Royal Air Force. He attended officer school at Maxwell Air Force Base, in Montgomery, Alabama, and later took courses to become a pilot instructor at Randolph Air Force Base, in Universal City, Texas, and Williams Air Force Base, outside Phoenix, Arizona. He became not only a squadron commander and a trainer of other pilots but the kingdom's chief acrobatics flyer at air shows for the royal family and Saudi public. His skill as a stunt pilot gave him the greatest joy because, as he noted, "it really appealed to [his] ego and self-satisfaction" to know that he could fly a hundred feet above the ground and roll the aircraft 360 degrees without killing himself.[16] He felt his ability to execute such a daring maneuver provided proof of his personal accomplishments and made it clear that he was not relying on his status as son of the defense minister to get ahead.

The young prince's love for risk taking, however, eventually put an end to his flying career—at least as a fighter pilot. In 1977, the year before he first became entangled in Washington politics, he crash-landed his disabled F-5 during an air show in Abha, the capital of Asir Province, in southwestern Saudi Arabia. The jet's landing gear failed to come down, and he probably should have ejected from the aircraft. Instead, Bandar executed an emergency landing, hitting the runway hard and seriously injuring his back. The injury was destined to become a lifelong problem requiring repeated operations. At the time, Bandar refused to allow the accident to deter him from pursuing his air force career and kept his sights on going back to the United States for ever more advanced officer training. Crown Prince Fahd and President Carter had their own designs on him, however.

EVER SINCE COMING into office in January 1977, the Carter administration had focused on three issues—a national energy policy to cope with escalating gasoline prices and growing dependence on foreign oil; the launch of a Middle East peace process; and the sale of billions of dollars in arms to Middle Eastern countries, particularly Iran and Saudi Arabia. Washington policy makers generally felt that Saudi Arabia had the United States over the proverbial oil barrel. State Department secret documents from this period certainly reflect this assumption. "The Saudi role in oil prices and supply is crucial in both the short and long term," said one briefing paper prepared for the incoming Carter administration. "It alone has the capacity to ensure that sufficient oil supply is available to meet essential world demand in the 1980s."[17] The Saudis were already producing more than nine million barrels a day and had plans to expand their capacity to twelve million. Israel's supporters in Congress were convinced Carter was ready to make deals at the Jewish state's expense to solve his energy problems.

Arms sales to the Middle East were just as problematic. Legislation passed in 1974 gave Congress for the first time a veto power and obliged the president to inform Congress of pending sales of $25 million or more thirty days in advance. Carter had first fought with Congress over the sale of seven Airborne Warning and Control System (AWACS) aircraft to Iran and was facing a similar battle over his plan to provide Saudi Arabia with the F-15 Eagle fighter jet. At that point, the United States had made only one major aircraft sale to the kingdom—the F-5 Freedom Fighter. But as oil prices and Saudi earnings began spiraling upward in the wake of the 1973 Arab oil boycott, so, too, did the Saudi appetite for American arms, increase—from $300,000 to $2.2 billion in just one year.[18] Then, between 1974 and 1978, the Saudis signed up for $16 billion more, plus nearly another $10 billion in military construction projects.[19] The kingdom had become a huge market for U.S. arms manufacturers and contractors. However, Congress was becoming increasingly critical of the U.S.-fueled arms race between both Israel and its Arab neighbors and Iran and Saudi Arabia. Every country in the Middle East wanted the latest model aircraft, with the most sophisticated avionics, bombs, and missiles in the American arsenal. The AWACS sale to Iran had proved particularly controversial. While it was finally approved, and though the planes were never delivered because the shah was overthrown in 1979, Congress as a whole questioned the justification of each and every aircraft, missile, and bomb.[20]

Israel's supporters, led by the powerful American Israel Public Affairs Committee (AIPAC), were ramping up to kill, or emasculate, any sale of advanced aircraft to hostile Arab countries. AIPAC literature termed the F-15 Eagle "the most advanced air-superiority fighter in the world" and claimed it would enable Saudi Arabia to "strike deep into Israel."[21] Carter, however, had inherited secret pledges made in 1976 by the Ford administration to sell Saudi Arabia the F-15s as a replacement for its aging British Lightning interceptors. The president had reaffirmed this pledge to Crown Prince Fahd during his visit to Washington in May 1977, but then dragged his feet. Not until February 1978 did he notify Congress, at first informally, that his administration intended to sell sixty of the aircraft to Saudi Arabia, balanced by the sale of seventy-five F-16s to Israel and fifty F-5Es to Egypt, all in one package deal. He then waited until April 28 to formally notify Congress, thereby setting the clock ticking on the thirty-day window it had to veto the sale. Such was the tricky political landscape Bandar entered when he was ordered by Fahd to return to Washington.

Bandar proved a quick study of the rough-and-tumble politics there, thanks to a set of excellent American tutors, in particular Frederick Dutton, who had served as President John Kennedy's special assistant for intergovernmental affairs and assistant secretary of state for congressional affairs; John West, a former South Carolina governor and Carter's ambassador to Riyadh; and David Long, a State Department Middle East specialist and professor of international affairs. Dutton was a Washington political pro who had worked on five Democratic presidential campaigns. He was so close to the Kennedy family that he rode in the ambulance carrying Robert Kennedy to the hospital after he was fatally shot at the Ambassador Hotel in Los Angeles in 1968. Kennedy's death put an end to Dutton's aspiration of working at the White House, and through his connections with Mobil Oil, he began working first for the Saudi Oil Ministry and then for the Foreign Ministry. While Dutton served as a political adviser, his wife, Nancy, began doing legal work for the Saudi Foreign Ministry in Washington.*

Bandar first met Dutton at the Madison Hotel during his stopover in April 1978, and Dutton taught him Washington politics, especially how to deal with the Israeli lobby. Bandar was fascinated by AIPAC and its workings. He wanted to adopt its tactics in dealing with Congress, inverting its goals to create a countervailing Arab lobby. Carter's staff had early on conducted a detailed study of the Jewish lobby that carefully noted that AIPAC could count on sixty-five to seventy-five votes in the Senate whenever it needed them. The study proposed a strategy of dealing with this formidable challenge largely through making personal contact with as many of these senators as possible.[22] Dutton also encouraged Bandar to make as many overtures to Congress as possible, but believed strongly that the White House and the

---

* The Dutton team became part of Bandar's inner circle, Frederick earning the sobriquet Fred of Arabia in the Washington press corps. He remained Bandar's chief political adviser for twenty-seven years, until his death at the age of eighty-two in June 2005. Nancy was still working as the Saudi embassy's legal adviser in late 2007.

president himself had to take the lead in pressing for Saudi arms sales in Congress and making it a matter of U.S. strategic national interest.

While the Duttons were busy promoting Bandar's career in Washington, John West was playing the same role for the young prince at the royal court. West was a Southern governor like Carter and an early supporter of his campaign for the presidency. The two were close friends, and West sent Carter handwritten, insightful letters once a month during the four years he served as the American ambassador to the kingdom, recounting in these dispatches and a separate daily diary his dealings with the royal family. West had regular access to Crown Prince Fahd and other senior Saudi leaders and used it frequently to make the royal family aware of Bandar's exploits in Washington and to urge that the young prince be given more and more responsibility for representing Saudi interests.

West took credit for convincing Fahd and Defense Minister Sultan to order Bandar back to Washington to lobby for the F-15 sale, telling them that the prince "was the best thing that had happened to the F-15 fight" and that he had to stay.[23] West himself returned to Washington to help Carter lobby and thus saw Bandar in action firsthand during the final chaotic weeks leading up to the F-15 vote. After Congress approved the sale on May 15, West wrote to Fahd heaping kudos on Bandar for his "boundless energy" and "utter politeness and courtesy" in dealing with members of Congress. "Prince Bandar evinced such enviable maturity as to rank him among prominent international statesmen and diplomats," he told the crown prince.[24] He urged Fahd to award Bandar "a Certificate of Superior Merit." And he asked Jordan to arrange for Carter to thank Bandar personally for his efforts. Earlier in April, Jordan had tried to do just that, but Bandar had refused out of concern that he would further alienate Saudi ambassador Ali Alireza, whom he had already miffed by seizing the initiative in the Saudi lobbying campaign.[25]

Bandar remembered his first engagement with American politics as a struggle to convert his skills as a pilot—"counting my fighters, bombers, and air cover"—into new political ones that would help him navigate successfully in Washington. "If Dutton said AIPAC was the main danger, I said, 'OK. Now I must get some jamming system to neutralize AIPAC so they don't shoot down my airplane.' "[26] He learned to deal with aggressive reporters and discovered how to engage people he presumed would be hostile to him, like Jewish senators. He discovered that the White House, the State Department, and the Pentagon were competing power centers with conflicting views, each hiding information from the other.[27] He discovered Democratic senators and House members didn't necessarily support a Democratic president. He was appalled to see congressional committees openly discuss what in Saudi Arabia would be regarded as top secret information, such as what avionics and missiles the F-15 would carry. "I was taken aback by the process. To me, it was too strange." But he also became "fascinated by the organized confusion of Washington."[28] Particularly fascinating was that a U.S. president would use a foreigner like himself to lobby the American Congress.

Bandar's description of his exploits in Washington needs to be treated with some caution. He is a born storyteller, but one prone to easy hyperbole and self-aggrandizement. Often there is no way to confirm his account of events because other participants have died or will not comment. At other times, available documents do not substantiate his version, or he contradicts himself in the repeated telling of his tales. All of the characteristics for which he became known—such as a willingness to massage the truth to suit his personal glory and a penchant for manipulating people and engaging in freelance diplomacy—emerged at the start of his involvement in American affairs. But so did his desire to serve Saudi kings and American presidents. Long before he was dubbed Bandar Bush because of his almost filial relationship with President George H. W. Bush, the young Saudi prince made himself indispensable to President Carter and learned to parlay this into favor with his king and crown prince.

The battle over the F-15 sale was the first demonstration of the ingenuity, tenacity, and daring that Bandar naturally possessed. Dutton had explained to him how all American foreign policy was rooted in domestic constituencies. But Saudi Arabia didn't have anything in America comparable to the Jewish community to muster support for the Saudi cause. So Bandar decided to create a constituency for the F-15 sale. He did this by contacting McDonnell Douglas, the F-15 manufacturer, and all other contractors, subcontractors, and labor unions that had a stake in the vote. He even mobilized union members' families, "their cousins and the cousins of their cousins," to flood Congress with telegrams and telephone calls in support of the sale.[29] At the same time, he became the White House's "answer man" for every senator, influence peddler, and national newspaper and TV station asking questions about why Saudi Arabia needed the aircraft.

Three experiences in particular remained fixed in Bandar's mind after lobbying for the F-15 sale. The first occurred in April 1978 and would prove of greatest benefit to his future diplomatic career. Carter's congressional strategists asked that Bandar fly out to California to lobby its retired Republican governor Ronald Reagan, who was already weighing a run for the presidency.[30] Bandar had no idea who Reagan was, which, according to him, amused Carter to no end. The president thought Reagan might just back the F-15 sale because of his strong anticommunist sentiments and felt his endorsement would carry a lot of weight with conservative Republican senators.

Bandar didn't have the foggiest idea either of how to contact Reagan, and he needed Dutton to fill him in on his career and political views. Through his U.S. Air Force contacts, the prince had befriended one person in California he felt might be able to help him: Thomas Jones, chairman of Northrop Corporation, the maker of the F-5s he had been flying back home. Unbeknownst to Bandar, Jones and Reagan were close friends. So when the prince asked if Jones could arrange for him to see Reagan on short notice, Bandar got a reply within half an hour. However, Jones told him he had to come to California immediately, because Reagan and his wife, Nancy, were about to leave on a trip to Iran to see the shah. So Bandar rushed west, reaching the Reagan home on the eve of their departure.

Bandar's account of his first meeting with Reagan may provide insights into the future president's thinking about Saudi Arabia, though it may also illustrate Bandar's occasional embellishment when telling a story.

"I sat down with Governor Reagan, and we chatted a little bit. Then I explained why we needed the aircraft. He said to me at the end of it, 'Prince, let me ask you this question. Does your country consider itself a friend of America?'

"I said, 'Yes, since King Abdulaziz, my grandfather, and President Roosevelt met. Until now, we are very close friends.' "

Then Reagan asked him a second question. "Are you anticommunist?"

"I said, 'Mr. Governor, we are the only country in the world that not only does not have relationships with communists, but when a communist comes in an airplane in transit, we don't allow him to get out of the airplane at our airport.' "[31]

Bandar was prepared for another lively discussion about the Saudi request for sixty F-15 Eagles. But there was none. "That was it. Two things were important. Are you friends of ours? Are you anticommunist? When I said yes to both, he said, 'I will support it.' "

Bandar said he then asked Reagan if he would mind saying that publicly to a reporter from the *Los Angeles Times* whom Dutton had prompted to pose the question at the airport as the Reagans left for Iran.

"Do you support the sale of the F-15s to Saudi Arabia that President Carter is proposing?" the *Times* reporter asked, according to Bandar's account.

"He said, 'Oh yes. We support our friends and they should have the F-15s. But I disagree with him [Carter] on everything else.'" Bandar added that the *Times* went with the story the next day under the headline REAGAN SUPPORTS CARTER ON F-15S TO SAUDI ARABIA.

When Bandar got back to Washington, Carter's people pummeled him with questions about how he had managed to get Reagan's endorsement and even get it into the *Los Angeles Times*. "I didn't know how big a hero I was in Washington," recalled Bandar.[32]

The only problem with Bandar's version of these events is that there is no record that the *Times*, or any other major U.S. newspaper, carried a story of Reagan's endorsement of the F-15 sale, then or later. However, on April 14, the *Times* did report in a two-paragraph story that the Reagans had left on a seventeen-day trip to the Far East and were stopping over in Honolulu, where the former governor was to address an auto dealers' convention. There is no mention in John West's daily diary of this event, either. It is, of course, entirely possible that the *Times* sent a reporter to the airport who asked Reagan about his views on the F-15, but that the newspaper did not think them sufficiently newsworthy to publish. Yet this is hard to believe given the media attention to the F-15 sales debate, and the fact that the newspaper did provide its readers with the much more mundane report about the Reagans' trip to the Far East. Apparently, Bandar was not ready to allow the facts to get in the way of his telling a great story, which his version certainly was.*

His other two lasting memories of the F-15 battle involved lobbying the Senate. The first was of an encounter with Senator Russell Long, son of the infamously corrupt governor of Louisiana Huey Long and one of the Senate's most powerful figures as Finance Committee chairman. When Bandar went to his Senate office, he was surprised by Long's request to talk with no aides present.[33]

---

* Unfortunately, by the time I discovered in the fall of 2006 that there was no *Los Angeles Times* story to substantiate Bandar's account, the only other two people who could have, Ronald Reagan and Frederick Dutton, were both dead.

"You want my vote, don't you?" said Long.

Bandar said, "Yes."

Long said, "It will cost you ten million."

Before Bandar could decide whether to stay or leave, Long threw his arm around Bandar's shoulder and eased him into a chair, commenting, "Did I shock you?" He then proceeded to reassure the young prince that he was not seeking the money for himself but for a bank in Louisiana that was one of the biggest financial backers of his reelection campaign that year. The bank, he told Bandar, needed to have Saudi Arabia's central bank, known as the Saudi Arabia Monetary Agency (SAMA), ask to make a ten-million-dollar deposit there so that the Louisiana bank could be certified to do business abroad. Bandar agreed to ask his government to arrange the transfer. Whether SAMA in fact made the investment is unknown, but Long did vote for the F-15 sale and was reelected.*

His second memorable experience in dealing with the Senate was an appearance he was asked to make to answer questions about the F-15 sale. "Suddenly they invited me to address—think about it—the Foreign Relations Committee for the United States Congress for a luncheon, and I was to sit with them behind closed doors."

In retrospect, Bandar said he understood the significance of that meeting, but at the time "it was almost like *Mr. Smith Goes to Washington*."[34] He remembered in particular his exchange with Senator Frank Church, who was leading the opposition to the sale, over whether the Saudis intended to base the F-15s at Tabuk airport, in northwestern Saudi Arabia.

"Suddenly, Church starts banging on the table. He said, 'But Bandar, Prince Bandar, Major Bandar, whatever I should call you, Tabuk is only five minutes, five minutes from Israel. You could destroy those people in five minutes.'

"I didn't know what to tell him. Suddenly, I thought a second and said, 'Senator, please calm down,' and everybody started laughing."

Tabuk, he told Church, had been there thousands of years, and it was Israel that kept coming closer as its territory expanded with each Middle East war. "They [the Israelis] kept coming closer and closer to me, I said, 'That's the only thing I can tell you.' And everybody started laughing again."[35]

Bandar's personal contribution to the F-15 lobbying campaign is difficult

* Long's version of this encounter is destined to remain unknown since he died in 2003.

to assess because the entire Carter cabinet became involved, along with a star-studded cast of political notables from outside. Carter, whose presidential authority and prestige were on the line, personally led the final push to block a veto, calling in a score of senators for visits and telephoning many others in the final days. The Saudis also lobbied hard. The king sent not only Turki and Bandar but his Princeton-educated foreign minister, Prince Saud al-Faisal, and two other American-educated cabinet ministers. They collectively put on a display of Saudi diplomatic panache never seen before in Washington.

West watched Bandar's response to the new challenge of dealing with American politics with acute interest. The prince became "terribly concerned about the lack of coordination" in the lobbying campaign and basically took over the Saudi end of the effort, West reported.[36] Supporters and opponents of the sale buried senators in an avalanche of forty thousand telegrams and letters, and AIPAC was "around like an army," according to West.[37] AIPAC sent every member of Congress a copy of *Holocaust,* a novel based on a television series that had just aired about the Nazi extermination of Jews during World War II, as a none-too-subtle reminder of the Arab threat Israel lived under.[38] The Saudis countered with full-page ads in major newspapers marking the observance of the American environmentalist movement's Sun Day, in which they touted their financing of solar power projects in the United States. The media treated the slugfest between the Israeli and Arab lobbies over the F-15 sale as an unprecedented spectacle, noting with great interest the emergence of the Saudi-led Arab lobby as a new force on the Washington political scene.[39] Bandar was learning how to operate in an environment that was the polar opposite of the highly secretive Saudi political culture.

The hero of the day in the U.S. media's eyes, however, was clearly Carter himself, though the vote seems never to have been in serious doubt. The White House knew two days before the Senate showdown on May 15 that it had ample votes. West reported that Carter had "half a dozen or so in reserve."[40] The *Washington Post* credited Senator Howard Baker Jr., the Senate Republican minority leader, with playing the key role in the final 55–44 tally and described the victory as "something of a first for Carter's White House," because it was the first time his administration had "plotted a sophisticated strategy to win congressional approval for a controversial policy."[41] The strategy it was referring to was Carter's insistence on a package vote that included simultaneous approval for the sale of seventy-five F-16s to Israel, fifty F-5Es to Egypt, and the sixty F-15s to Saudi Arabia. The bottom line was that the Carter administration and its Saudi allies had prevailed over AIPAC in a pitched battle, and Congress had faced "the new facts about Saudi Arabian oil and dollar power."[42] Carter's tenacity had also thoroughly impressed the Saudi royals. "They cannot refuse the president anything now because of the stand he has taken," Bandar assured West.[43] Before long, Carter would be asking plenty of the Saudis, including their help in getting him reelected.

CHAPTER 3

Return of the Messenger

AFTER THE F-15 BATTLE WAS OVER, Bandar returned to the kingdom to pursue his air force career. By then, he had become good friends with Ambassador John West, and the two continued to meet regularly to discuss the latest developments in Washington and, above all, the fast-moving events taking place in the Middle East. The peace process was being propelled forward at breakneck speed by Egypt's dynamic leader, president Anwar Sadat, who had taken over upon the death of Gamal Abdel Nasser in October 1970. Sadat had managed to keep the eyes of the world riveted on him. First, he had dared to take on Israel militarily, becoming an instant Arab hero after the Egyptian army broke through Israeli lines along the Suez Canal at the start of the fourth Arab-Israeli War in October 1973. No matter that Israel ultimately won the war, nearly annihilated the Egyptian army, and still occupied Egypt's vast Sinai Peninsula at the end of hostilities. Sadat's standing as *the* leader of the Arab world was uncontested.

The Egyptian leader had then turned his energies to making peace with Israel in order to recover the Sinai and launch a broader Arab-Israeli peace process. He had again astounded the world in November 1977 by becoming the first Arab leader to dare to travel to Jerusalem and address Israel's parliament, the Knesset, in a direct call for peace. His bold unilateral diplomacy toward the Jewish state, however, had provoked Egypt's expulsion from the Arab League and severe strains in relations with the Saudis, who feared Sadat was much more interested in recovering the Sinai for Egypt than resolving the Palestinian issue for the entire Arab world. Still, the Saudis welcomed the revival of the peace process.

President Carter, who had come into office in January 1977, was also intensely interested in revitalizing the peace process and had spoken out early on the need to create a Palestinian homeland as part of a settlement. He had at first pushed for reconvening the Geneva Conference launched after the 1973 war partly for this purpose. But Sadat's initiative had led Carter to reorient his efforts toward securing a peace agreement between Egypt and Israel. After twelve arduous days of talks at Camp David, outside Washington, Sadat and Israeli prime minister Menachem Begin had made history by signing a set of accords on September 17, 1978, paving the way for a peace treaty between Egypt and Israel. This whirlwind of diplomatic activity had made it ever more imperative for Crown Prince Fahd, the kingdom's de facto ruler under a kindly but passive King Khalid, to establish his own direct line into the White House to keep himself informed of what was likely to happen next.

IN THE FALL of 1978, Carter sent a message to Fahd telling him he had "something sensitive" he wanted to discuss and asking for Bandar in particular to come see him.[1] Fahd was puzzled as to why Carter wanted to discuss "something sensitive" with Bandar rather than directly with him, and he summoned the prince for an explanation. An equally puzzled Bandar asked to see the original English text of Carter's message and instantly realized that what he wanted was for Bandar to come pick up a sensitive message for Fahd. Fahd ordered him to take the Pan Am flight from Dhahran to New York that same night. Bandar was not to tell the Saudi embassy he was coming and was met by a White House aide at Washington National Airport. Bandar brought back the message from Carter to Fahd. After reading it, the crown prince sent Bandar back to Washington with his answer. Carter, in turn, gave him another message for the crown prince. In the process of shuttling messages back and forth, Bandar discovered that Carter was anxious to make peace between Sadat and the Saudis after the signing of the Camp David Accords and was seeking to serve as an intermediary. Fahd had summarily rejected Carter's offer, bluntly telling him, "We will sort out our problems with Egypt directly, not with you."[2]

Bandar also learned, however, how important the role of messenger was to putting himself at the center of royal diplomacy. The job had brought him repeatedly into direct contact with Fahd, who had clearly taken a liking to Bandar. In fact, the crown prince was about to make Bandar his personal envoy. He also intended to have him work behind the back of the Saudi ambassador to Washington, Ali Alireza, who did not belong to the royal family or have much standing at the royal court. Furthermore, Alireza had proved ineffectual in dealing with the pro-Israeli lobby and rallying support in Congress for the Saudi F-15 purchase. Naming the ambassador to Washington was the prerogative of the king, not the crown prince, and King Khalid seemed oblivious to Alireza's shortcomings. So Fahd simply bypassed the king and Alireza by using Bandar as his backdoor channel to the White House.

Bandar's decision to attend Maxwell Air Force Officer Training School starting in June 1979 brought him back to the United States, but to Montgomery, Alabama, not Washington. However, his academic ambitions served to get him there. The British Royal Air Force College at Cranwell had taught Bandar how to fly, but it had provided him with no general college-level education. This bothered Bandar, who was well aware that some of his cousins had gone to elite American universities. Bandar mentioned his desire for a higher degree to Ambassador West, who in turn contacted David Long, the State Department official, who had briefed West on Saudi Arabia before he took up his posting in Riyadh. Long had become a regular visitor to the embassy in Jeddah on periodic consultancies. A diplomat with a markedly scholarly bent, he was a specialist in both Saudi Arabia and international relations, with teaching stints at George Washington, Johns Hopkins, and Georgetown universities. West asked Long to arrange for Bandar to take courses somewhere in the Washington area.[3] This Long did by convincing Robert Osgood, then dean of the Johns Hopkins School of Advanced International Studies, to allow Bandar to enter "a special program" leading to a master of arts degree in international public policy.[4]

The proposed one-year program was designated "special" because Bandar was to commute from Montgomery twice a month over weekends for one-on-one tutorials with selected professors paid extra for the sessions. Osgood was hard put to refuse the special arrangement since Long told him in a May 1979 memorandum that he was acting "with the encouragement" of White House chief of staff Hamilton Jordan and Secretary of State Cyrus Vance.[5] Long served as the prince's chief professor and academic overseer. Starting in the fall of 1979, Bandar took eight courses in international economics and politics, political theory, U.S. foreign policy, and Middle East politics, scoring four As and four B pluses, according to a transcript of his school records.[6] Mystery still surrounds his master's thesis, which focused on the domestic origins of U.S. foreign policy. Though apparently it was extremely well written, Bandar received only a B plus. West said in one of his daily diary entries that the thesis was "exceptionally good" and had inspired him to write about the "impending crunch in US-Saudi relations."[7] But in another entry, he said, "I cannot help but wonder how much help he might have had with it."[8] One person who almost certainly helped Bandar was Fred Dutton.

West kept Bandar's father informed about his progress. When he went to tell Sultan about Bandar's final grades in June 1980, Sultan joked that Bandar had "spent a lot of money" on getting his degree, in response to which West quipped, "That was the reason he received a B plus instead of an A in economics."[9] Even Carter's national security adviser, Zbigniew Brzezinski, read the thesis, commenting that Bandar had learned a lot about the U.S. decision-making process and explained how it affected Saudi Arabia's interests "in an interesting and imaginative way."[10] When West took Long on one of his visits to see Fahd, the crown prince also joked about Bandar's new degree, saying, "People with much wisdom but no learning are like donkeys carrying weighty tomes on their backs."[11]

ALMOST IMMEDIATELY AFTER his return in June 1979, Bandar found himself called upon for help by President Carter once again. The United States was facing its worst gasoline shortage since the 1973 Arab oil boycott, and Americans were clamoring for relief. Lines at gas stations across the country had become infuriatingly long, and customers were paying sky-high prices when gasoline was available. The immediate cause of the energy crisis this time was Iran. The shah, Mohammad Reza Pahlavi, had fled the country in January to escape the furor of an Islamic revolution led by the Iranian spiritual leader Ayatollah Ruhollah Khomeini. The ensuing chaos had created doubts about sufficient oil supplies worldwide, since Iran had been a major oil exporter. Making matters worse, the Saudis had cut production by nearly 1 million barrels a day to 9.5 million at the start of the year, and in April 1979 they made a second cut to 8.5 million. The Saudis had the capacity to produce 12 million barrels a day at that point.

On July 15, Carter delivered what was to become known as his "Malaise Speech," devoted to the "serious energy problem" and "crisis of confidence" facing the nation.[12] In his speech, he called upon Americans to make numerous personal sacrifices to reduce their use of gasoline, oil, gas, and electricity, setting the very ambitious goal of cutting foreign oil imports by 4.5 million barrels a day by 1990. Secretly, Carter had already turned to the kingdom for help, calling in Bandar and asking him to deliver a message to Fahd pleading for an increase in Saudi production. Fahd's reply, according to Bandar, was "Tell my friend, the president of the United States of America, when they need our help, they will not be disappointed."[13] The king was true to his word. As the thirteen-nation Organization of the Petroleum Exporting Countries (OPEC) was meeting in Venezuela in late June, the Saudi oil minister, Sheikh Ahmed Zaki Yamani, announced that Saudi Arabia was increasing production by one million barrels and keeping its price below the official OPEC one.

West's diary corroborates Bandar's account of how Saudi Arabia came to Carter's rescue. West wrote that on May 30 he began discussing with Hamilton Jordan what they could do to help get Carter reelected.[14] Jordan told West that solving the energy crisis was "not only critical but decisive." West replied that he thought Fahd, if "properly approached, would do anything necessary to re-elect the president." Jordan then asked West to talk to Carter about an appeal to the Saudis because "he [Carter] was adamant he would not do anything politically motivated." Maybe West could persuade Fahd that "both the politics and the good of the country were at stake." West went to the White House on June 1 to discuss a draft letter to Fahd, and the president asked him whether the Saudis were "really interested in seeing him reelected." West said he was sure "any reasonable request would be granted." Carter then replied, "Well if they are, they've got to help on energy."[15]

On June 6, Carter sent the carefully drafted letter to Fahd, imploring him to consider how Saudi Arabia "might best serve its own long term national interests and those of the community of nations in this crisis" by increasing production and holding down prices.[16] Bandar had suggested some of the wording as well as the general approach the president should take in making his plea, according to West, who returned to Saudi Arabia for a follow-up meeting with Fahd. The U.S. envoy proposed that Saudi Arabia increase production by one million barrels a day for six months and keep any price increases to "an absolute minimum." Fahd replied that he would do "anything in his power externally or internally to help insure your [Carter's] re-election," since he felt this was "essential if there was ever to be a just and lasting peace in the Middle East."[17]

Fahd's laudatory words for Carter as reported by West might seem suspect in light of the Saudis' critical attitude toward the Camp David Accords and opposition to the Egypt-Israel peace treaty, which the U.S. president had brokered. The Saudis had even severed diplomatic relations with Cairo. Yet the Saudi response to his plea clearly indicated that Fahd deeply appreciated Carter's commitment to peace and believed he was the best chance the Arabs had for solving the Israeli-Palestinian problem. At the June 26 OPEC meeting, the Saudis announced they would hold their prices to between seventeen and eighteen dollars a barrel despite opposition from other OPEC members and even Saudi "technocrats." West told Carter that the eighteen-dollar ceiling was seen in Riyadh as "a major concession to the U.S." and amounted to a subsidy of thirty million to forty million dollars a day, since other producers were charging twenty-two to twenty-three dollars.[18] By October, the extra Saudi oil had created an oil glut that was forcing prices downward sharply.

The success of this venture in oil diplomacy gave Bandar enormous standing in Washington. In early December 1979, Carter asked the prince to come to the White House so that he could thank him personally for the Saudi help in alleviating the U.S. energy crunch. They spent forty-five minutes together, and their discussion ranged from ways the two governments could work together to heal the rift between Saudi Arabia and Egypt to ideas on how to deal with the revolutionary government in Tehran. In November, Iranian students had overrun the U.S. embassy there and taken sixty-three American diplomats hostage, demanding that Washington turn over the deposed shah, who had taken refuge in the United States. Carter was desperately seeking ways to gain their release before the onset of the 1980 presidential campaign. This tête-à-tête between Bandar and Carter was the first instance of his dealing directly with a U.S. president in such a fashion, bypassing all normal diplomatic channels. He was becoming a presidential adviser and confidant, a role he would come to relish and play repeatedly throughout his diplomatic career, which would not formally begin for another four years. Their meeting was kept secret even from the State Department, which was reduced to calling West in Jeddah to find out what had transpired.[19]

From West's diary, we know that they discussed the impasse between the Saudis and Sadat in some detail, and that they mulled over a daring scheme for resolving the hostage crisis. Bandar suggested that Carter turn to the Palestine Liberation Organization (PLO), which the U.S. government refused to recognize at that point, for help in gaining the release of the American diplomats. According to Bandar's plan, King Khalid would send his personal plane to pick up PLO chairman Yasser Arafat and fly him to Tehran, where Arafat would make a personal plea to Ayatollah Khomeini for the release of the hostages. With the hostages and Arafat aboard, the king's plane would then proceed to Washington, where Carter would personally meet them and thank Arafat for his "humanitarian gesture." West noted with some understatement that this would be "a dramatic deal."[20]

Bandar was apparently hoping the ploy would lead Carter to recognize the PLO as the sole legitimate spokesman for the Palestinian people, then a primary objective of Saudi diplomacy and one vehemently opposed by Israel and its U.S. congressional supporters. In the event, the Bandar plan never came to fruition. But the prince and Carter nonetheless were developing an ever-closer relationship. West described Bandar as "bubbling over" about the meeting afterward. Bandar had joked with Carter, too, about his close friendship with West, telling the president he was "the only [American] ambassador who had a prince for an aide."[21]

Bandar, still only a pilot and with no diplomatic standing, was becoming involved in every aspect of Carter's Middle East policy. When the PLO gambit did not pan out, the prince redirected his energies to brokering a breakthrough with Sadat, which was very much on Carter's mind because of the Egyptian leader's isolation in the Arab world after its peace treaty with Israel. The prince had taken it upon himself to contact and meet with Egyptian vice president Hosni Mubarak while he was visiting Washington in November 1979.[22] This meeting occurred after Carter sent his ambassador to Cairo, Hermann Eilts, to Saudi Arabia to try to convince the Saudi leaders to restore diplomatic relations with Cairo, a gesture they rebuffed. Bandar then met secretly with Mubarak without first asking for permission from his own government. But after Fahd was told about the meeting, he authorized the prince to continue with his initiative.

Bandar even tried to broker a truce himself. While visiting Washington in mid-March 1980, the prince broached the subject of, in West's words, "what we can do to get him [Bandar] to intercede" to ease tensions between Sadat and the Saudis.[23] Bandar proposed that Carter write a letter to Fahd asking the crown prince to extend an olive branch to the Egyptian leader. If Fahd would write a conciliatory letter, it could be presented to Sadat in Washington, where he was scheduled to travel in early April for a meeting with Carter and Israel's Menachem Begin to discuss the next steps in the peace process.

Bandar's plan set in motion a dramatic diplomatic scramble. On April 2, West saw Carter finalize the presidential letter to Fahd "to hopefully bridge the relationship upon Sadat's arrival" in Washington.[24] The next night, Bandar left for Riyadh with Carter's letter. Time was of the essence, since Sadat was scheduled to be at the White House the morning of April 9. Once in Riyadh, however, Bandar ran into resistance from Fahd, who dragged his feet at the last moment about writing a friendly letter to the likes of Sadat. Carter wanted the Saudis to agree to a temporary truce in their attacks on the Egyptian leader, and vice versa, while he made a final attempt to break the deadlock in negotiations over Palestinian autonomy. The Camp David Accords had set a deadline of May 26 for reaching an agreement. Bandar had to wait three days and did not get Fahd's reply letter until the evening of April 8.[25]

Carter had arranged for Bandar himself to present Fahd's letter in the Oval Office while Sadat was there, at a meeting scheduled to start at precisely ten twelve in the morning. The White House log for April 9 indicates that the plan for Bandar to break into the Carter-Sadat meeting was "very off the record."[26] West later recounted that "they brought Bandar in, and that he, Carter and Sadat had quite a session."[27]

There was one sour note in Bandar's performance, however. He had taken it upon himself to alter Fahd's letter to Sadat, apparently to make it sound more conciliatory than the crown prince had intended. The Americans, of course, eventually saw the Arabic text and realized what Bandar had done. West described Carter's national security adviser, Brzezinski, as "furious" over the mistranslation, while the prince defended himself by glibly commenting, "Well, I knew what Fahd wanted to say, and needed to say, so I translated it that way."*

It was an early display of Bandar's penchant for creative diplomacy, as well as his willingness to freelance. His intentions were laudable—he was

---

* West only disclosed Bandar's misdeed long after he had retired. In a barely legible handwritten note attached in June 1998 to a draft of Carter's letter to the Saudi crown prince, West quoted Bandar as saying he decided to change the text because "Fahd couldn't afford to say it as strongly as needed in a letter and I helped him."[28]

trying to help Carter solve what the president had told Fahd was "one of the most serious problems" he faced at the time, the deep rift between Saudi Arabia and Egypt over the Egypt-Israel peace treaty. Carter had even described the rift as a "severe threat" to the goal of finding peace in the Middle East.[29] Bandar was clearly ready to take diplomatic risks in what he would later describe, somewhat contemptuously, as "the game" of Washington politics. As it turned out, his efforts were for naught. Even before May 26, the Egyptian government-controlled press resumed its attacks on the Saudi leadership, and the deadline came and went without any agreement on the Palestinian issue.

THE SAUDI WILLINGNESS to manipulate oil prices to help Carter continued right up to the eve of the 1980 presidential elections, even though U.S.-Saudi relations went through a rough patch earlier in the year. The shah's downfall had touched off a debate within U.S. policy-making circles and the media about prospects for the survival of the Saudi monarchy next door. The debate seemed even more relevant after several hundred Wahhabi fanatics took over the Holy Mosque in Mecca in November of 1979 and engaged in a prolonged, bloody battle with Saudi security forces before being defeated. The following month, the Soviets invaded Afghanistan to install a communist government, heightening fears of Soviet expansionism in the Persian Gulf. In response, Carter used his last State of the Union Address, on January 23, 1980, to proclaim what would become known as the Carter Doctrine. The Soviet presence in Afghanistan was "a grave threat" to the free movement of oil from the Persian Gulf. "An attempt by any outside force to gain control of the Persian Gulf region will be regarded as an assault on the vital interests of the United States of America, and such an assault will be repelled by any means necessary, including military force."[30] The U.S. security guarantee King Faisal had sought in 1972 was taking shape.

Yet this new U.S. commitment to the gulf's security could not allay growing Saudi doubts about the American attitude toward the kingdom. The Saudis discovered that West had produced a detailed analysis examining the royal family's stability and capacity to stay in power that was not totally reassuring.[31] The Saudis reacted by letting West know the royal family was extremely offended that the Carter administration thought "its days numbered."[32] Making matters worse, the al-Saud family felt itself to be personally under siege because of a British-made film, *Death of a Princess*, that the U.S. Public Broadcasting Service planned to show in May 1980 on all its affiliates across the United States. The dramatized documentary recounted the travails of a Saudi princess who was publicly executed for committing adultery. The Saudis expelled the British ambassador in Riyadh over the film's showing in England and mounted a massive campaign to stop its airing in America. In the end, PBS aired the film on schedule, to the deep chagrin of the Saudis.

On another front, the Saudis were pressing Carter for the sale of aerial tankers to refuel their F-15s but getting nowhere. To show their displeasure over the state of U.S.-Saudi affairs, the Saudis increased the price of oil by two dollars in mid-May and refused to provide oil for the U.S. strategic reserve. By early June 1980, West was again pleading with Fahd to hold oil prices down, at least until after the November presidential election. His case was undermined by a report in the *Washington Post* on June 23 that Carter had decided to postpone a decision on the latest Saudi arms request until after the elections. AIPAC had mobilized seventy senators to send a letter putting the president on notice regarding their strong opposition to the sale.

However, the unexpected onset of full-scale war between Iraq and Iran in September 1980 changed the atmosphere dramatically. The Saudis became anxious that the fighting would spread to engulf the kingdom and turned to Washington for protection. Bandar was again the messenger. In late September, West asked Defense Minister Sultan whether the Saudis "wanted equipment such as AWACS and an anti-aircraft Hawk missile battery."[33] Bandar relayed the message that they indeed did, and West sent that message on to Washington. This exchange represents the origins of what was to become an epic battle in Congress over the AWACS sale at the start of the Reagan administration.

West was the one who first planted the seed in the Saudis' minds that it might be possible for them to obtain what was then the most sophisticated American airborne surveillance and command-and-control system, one that no non-NATO country had at the time, including Israel. The ambassador and Bandar teamed up to make sure the Saudis would make a request to purchase the AWACS. West proposed that the Saudi Royal Air Force "brass" be given a promotional ride in the aircraft. Bandar thought that was a great idea, telling West it would be like "selling them a new car. Once they went up in it, there would be no talking them out of it."[34] A three-hour ride for the brass was duly arranged for October 14, and as Bandar had predicted, the Saudis were hooked. West then pressed for the Carter administration to commit to the sale immediately, arguing that "it was too good a chance to pass up. They've [the Pentagon] been wanting bases here for a year and here in effect the Saudis are offering them to us."[35] Bandar had reassured West that the Saudis no longer cared if the U.S. military presence became public, as the stationing of AWACS in the kingdom surely would since scores of American support personnel would come, too.[36]

The Saudi formal request set off another heated debate within the administration over how to respond in the middle of the presidential campaign. In the end, the decision was made to send four AWACS manned by Americans as a sign of U.S. commitment to Saudi security. A last-minute debate over whether to state publicly that the United States had "offered" the planes or that Saudi Arabia had "requested" them was resolved by Bandar, who suggested they finesse the issue by publishing different versions in Arabic and English.[37] Fahd was so pleased by the U.S. response, according to West, that he gave the green light "on just about everything" the Pentagon was seeking in Saudi Arabia, including joint military planning, the prepositioning of U.S. war matériel, and access to Saudi bases for the AWACS. West called it "a grand sweep."[38]

Just as importantly, the crown prince responded to Carter's request that the kingdom avoid cutting its oil production or pressing for a price increase. West reported back that Fahd was "favorable on both requests" and had said that Carter's reelection was "so vital to the whole world that there was nothing he wouldn't do to help achieve that result."[39] West informed Carter in late October that both Fahd and Prince Abdullah, the Saudi Arabia National Guard commander and future king, had gone to Mecca and offered special prayers for Carter's reelection.[40]

CHAPTER 4

"You Came a Long Way"

CARTER'S FAILURE TO RESOLVE the Iranian hostage crisis produced an overwhelming victory in 1980 for his Republican opponent, Governor Ronald Reagan, whom none of the top Saudi royals had ever met. None, that is, except Bandar. "So it was decided maybe I should go and make contact with him," Bandar recollected.[1] The prince needed a cover for being in Washington and quickly engineered one. He would attend the National War College on the banks of the Potomac and use this as his excuse for being within a mile of the White House. Despite the fact that the college had no program at that point for training foreigners, Bandar used his connections to the U.S. Air Force and called upon General David Jones, whom he had come to know both in Washington and Saudi Arabia and even played squash with. Appointed under Carter, Jones was still chairman of the Joint Chiefs of Staff in early 1981. The prince asked Jones if a way could be found for him to attend the college. Jones obliged, jury-rigging an air force officers program for just three foreigners—one from the Arab world, one from Israel, and one from Brazil. Bandar, of course, was Jones's pick to represent the Arab world.

In the end, the ruse was not necessary, and Bandar never attended the college. Three months after Reagan took office in January 1981, his secretary of state, Alexander Haig Jr., made his first swing through the Middle East to drum up support for the president's hallmark crusade against the Soviet Union and communism. While in Riyadh on April 6–7, Haig discovered the

Saudis cared a lot more about the unresolved Palestinian issue and the pending sale of AWACS than they did about Reagan's communist menace. During a late-night talk with crown prince Fahd, the secretary of state discussed
the difficulties facing the sale and suggested that "maybe Prince Bandar
could come back and help [them] with Congress" the way he had with the F-
15s. Fahd readily agreed.[2] This time, Bandar would return with an official
royal mandate as chief Saudi lobbyist. In late August, Faisal Alhegelan, who
in mid-1979 had replaced Ali Alireza as the Saudi ambassador in Washington, officially informed the White House that Bandar had been chosen to
head up the Saudi end of the lobbying campaign "in a way guaranteeing
progress and the best of results."[3]

Selling AWACS to Saudi Arabia had not been Reagan's idea, carried over
from Carter's negotiations and championed by his ambassador in Riyadh,
John West, as it was. To West and others, including General Jones, selling
the aircraft to the Saudis seemed obvious, a golden opportunity for the Pentagon to fulfill its cherished dream of establishing an "on the ground" presence in the kingdom. Carter had never formally committed to the sale before
leaving office, but his secretaries of state and defense, Edmund Muskie and
Harold Brown, assured the incoming Reagan administration that they had
all been "favorably disposed toward an eventual future sale of AWACS."[4]
Carter even proposed a "joint representation" by officials of the two administrations to the Saudis. Though Reagan's transitional team declined the offer, a few months after arriving in office, the new Republican administration
enthusiastically embraced the Carter proposal. For Reagan, the rationale
was simple: "It was important to strengthen ties with this relatively moderate Arab country, not only because its oil exports were essential to our economy, but because, like Israel, it wanted to resist Soviet expansionism in the
region." The Saudis needed the help of a great power to defend their oil
fields, and "to put it simply, I didn't want Saudi Arabia to become another
Iran."[5] Reagan clearly was determined to demonstrate that he, unlike
Carter, would stand by America's allies. He was using the AWACS as a symbol of the U.S. commitment.

To consummate the deal, Reagan had to square off directly with Israel's
prickly prime minister, Menachem Begin, and his powerful ally in the United
States, AIPAC.[6] Israel regarded the super-sophisticated spy aircraft as a real
problem for its security, arguing that the Saudis would be able to track land
and air movements throughout the Jewish land. There were other items as

well in the Saudi arms package that worried the Israelis. Reagan was breaking Carter's promise not to sell enhancements to the F-15 that would make the jet fighter potentially a long-range attack aircraft, not just a defense one. Washington was proposing to sell fuel tanks to extend the F-15's range as well as AIM-9L Sidewinder missiles to make it more deadly in aerial combat. In addition, the package included Boeing 707 aerial refueling tankers for the AWACS. Altogether, it was worth a whopping $8.5 billion.

The AWACS debate has become a classic case study of clumsy lobbying by the White House in pursuit of foreign arms sales. At most, the process was supposed to last fifty days in two phases—twenty days for the informal notification of a pending sale to Congress and then thirty more for debate before a vote. For the AWACS, the White House managed to drag out the controversy for nearly nine months.[7] After announcing its intention to make the sale in early March, the administration did not formally submit the request until October 1 because it knew that a majority of senators opposed the deal. In fact, more senators were against the sale than for it until the last moment. In the end, it only passed by a two-vote margin. Just hours before the vote of October 28, Reagan wrote to friends that the "count looks about even" and that he was praying to God for success.[8] Reagan found himself obliged to commit his personal prestige and presidential authority in matters of foreign policy in order to round up enough votes. He met personally with half the Senate's members before the debate was over. Even then, if Senator William Cohen, a Republican with a Jewish father, had not changed his mind at the last moment, the sale would probably have been defeated.[9] The crisp slogan created by Bandar's politically savvy adviser Frederick Dutton to rally support seemed to say it all: "Reagan or Begin."*

The Senate vote was so close that the sale might well have been defeated—thereby crippling U.S.-Saudi military cooperation as AIPAC intended—had Israel played its hand better. Instead, Begin did everything possible to antagonize Reagan personally throughout the summer and fall of 1981. First, the Israeli leader in early June ordered a spectacular air raid on the Iraqi nuclear reactor near Baghdad without consulting, or even informing, Reagan beforehand.

---

* Dutton wanted to create bumper stickers with that slogan, derived from a statement by former president Richard Nixon published on October 4 that criticized opponents of the sale. They had "fallen into the trap of forcing members of Congress to choose between Reagan and Begin."[10]

Then, he further infuriated the U.S. president with his performance during a trip to Washington in September. While feting the Israeli prime minister at the White House, Reagan asked him explicitly not to lobby against the AWACS sale while he was in the country. Begin promised Reagan he would not. But once outside the White House gates, the Israeli leader did just that.[11] Reagan felt betrayed, and he let Begin know it. The struggle over AWACS really did become a question of "Reagan or Begin."

Bandar played the same role he had during the Senate debate on the F-15s, answering questions patiently and at great length from senators about the Saudi rationale for wanting to purchase the AWACS. He also sought to allay fears regarding Saudi stability and reliability as an ally, showing a picture to wavering senators of his grandfather, King Abdulaziz, and Roosevelt at their 1945 meeting aboard the American president's ship in Egypt's Great Bitter Lake. Once again, the prince attracted attention and praise from the media, who were fascinated by his skills at social networking. Reporters had never seen anything quite like the thirty-two-year-old Saudi pilot, not even an accredited diplomat but negotiating with the White House and Senate leaders and referring casually to Secretary of State Alexander Haig as Al and Reagan's national security adviser, Richard Allen, as Dick.[12] Bandar turned his home on Kalorama Street in northwest Washington into a reception center, impressing everyone with his polite, nonroyal approach to America's political "commoners." *Newsweek* noted that he had "dazzled senators with his grace, wit and charm" and that he had taken up regular squash playing with Joint Chiefs of Staff chairman Jones. With the former pilot and astronaut Democratic senator John Glenn, he mimicked aerial dogfights as if they were "old pilot buddies."[13] Stories were devoted to his lobbying activities, which included a weekend trip to see Republican Senate Majority Leader Howard Baker Jr. at his home in Huntsville, Tennessee.[14]

But Bandar's main input was negotiating on behalf of the Saudi government the terms of a compromise deal regarding the degree of U.S. control over, and presence on, the aircraft. These negotiations required him to work closely with Baker, as well as with Reagan's chief of staff, James Baker III. The experience created personal bonds that would serve him well later on, particularly those with the White House chief of staff, who would become President George H. W. Bush's secretary of state. At one point, Bandar was negotiating directly with Reagan himself, or at least relaying to him King Khalid's message that Saudi Arabia could not accept joint U.S.-Saudi command of the AWACS.[15] In the end, Bandar helped work out terms acceptable to the Saudis, which were contained in a presidential "letter of certification" specifying various conditions under which the sale would go forward. These included sharing of information with U.S. authorities and various safeguards to block third parties from access to the AWACS. For all the maneuvering by opponents to the sale, the Senate pretty much ended up approving the same package of AWACS, F-15 enhancement equipment, and missiles that Reagan had submitted in the first place. And, unlike Carter during the F-15 vote in 1978, Reagan retained the option to upgrade the package at a later date.[16]

The successful AWACS sale set the stage for a new level of military cooperation between the United States and Saudi Arabia, putting the U.S. Air Force on the ground visibly in the kingdom for the first time since its expulsion from Dhahran in 1962. A blockbuster story just days after the vote described the Pentagon's "new grand strategy for the Persian Gulf," which involved plans for surrogate bases "equipped and waiting for American forces to use."[17] The United States would build a state-of-the-art command, control, and communications system; an integrated air defense umbrella over the kingdom; and even a Central Command headquarters. Basically, U.S. and Saudi defense planners were turning the kingdom into one big land-based aircraft carrier that the U.S. Rapid Deployment Force, created by Carter at the end of his administration, could use when called upon to defend the Arab states of the Persian Gulf. The Saudis would even pay for the necessary infrastructure.

In fact, planning on a grand design for building a U.S. security umbrella over Saudi Arabia had begun as early as 1974 when the two countries had established a Joint Commission on Economic Cooperation; its military subcommittee had even outlined the sequence in which the Saudis would obtain ever-more-sophisticated aircraft, starting with the F-5s and ending with the AWACS. The Saudis would also build a series of "military cities" that U.S. forces could use if needed to protect the kingdom.[18] Work on building the infrastructure of the security umbrella had begun in the mid-1970s with the signing of over eight billion dollars in military construction agreements.[19]

The "new grand strategy" story was flatly denied by the Pentagon, but West had made it clear in his diary back in October 1980 that such a deal had indeed been worked out, and approved by top Saudi leaders as a result of the quick dispatch of AWACS that month.[20] The final proof of the story's accuracy would come during the first Gulf War, in 1990–91, when Saudi

Arabia accommodated hundreds of thousands of U.S., Western European, and Arab soldiers and hundreds of aircraft in preparation for the ouster of Saddam Hussein's army from Kuwait. Bandar noted that the first U.S. Air Force contingent to arrive became operational within six hours—not the forty-eight hours the Pentagon had anticipated—because "all our facilities" had been built to U.S. specifications, even the secret underground command post at the Dhahran airport.[21]

AMERICA'S GROWING MILITARY presence inside the kingdom starting in the early 1980s coincided with an upsurge in Saudi religious activism. The main cause of this Wahhabi awakening, however, was not the new American footprint on the Land of the Two Holy Mosques. Rather, it was the challenge from the Iranian revolution led by that country's supreme Shiite religious leader, Ayatollah Ruhollah Khomeini, who was out to overthrow the Sunni Saudi monarchy. As if the Iranian challenge was not enough, the al-Sauds had to deal simultaneously with the fallout from the 1979 takeover of the Holy Mosque in Mecca by Wahhabi fanatics who questioned the royal family's religious credentials for leadership. These two events convinced Fahd, who became king in June 1982 upon the death of Khalid, that he had to reinvent himself and reshape his image.

Fahd had won a well-deserved reputation for being something of a playboy and pleasure seeker as a young adult, and his reputation for "excess" was embodied in the marble and gold replica of the White House he had built in Marbella, the coastal summer playland of the Spanish rich that he frequently visited. But Fahd was also a chief architect of the modern Saudi state and even an aspiring religious reformer. A year after ascending the throne, he boldly proposed that the kingdom's Wahhabi establishment reexamine some of its interpretations of the Koran, a practice known as *ijtihad*, to accommodate the needs of modern Saudi society. He immediately ran into stiff opposition, however, and did an about-face.[22] Instead of pushing for badly needed religious reform, Fahd sought to reassure the Wahhabi clerics of his religious credentials by pandering to their fundamentalist demands. He also postponed for a decade a plan to introduce a Basic Law of government that was supposed to modernize the kingdom. When finally promulgated in 1992, it instead declared the Koran the law of the land.

Fahd sought by all means to transform himself into a paragon of Islamic virtue. He staunched criticism from Wahhabi clerics by giving free rein to their morality police, known as the *mutawwa'in*, whose mission it was to ensure rigid adherence in public to fundamental Islamic precepts, particularly strict separation of unmarried men and women. Westerners, and even visiting foreign reporters, often had unpleasant run-ins with these bearded, humorless guardians of the faith, and during Fahd's reign little was done to curb their excesses. They would even try to separate American male and female reporters eating together in restaurants. The king also turned over to the Wahhabi establishment control of the education system and its curricula, which resulted in a plethora of university graduates steeped in Wahhabi fundamentalism and hostile to any kind of reforms, Western culture, and even other Islamic sects. To make clear his own commitment to defending Islam against all foreign threats, Fahd decided in 1986 to change the title of Saudi monarchs from "king" to "custodian of the Two Holy Mosques."

The worst foreign threat for Fahd came from neighboring Shiite Iran, presaging the intense Saudi-Iranian rivalry for regional leadership that continues today. Tens of thousands of Iranian Shiites, who took advantage of the annual pilgrimage to Mecca after the Iranian revolution in 1979, spread Iran's anti-American and pro-Khomeini message and staged demonstrations challenging Saudi Arabia's claim to be sole custodian of Islam's holiest sites. Clashes between these pilgrims and the Saudi police for a while occurred annually and culminated in the death of more than 400 people, 275 of them Iranians, in July 1987. The Iranians even planned to seize control of the Holy Mosque and declare Khomeini leader of the Muslim world after the ayatollah denounced the al-Saud family as "devious," "ungodly," and "not worthy of being in charge" of the holy sites.[23] In response to the Iranian provocations, the Saudis for some years banned Iranian pilgrims altogether and then sharply limited the number allowed to come into the kingdom on pilgrimage.

The Saudis had to contend with Iranian military provocations as well. On one occasion in June 1984, Iranian American-made Phantom jets ventured into Saudi airspace, probably seeking to attack Kuwaiti or Saudi oil tankers headed for Iraq. The Saudis decided to respond with strong backing from the United States. They sent two F-15s, guided by a U.S.-manned AWACS, to intercept the Iranian jets and shot down two of them. The Iranians launched more Phantoms as if planning to attack the kingdom, but then recalled them, possibly because they feared provoking U.S. retaliation. Bandar was delighted with the Saudi performance and issued a sharp warning to the Iranians from Washington that the kingdom was determined to defend itself and its interests in the gulf.

The United States would eventually put American flags on Kuwaiti tankers and provide military escorts for them. The Saudis, anxious to avoid inciting the Iranians any more than necessary, never accepted U.S. naval escorts. They did, however, sever their diplomatic relations with Tehran until Iran finally sued for peace with Iraq in 1988. By then, the Iranian model of Shia theocracy had lost its luster throughout the Sunni Islamic world. But the Saudi distrust of Iran and its imperial ambitions has endured ever since, and it explains the sharp Saudi reaction to Iran's bid to extend its political influence westward into Sunni-dominated Arab lands in the wake of the 2003 U.S. invasion of Iraq.

The Iranian religious challenge evoked a different response than did the military threat. Fahd set out to spread the Wahhabi message worldwide to counter it. He built a huge publishing house in Medina to produce tens of millions of copies of a Saudi-approved Koran in a bid to make it the standard version for the entire Islamic world. Starting in 1985, they were handed out as gifts to every pilgrim coming to Mecca and sent to Saudi embassies around the world for further distribution. This version remains less controversial, however, than the Noble Koran, upon which the top Wahhabi religious authority, grand mufti Sheikh Abdulaziz bin Baz, bestowed his official blessing in 1983. The commentary accompanying the opening verse makes clear that those who earn Allah's anger include people "such as the Jews" and those who have gone astray, "such as the Christians."[24]

The Saudi drive to export its religious influence eventually reached the United States and the heart of Washington, where the Saudi embassy became the main supporter of the Islamic Mosque and Cultural Center on Massachusetts Avenue. In November 1980, a group of pro-Khomeini Iranian activists had seized control of the site and ousted its Egyptian (Sunni) imam. They held on to the mosque until early 1983, when Washington police finally ousted them. The Saudis then moved in to appoint their imam, and Bandar eventually became chairman of the mosque's governing council.

In the turbulent decade after the Iranian revolution, the U.S. government welcomed this new Saudi religious activism, viewing it as a badly needed counterweight to help contain Iran's drive to expand its religious and political influence. The Saudi export of Wahhabi Islam would eventually develop into an impressive soft power that the House of Saud could extend across the Muslim world far beyond its limited military might.[25] The kingdom not only became the Islamic world's number-one publisher of the Koran, but also sent out thousands of missionaries and built hundreds of mosques, schools, and cultural centers around the world to combat Iran's revolutionary Shiite message. Before long, this international activism took concrete form in a jihad aimed at the Soviet occupation of Afghanistan, which had begun the same year as Iran's revolution.

As in Washington, Afghanistan became a cause célèbre in Riyadh, fueling Wahhabi zeal to new heights and offering a concrete outlet for thousands of young Saudi mujahideen, or "holy warriors," eager to perform what was regarded as a religious duty. Starting in the early 1980s, the Saudi government provided several billions of dollars in arms and other assistance to the cause of freeing Afghanistan from godless communists. Reagan, of course, was careful to call them "freedom fighters" rather than "holy warriors." But he bestowed the White House's official blessing on their Islamic fervor whenever their turbaned leaders came to Washington to rally Congress and the American people to the cause. No Reagan administration official, neoconservative, or Washington think tank paid any attention to the potential consequences of stoking the fires of Islamic militancy for the sake of Soviet rollback.

BANDAR RETURNED HOME after the AWACS vote in October 1981, but again not for long. Secretary of State Haig was responsible this time for convincing the Saudis to send him back to Washington. At a meeting with King Khalid in Marbella in early February 1982, Haig revived the idea of Bandar's attending the war college in Washington. By then a lieutenant colonel, Bandar was present at the meeting, and upon Khalid's assent, he immediately headed back. This time, Bandar got as far as enrolling and attending for two weeks before the king changed his mind, naming him defense attaché at the Saudi embassy. Bandar was taken aback by this unexpected appointment. Anticipating a senior staff position within the Saudi Royal Air Force, he had been assigned instead to a job that was "usually a kiss of death for a career." Bandar decided the king was putting him to some kind of test and accepted the position.[26] As events would have it, the prince took up his new post just as Reagan was facing the first Middle East crisis of his presidency—Israel's massive invasion of Lebanon, which began on June 6, 1982. The Israeli aim was to drive the Palestine Liberation Organization (PLO) and its guerrilla army out of that country and, if possible, kill its leader, Yasser Arafat, in the process. One week after the invasion began, King Khalid died unexpectedly, and Fahd ascended to the Saudi throne. The new king's private messenger was ready for duty.

Bandar's account of his role in the torturous negotiations that finally led in late August to the PLO's evacuation from Beirut is another example of his penchant for stretching the truth. Bandar claimed he was responsible for negotiating the complicated conditions under which Arafat and his guerrillas agreed to leave, but complained that "nobody gave us credit for it."[27] Indeed, neither Reagan nor his two secretaries of state during the crisis, Haig and George Shultz, give more than passing mention to Bandar regarding these negotiations in their memoirs, though the president did later acknowledge his role. Bandar traveled to Beirut repeatedly and dealt extensively with Reagan's deputy national security adviser, Robert "Bud" McFarlane, in the initial search for a solution. Since the Saudis were presumed to have a lot more influence with Arafat than it turned out they did, reporters covering the war watched closely Bandar's comings and goings for signs that Arafat might be preparing to leave.

Bandar's chief memory of that long, hot summer ordeal was his confrontation with Haig at the State Department in mid-June. One of the issues at stake involved whether PLO fighters would be allowed to take their arms with them if they agreed to evacuate. The prince had taken on the role of intermediary and was trying to strike the best terms possible for Arafat. Bandar remembers that at one point he and Haig engaged in more or less an all-out shouting match.[28]

The prince argued that Arafat's men should be allowed to leave with any weapons they could carry with them. Haig at first flatly refused, reminding the prince that the Israeli army had Beirut surrounded and that Defense Minister Ariel Sharon was poised to send his troops into the city's heart to crush its resistance. Bandar thought Sharon's threat to invade Beirut was an empty one, as the price in loss of Israeli soldiers would be too high.

In increasing exasperation, Bandar finally got up to leave, shouting as he did, "Tell Sharon to go away. There is no more discussion. I have nothing more to tell you!" As Bandar remembers, Haig at that point asked, "If I agree to this, do we have a deal?"

"We have a deal," replied the prince.

Haig said he would get back to Bandar shortly. An hour later, he called him to formalize the agreement. Bandar called Fahd, who in turn relayed the tentative departure terms to Arafat. But the PLO leader then asked for U.S. protection of the ships that were to transport his eighty-five hundred fighters and personnel to Egypt, which was initially mentioned as their destination, though later it ended up being Tunisia.

Bandar said he thought Haig "was going to faint" when he told him, " 'We need the U.S. Navy to protect us from Beirut to Alexandria.' " The deal worked out, according to Bandar, was that the U.S. Navy would escort the ships halfway across the Mediterranean, and then the Egyptians would provide for their protection until they reached the port of Alexandria.

Yet other accounts do not accord the prince such a central role. On June 25, Reagan announced what amounted to Haig's forced resignation. Haig had strongly disagreed with other senior administration officials, even Reagan himself, about whether to stop the Israeli army or encourage it to press on into the center of Beirut. Nothing had been settled regarding PLO departure terms by the time of Haig's resignation. Haig later took strong exception to Bandar's portrayal of the argumentative tenor of their meeting and claimed he had never used the threat of the Israeli army moving into Beirut, because he wanted to be careful not to feed the Saudi "paranoia" that the United States was "pulling the Israeli strings." He chalked up Bandar's account of their meeting to his "impressive dramatic talent," commenting that "he let his imagination run away with him on this one."[29]

One central element in Bandar's account was accurate, however: After nine more weeks of negotiations, the PLO fighters were allowed in the end to depart with their individual arms. They scattered in all directions— overland to Syria and by ships to half a dozen Arab nations. A few went to Egypt, but not under U.S. escort. In the end, the only U.S. protection covered Arafat's personal departure aboard the Greek merchant vessel *Atlantis*, which sailed for Piraeus, Greece, on August 30 accompanied by a Greek, not an American, warship. The U.S. Sixth Fleet offered only general air coverage.[30]

In the U.S. media, the main hero of the day was not Bandar but Philip Habib, a veteran State Department peace negotiator who had come out of retirement in ill health at the age of sixty-two, risking life and limb under Israeli shells and gunfire in Beirut to negotiate the final conditions for the PLO evacuation. A week after the last PLO contingent left Beirut, on September 1, Reagan held a ceremony at the White House where he awarded Habib the highest civilian honor, the Presidential Medal of Freedom. However, Reagan did mention years later, in a 1986 presidential certification to Congress required for the transfer of AWACS, that Saudi Arabia had played "a major and highly visible role" in attempts to bring peace to the warring factions in Lebanon in the aftermath of the PLO's withdrawal, and he praised Bandar by name for his efforts.[31] In *The Reagan Diaries*, finally published in 2007, the president praised Bandar again, writing that he had done "a great job" in helping to broker a cease-fire.[32]

Bandar's relationship with Haig, the first of eight secretaries of state he would come to know intimately, was not always confrontational. Before Haig's resignation, Bandar had scheduled a large dinner party in his honor. Upon learning of his unceremonious dismissal, Haig called Bandar and asked him to cancel the party. But Bandar invited the secretary and his wife to come anyway. After dinner, Haig vented his bitterness in private to Bandar about how he had been driven out of office by his enemies inside the administration.

"I've been had," he lamented. "I shouldn't have let them have me, but I've been had today. Foolish."[33]

ON OCTOBER 24, 1983, Prince Bandar formally became his country's ambassador to the United States. In Bandar's recollection, his presentation of his credentials to the president on that fall day was anything but formal.[34]

Reagan cut short Bandar's presentation to exclaim, "You know something? You came a long way. When I first met you, you were a young major in your air force. And now, you are an ambassador of your country to the United States of America."

Not certain how to respond, Bandar decided to be sassy.

"Well, Mr. President, you didn't do too shabbily yourself. When I first met you, you were an unemployed governor, and now you're president of the greatest country in the world."

The Reagan years would see the epic struggle of the Cold War reach its climax, and Bandar put himself at the center of the U.S.-Saudi joint effort to ensure that America came out on top, becoming involved in various CIA schemes to roll back communist influence around the world, from Africa to

Afghanistan to Central America. Bandar the diplomat became Bandar the master covert operator.[35]

According to Bandar, the Saudis long harbored doubts about the tenacity of U.S. commitments to their third world allies and friends in America's struggle against communism.[36] "Everybody says America always cuts and runs. America does not sustain a policy. America does not go all the way," said Bandar, citing as a classic case the U.S. abandonment of Vietnam. Washington's constant "flip-flopping" was a real problem for Saudi Arabia, since it tended to discredit America's allies as well: "When you catch cold, we catch pneumonia." When the United States abandoned the contra cause in Nicaragua, this raised questions about its willingness to stick it out in Afghanistan, which the Saudis viewed as their biggest commitment and primary battleground in the Cold War. "If the other side believes that you really are wavering or [you] give the wrong message through losing, say in Nicaragua, we pay for it," Bandar noted. The only reason the Saudis willingly anted up for the contra cause in Nicaragua, he said, was to make sure that when Reagan said he was taking a stand there, that "he can stand." The Saudi concern was not academic. One of the kingdom's neighbors, South Yemen, was avowedly communist and providing facilities to the Soviets, and across the Red Sea there were thirty-five thousand Cubans in Ethiopia. "For us, it was important to modulate that picture [of flip-flopping] within our region by showing they [the United States] have staying power."

A decade later, the prince was still peeved about the bad press Saudi Arabia had received for its secret funding of the contras. He was particularly rankled about the behavior of Reagan's then national security adviser, Bud McFarlane, who had divulged the Saudi role to Congress in 1987 after insisting the Saudis keep it secret and promising he would do the same. Having arranged for the secret Saudi funding directly with Bandar, McFarlane had told him, "I'm a Marine. I will fall on my sword before I talk," and Bandar had gone to the extent of lying to American reporters and editors. "We were hurt because we felt a trust was betrayed."[37]

The Saudi sense of U.S. betrayal was nothing new, but the Nicaragua story was personal for Bandar. From the Saudi viewpoint, there was nothing illegal in their decision to send at least one million dollars a month to the contras after Congress cut off all U.S. funding in 1984. Altogether, the Saudis provided thirty-two million dollars. "We broke no U.S. law per se," said Bandar, ignoring the fact that Congress had explicitly banned U.S. solicitations from other countries. "Why would I come and volunteer to do something for Nicaragua? I didn't even care about Nicaragua. So it left a bad taste in people's mouths. You are a very difficult ally to handle."[38]

Nicaragua stands as a good example of the lengths Bandar was willing to go in order to stack up chips with the Reagan administration. It is also highly illustrative of the way Reagan's byzantine CIA director, William Casey, turned the Saudis into a surrogate agent for U.S. covert activities that he wanted to keep hidden from Congress or carry out despite its explicit prohibition. Casey was extremely careful not to leave any paper trail in his dealings with the prince. For example, when Casey wanted to tap the Saudis for contra money, he never dealt directly with Bandar. "He always said that he had never discussed the contra deal with me, and he was telling the truth," the prince said. "Once I asked a question about the contra aid, and he told me, 'I cannot discuss this with you because we are forbidden to discuss this.' " Instead, Casey used a third party who shuttled back and forth between him and Bandar to discuss Saudi funding. "He knew what I would do. I know what he knew." Bandar called Casey "a political enigma" ("He would have been a great CIA director in the 1950s at the height of the Cold War") and too "dogmatic" in the pursuit of what he perceived as U.S. interests around the world.[39]

The dogmatism shared by Reagan and Casey toward defeating the Soviet Union and its allies anywhere in the world was further revealed in their attitude toward the Communist Party in Italy. The party was taking its distance from Moscow and promoting Eurocommunism, but to Reagan and Casey, a communist was a communist, with or without a "Euro" in front of the name, and all were a threat to America. So the CIA director enlisted Bandar, who confessed to knowing nothing about Italian politics, to carry out another "off the book" operation in the name of stemming the communist tide. Bandar looked back on that episode as somewhat surreal. "I close my eyes, and I see it, but it must have been in a movie. It cannot be real, but it was real."[40]

According to Bandar, Reagan's longtime friend and the ambassador to the Vatican, William Wilson, asked him to provide and deliver ten million dollars to help the Christian Democrats defeat the ascendant Communist Party in the local elections of May 1985.* Shortly before those elections,

---

* Bob Woodward wrote in his book *Veil: The Secret Wars of the CIA 1981–1987* that the elections in question occurred in May 1985 and that the Saudis provided two million dollars.[41]

Reagan had given an interview to European correspondents in Washington in which he urged Italians not to vote for the largest Marxist party in the West. Bandar recalled that he packed up the Saudi "donation" in a suitcase, flew in his private Airbus from Washington to Rome, and drove in a Saudi diplomatic car to the Vatican Bank, where a priest came to the bottom of the stately building's steps and relieved him of the bulging suitcase, no questions asked. The Vatican was responsible for dispersing the donation to the Christian Democrats, who in fact managed to edge out the communists by 4 percent of the vote in the local elections.

However, the veracity of Bandar's enthralling account of this Italian caper on behalf of Casey could not be determined. Bandar has told this story to only four people, three of them from the *Washington Post*.[42] Attempts to verify it for a series of articles on U.S.-Saudi relations after 9/11 proved impossible.[43] The late Maxwell Rabb, U.S. ambassador to Rome in the mid-1980s, said he had never heard about Saudi funding of the Christian Democratic Party. But he did note that the Saudis were "very close friends" of the Christian Democratic–led government.[44] Wilson, Reagan's Vatican ambassador, also denied any knowledge of the event, commenting that if it had occurred, "it sure took place without my knowledge."[45] He said that he had seen Casey "often" and had rejected his request that CIA agents be assigned to the U.S. mission to the Vatican. Reagan's national security adviser, McFarlane, also denied any knowledge of the Saudi role, but admitted that Casey didn't let him in on "any of his Rome shenanigans."[46] Assuming it happened, unlike Nicaragua, Bandar's Italian caper at least did not cost him, or Saudi Arabia, any embarrassment because it did not become known until years later.

On the other hand, another Casey covert operation undertaken that same year involving Bandar backfired badly, causing the prince a lot of grief at the royal court. The operation was aimed at no less than the assassination of Sheikh Mohammed Hussein Fadlallah, the spiritual leader of Lebanon's newly formed militant Shiite group Hezbollah, or Party of God. On March 8, 1985, a massive car bomb blew up outside a mosque near his apartment building in the southern suburbs of Beirut, killing eighty people and injuring two hundred others. The bombing was particularly insidious because it took place as people were leaving the mosque, and many of the victims were worshippers. But Fadlallah escaped unharmed. The sheikh had come onto the U.S. radar screen because he was said to have blessed the bombers of the U.S. military barracks at the Beirut airport in October 1983, who killed 241 Marines. Bob Woodward, in his book *Veil: The Secret Wars of the CIA, 1981–1987*, claimed that Casey and Bandar had met and conspired together to carry out the attack on Fadlallah, outsourcing the operation to a former commando in the British special operations forces, with the Saudis footing the three-million-dollar cost.[47] Bandar emphatically denied that such a meeting ever took place or that the Saudis were involved in any way in the attempt on Fadlallah's life.*

Bandar had good reasons to deny Woodward's account, namely his own credibility at the royal court and the fate of his career. Crown Prince Abdullah, who had a special interest in Lebanon, had apparently never been told that the Saudis might have been involved in the Beirut fiasco. After Woodward's account appeared in October 1987, Abdullah, according to a story in *Mideast Markets*, blocked Bandar's hopes for leaving Washington to become the king's national security adviser.[49] If King Fahd withdrew him from Washington, it would appear to be an implicit confirmation of Saudi involvement and raise questions about official Saudi denials.†

For all his involvement in U.S. Middle East and Cold War policies during the Reagan years, Bandar's standing with the elderly president was never intimate. Over the eight years Reagan was in office, the president mentioned in his diaries dealing with the prince on just ten occasions, often merely to receive messages from King Fahd. Playing on Reagan's hatred of communism, Bandar did try several times to talk him into making a deal to wean Syrian president Hafez al-Assad from his dependency on the Soviet Union. Bandar told Reagan that Assad wanted "to trade the Soviets for U.S. help and influence." But the president turned him down because he feared Bandar's proposal would require the United States' "separating [itself] somewhat from Israel," and that, said Reagan, was a "no can do."[50]

Bandar was closer to Reagan's wife, Nancy, and he was reported to have

---

* Woodward has stood by his assertion. In an interview on PBS's *Frontline* in October 2001, he said the Casey-Bandar meeting took place during "a stroll in the garden" at the Saudi embassy residence in McLean, Virginia. They agreed that the Saudis would "put up the money to hire some professionals to go and try to car-bomb Sheikh Fadlallah." Casey kept the operation so "off the books" that even Reagan did not know about it, according to Woodward.[48]

† The *Mideast Markets* story is interesting because it constitutes the earliest report that Bandar, after only four years as ambassador in Washington, was aspiring to become the king's national security adviser. It would be nineteen more years before he achieved this goal.

used his access to her to try to influence U.S. foreign policy, and at one point even Reagan's appointment of his national security adviser. When the president was considering in October 1983 whom he should name to replace William Clark, he wavered between Bud McFarlane and his ultraconservative and highly outspoken U.N. envoy, Jeane Kirkpatrick. In the end, he chose the former. Asked about reports that he had weighed in with Nancy in favor of McFarlane, Bandar conceded he had made his views known "to certain people," but said he felt this had been "a minor fact in the decision, to be honest."[51] Still, the Saudi ambassador's having tried to influence the outcome of Reagan's choice seemed an intrusion into U.S. foreign policy way beyond what was appropriate for an Arab, or any other, foreign envoy to Washington.

CHAPTER 5

"Trust but Verify"

STARTING IN 1985, THE SAUDIS were forced to begin looking elsewhere than the United States for their most advanced weaponry, and King Fahd put Bandar in charge of spearheading the search. The Saudis had enjoyed two stunning victories in hard-fought battles with the American Israel Public Affairs Committee (AIPAC) over the sale of F-15s and AWACS. But Saudi good fortune, always dependent on White House resolve, was waning. Fahd asked Reagan for forty-eight additional F-15s during his state visit to Washington in February, but the president replied that while he supported the request, he didn't think he could get Congress to support it.[1] The king then warned Reagan that he would have to go elsewhere, and according to Bandar, Reagan said he understood and agreed. During the summer, the Saudis turned to Britain to purchase forty-eight Tornado fighters and thirty Hawk trainers in a deal initially worth four billion dollars but ultimately more than twenty times that amount.

The prince said the Saudis had also been interested in purchasing the U.S. Pershing, a mobile, intermediate-range, two-stage missile with a range of more than one thousand miles. The Pershing was a mainstay of NATO defense against Soviet forces in Europe, and the subject of endless U.S.-Soviet disarmament negotiations. "We asked for Pershings also, and America said no."[2] The request must have shocked the Reagan administration, since the Pershing was armed with a nuclear warhead, though it could be adapted to carry a conventional explosive as well. Bandar said the Saudi concern was countering the Soviet-built Scud missiles that both the Iranians and the Iraqis had modified to produce longer-range versions capable of flying up to six hundred miles. Both sides were firing them off at each other's capitals. The Iranians started using their Scuds against Baghdad in 1985, and that triggered the Saudi search for missiles. "The Iranians at that time could have put a Scud right in the gulf and fired at our oil facilities with impunity," Bandar explained. "His majesty's feeling was 'I must get a weapons system that I can [use to] hit deep into the heart [of Iran] and deter.' "[3]

The prince's first mission was to obtain the Tornados, and Bandar later remembered the al-Yamamah, or "dove of peace," contract as the easiest arms deal he had ever clinched.[4] King Fahd sent Bandar in the summer of 1985 to Austria to seek out British prime minister Margaret Thatcher, who happened to be on vacation in the mountains outside Salzburg. Bandar carried a letter from the king containing a formal request for the Tornado purchase. Without asking for the Saudi rationale or posing any other questions, Thatcher immediately replied, "You have a deal."[5] Their conversation about the purchase lasted just twenty-five minutes, and Bandar noted the difference between buying arms from the British, with no questions asked, and buying from the Americans, which required months of protracted battle with Congress. For Britain, it was a veritable bonanza, the biggest military sale in the country's history, eventually worth eighty-six billion dollars for seventy-two jets, two air bases, and innumerable service contracts. Nonetheless, the al-Yamamah deal, which the Saudis paid for in oil rather than cash, would become the subject of much scandal later, with Bandar at the center of it.

The deal signaled the end of the U.S. monopoly on military jet sales to the kingdom—at least for the Royal Saudi Air Force's most advanced aircraft—and the start of a new diversification policy for the Saudis. AIPAC had won its battle, but at a price dear to Israel's own security—the loss of U.S. control over where in the kingdom the Saudis installed the weapons most threatening to Israel. AIPAC's clout became clear in May 1986 when the Senate and the House voted overwhelmingly to deny the $354 million sale of even air-to-air missiles to the Saudis. This time, neither Reagan nor Bandar made any attempt to lobby for the sale; Reagan was out of the country when the vote was taken, and the prince was back home during the entire fifty days of informal and formal notification to Congress of the sale. The Saudis left the lobbying to six high-powered Washington public relations firms they were collectively paying $1.5 million a year to make their case.[6] Their displeasure with the turn of events even prior to the vote was made known in the subtle, arcane ways for which the Saudis are famous: The day Vice President George H. W. Bush arrived in Riyadh for a visit, on April 5, Crown Prince Abdullah left for Dhahran to join King Fahd, who had also gone out of his way to be absent from the capital.[7]

Bush's visit marked the only time the U.S. government has pushed Saudi Arabia to actually increase, rather than decrease, oil prices, a strange episode in the history of American oil diplomacy. Gasoline prices at the pump had hit a seven-year low in April, falling below one dollar, and the U.S. oil industry, for once hurting badly, was pressing Washington to do something. Bush's mission was to jawbone the Saudis into cutting production so that prices would go back up. Bandar escorted the vice president around the kingdom and tried to smooth his meetings with a Saudi leadership already very unhappy with Washington. For those who held that Bush was Big Oil's man in the Reagan administration, his mission to the kingdom was proof positive.

At the time, the Saudis were in an all-out price war with other members of the thirteen-nation Organization of the Petroleum Exporting Countries (OPEC), which were overproducing and selling below the group's mandated prices. To show they had the muscle to mainstain discipline in and control over OPEC, the Saudis had decided in October 1985 to pump an extra million barrels a day at a discount price of three dollars per barrel. Their idea was to punish OPEC's cheaters and force them to cut back their production and adhere to official prices. But the immediate effect was to flood the market and send oil prices plummeting first to twelve dollars a barrel and then to ten.[8]

Bush was finally granted a meeting with Fahd, but he had to fly to Dhahran to see him. During their two-and-a-half-hour meeting, Bush bemoaned the free fall in oil prices, telling the king it had become a threat to U.S. national interests, by which, of course, he meant specifically a threat to the U.S. oil industry. Here was an attempt at official U.S. price-fixing if there ever was one, though Bush denied he had come to Saudi Arabia on a "price-fixing mission" and insisted he was rather trying to reestablish "stability" in the chaotic oil market.[9] However, the king was more worried about Saudi clout over OPEC than low gasoline prices in America, and the two leaders reached no agreement on a desirable price for oil, mostly because the Saudis had just begun playing hardball with their OPEC rivals. Four months later, though, OPEC agreed to cut production by a huge five million barrels a day, and the price rose quickly to seventeen dollars a barrel. The evidence suggests that the Saudis were acting far less to please Washington than to show who was boss of OPEC.[10]

HAVING BEEN REBUFFED by Congress, the Saudi leadership remained determined to obtain missiles. Bandar argued that the kingdom had no choice other than to turn to communist China, because no Western European nation produced an intermediate-range missile, and the Saudis did not want to deal with the Soviet Union. That, he said, "would have really alienated our American friends."[11] As events turned out, the Saudi decision to seek Chinese missiles not only seriously alienated the Reagan administration, but also brought Saudi Arabia to the brink of war with Israel, or at least the closest the two nations have ever come to open hostilities. That China should have been the cause came as no small surprise to both U.S. and Israeli intelligence services, which were caught flat-footed. Still, Saudi Arabia and China shared some natural affinities. Though communist in ideology, China was ruled by a similarly secretive autocratic elite with no tolerance for Western-style democracy and a strong sense of being the center of an ancient civilization and culture. But the Saudis had no relations of any kind with China, recognizing its rival Taiwan instead. So Fahd decided to use Bandar, the same way President Nixon had Henry Kissinger, to make a series of secret trips to Beijing.

Bandar's opening to China began, ironically, in Washington right under the nose of the Reagan administration. In the spring of 1985, Bandar casually mentioned to the Chinese ambassador, Han Xu, that Saudi Arabia was interested in buying missiles from his country.[12] To say the least, the ambassador must have been astounded by the request and even more so by the prince's offer to go personally to Beijing to discuss the matter if the Chinese agreed. Bandar wanted a "yes-or-no answer," but not surprisingly the ambassador came back with an ambiguous reply. Bandar agreed to further talks, and the two ambassadors concocted what seems in retrospect a highly unlikely cover story for their ongoing contact. Bandar would go with a large Saudi delegation to Pakistan to discuss cooperation with China in the development of their petrochemical industries—a subject the prince knew nothing about. In Islamabad, during a brief walk in the garden of the Chinese embassy with the head of the delegation, Bandar was given a short message: "Yes" to the missiles and "Come to Beijing to discuss the details." A few weeks later, Bandar embarked on the first of three secret and two public trips he would make to the Chinese capital, to discuss first missiles and then the opening of diplomatic relations between China and Saudi Arabia. He dealt directly with Prime Minister Zhao Ziyang and, when Zhao was removed in 1989 after opposing the use of force to crush the pro-democracy student demonstrators in Tiananmen Square, with Communist Party strongman Deng Xiaoping.

On Bandar's first trip to Beijing, in July 1985, much of his time was devoted to parrying Chinese insistence that the Saudis cut diplomatic relations with Taiwan as part of the deal. "We told them we cannot have a deal like that. If we change our relationship with Taiwan, it will have to be our decision, not imposed on us. We just got stuck on that point for a long time."[13] He recalled that he finally broke the stalemate by asking the Chinese whether they really wanted the Saudis to sell their friends so cheaply, suggesting that Saudi diplomatic relations with China might well be "sold" one day for a higher price. At that point, the Chinese backed off, and the missile deal was concluded with the understanding that the Saudis would maintain their ties with Taiwan for the time being. The Chinese ability to keep Bandar's visit a secret was put to a severe test by the presence in a neighboring guesthouse to the Saudi one of an Iranian delegation, but it never discovered he was there.

On another of his secret missions, in early July 1986, Bandar was taken to see the factory near Xi'an, in Shaanxi Province, where the East Wind CSS-2 missiles were manufactured. Again, he was posing as a Saudi petrochemical salesman. The factory was located near the site of China's famous tomb housing thousands of terra-cotta soldiers and horses dating back to the third century B.C. The Chinese took the whole Saudi delegation to visit the statues. Then afterward, while other members were resting, Bandar was driven alone to the complex for a quick tour and briefing. By pure chance, the *New York Times* correspondent in China, John Burns, happened to be passing through Xi'an on a motorcycle trip with a friend. The police stopped and detained the two for two days. Burns was subsequently expelled from China on suspicion of espionage. According to Bandar, the Chinese thought Burns was spying on their Saudi visitors because "the only thing they were hiding at that time was my visit around Xi'an." Bandar and the Chinese were so convinced that Burns was on to the prince's secret visit that they concocted a press release in case the *Times* published a story.*

The missile deal laid the groundwork for later diplomatic and economic relations with China that would eventually become a counterbalance to Saudi dependence on the United States. Bandar was not the only one involved in forging the kingdom's first opening to a communist power. So, too, was his half brother General Khaled bin Sultan, who was head of the Saudi Air Defense Forces in the mid-1980s. Khaled would later become co-commander with U.S. general Norman Schwarzkopf of the coalition forces assembled to drive Saddam Hussein out of Kuwait during the first Gulf War, in 1990–91. Khaled worked out the details of the missile purchase in secret meetings held between December 16 and 23, 1986, at a Saudi air base with Lieutenant General Cao Gangchuan, deputy chief of the People's Liberation Army's general staff. Khaled made four secret trips to China himself starting in February 1987. In his own account of the Saudi rationale for acquiring the missiles, the general put as much emphasis on the kingdom's need for a deterrent against Israel as against Iran, because of the Israeli nuclear capability.[14] Bandar never mentioned Israel. The two accounts of these sometime rival brothers make clear that there was a lot of traffic between Beijing and Riyadh for almost three years without the CIA, or any of the other fifteen U.S. spy agencies, ever becoming aware of its real purpose.† The deception was completely successful, and Bandar, the linchpin of the U.S.-Saudi relationship, had initiated and carried it off at the same time that he was working secretly with Casey and the CIA on various covert operations.

The Reagan administration became aware of Bandar's masterful deceit only in early 1988. Assistant Secretary of State Richard Murphy confronted Bandar on March 6 with U.S. satellite pictures of the missile sites in the Saudi desert and demanded an explanation. By then, half of what was later determined to be the purchase of fifty Chinese East Wind CSS-2 missiles and nine

---

* Many years later, when both Burns and I were covering the 1992–95 civil war in Bosnia, I asked him about the incident. He said he had had no idea that Bandar was in Xi'an at the time and had never been told his expulsion was linked to Bandar's visit there.

† The Americans had been aware of Bandar's trips to Beijing, but Bandar told them he had gone there to help Iraq by trying to convince Beijing to halt its arms sales to the Iranians, which had included deadly Silkworm shore-to-ship missiles. He told the Americans that China had agreed to sell the Silkworms instead to Iraq, and that Saudi Arabia was picking up the tab.

launchers had already reached Saudi Arabia. Late the previous year, they had been smuggled in by ship and mixed together with Chinese missiles headed for Iraq under another ruse, to avoid Iranian interception. The Saudis had asked the Chinese to deliver the weapons to a Saudi port so they could be taken overland to Iraq to avoid possible Iranian detection and attack. What the CIA never discovered until it was too late was that upon the arrival of the Chinese arms in the kingdom, the shipment had been split up and sent in two different directions: The Iraqi Silkworm missiles had been hauled overland to Iraq, while the CSS-2s had been trucked southwest to a site in the kingdom's desert Rub' al-Khali "empty quarter." When the CIA had first begun asking questions about the activities under way there, Bandar had told the agency that the Saudis were building a huge new "ammunition depot" to keep their munitions far from populated areas for safety's sake.[15]

The *Washington Post* broke the story on March 18 after Bandar tipped the newspaper off to avoid having it appear in the rival *Washington Times* first. The prince was convinced the Israelis had leaked the news to the *Times*. The *Post* article made the point that the missiles had a maximum range of twenty-two hundred miles, making them capable of reaching "any part of the Middle East with a nuclear warhead." (Later reports said they had less than half that range.) Both China and Saudi Arabia were quick to provide Washington with assurances that they would never carry such warheads, but the missiles were so inaccurate that doubts remained in U.S. intelligence circles about their ability to come close enough to hitting a target with only conventional explosives.[16] A week later, a top aide to Israeli prime minister Yitzhak Shamir let it be known that the "possibility always exist[ed]" that Israel would strike the Saudi missile site if the United States failed to deal with the problem. He noted that Israel had "a tradition of not standing by quietly when there [was] a real threat against it."[17] The message was not lost on Bandar, who felt the political temperature rising fast and the heat suddenly concentrated on him.

Reagan, who was furious, gave the Saudis three options—ship the missiles back to China, dismantle them temporarily and negotiate terms for their use, or allow U.S. monitors to be stationed at the launching site. The king refused all three. "Things were tense," Bandar recalled. "We were not talking."[18] Then, when the Israeli air force began maneuvers suggesting it might be preparing to strike the missile site, Bandar approached Reagan's national security adviser, Colin Powell, who was by then a good friend and another of his racquetball regulars, for help.

Powell thoroughly chewed Bandar out for causing the crisis in the first place and said the missiles were causing the Saudis more trouble than they were worth.[19] Bandar reiterated the threat his country perceived and reminded Powell that the Saudis had asked the United States for missiles and been turned down. He also assured Powell they would not be used offensively against anybody in the region, only to defend against an attack on the kingdom. Powell told Bandar he would relay the Saudi message to the Israelis and get back to him. The same afternoon, Bandar learned from Riyadh that Saudi radar had picked up a huge Israeli air force maneuver. He went immediately to see Powell and reminded him to tell the Israelis that Saudi Arabia had no incentive to fight, but that if attacked, it would have no option but to retaliate.

Powell passed the Saudi message on to Reagan and Israel, but the Israelis would give Washington no commitment not to bomb. Uncertain whether Powell was telling the truth or using the Israeli evasiveness to pressure the Saudis into giving up the missiles, Bandar relayed to King Fahd that the United States had been unable to obtain any commitment from the Israelis not to attack. In response, the king ordered the entire Saudi air force to move north and to do it in such a way that the Americans who were on training missions in the kingdom were aware of it.

At midnight Washington time, Powell called Bandar demanding to know why the Saudi air force was on the move. The White House security adviser warned that the Saudi action could lead to a disastrous miscalculation by one of the two countries, to which Bandar replied again that his country had no incentive to initiate hostilities with Israel, but would retaliate if attacked. Powell asked Bandar to come over to his home for more talks. In the meantime, he called the White House and Israel to discuss a way out of the looming confrontation. Finally, Bandar recalled, both countries agreed to back off and announce that their air forces were just engaged in "night exercises."

"We came to the brink," Bandar said.

The actions of others confirm that the two countries were indeed close to war. Reagan issued a public warning to Israel not to make a preemptive strike, making it clear that he was "totally opposed to any such thing."[20] Egyptian president Hosni Mubarak sent what was described as an "urgent message" to Reagan asking him to intervene and warning that an Israeli strike would "blow up peace."[21] The Israeli air force did engage in low-level bombing practice runs, and U.S. intelligence officials were telling reporters they could be in preparation for a preemptive strike.[22] Reagan officials were sufficiently concerned about a possible clash to move quickly to obtain guarantees from both the Saudis and the Chinese that the missiles would never be armed with nuclear or chemical warheads. Powell's own recollection was that the situation was "every bit as tense" as Bandar had described it, but he still judged the two countries "well short of actually going to war."[23]

One casualty of the Chinese missile saga was the U.S. ambassador to Saudi Arabia at the time, Hume Horan. One of the State Department's most seasoned Middle East hands and a fluent Arabic speaker, Horan was caught in the cross fire between Washington and Riyadh in what he later regarded as the most serious crisis in U.S.-Saudi relations prior to 9/11. The State Department first ordered him to see Fahd immediately and convey U.S. "surprise and disapproval" regarding the missile purchase. He did as instructed, to the great displeasure of the Saudi king, whom Horan described as "furious with him" over the reprimand. The king bluntly told him "to keep my nose out of it."[24]

No sooner had Horan delivered the formal U.S. protest than he received a directive to disregard his earlier instructions, but it was too late. Fahd was so furious he asked for Horan's removal. By the end of March, he was gone. According to U.S. Middle East historians, it was the first time since the United States had established diplomatic relations with the Saudi kingdom in 1933 that an American ambassador had been fired at Saudi request.[25] Horan said the Saudis had already been suspicious of him because he spoke fluent Arabic. In addition, his father was Persian and had been a foreign minister under the deposed shah. His Persian pedigree was "offensive" to the king. Bandar had never liked Horan and had stayed away from the ceremony at the State Department marking his departure for Riyadh in mid-September 1987.[26] The prince had thereafter pressed for his removal at the State Department and the White House. In the end, Washington had bent as much to Bandar as to the king, in Horan's eyes. He believed his removal marked a turning point after which the clout of all future U.S. ambassadors to the kingdom was seriously diminished. "It hardly mattered what an American ambassador said or wrote back out there. U.S.-Saudi relations were handled by Bandar here [in Washington]. The U.S. ambassador's influence ended in Riyadh."[27]

BANDAR'S ACCOUNT OF his impact on the shaping of America's Middle East policy during the Reagan years does not jibe with those of others involved. One of the biggest shifts to occur was the United States' decision in December 1988 to formally recognize the Palestine Liberation Organization (PLO) as a legitimate voice in the peace process. America had long insisted that the group recognize Israel's existence and renounce terrorism as preconditions for any kind of dialogue with Washington. On the other hand, Reagan was hamstrung in moving forward with his own proposal for a settlement to the Israeli-Palestinian conflict without having a Palestinian partner in the negotiations. The so-called Reagan plan, announced in September 1982 immediately after the PLO departure from Beirut, had called for the creation of a self-governing Palestinian authority over the West Bank and the Gaza strip that would be in association with Jordan. Israel and Jordan were supposed to negotiate the details without PLO participation.

Bandar claims that he played a central role in convincing Reagan to recognize the PLO, and that it was the quid pro quo he extracted from the White House for Saudi funding of CIA anticommunist covert operations around the world. Specifically, he says the Saudis agreed to fund the contras after Congress cut off money for them in 1984 in return for U.S. recognition of the PLO. The outlines of the deal were sketched in his mind when Bud McFarlane, the national security adviser, came to him asking for help with the contras, and Bandar proposed to King Fahd that the Saudis make this demand. Fahd gave Bandar a green light to make a "deal," and Bandar claims he went back to Riyadh with a letter signed by Reagan recognizing the PLO as the sole Palestinian representative in peace talks with the authority to veto anything.[28]

To date, however, no evidence has come to light to substantiate that Reagan made any such deal. Based on what is known, the breakthrough came about only after enormous U.S. and international pressure had been brought to bear on the PLO and Yasser Arafat to accept the existence of Israel. According to Nicholas Veliotes, an assistant secretary of state at the time, the effort began as early as 1981, just after Reagan came into office, and had nothing to do with Saudi funding for the contras. Veliotes said that he launched the initiative with Reagan's approval, but that it was scuttled after the Israeli invasion of Lebanon in June 1982. Veliotes worked through a private intermediary to avoid direct contacts with the PLO. Bandar played no role, he said, but the Saudi government did act to assure the PLO of the bona fides of Veliotes's chosen intermediary.[29]

Bandar did become involved later, according to Veliotes, when the United States was seeking Arafat's approval of the Reagan plan. In April 1983, Arafat had finally agreed to support the plan, but then said he needed the approval of the PLO National Council, which was meeting in Kuwait at the time. So Arafat flew there ostensibly to confirm the council's acceptance of the plan. When the time came for a vote, Veliotes had Bandar on one telephone line and Hasib Sabbagh, a close friend of Arafat, on another. Both were in direct contact with Palestinians attending the meeting. Bandar reported that the council had approved the Reagan plan, but Sabbagh told Veliotes it had been turned down, and Sabbagh was right. According to Veliotes, Bandar had heard what he hoped to hear and had totally misread Arafat, who was in the process of ensuring that the meeting actually disapproved PLO acceptance of the Reagan plan. For Veliotes, Bandar's "bad judgment" was part of a more general problem in dealing with the Saudis as brokers. "You had to be very careful when they told you X told them something, say Arafat, whether it was really what Arafat meant, or what he had really told the Saudis, or what the Saudis wanted us to hear." Veliotes felt this problem was compounded by doubts about whom Bandar was speaking for, himself or the king. "You were never quite sure whether you were talking to Bandar the wing commander or Bandar the Saudi prince who was representing the royal apparatus."[30]

In its final months, the Reagan administration did recognize the PLO as a result of seven years of on-again, off-again talks through various intermediaries. Neither Bandar nor other Saudis played a noticeable role. Instead, Sweden's foreign minister, Sten Andersson, served as a key mediator between the PLO and Washington.[31] The issue of U.S. recognition came to a head in November 1988 when Arafat applied for a visa to attend a U.N. General Assembly session in New York. Blaming Arafat for the lack of progress in the peace process, Secretary of State George Shultz personally refused his request. A diplomatic commotion ensued over the U.S. right to take such an action. But it got results. At a Geneva press conference on December 14, Arafat proclaimed the magic words: The PLO "totally and absolutely re nounce[d] all forms of terrorism including individual, group and state terrorism" and agreed that all parties to the Middle East conflict had a right "to exist in peace and security, including the state of Palestine, Israel and their neighbors."[32] The United States then recognized the PLO, but Israel was still not ready to talk to Arafat, and the impasse dragged on into the first Bush and then the Clinton administration.

In the end, while no documents proving Bandar's assertion of a contras-for-PLO deal have come to light so far, there may have been an implicit one, as suggested by the testimony of a Palestinian American businessman, Sam Bamieh. He was called to testify before the House Subcommittee on African Affairs in the summer of 1987 about secret U.S. funding for the Angolan anticommunist movement, the National Union for the Total Independence of Angola, led by Jonas Savimbi. Bamieh informed the panel that he had met then crown Prince Fahd at his home in Riyadh in November 1981 and been told that in exchange for the American AWACS, the kingdom was ready to fund "anti-communist movements around the world." Fahd had promised to do "whatever" the Reagan administration wanted the Saudis to do.[33] Bamieh also testified that Bandar had been put in charge to make sure it happened. He had met the prince in February 1984 in Cannes, France, where they had discussed setting up a shell company to funnel funds to anticommunist rebels not only in Angola but also in Afghanistan. Bamieh said that Bandar had told him that even as they were meeting, Fahd was discussing the same issue with CIA director William Casey aboard his royal yacht. The Saudis, Bamieh told the House hearing, had already provided Morocco with fifty million dollars to train Savimbi's guerrillas, who were seeking the overthrow of the communist government in Angola.[34]

ONE OF THE more ironic twists to Bandar's activities in Washington during the Reagan years was the time and energy he spent opening up Saudi relations with the United States' chief Cold War adversaries, the Soviet Union and China. Bandar claimed to have been the secret envoy King Fahd used to initiate a dialogue with both. The opening with China came first because of the missile agreement and because China supported the Saudi position on Afghanistan.[35] Bandar oversaw the first step on the road to full diplomatic relations between China and Saudi Arabia in Washington, where in November 1988 he signed an agreement with the Chinese ambassador allowing the two nations to open trade offices in each other's capital. The Saudis still kept their ties to Taiwan for a while, but informed the Taiwanese of their intention of switching sides shortly. Bandar said both he and his half brother Prince Khaled had argued at the royal court for establishing ties with Beijing "because the Chinese were really treating us very well."[36] Bandar particularly appreciated that "they never forget their friends." The best example of this was the near veneration in which the Chinese still held Henry Kissinger for his role in Richard Nixon's opening up diplomatic relations with China nearly two decades earlier. The Chinese were treating Bandar the same way, maybe even better.[37] China and Saudi Arabia formally opened up diplomatic relations on July 21, 1990. Bandar planned to fly to Beijing ten days later for a vacation, but the first Gulf War broke out.

Establishing relations with the Soviets was much more complicated because of a long-standing Saudi decision not to have any ties until they withdrew from Afghanistan. Bandar recalled that technically Saudi Arabia never formally broke diplomatic relations, and that the Soviet Union was one of the first nations to recognize the present-day Saudi kingdom in 1932. But when the kingdom's founding father, King Abdulaziz, discovered there was a single Soviet communist diplomat present in the country, he ordered him out of the kingdom. After that, relations remained frozen, first because the Soviet Union backed all of the Saudi monarchy's radical Arab foes for three decades and then because in 1979 it invaded Afghanistan.

The Afghan cause was, of course, the keystone of Reagan's anticommunist crusade and what drew U.S., Saudi, and Pakistani intelligence services into a tight alliance during the 1980s.[38] The Saudis spent several billion dollars on arms purchases and economic assistance and agreed to match the Reagan administration dollar for dollar during the latter years of the struggle. It offered air tickets and official encouragement for thousands of young Saudis to go join the jihad against the godless Soviets. Among the most prominent holy warriors was Osama bin Laden, son of one of Saudi Arabia's wealthiest construction magnates and the future leader of the terrorist organization al-Qaeda, founded in the last year of Reagan's administration. But the Saudi who played the most instrumental role in the campaign to drive the Soviets out of Afghanistan was Prince Turki, the American-educated head of the Saudi intelligence service.[39] Bandar claimed he, too, played a crucial role at the very end by helping to convince Mikhail Gorbachev, the reform-minded Soviet president, to withdraw.

As with the Chinese, Bandar's first contacts with Soviet diplomats took place in Washington. Initially, they had nothing to do with opening diplomatic relations with Moscow, as the Washington media first surmised. Bandar went to see the long-serving Soviet ambassador Anatoly Dobrynin on a courtesy call after his official appointment as Saudi ambassador in October 1983. At the time, Dobrynin was dean of the diplomatic corps, and that, said Bandar, was the sole reason for his visit. Bandar said he had no further contact regarding a diplomatic relationship until 1988. In February of that year, he went to Moscow, where he again met with Dobrynin, who by then had become Gorbachev's national security adviser. The reason for his trip, he said, was a decision by Fahd and Reagan to press jointly for a Soviet withdrawal from Afghanistan.[40]

Bandar's first talks took place with Gorbachev and his advisers together, during which the Soviet leader blustered that they had "better quit" or the Saudis would find themselves "in deep trouble." To impress Bandar about Soviet intelligence on what the Saudis were up to in Afghanistan, Gorbachev said he knew they were providing two hundred million dollars annually to arm the Afghan mujahideen.

"I said to him, 'You are absolutely wrong, Mr. President.'"

"He said, 'I am not wrong. My information is solid.'"

"I said, 'You are wrong. We are paying five hundred million, not two hundred million, and we're willing to pay a billion if you don't get out of Afghanistan.'"

At that point, Bandar recalled, Gorbachev asked him to go for a walk alone outside the meeting room. He thanked the prince for his warning, telling him he could now "use that as a club against his people." According to Bandar, the Soviet leader assured him he would be out of Afghanistan by the following March. Indeed, on February 15, 1989, the Soviet Army began its withdrawal, and by the start of March it was complete.

Was Bandar's escalation threat as decisive as he claimed? He was clearly knocking at a wide-open door at Gorbachev's reform-minded Kremlin. Peace negotiations sponsored by the United Nations had been under way for months and were verging on closure by the time of the Bandar-Gorbachev meeting. Transcripts of Soviet Politburo sessions from that period indicate that Gorbachev had resolved to leave Afghanistan by the fall of 1986, when he first stated that his strategic objective was to get out "in one, maximum two, years."[41] The documents reflect little opposition to a withdrawal among Politburo members. By the end of 1987, Gorbachev and Reagan were trying to resolve not whether Soviet troops would withdraw but whether U.S. aid for the Afghan resistance would stop when they left.[42] In the end, the Soviets left with no U.S. assurance of a cutoff of that aid.

On April 14, about two months after Bandar's talk with Gorbachev, the Soviet Union signed a formal agreement in Geneva committing itself to withdrawal. The pact was also signed by the Soviet-backed regime in Kabul and representatives from Pakistan and the United States. The Geneva signing ceremony excluded all the Afghan resistance leaders as part of a face-saving formula that also involved U.N.-conducted indirect talks between the Afghan mujahideen and the Soviets and their Kabul allies, to avoid humiliating face-to-face negotiations.

The Soviet departure from Afghanistan did not lead the Saudis to immediately reestablish their relations with Moscow. It would take another two years and the imperative need to win Soviet support at the United Nations for the U.S.-Saudi campaign to oust Saddam Hussein's army from Kuwait by force. Bandar spearheaded the negotiations, holding secret talks first with the Soviet ambassador to Washington, Alexander Bessmertnykh, and later in Moscow with Soviet foreign minister Eduard Shevardnadze. The contacts had begun shortly after the Iraqis took over Kuwait in early August 1990. In the end, the Saudis basically had to bribe Gorbachev with a four-billion-dollar letter of credit to gain Soviet backing for a U.N. resolution authorizing the use of force against Saddam. They also had to agree to resume full diplomatic relations with the Soviet Union and did so on September 17. Despite the Afghan war, Moscow was only about two months behind Beijing in establishing relations with Riyadh.

Bandar came away with one unique souvenir from his dealings with Gorbachev: a photograph of the Soviet leader and President Reagan with the words "Trust But Verify" written on it. Reagan had become famous for this adage and used it at a press conference, even speaking in Russian (*"doverey no proverey"*), at the U.S.-Soviet Iceland summit in October 1986. While Bandar was in Moscow in early 1988, he said, Gorbachev gave him one of only fifty copies made of a photograph of the two leaders standing together. The next time he saw Reagan, the prince showed him the picture.[43]

Bandar asked him, "Why do you think he gave it to me, Mr. President?"

"What did he tell you?" asked Reagan.

"He said, 'I want you to know I'm a friend of your friend, too.'"

Reagan then picked up his pen and scrawled on the picture, "Prince Bandar, Trust But Verify."

When Bandar next saw Gorbachev in Moscow after the attempted coup against the Soviet leader in August 1991, he showed him the same picture. Gorbachev, too, picked up his pen and inscribed in Russian, "*Doverey no Proverey.*" Bandar kept this unique photograph on prominent display in his office at the Saudi embassy in downtown Washington.

CHAPTER 6

"Going All the Way"

NO EVENT LEFT A DEEPER imprint on Bandar's soul than the outbreak of the first Gulf War on August 2, 1990. Watching one Arab country occupy another was something the prince had thought he would never see in his lifetime. Making it even worse, Bandar was the victim of deception at the hands of an Arab "brother" who had benefited from twenty-eight billion dollars in Saudi aid during its war with Iran.* In the days immediately preceding the outbreak of war, Saddam Hussein provided personal assurances to King Fahd, President Hosni Mubarak of Egypt, and King Hussein of Jordan that he would not invade Kuwait, at least until after a high-level Arab meeting in Baghdad in early August to resolve Saddam's grievance over Kuwait's alleged theft of Iraqi oil from the Rumaila Field, which straddled the two countries' border. Based on the assumption that Saddam was still open to mediation for a peaceful end to the crisis, the Saudi message back to the White House and 10 Downing Street was "not to worry, we will find an Arab solution." Unfortunately, Bandar was thus the messenger with the news that the crisis had been defused.[1] He ran into considerable apprehension from General Colin Powell, then chairman of the Joint Chiefs of Staff, who had in hand satellite reconnaissance photos of the Iraqi army's buildup

---

* Bandar would never forgive Saddam Hussein for his treachery. His desire to get even with the Iraqi leader helps explain why he would become part of the neoconservative "war party" in Washington pressing to invade Iraq in the early spring of 2003.

of a force of more than one hundred thousand troops along the Kuwaiti border. But Bandar was confident Saddam was bluffing and using the buildup to pressure, not invade, Kuwait.

He then went on to London on August 1 to brief Margaret Thatcher on the pending Arab solution before taking his whole family on a vacation in China for the first time with Frederick and Nancy Dutton.[2] Bandar found that Thatcher shared Powell's mistrust of Saddam, and she told him to "expect the worst."

Bandar planned to leave for Beijing the next morning, but shortly before midnight he received a call from an aide to Bush's national security adviser, Brent Scowcroft, who told him the Iraqi army had crossed the Kuwait border. The prince still didn't believe Saddam was serious and brushed off the aide.[3] A half hour later, Bandar got another call and learned that Iraqi tanks were on the roll and not far from Kuwait City. Bandar was stunned by the news and still reluctant to believe it. But King Fahd also called him with the same information and instructions to get back to Washington as quickly as possible.

In the end, an alliance of thirty-seven nations and 750,000 soldiers commanded jointly by Americans and Saudis—Christians and Muslims allied—used the Land of the Two Holy Mosques to destroy a onetime Arab national hero. This was unlike anything the Arab and Muslim worlds had ever seen— a dream-shattering event, as Bandar called it. Two months before the war, the prince had gone to Baghdad to see Saddam and listened to him sing the praises of the Saudis as "true Arab nationalists" and an inspiration to the Muslim world. From one day to the next, the Saudis had become, for Saddam, American lackeys unfit to protect Islam's holy sites.

"The question became 'How can we say to Israel and the whole Arab world that Israel is wrong for occupying Arab lands and then accept that an Arab will occupy Arab lands?' He shattered everything," Bandar said.[4]

The religious and political fallout from the war was enormous. The seeds were sown for a Wahhabi revolt against the foreign presence in the kingdom that would come to haunt both the House of Saud and America for years to come. Osama bin Laden would come to life as an inspirational guide for thousands of Saudis. Al-Qaeda, born before the war, would be transformed into a world menace. But the war spawned other changes, too. The Saudis became far more cynical about Arab solidarity after King Hussein of Jordan and the Palestine Liberation Organization came out in support of Saddam. So did the Muslim Brotherhood despite years of Saudi protection for its persecuted brethren. The Saudis cut their political ties and financial aid to all of them. They became much more willing to define and pursue their own narrower national interest. After the war, they joined the Middle East peace process for the first time. They no longer insisted on the PLO being at the negotiating table. Bandar was in the middle of this postwar ferment and a prime promoter of a new Saudi realpolitik.

Upon reaching Washington on August 2, Bandar was given briefings and shown satellite photos of the Iraqi army's steady advance through Kuwait City and southward toward the Saudi border. His briefers included Scowcroft, Powell, and Secretary of Defense Dick Cheney, and their common message was that American forces had to be on the ground inside Saudi Arabia to stop Saddam's army from marching into the kingdom. The entire U.S. national security hierarchy was bent on convincing Bandar, and through him the king, of this imperative necessity. Bandar later remembered vividly his meeting with President George H. W. Bush on the afternoon of August 3. The prince by then had known him for ten years—eight as Reagan's vice president—and felt he knew him well. He found the president so down-to-earth and easygoing that addressing him formally as "Mr. President" had always been difficult for him. "He's almost like a buddy," Bandar remarked.[5] The prince also believed he knew Bush's moods and inner feelings. The man he saw before him that day harbored "quiet hidden anger" and determination to get Saddam out of Kuwait. "In my judgment, George Bush the person, George Bush the human being, whether he knew it or not, had made up his mind from day one."[6] The question in Bandar's mind was whether the president could rally others to a call for war. Ironically, Bush had the same doubts about the Saudis and feared they might back out rather than go to war over Kuwait.[7]

Bandar reflected all the Saudi ambivalence about relying on the United States. Scowcroft described him as "ill at ease" and evincing an "equivocal posture" when confronted by the U.S. offer to come to the kingdom's rescue. He wrote in his memoirs that Bandar's explanation for his ambivalence "really set [him] back."[8] President Carter had in Bandar's eyes humiliated the Saudis when sending a squadron of F-15s to the kingdom after the Iranian shah's overthrow in 1979. The planes had been meant as a show of U.S. resolve to defend the Saudi royal family, but Carter had emptied the gesture of all meaning by publicly declaring the warplanes were unarmed even before they reached the kingdom. Would Bush do the same?

Bandar reminded Scowcroft as well of the American "cut-and-run" performance in Lebanon. Reagan had sent U.S. Marines to serve as part of a multinational peacekeeping force after the PLO withdrawal from Beirut in August 1982. The idea had been to bolster the central Lebanese government and army against various Syrian-backed Lebanese factions. When Shiite radicals had begun firing on the Marines, Reagan had sent the battleship *New Jersey*, fresh out of mothballs, to Lebanon's shores as a show of American resolve. The *New Jersey* had fired some of its massive sixteen-inch shells into the Shouf Mountains behind Beirut. At one point, Reagan had declared a tiny village, Souk al-Garb, sitting on the crest of the mountains to be of "vital interest" to the United States. But the death of 241 Marines in a massive bomb attack at their Beirut airport barracks in October 1983 had suddenly changed Reagan's mind about how "vital" even the whole of Lebanon was, let alone Souk al-Garb. Overnight, he had withdrawn all U.S. military forces and ceded Lebanon to Syria. For the Saudis, this was the recent record of "American resolve" in the Middle East—unarmed F-15s and cut-and-run under fire in Lebanon.

Bandar asked Scowcroft whether, if the "going got tough, the United States would behave in the same manner once again."[9] On the other hand, the prince was keenly aware of the Kuwaiti mistake of waiting too long before asking for outside help. "The Kuwaitis lost their country because they wanted to be 'good Arabs' and not bring the Americans in."[10] Bandar was in a real dilemma. The Americans needed a formal Saudi request if they wanted help, but the Saudis didn't want to ask unless they were sure the Americans would "go all the way" with their commitment to defend the kingdom.[11] Bandar and Scowcroft went round and round about how to resolve this catch-22 with no success. Suddenly, Bush walked into the meeting "in his old awkward way," leaning against the wall with his hands folded and with "a touch of sadness in his face."

"You know, Bandar, it hurts when your friends don't trust you," Bush said for an opener.[12]

"Mr. President, oh, we trust you," Bandar responded. "This is nothing personal. My country's survival probably depends on this. It's very simple. If you tell me what you can do, then I can tell you what our position is. In any case, I have to go back to my boss, His Majesty, to get clearance."

Bush asked Bandar what exactly he needed to know.

"We need to know how far you're willing to go."

"If you ask for help from the United States of America, we will go all the way with you," Bush replied calmly.

At these words, Bandar said, the hair on his hands stood on end under the weight of the moment. He went over to Bush, shook his hand, and said, "I believe you."

"So?" said Bush.

"So, I still need to know," replied Bandar, and everyone broke out in laughter.

Bush then told Scowcroft to have Cheney and Powell brief Bandar on Operation Plan 1002-90, titled "Defense of the Arabian Peninsula."[13] It was a Pentagon emergency contingency plan for the Persian Gulf that had initially envisaged a Soviet invasion of Iran and had just been updated to deal with a possible Iraqi or Iranian attack against an Arab neighbor. The update was barely a month old. At the Pentagon, Cheney and Powell spelled out a mesmerizing scenario for the U.S. deployment of a massive force to the kingdom, including 220,000 troops and squadrons of fighter jets and bombers. Bandar was impressed. "I guess now I think we are in business," Bandar told Cheney and Powell.[14] He also suggested they provide King Fahd with the same briefing to convince him of the U.S. commitment to "going all the way." Bandar went back to the White House, where he found Bush talking to Fahd on the phone. Bush handed it over to the prince, and Fahd asked his assessment of the threat to the kingdom. Bandar described the satellite photos to the king as "ominous," but he hesitated to commit himself. He suggested the king allow a Pentagon team to come brief him personally. But the king wanted to know what Bandar thought then and there. "What's your assessment? Don't tell me what they tell you."[15] Bandar felt himself to be in an exceedingly tight spot. He saw the steady advance of Iraqi troops from the U.S. satellite photos, but inviting America's Christian troops in to defend the Land of the Two Holy Mosques was a decision of existential proportions. Finally, they all agreed to send a high-level U.S. team to brief the king.

Bush wanted Cheney dispatched immediately. But Bandar advised that he go first and prepare the way. He felt neither country could afford a Saudi refusal of an offer by the U.S. secretary of defense without encouraging Saddam to make a grab for the Saudi oil fields just forty miles away from Kuwait's border. The answer had to be "yes" before Cheney left Washington. Bandar favored "a decisive American intervention," but he still had to convince his king and other senior royal family members of that.[16] Within twelve hours of being home, he sent word back for Cheney to come ahead. The king's answer would indeed be "yes."

Cheney did not disappoint. He reaffirmed to the king that the United States was "willing to go all the way with you."[17] He showed Fahd the latest overhead satellite photos of Iraqi forces, illustrating a continuing buildup, and outlined U.S. military plans to protect the kingdom. Bandar was convinced that the event that ended the debate within the royal family about whether to invite in the Americans took place while he was flying back to Riyadh.[18] On August 4, several Iraqi reconnaissance patrols penetrated ten to twelve miles across the Kuwait-Saudi border, while two divisions of Saddam's elite Republican Guard continued moving toward the border as well. Bandar said the incursions included tanks.[19] Saudi military leaders at first wanted to engage, said Bandar, but the king demurred and ordered them to use the Saudi hotline to Iraqi military headquarters in Baghdad to inform Iraqi commanders about the incident.

At first, the Iraqi chief of staff was effusively apologetic.[20] Within half an hour, the tanks were withdrawn. But six hours later, another incursion took place. Again the king ordered the Saudi military to call Baghdad. This time, a junior officer answered, not the chief of staff, with another apology. Again, the tanks turned around and went back across the border into Kuwait. Then, for the third time the same day, the tanks came rolling back across. Saudi officers again picked up the phone, but this time the hotline was dead. "This is where the Saudi leadership began to think something ominous was going to happen," said Bandar. The Iraqis had been probing one of the few passageways through sand berms and border obstructions leading to the Saudi oil heartland. "History would never have forgiven King Fahd had he asked for no help and we didn't take any precautions and he [Saddam] went through."

Once Cheney and his briefers had finished, Fahd remarked, "God knows that Saddam Hussein did not leave us any way out of confrontation." He then asked his assembled advisers to give their opinions, and they all deferred to the king.

"We will rely on Allah, and we will go ahead. You have the formal request," the king told Cheney.[21]

Chas. Freeman Jr., the U.S. ambassador to the kingdom at the time, recounted some of the conversation that took place among the Saudis at that historic meeting.[22] He listened to an exchange in Arabic between Fahd and Crown Prince Abdullah, who had suggested the royal family needed more time before making a decision. "We have to make the decision now," insisted Fahd, "or what happened to Kuwait will happen to us." When Abdullah tried to argue that there was "still a Kuwait," the king retorted, "And its territory consists solely of hotel rooms in London, Cairo, and elsewhere." Abdullah then agreed, and so did his other advisers. But Fahd later told Freeman that it was the only time in his "many decades of public life that he had ever made a decision on his own without waiting for consensus."[23]

THE WAR PROVED to be an extraordinary bonding experience for Bandar with President Bush and his senior security team—Scowcroft, Cheney, Powell, and Secretary of State James Baker III. The prince called it his "dream team for crisis management."[24] By then, he had already known its members in various capacities for a decade or more, played racquetball with some, hunted with others, and dined repeatedly with all of them. He had served as their translator when they went to Saudi Arabia to see the king and briefed them on Saudi views of the world. But in the ensuing weeks and months of consultations over how to deal with Saddam, Bandar practically became part of the Bush administration. He was in and out of the White House, Pentagon, and State Department at all times of day and night. He was given the rare privilege for a foreign diplomat of access to the State Department underground garage. And U.S. national security people installed a high-security telephone on his desk linking him instantly to all decision-making centers in the U.S. government. Bandar said he ate more pizza at late-night meetings during the fall and winter of 1990–91 than in his entire life before or since. He would order takeout from Pizza Hut and have it delivered by an aide to wherever they were meeting. Bandar found it somewhat ironic that in the richest nation on earth, the favorite food of its highest officials should turn out to be fast food at a time of crisis. He quickly adjusted, keeping a can of jalapeños in his car to add to the otherwise bland pizzas.

Of all the members of the Bush dream team, he had perhaps the highest regard for Scowcroft, the president's national security adviser. He found him "extraordinarily intelligent and humble at the same time," a man who "doesn't wear around the sleeves" over time.[25] He realized quickly that Scowcroft was the closest to Bush of any of his advisers, but Bandar found he never flaunted this. "If he tells you something, you can count on it. If he can't deliver, he tells you." Bandar contrasted him to Reagan's first national security adviser, Richard Allen, whom he found "extraordinarily sharp intellectually" but aggravatingly "cocky." Fortunately, Allen did not last long. Baker, on the other hand, was a fixture in Bandar's life for twelve years, starting with Reagan and continuing through the Bush years. Bandar found Baker to be "full of life," with a mind that never stopped working.[26] Baker loved "the panache" of being secretary of state and came the closest to acting like a prime minister of any American official Bandar dealt with. In this regard, the prince was strikingly similar, loving the panache of royalty and the trappings of power.

Bandar was perhaps closest to Powell because of their common military background and way of thinking. The two had begun playing racquetball together in 1979 when Bandar was studying at the Johns Hopkins School of Advanced International Studies. The African American general was aware of the vast social distance between the two, "a kid from the South Bronx and prince from a royal palace," as he put it.[27] Yet they treated each other with a familiarity that approached "the outrageous and the profane." Powell called the prince "Bandar the Magnificent" and "you Arab Gatsby," while Bandar called Powell "Milord."[28] The day of decision for the first Gulf War, however, Powell seemed to be somewhat peeved by Bandar's nonchalant attitude when he came to Cheney's office for a briefing. The general noted that "Bandar played his usual Americanized, jaunty fighter pilot role, drinking coffee from a foam cup and stirring it with a gold pen" while he studied the reconnaissance photos with an unlit cigar clenched between his teeth.[29]

The Gulf War put the Bandar-Powell friendship to a serious test. They had to work out the difficult issues posed by sending Christian, Jewish, and female troops into a country dominated by a religion hateful toward the first two and dedicated to keeping the latter out of public sight and in a subservient role. The massive American presence in the kingdom made starkly clear for the first time the yawning chasm between the two countries' cultures and mores. One issue was whether Christian soldiers would be allowed to bring Bibles into Saudi Arabia. Bandar told Powell that Saudi customs officials would confiscate them. Powell warned him that it would be a public relations disaster if word got back that "the Arabs will take your sons, but not their Bibles."[30] So they agreed the Bibles would be flown directly to air bases being used by the U.S. Air Force, thus circumventing Saudi customs officials.

Bandar also warned that Jewish services would never be allowed on Saudi soil. Powell foresaw another public relations disaster: Jewish American troops would be asked to defend the kingdom "but they can't pray in it?"[31] In the end, Powell agreed to helicopter Jewish personnel out to American ships in the Persian Gulf to hold their services. (Freeman maintains that both Christian and Jewish services ended up being held inside the kingdom without any problem.) Bandar was even worried about American soldiers accidentally displaying crucifixes. Powell told him he would order them to be worn inside soldiers' shirts to hide them. Miraculously, none of these religious issues caused any serious flap. Powell also agreed to the Saudi ban on alcohol for all foreign troops, even on U.S. bases. But Bandar and Powell found no solution to female American GIs driving vehicles other than to keep them restricted to bases as much as possible. Still, the word got out and had serious ramifications. On November 6, a group of seventy Saudi women, inspired by the example of foreign female drivers, staged a brief run-about in the streets of Riyadh before being arrested by Wahhabi religious policemen. They were detained, stripped of their passports and jobs, and shamed publicly. Wahhabi clerics seized on the incident as evidence of the subversive influence of the American presence and used it to incite a backlash for their fundamentalist cause.

Bandar did not have to manage the military side of the war, just the multiple strains on the Saudi-American relationship. They came in all forms. One was a near public relations disaster at the start of the American military buildup stemming from the attempt by the Saudi information minister, Ali Shaer, to keep American and other foreign reporters out of the kingdom. He wanted to attract as little attention as possible to the swelling western presence in the Land of the Two Holy Mosques, hoping to minimize criticism from the Muslim world. As a result, there was no television coverage of the arrival of the first U.S. troops in the kingdom on August 8. Even the publicity-conscious Pentagon would not allow a press pool on the planes transporting them there.* Shaer's idea was to restrict the foreign press corps

---

* I was among the first six American reporters allowed into the kingdom on August 6, armed with just a two-week visa.

to a small number of reporters at a time who would be allowed into the kingdom for just a few days. Major U.S. newspapers and television networks staged a revolt. Their publishers and owners collectively wrote to the White House to complain. Not until August 13 was the first Pentagon press pool allowed in. Bandar sought to handle the looming PR crisis by sending nine of his best and brightest embassy aides, led by the young, Texas-educated Adel al-Jubeir, to intervene with Shaer and calm the storm. Between the bad publicity and the combined pressure from Bandar and the White House, Shaer finally relented. A steady flood of reporters poured into the kingdom, reaching as many as sixteen hundred on the eve of battle.

Bandar had no doubt the coalition would prevail. Rather, he was worried Bush would be undermined in his resolve, even blocked from declaring war, by a skeptical Congress. As a result, he spent most of the time lobbying domestically in America.[32] The prince went into high gear blitzing Congress, the media, and the public in speeches and meetings across the United States. He remembered one particular ordeal—spending five hours in the office of Democratic senator Paul Sarbanes, who had opposed Bush's decision to send troops to the kingdom and favored economic sanctions only. Bandar refused to leave until Sarbanes more or less promised to support stronger action.

The prince found himself in a battle royal not only with American opponents to a war. He had to contend as well with King Hussein of Jordan, probably the most beloved Arab leader in the eyes of Congress. In a surprise appeal to the American people during a CNN broadcast on September 22, the "plucky little king," as he was affectionately known, called for understanding of Saddam's invasion of Kuwait because the emirate was just a British colonial fiction anyway. The presence of foreign forces in Saudi Arabia was desecrating the Muslim world's holiest sites, and they should be withdrawn immediately. The Saudis were livid. Bandar responded with a blistering "Open Letter to King Hussein," published four days later in the *Washington Post*. His op-ed piece stands to this day as probably the most devastating critique of one U.S. ally by another ever to appear in the U.S. media. Bandar, a mere prince, basically put Hussein, a majestic king, in his place. What had the Jordanian king done to protect the al-Aqsa Mosque, lost to the Israelis in the 1967 Arab-Israeli war? Was that the kind of protection His Majesty was proposing for the Two Holy Mosques in Saudi Arabia by relying on Saddam Hussein? He reminded the king that Jordan was even more artificial than Kuwait in its borders, and that he had relied on British troops to stay in power in 1958. So Saudi Arabia didn't need any lessons from him about calling in foreign troops to protect itself.

Bandar's main contribution to bolstering the Washington "war party" was probably the unusual alliance he formed with Jewish groups. The prince had started cultivating American Jewish leaders in 1988, at first secretly and, he admitted, "on his own." But after a couple of clandestine meetings facilitated by the Egyptian ambassador to Washington, Abdel Raouf el-Reedy, Bandar approached King Fahd for formal permission to continue developing his contacts. His argument: that something good might come out of it, while nothing bad could come out of it. The king, noting that he himself had met Henry Kissinger, told him to "press on but make sure it's quiet" until they could assess the value of the initiative.[33] By the time of the Gulf War, Bandar had held half a dozen meetings with leaders of almost all the major Jewish groups in America, and they had become very public affairs. The prince recounted that at one of these meetings he was pressed to take the next step and meet with Israeli officials. He demurred, offering to meet with the Israelis if they agreed to meet with PLO chairman Yasser Arafat. Bandar said that the two sides learned how to disagree but still keep talking, remain friends, and search for common ground.[34]

The war provided it. It even brought together an unlikely mix of previous archenemies—Saudis and pro-Israel hawks. This time Bandar, the powerful American Israel Public Affairs Committee (AIPAC), and Jews in Congress were on the same side and even working together. They formed the Committee for Peace and Security in the Gulf. Its founder was Representative Stephen Solarz, a New York City Jewish Democratic activist and at the time one of the most influential members of the House International Affairs Committee. Bandar attended one of the first meetings where the idea of setting up the committee was discussed. Other members included Frank Carlucci, Reagan's former secretary of defense, and his acerbic U.N. ambassador, Jeane Kirkpatrick. Another leading light was Richard Perle, a senior Pentagon official during the Reagan administration, at the time a fellow at the American Enterprise Institute in Washington, and already a super-hawk on Iraq. Perle was the committee's chief fund-raiser and drew most of his funds from defense contractors.[35]

Bandar lobbied AIPAC, the American Jewish Congress, the Conference of Presidents of Major Jewish Organizations, Jewish Democrats in Congress, and Jewish think tank intellectuals alike. Henry Siegman, then AJC executive director, remembered the smooth-talking prince making an extremely favorable impression on his new Jewish friends, wooing them with the lure of better Arab-Israeli relations and assurances that Saudi Arabia would acknowledge that "Israel was a fact in the Middle East" after the war. The Bandar initiative did at least result in the first visit ever by a Jewish delegation, led by Siegman, to the kingdom in January 1992. Others followed.

His overtures to Jewish groups would also lead to a sharp disagreement with some of their leaders about whether he had made an explicit commitment to Saudi, and even Syrian, recognition of Israel's legitimacy after the war. Siegman publicly accused Bandar later of breaking his promise to American Jewish leaders on this point.[36] Solarz said he did not remember Bandar ever making such a commitment except in the context of an agreement on the Palestinian problem.[37] In any case, the Jewish lobby threw its considerable weight behind the effort to gain Senate approval of what amounted to a declaration of war on Saddam. Even with AIPAC's support, it was a very close call: The resolution squeaked through by a three-vote margin at 52–47. Bandar was absolutely correct to have been apprehensive about Bush's ability to carry the day in Congress.

THE SCARIEST DAY of the Gulf War for Bandar happened long before the first shots were fired. In September of 1990, as the military buildup was gathering momentum, Bush called Bandar to tell him there were unconfirmed reports that Saddam had anthrax in his biological weapons arsenal. Bandar described the reports as causing a major crisis within the coalition, whose members were already worried about the possible use of chemical weapons by Saddam. General Khaled, the Saudi coalition co-commander, attributed this fear to what he regarded as a vastly exaggerated American assessment of the Iraqi threat right up until the coalition offensive was launched.[38] According to Bandar, however, Bush was concerned specifically about Saddam's possible use of anthrax. Bandar became just as worried, imagining the effect if an anthrax bomb were exploded over Dhahran, the hub of the military buildup, making it unlivable for weeks or months.[39] The prince kept the knowledge of the threat to himself, though it was hardly a secret. On September 29, both the *Washington Post* and the *New York Times* published front-page stories reporting that U.S. intelligence agencies believed Iraq had a stockpile of biological weapons, including anthrax, and would have the capability by early 1991 to use them on the battlefield. They both quoted CIA director William Webster, who had just made this public a few days before in congressional testimony.[40]

Whatever the facts were, the anthrax scare rattled the White House. Bush continued to have doubts about Saudi war resolve. He asked Bandar what he thought Fahd's reaction would be in the face of a public panic about a possible anthrax attack. The prince reassured him that the king's determination to see Saddam rolled back remained rock solid. "He will do it. Period. But it is a tough, tough decision," Bandar told Bush.[41] Since Bandar at that point had not had time to consult with Fahd, he apparently had decided to speak for him. He and Bush finally agreed there was not much they could do other than step up their surveillance for signs of chemical weapons being brought into the war theater and hope for the best. Bandar said the anthrax specter hung over him like a nightmare, giving him serious doubts about the potential impact of the threat on both governments' resolve.

Bush took the chemical weapons issue seriously enough to warn Saddam against using them in a way that implied the United States might just possibly resort to nuclear retaliation. Secretary of State Baker delivered the veiled threat to Iraqi foreign minister Tariq Aziz at their "last-chance meeting" in Geneva on January 9, 1991. "If the conflict involves your use of chemical or biological weapons against our forces, the American people will demand vengeance. We have the means to exact it," Baker told Aziz.[42] Saddam never did resort to such weapons, either during the air war from January 17 to February 24 or during the ensuing land war that lasted just one hundred hours. Still, there was grave concern that some of the eighty-eight Scud missiles Iraq fired off during the war—forty-two of them at Israel and forty-three at Saudi Arabia—would be tipped with chemical warheads.[43] But as it turned out, none were, and Saddam's army was laid waste across the desert with little resistance. The dictator himself, however, was allowed to hold on to power in Baghdad.

For Bandar, the Gulf War had been one long emotional high, an unparalleled, exhilarating experience and what he called a "defining moment" of his life.[44] He had accomplished his goal of building strong political and military foundations for the U.S.-Saudi alliance. The two governments and their militaries had worked together amazingly well to assemble a multinational coalition that had included even troops from Syria, despite its close political links to Iraq. Bandar had helped Baker raise over sixty billion dollars to finance the war. He had helped secure support for military action from the Soviets by going to Moscow to arrange for the resumption of diplomatic relations and a four-billion-dollar line of credit. He was amazed at how easy it had been to work out a formula for stationing ultimately 540,000 U.S. troops in the kingdom.

The Saudis had asked for a very simple agreement. Bandar said it had consisted of just three sentences and contained just three conditions: One, American forces would come at the invitation of the Saudi government and would depart at the request of the Saudi government; two, no U.S. forces would be used offensively from land, sea, or air territory of Saudi Arabia without the prior consent of the Saudi government; and three, visiting friendly forces would respect the cultural and religious traditions of the kingdom. "The Americans could not believe we would sign an agreement without lawyers. We said, 'No, no. It's just three sentences. We don't need lawyers.' "[45] True to the agreement, the Pentagon had all U.S. land forces out of the kingdom by June 1991. But it left behind some air force units soon to become a festering sore.

SHOCK WAVES FROM the war traveled across the Middle East and shook Saudi Arabia to its desert roots. The kingdom was propelled at once in diametrically opposite directions. On the one hand, it moved toward direct engagement in the peace process under U.S. prodding and closer to de facto recognition of Israel. On the other hand, the massive foreign presence roiled up Wahhabi clerics and scholars, setting off an "awakening" among the more militant ones bent on contesting all things American, Jewish, or Western.

In the immediate aftermath of the Gulf War, Secretary of State Baker was determined to relaunch the dormant Middle East peace process with an international conference that would bring all belligerents to the same table for the first time. Initially, innumerable objections and conditions were raised as Baker undertook eight shuttle trips among the region's capitals during the spring and summer of 1991. The Saudis at first showed no interest in the idea at all. Then, suddenly, the king changed his mind.

In his memoirs, Baker gives considerable credit for this turnabout to the prince, whom he appreciated both for his "aura of charming roguishness" and for his "extraordinary influence" with King Fahd.[46] Because of the latter, the U.S. secretary of state had taken to using Bandar as his personal advance man at the Saudi royal court. He would ask the prince to precede him on his visits to Riyadh to brief Fahd and get his support for whatever proposal or initiative Baker was pressing at the time. "His powers of persuasion in these situations were frequently decisive," the secretary noted.[47] But Bandar wasn't always ready to play ball. At one point, Baker became furious with the prince's famous diplomatic disappearing acts. These were sometimes related to his health but sometimes, too, to his lack of interest in being helpful.

In the spring of 1991, the secretary found himself in the strange position of being closer to convincing the notoriously obstreperous Syrian leader Hafez al-Assad to attend the peace conference than the Saudi king. This annoyed Baker greatly. He felt Saudi Arabia owed the United States a big debt of gratitude for saving it from Saddam's rampaging army. But the king kept putting him off, and Bandar was refusing to return his phone calls. His excuse was that he was recuperating from a flare-up of his recurring back injury at his father's retreat outside Geneva. On one trip to the region in April, Baker finally lost his temper, telling an aide to leave a tart message on Bandar's phone that he was fed up busting his "commoner's ass out here" while Bandar sat "on his royal butt."[48]

Still, Bandar was slow to engage. Finally, in early May, Baker dispatched Dennis Ross, the State Department's director of policy planning, to see Bandar and light a fire under the royal Saudi throne to support the Middle East conference. Ross went to see Bandar at his residence in McLean, Virginia, on a Saturday afternoon and did not mince words: "In this country, there is a collective sense that we did not just liberate Kuwait, we saved your butt. No one can understand, especially on the Hill, that Saudi Arabia is doing nothing for peace." Ross warned Bandar that his own credibility was at stake and that unless the Saudis did something, "we are going to see a very strong anti-Saudi campaign emerge soon." Bandar asked what Ross had in mind. Ross suggested the Saudis signal their support for the conference publicly and also agree to send at least one observer to attend. If they needed some diplomatic cover, they could send a delegation from the Gulf Cooperation Council, (GCC), which was led by Saudi Arabia and included six Arab gulf states. Ross wrote that the prince "loved the idea and promised to make it happen."[49]

The U.S. pressure didn't stop there. On May 7, Bush and Baker met Bandar at the White House and again pressed him hard to convince Fahd to attend. "Tell my friend the king I need his help," Bush said.[50] Baker was even more explicit. "When you needed us, we came. Now we need you." The prince left immediately for home, this time reversing his normal role to serve as Bush's messenger. Fahd called together his senior advisers, including Crown Prince Abdullah and Defense Minister Sultan, for a royal family conclave. Toward the end, Fahd turned to Bandar and asked his opinion.

"I can't be sure of the consequences if we say 'Yes,' but if we say 'No,' we will have hell to pay in American domestic politics," Bandar replied.

Fahd then turned to the others and said, "If you can tell me that we'll never need the Americans again, I'll tell them to go away. If not, then we have to help them."[51]

Three days later, the Saudis declared their support for the conference and announced that an observer delegation from the GCC would attend. Baker called the Saudi decision "a stunning development."[52] Bandar would even end up leading the GCC delegation, and the *New York Times* remarked that it was "the first time that any senior Saudi official has attended any sort of negotiations with the Prime Minister of Israel."[53] Unfortunately, the conference, held in Madrid at the end of October, turned out to be another dry hole in the quest for a Palestinian settlement, partly because the PLO had been left out in the cold. But the conference did pave the way for secret Israeli-PLO talks in Oslo two years later, a process in which Bandar would play no part.

THE OTHER MAJOR consequence flowing from the Gulf War unfolded inside the kingdom. On August 14, 1990, a few days after American troops began pouring into Saudi Arabia, the kingdom's Council of Senior Ulama issued a religious decree, or fatwa, bestowing its blessing on their presence in the Land of the Two Holy Mosques. Official Wahhabi clerical support for controversial decisions by al-Saud rulers was nothing new; even the kingdom's founder, King Abdulaziz, had used British air might to help crush the fanatical Wahhabi Ikhwan, or "brothers," in the late 1920s. But justifying Saudi reliance upon a whole army of mostly Christian soldiers was a religious matter of a whole different magnitude. The decree carefully avoided any mention of the fact that these were Christian soldiers coming to the kingdom's defense. The Wahhabi clerics justified their decision by noting what had happened to

Kuwait, arguing that "fortunate is the one who learns his lesson from the fate of others." They stated that it was the king's "obligation dictated by necessity" to invite in "qualified forces with equipment that bring fear and terror to those who wish to commit aggression against this country."[54]

Little did anyone understand at the time what forces they were setting loose. The decree became the center of a theological dispute that fueled a revival of Wahhabi fervor and a wave of political agitation unlike anything the House of Saud had seen previously. For Osama bin Laden, it was nothing less than a casus belli, a cause for launching a religious holy war. Both Saudi liberals and Wahhabi traditionalists, while arguing with each other, joined hands to demand sweeping political reform. They did so in the Saudi way of protest, not by marching in the streets or holding rallies but by firing off petitions and letters to their king.

The opening shot heard around the kingdom came on May 18, 1991, as the last American troops were leaving and Bandar was busy with Baker reviving the peace process. A letter to the king, signed by five hundred Islamic clerics and scholars, set forth twelve demands, including the creation of a consultative council, the strict application of religious laws, a war on corruption, and a new foreign policy "avoiding alliances that violate the Shariah, Islam's legal codes."[55] Among the signatories were those who would lead the challenge to al-Saud authority throughout the rest of the decade and into the twenty-first century—Sheikhs Safar al-Hawali, Salman al-Audah, and Nasir Umar. They had already established their credentials by attacking the Wahhabi establishment for its fatwa approving Saudi reliance on foreign forces. The agitation did not let up. In September 1992, 107 Islamists sent a forty-five-page "Memorandum of Advice" to the Saudi grand mufti, Sheikh Abdulaziz bin Baz, demanding greater authority for clerics over Saudi society, censorship to prevent "the dissemination of infidel and secular ideas" from the West, and the creation of a half-million-strong army to "protect the holy country, fight the Jews and help the Muslims."[56] Basically, they were calling for the restoration of an Islamic puritanical society swept clean of all traces of the American presence.

The religious ferment engulfing Saudi Arabia came to be known as the Islamic Awakening (al-Sahwa al-Islamiyya). It had its origins in the 1979 takeover of the Mecca Holy Mosque by Wahhabi fanatics and had been fueled by the long jihad in Afghanistan throughout the 1980s. But the Awakening took on far greater scope and depth after the Gulf War, "the most

critical event in the history of Saudi Islamism," as one study of the movement described it.[57] The war clearly had emboldened Wahhabi militants to
take their opposition public and to defy the government openly in a way
they had not dared before. Suddenly, highly respected Wahhabi scholars like
al-Hawali and al-Audah were challenging the regime's legitimacy in religious terms that could not easily be refuted. They were delivering fiery sermons attacking the al-Sauds for allowing "infidels" into the Land of the Two
Holy Mosques. They became far more popular and credible than official
government clerics.

King Fahd at first sought to pacify them by giving the *mutawwa'in*, the
official religious police, free rein to impose ever-more-strict religious behavior on Saudi society and above all on foreigners living in the country. Chas.
Freeman, the U.S. ambassador in Riyadh, recounted that American women
found themselves subjected to "frequent and escalating harassment" by
what he called "religious vigilantes," and he spent a lot of time trying to
persuade Saudi authorities to restrain their activities.[58] They were not vigilantes, however. They belonged to the *mutawwa'in*, and they also turned on
the kingdom's minority Shiite population; one Shiite, charged with apos-
tasy, was beheaded.

By the end of 1992, Fahd had decided his Wahhabi critics were becoming
too much of a challenge, and he issued a stern warning for them to cease
and desist or go to jail. The result was a three-way split in the Wahhabi opposition, with one group going underground inside the kingdom; another,
led by bin Laden, moving to the Sudan; and a third fleeing to London to organize the Committee for the Defense of Legitimate Rights, led by Mohammed al-Masari and Saad al-Faqih. One of the issues all these groups
had in common was their denunciation of what they regarded as an unholy
alliance between the House of Saud and the White House. This was becoming a defining issue.

THE GULF WAR left behind much unfinished business leading to the residual
American military presence that would cause so much harm to the "special
relationship" for years afterward. The coalition never forced Saddam to accept surrender terms or acknowledge his defeat. Much of his army, notably
many of his elite Republican Guard brigades, remained intact. Within six
weeks, they were engaged in a bloody massacre of rebellious Shia in southern

Iraq and rebellious Kurds in the north, without the United States or the United Nations lifting a finger to stop it. U.S. troops were still present in southern Iraq in March when Saddam's forces slaughtered twenty thousand Shia who had been led to believe the Americans would support them in their revolt. Saddam not only crushed the two rebellions and rebuilt his army, but also successfully opposed any kind of U.N. inspections to track down and dismantle his chemical, nuclear, and biological weapons. Suddenly, the celebrations over the coalition's smashing victory morphed into a heated controversy over why the United States had not "gone all the way" to Baghdad to depose the Iraqi dictator.

Schwarzkopf, the U.S. coalition co-commander, ignited the debate within a month of the war's end. During a television interview, he said he had recommended to Powell and Bush that the coalition "continue the march," but did not indicate where he thought "the march" should have stopped. Powell was furious. After consulting Bush, he put out a statement that there was "no contrary recommendation. There was no disagreement. There was no debate."[59] But Powell had to concede for years afterward that it was "still hard to drive a stake through charges that the job was left unfinished." Powell emerged with a reputation of being "a reluctant warrior."[60] Bush and Scowcroft argued in a memoir they coauthored that the coalition had never had a mandate to depose Saddam and that its Arab partners were against such a step because they feared "the breakup of the Iraqi state."[61] They wrote, "We felt a sense of urgency on the part of the coalition Arabs to get it over with and return to normal."[62] It was certainly true that the Saudis were emotionally, physically, and financially exhausted, as those few reporters remaining there at the end of the war can attest. Saudi officials closed down the kingdom to the outside world as fast as they could. The royal family and government went on a collective vacation. Bandar disappeared to nurse his back in Geneva. The main Saudi concern was to see American and other Western troops clear out of the kingdom to appease growing Wahhabi restlessness. General Khaled later wrote in his memoirs, "Our war aims were achieved." King Fahd had no wish "to invade or conquer" Iraqi territory. Saudi troops had strict orders "not to set one foot inside Iraq."[63]

While the Saudis wanted the United States back "over the horizon" as fast as possible, the Pentagon was pressing for just the opposite—a permanent foothold in the kingdom in preparation for the next crisis. It hoped to establish a forward headquarters in Saudi Arabia and to pre-position war matériel to equip at least six brigades in the Arab states of the Persian Gulf, primarily in the kingdom. Pentagon planners wanted to be ready to go into battle next time in days or weeks, not the five months it had just taken to build up for a counter-offensive against Iraq. The Saudis, however, refused to cooperate.

Freeman maintained that Washington badly bungled its attempt to establish a new postwar security order for the Persian Gulf. He blamed Secretary of Defense Cheney for the Saudi rejection. The former U.S. ambassador said there had been a lot of discussion during the war buildup among himself, Schwarzkopf, and U.S. Central Command planners about establishing a plan that would preclude the need for keeping any American forces in the region. They had sketched out what he described as a three-tier defense structure.[64] Freeman made no mention of Bandar playing any role in these discussions. The first tier would depend entirely upon a collective defense pact among the six Arab states belonging to the Gulf Cooperation Council, backed by U.S. logistical support. The second tier would be the GCC states plus the forces of Egypt and Syria. The third—and then only "in dire need"—would be the addition of non-Arab and non-Islamic forces from the United States and other Western countries. The plan did envisage, however, pre-positioning of U.S. war matériel and equipment in the region so that American troops and aircraft could be up and running as soon as they arrived. In the meantime, U.S. forces would periodically carry out joint exercises with the Arab gulf states to demonstrate to all potential future aggressors, notably Iraq and Iran, that there was a credible deterrence in place. This three-tier defense plan is what lay behind the "Damascus Declaration" issued by the six GCC states, Egypt, and Syria just two weeks after the war's end, according to Freeman. It called for a "new Arab order" and an "Arab peace-keeping force" led by the Egyptians and the Syrians to assure peace in the gulf.

But the victorious Bush administration never moved to help make this postwar gulf security plan possible. Freeman and Schwarzkopf only drew up the draft of an umbrella agreement that was deliberately short (a page and a half), spelling out the basic concept, including the pre-positioning of some U.S. war matériel. Freeman said the idea was to get Saudi agreement in principle and then negotiate details later.[65] That was the way the Saudis preferred to operate with the Americans. Instead, when Cheney came out in

early May 1991 to discuss postwar security arrangements, he presented the
Saudis with such a long, detailed pre-positioning scheme that Saudi hackles
were immediately raised. Cheney, Freeman said, even had the gall to ask the
Saudis to pay for the American equipment that was to be stowed in giant
desert depots and maintain it at their expense. Freeman blamed Paul Wolfowitz, then undersecretary of defense for policy, for rewriting the initial
plan at the last moment during their flight over to Riyadh. "Somehow on the
plane, a modest scheme became an enormous demand." The result was, of
course, that the Saudis refused what looked to them very much like a permanent U.S. presence.[66] Bandar was not present at this critical meeting, and
whether his mediating skills would have made any difference to the outcome
is unclear.

The Saudi strategy was the exact opposite—to become less dependent on
the U.S. military umbrella. They made plans to expand the Saudi army and
air force, above all the latter. They made known that they wanted to buy the
F-15E Strike Eagles denied them a decade earlier by AIPAC and Israel, and
they took advantage of the reservoir of goodwill toward the kingdom in the
wake of the war to press for them. The Pentagon had already endorsed the
idea of the Saudis obtaining the more advanced F-15s in a new postwar assessment of their security needs.[67]

As it turned out, events in Iraq were pushing the United States and Saudi
Arabia into adopting a postwar containment policy toward Saddam's embattled regime that would require the U.S. Air Force to remain in the kingdom whether the Saudis liked it or not. In August 1992, the United States,
Britain, and France agreed to establish two separate no-fly zones over southern and northern Iraq where Iraqi planes and helicopters would be forbidden to enter. They declared they were doing this to enforce a U.N. Security
Council resolution adopted in April 1991 condemning the "repression of the
Iraqi civilian population in many parts of Iraq," namely in the Shiite south
and the Kurdish north. But the council had approved no measures to halt
this repression, certainly not military action by U.S. and other Western
countries.

Almost all the Arab states opposed establishing these zones, as a dangerous precedent and the first step toward the de facto partition of Iraq into
three separate regions. Kuwait was the only Arab country that had a good
word for the plan.[68] The Saudis said nothing, a sign of their desire to avoid
public exposure of their embarrassing association with what came to be

known as Operation Southern Watch, which called for the use of Saudi AWACS protected by U.S. fighter jets to orchestrate U.S., British, and French warplanes operating from Saudi air bases to make sure Iraqi aircraft did not fly over southern Iraq.[69] Initially, the Saudis were reported to be "equivocating" on the use of their bases and even to have barred British Tornados from using them.[70] They relented, but Saudi doubts about Operation Southern Watch would grow with each passing year. Part of their unease stemmed from the ever-expanding U.S. military presence in the kingdom, which became increasingly visible and controversial. Eventually, it would include eighty to ninety aircraft and four thousand to five thousand air personnel stationed in Dhahran and Taif. There was no U.S. exit strategy from Southern Watch, either. In effect, the United States had reestablished its old Dhahran air base, though without any formal agreement to do so.[71] In frustration, Freeman sent a telegram back to Washington in which he described the U.S. postwar posture in these terms:

"We're in the position of someone who has gone to dinner, and dinner is over. Everyone else has left, and we're sitting there. The host has turned the air conditioner off and said, 'I think I'd better take the dog for a walk' and begun to turn the electricity on and off, and we're still not leaving. Our host is too polite to say, 'Shouldn't you be taking your leave?' "[72]

The quid pro quo for Saudi Arabia's reluctant cooperation became clear in September of 1992 when Bush announced that his administration intended to sell the kingdom seventy-two F15s, forty-eight of them the E model Strike Eagles. The package of planes, support services, infrastructure, and munitions was worth nine billion dollars. As usual, AIPAC and Israel protested, but they could not stop the sale in the wake of the unprecedented Saudi cooperation during the Gulf War and then with Southern Watch. Bush cleverly made the sale an issue in the presidential campaign, noting that it involved forty thousand jobs for Americans. His opponent, Bill Clinton, did not oppose the sale, either. Opponents could not muster enough votes in either the House or the Senate to block the sale, and it was approved. The only compromise was an agreement to provide a slightly less sophisticated export version known as the F15S, with "S" standing for Saudi Arabia. Bandar did not play a major role in the administration's lobbying effort this time, but he could still savor the third defeat of AIPAC on his watch as ambassador in Washington.

Another legacy of the Gulf War did have a big impact on the sale, in fact on the entire U.S.-Saudi relationship—Saudi bankruptcy. The cost to the Saudis had been staggering. They had paid out billions of dollars for Soviet and other votes in support of the war at the United Nations; for the transport of troops contributed by Syria, Egypt, and a dozen African countries; for jet fuel, food, housing, and water for the entire 750,000-man coalition army while present in the kingdom; for Kuwaiti refugees; and finally, for a good portion of the U.S. military presence. Freeman said he had personally collected $16.9 billion from King Fahd, "including $3.2 billion that he had never agreed to."[73] Secretary of State Baker had literally forced the additional Saudi contribution out of the king at a meeting in which the secretary had "grabbed King Fahd by the equivalent of his lapels and said, 'I want to understand that I heard yes to that question" of whether he would ante up as requested. The startled king had then said, "Yes," but dragged his feet on coughing up the money. So Baker had called upon Bandar to collect the $3.2 billion, which he had dutifully done. The prince had become Washington's bill collector, too.[74]

The U.S. ambassador had conducted a running argument with Washington right from the war's start over the true state of Saudi finances. Saudi reserves were down to between three billion and seven billion dollars, which "were essentially exhausted in the first week of the war," Freeman said. No one in Washington believed him. "There was simply disbelief at the idea that Saudi Arabia could be cash poor."[75] The price of oil, however, had gone down by two dollars a barrel because Arab oil producers led by Saudi Arabia had pumped more to compensate for the loss of Iraqi oil. (Saudi production alone jumped from five million to eight million barrels a day.) Making matters worse, the Saudis went on a reckless spree of buying emergency war matériel for their own forces with Bandar in the lead. The king had given the prince authorization to sign contracts with U.S. companies, and Bandar had spent lavishly with no regard for the kingdom's financial straits. The Saudis signed more than twenty-seven billion dollars in military sales agreements between 1990 and 1993.[76] After the war, when the king finally realized the kingdom faced financial disaster, he revoked Bandar's authorization, forcing the cancellation of various contracts that Bandar had signed on behalf of Saudi Arabia.[77] Freeman's own estimate of the war's cost to the Saudis was "something in the order of sixty-five billion dollars," at a time when their grass domestic product (GDP) was one hundred billion dollars.[78] The Saudi national debt went from virtually zero to 55 percent of the country's GDP in less than one year.

The situation only became worse after the war. The Bush administration kept up a steady stream of requests for the Saudis to pay for various U.S. policy initiatives, "in many cases very remote from Saudi Arabia," Freeman said.[79] Just before he left the country in August 1992, Freeman made a list of all Washington requests for Saudi financial contributions since the war's end and discovered they numbered no less than fifty-two. Many were absurd from a Saudi viewpoint, such as aid for Christian Armenia in its struggle with Muslim Azerbaijan, and the purchase of pork, which Muslims refuse to eat on religious grounds, to feed starving Russians. The Saudis rejected every one of the American requests. In the process, enormous resentment built up in Riyadh over what Freeman termed "this flow of uncoordinated and ill-conceived requests." It had become, in his words, "the principal point of friction" between the two governments. Washington assumed that since the Saudis had been able and willing before the war to pitch in on financing U.S. foreign policy ventures, "this behavior would continue even when the Saudis were broke."[80]

Would the history of the U.S.-Saudi relationship have turned out differently had the coalition marched on to Baghdad in February 1991? Would the fall of Saddam Hussein then have spared Iraq the chaos engendered by the U.S. invasion twelve years later? Could the terrorism that became such a threat to U.S. interests a few years later have been avoided? It seems doubtful. The overthrow of Saddam then would probably have just accelerated what was to happen with the toppling of Saddam in March 2003. If there was little postwar planning by Washington in 2003, there was absolutely none in 1990. U.S. forces would still have become bogged down in Iraq, spawned an insurgency, and birthed al-Qaeda in Iraq. The reflections of Bush and Scowcroft on why they decided to stop the "march" at Kuwait's border revealed these concerns. There was no exit strategy, and in words that today sound prophetic they noted, "The United States could conceivably still be an occupying power in a bitterly hostile land."[81] Worse yet, the U.S. military presence in Saudi Arabia would have remained far larger; this would just have hastened the Islamic Awakening that would prove such a challenge to the House of Saud and the United States a decade later.

CHAPTER 7

Strategic Asset or Strategic Liability

BUSH'S DEFEAT BY CLINTON in the November 1992 election came as a great shock and disappointment to the Saudis, Bandar in particular. The American president he had been closest to had lasted only one term in office. He couldn't understand why an American leader who had presided over victory in war would be repudiated so quickly by his own people, though he remembered that the same thing had happened to Winston Churchill at the end of World War II. He reminded Bush of that in an emotional letter he wrote the president the night of the presidential election.[1]

The prince had flown to Houston to watch the returns and be ready to congratulate Bush on his reelection. Frederick Dutton, his closest political adviser, had warned him against going there, because it would brand him as blatantly partisan in an American presidential election, which was out of order for the dean of the Washington diplomatic corps. The prince didn't care. Bandar told Bush that, win or lose, he was a "friend for life" and "one of my family."[2] When Bush called to tell him he had lost, Bandar felt like he was being told about a death in the family.

Bandar had known Bush by then for twelve years, since he had become Reagan's vice president. The prince had escorted him on his contentious trip in April 1986 to Saudi Arabia; they had even become stuck in the sand dunes together there on a desert ride.[3] He had bonded with Bush in war, and their two families had grown close as well. Bandar had become a frequent and welcome visitor to the White House and the Bush summer home in Kennebunkport, Maine. When the Bushes had been in Saudi Arabia visiting U.S. troops during Thanksgiving in 1990, Bandar's wife, Princess Haifa, had taken in their daughter, Dorothy, and her family, who were passing the holiday alone at the White House. Bandar was by then well on his way to earning the moniker Bandar Bush, which he would later inherit in the U.S. media.

At the same time, his relations with Bill Clinton had been rocky from the start. That was when Clinton was still Arkansas governor and in search of donations for his state university. He first approached the Saudi embassy in 1989 in connection with the University of Arkansas's drive to raise twenty-three million dollars to establish a Middle East studies center. The Saudis had never given this large a donation to any American university and were uncertain why they should invest such an amount in what was to them a little-known institute located in a backwater state. "I don't think even prophets knew that Bill Clinton was going to run for president, [much less] be elected," said Bandar, reflecting back on this embarrassing episode in his career.[4] But Clinton kept badgering Bandar. The king, at the prince's request, had previously made a number of charitable donations to presidential causes, or those of their wives: In 1985, he had donated one million dollars to First Lady Nancy Reagan's "Just Say No" antidrug campaign and offered several prize Arabian horses to the president.* In 1989, he had given another million dollars to First Lady Barbara Bush's campaign against illiteracy. And the Saudis had given millions to help build presidential libraries. But the Clinton request was far more than the Saudis had ever had to deal with. Clinton may have thought he had a Saudi connection because Prince Turki, Bandar's brother-in-law and the longtime Saudi intelligence chief, had been a Georgetown University classmate and a casual acquaintance. Bandar finally passed on Clinton's request to the king, who, surprisingly, approved it. The request was then sent to the Saudi Ministry of Higher Education and various Saudi universities that were asked to make contributions.

By the time of Saddam's invasion of Kuwait in August 1990, the University of Arkansas had received word that three million dollars was on the way. The fate of the other twenty million dollars remained unknown. Despite the war, Clinton kept pressing Bandar for an appointment to find out. Twice Bandar gave him one and then had to cancel it. On one of these

---

* Reagan had to refuse the horses because of government-imposed limitations on the value of gifts to a president.

occasions, he stood up Clinton and a university delegation when they were already in Washington because of war business. He simply forgot about a third appointment and saw Clinton only briefly. Bandar recalled listening politely and trying to put Clinton off by suggesting the University of Arkansas and Saudi universities first do a study outlining a collaborative proposal. Clinton had such a study already in hand and turned it over to Bandar, who dutifully sent it back to the education ministry in Riyadh and "forgot all about it."[5]

Clinton's request finally made its way through the Saudi bureaucracy after a year and a half, and the remaining twenty million dollars was approved in October 1992 on the eve of the presidential election. (The money would not be delivered until January 1994.) Bandar said he then purposely held off disclosing the news until after the election because he felt he would look "odd" doing it beforehand, as if he were voting for Clinton to win.[6] So word of the gift had to await election results. The Democratic winner had already been told of the Saudi decision by the time King Fahd called on November 10 to congratulate him on his victory. Press reports at the time suggested Clinton was still soliciting the king for a donation, but Bandar said he was simply thanking Fahd. Clinton took advantage of the call to try to establish a personal tie with the Saudi monarch, knowing full well he was going to have major difficulties replacing Bush in the Saudis' affections. He told the king he was aware he had just "lost a friend" in the White House and assured him he wanted "to be just as good a friend . . . as Bush."[7]

But the Clinton White House would never forget where Bandar had spent election night and for whose victory he had been cheering. "When the Clinton administration came in, he was Bush's son for all intents and purposes," remarked Martin Indyk, who was dealing with the Middle East at the National Security Council at the time.[8] Clinton aides were determined to shut him out of the White House and make his meetings with Clinton as few and far apart as possible. There was a kind of vendetta against the prince, a deliberate campaign to cut him down to size, or rank, to the mere ambassador he was. "The kind of easy access Bandar had [with Bush] was gone. I mean gone. He couldn't get through the door," boasted Indyk.[9] Anthony Lake, Clinton's first national security adviser, said the prince was treated with all due respect for his ambassadorial position, but nothing more. But both Indyk and Lake made clear they had not allowed Bandar to replicate with Clinton the "absolutely extraordinary relationship" he had enjoyed with

Bush.[10] Cutting the prince down to rank also meant ending the security detail with which the State Department had been providing him since the Gulf War, as well as his automatic access to underground parking there. The new frosty attitude extended beyond Bandar to the kingdom itself; Clinton did not bother to appoint a new ambassador for nearly two years after Chas. Freeman's departure in August 1992.

The prince, for whom access to the White House was all important, insisted that nothing changed appreciably. He cited as proof his ability to become the first foreign dignitary to see Clinton after his inauguration. Clinton's aides were anxious to emphasize that the new president's priority was on domestic issues. So they rejected a request by Turkish prime minister Turgut Özal, who had been in a Houston hospital, to pay his respects to the new American president on his way home. But Bandar somehow snuck into the White House on January 26, which caught the attention of the media. "This is just to prove to you that I really have access," the prince said, recounting the incident to dispel the image that he had lost his enduring pull during the Clinton years.[11]

There were other reasons for Bandar's cool reception at the White House initially. First, no crisis or big event brought the prince and Clinton together to bond them. Both were left on the sidelines of the biggest breakthrough in the Middle East peace process in contemporary times. While administration officials engaged in lackluster peace negotiations in 1992 and 1993, the Norwegian government and a private peacemaker, Terje Roed-Larsen, secretly arranged face-to-face meetings between Israeli and Palestine Liberation Organization (PLO) negotiators in Oslo. In early September 1993, the news finally leaked that the two sides had reached agreement on mutual recognition and a Declaration of Principles that included establishing an interim government, called the Palestinian National Authority, to run the Gaza Strip and the West Bank. News of the Oslo Accords stunned the world, particularly U.S. policy makers who had played no role in bringing them about.

The accords led to a historic signing ceremony on September 13 at the White House, where PLO chairman Yasser Arafat and Israeli prime minister Yitzhak Rabin shook hands before a crowd of three thousand star-struck admirers, including most of America's past failed peace negotiators. Clinton and Bandar were reduced to acting like bridesmaids at the wedding of an extremely nervous couple, making sure both got to the altar on time and behaved properly. Both Rabin and Arafat threatened not to show up. Clinton had to nudge Rabin physically into a handshake at the last moment, and Bandar was tasked with making sure Arafat was dressed properly, which in the end he refused to do anyway. Bandar made one other contribution: a passage from the Koran for Clinton to cite in his speech: "If the enemy inclines toward peace, do thou also incline toward peace."[12]

Bandar was also handicapped at the start of the Clinton administration by the kingdom's dire financial straits. It was a highly embarrassing situation. Here was the world's leading oil exporter unable to pay its bills, basically declaring bankruptcy, and seeking protection from its creditors. Bandar had been largely responsible for the unaffordable shopping spree the kingdom had indulged in at the end of the Gulf War, which had resulted in $30 billion in new and old, still-unfulfilled arms orders. By May 1992, the Saudis owed the Pentagon $16 billion. Bandar found himself seeking new terms on the U.S. payment schedule; he wanted to stretch out the payments from four years to ten and also stretch out the schedule for the purchase of the F-15s and C-130 cargo planes on order.[13] Bandar didn't want to cancel any of the contracts. In late December 1993, he called his three biggest U.S. arms creditors to a five-hour luncheon at his retreat in Aspen, Colorado, to discuss a way out. Most concerned were General Dynamics, with a $2.9 billion order for 315 M-1A2 tanks, and McDonnell Douglas, holding a $9 billion contract for seventy-two F-15s. Raytheon Corporation also had a big order for Patriot missiles and Hughes Aircraft Company for a computerized air-defense network. Bandar told their executives that the kingdom needed more time to pay and assured them that the kingdom's cash flow problem was temporary.[14] The payments and delivery schedules were stretched out, as none of these companies was about to lose the Saudi account.

In the midst of this major financial crisis, Bandar made the situation worse, in a bid to salvage the kingdom's rocky standing with the Clinton administration and reestablish his access to the White House. The prince's power and influence at the royal court depended on that precious asset. The first opportunity to wedge his way back through the White House door came in mid-1993, when Clinton needed to secure the political support of Washington State for his reelection by boosting the fortunes of the Seattle-based Boeing Company. Boeing was pressing the administration to lift its economic sanctions on Iran so that it could sell commercial aircraft there, as well as to Saudia, the civilian Saudi Arabian airline. However, Clinton didn't want to change U.S. policy toward Iran. So Indyk, who had sought to isolate Bandar from the White House, found himself turning to him for a solution. After all, the Saudis had no interest in seeing U.S. sanctions on Iran lifted, either.

Saudia Airlines had drawn up a six-billion-dollar modernization program in 1989 that called for the renewal of its entire fleet of sixty airliners. The plan foresaw the state company obtaining 60 percent of its new aircraft from U.S. companies and the remainder from European ones, mainly Airbus. But after Clinton's election, the king came under enormous pressure to recalibrate this formula totally in America's favor. Clinton sent Secretary of State Warren Christopher, Secretary of Commerce Ron Brown, and Secretary of Transportation Federico Peña, one after another, to Riyadh to plead with Fahd. Bandar himself was set up for a staged "chance encounter" with Clinton during a meeting with other officials at the White House in July 1993 so that the president could press him to lobby the king on the six-billion-dollar deal.[15] Indyk had called Bandar in to discuss Clinton's political dilemma. "What if we get the king to buy all American aircraft and stop any sale to the Iranians. That would do the trick," suggested the prince.[16]

Bandar flew back to Riyadh immediately and brought back good news: Saudia would buy 100 percent American. Clinton called up Fahd to thank him profusely. Later, Bandar explained the king's decision by saying he had felt he needed to say "Thank you to our friends in America" for their help during the Gulf War. But Clinton turned the sale into practically the sine qua non for Saudi favor at the White House, telling the king that the plane sale was "something personally important to him" and his reelection chances.[17]

The problem was how to finance the six-billion-dollar purchase given Saudi Arabia's massive debt burden, low oil prices, and a ten-billion-dollar budget deficit. This turned out to be a huge problem. Clinton finally solved it by getting the U.S. Export-Import Bank to guarantee loans for the entire amount. It was the largest underwriting of an American sale abroad ever made by the bank. Bandar said the bank's guarantee was extremely important to the Saudi government because it was a sign of official American confidence in the debt-ridden Saudi economy. Still, the Saudia deal added six billion dollars to the Saudi government's foreign debt and continued to be an issue in the U.S.-Saudi relationship for nearly two years.

On February 16, 1994, Clinton and Bandar together made the announcement at the White House amid much feting of the U.S.-Saudi alliance and its future. Finally, the prince had his presidential photo to prove back home his good standing at the White House. But careful listeners sensed the two were talking about different deals. Clinton confidently announced that Fahd had told him the kingdom was buying "the entire replacement fleet" from Boeing and McDonnell Douglas. Noting that this would assure tens of thousands of jobs for workers in half a dozen Western states, the president hailed the news as "a gold medal win" for America.[18] Bandar, who had actually written Fahd's letter to Clinton and thus knew precisely what it contained, said something different. The king had only agreed to start negotiations with the two companies and for "a substantial number of aircraft," not necessarily Saudia's entire fleet. (A final agreement was not reached until November 1995.) Still, the prince was full of praise for American leadership in the new post–Cold War era, noting that as the world's only superpower, the United States was truly "the only game in town." Saudi Arabia, he assured Clinton, was "determined to be a strategic asset and not a strategic liability."[19]

THE FIRST TEST of this commitment came within months. Bandar found himself at serious odds with the Clinton administration over the breakout of civil war in newly united Yemen, on the kingdom's ill-defined western border. Until 1990, the country had been divided between North Yemen and South Yemen and ruled by two separate governments. The north was dominated by conservative Islamic tribes, and the south was ruled by Soviet-backed socialists and communists. Then, the two parts formed a fragile union. But in May 1994, remnants of the communist-led South Yemen announced they had had enough and were seceding. The larger and militarily more muscular north, under the wily president Ali Abdullah Saleh, decided to use force to crush the secessionist movement. The Saudis, still smarting from Yemen's support of Saddam Hussein during the Gulf War, jumped in on the side of the southern rebellion. This seemed an exceedingly strange choice for an Islamic fundamentalist monarchy, but the House of Saud had always been nervous about a unified Yemen on its border, because as such it became the most populous nation on the Arabian Peninsula. Other factors were a nagging border dispute and constant clashes with Yemeni tribesmen. A divided Yemen would clearly be less of a challenge to the House of Saud.

In Saudi Arabia, responsibility for foreign policy is divided into fiefdoms among the most powerful princes, and Yemen belonged to Bandar's father, Defense Minister Sultan. He was the principal advocate for what turned out to be the disastrous Saudi policy to back the communist-led rebellion. Not only were the rebels crushed by Saleh's northern army within less than two months, but the Saudis found themselves squarely on the opposite side of the Clinton administration in the Yemeni family feud. Clinton wanted to keep Yemen united, and he saw no good reason why the United States should recognize a reconstituted independent, socialist South Yemen.

In terms of U.S. domestic politics, there was one delicious irony at play in this otherwise obscure battle over distant Yemen's fate. The main U.S. company operating in northern Yemen was Hunt Oil of Houston. By discovering a respectable oil deposit there in 1984, Hunt had single-handedly put the nation on the world's map. A decade later, it had reserves estimated at 4 billion barrels (compared with Saudi Arabia's 260 billion barrels) and was producing 350,000 barrels a day. The owner was Ray Hunt, and he and his family had been major financers of President George H. W. Bush's two presidential campaigns. This was why Bush, as vice president, had bothered to stop in Yemen on his trip to Saudi Arabia in 1986; the only site he had visited outside the capital had been Hunt's new refinery. Clinton was therefore acting to protect the interests of his Republican predecessor and Bush's financial backer.

The diplomatic battle over Yemen occurred largely before the U.N. Security Council. Bandar was sent to lead the Saudi charge. He wanted to get the council to press for a halt to the fighting so that the embattled southern rebels could gain more time to maneuver for recognition. The prince more or less wrote the Security Council resolution calling for an immediate ceasefire and the opening of negotiations between the north and south to find a peaceful solution. It was considered a major success for Bandar when on June 1, 1994, the council unanimously adopted a resolution demanding an end to the fighting without any mention of Yemen's unity. But events on the ground quickly made Bandar's artful diplomacy irrelevant. The same day that the U.N. resolution passed, northern forces began a siege of the rebels' last stronghold, in the southern capital of Aden, and by early July the secession was crushed.

Bandar lobbied hard for U.S. support, including in meetings with Clinton himself. But the president would have none of it. He sent his chief of staff and close friend, Thomas McLarty, on a secret trip to Riyadh to explain the U.S. position and press Fahd to change his own in favor of a united Yemen. McLarty proved a hit with the king, regaling him with hilarious stories about Clinton. But neither leader changed the mind of the other.[20] Bandar kept chasing Clinton around the world trying to persuade him. The prince showed up at a G-7 summit in Naples in early July to lobby the president to get the G-7 members, the world's major industrial powers, to intervene on behalf of the southern Yemeni rebels. By that time, the secessionist movement was over, and Bandar was tilting at windmills and looking more than a little foolish.[21] The only token Bandar extracted from Clinton was standard "reassurances" of the U.S. commitment to Saudi security, as if that were the main issue.[22]

ON OCTOBER 7, 1994, Saddam Hussein suddenly moved ten thousand additional troops, including some of his elite Republican Guard units, close to the Kuwait border. Altogether, there was an Iraqi force of fifty thousand within striking distance of Kuwait City. The buildup set off alarm bells throughout the Persian Gulf and Western capitals. Clinton ordered the mobilization of thirty thousand U.S. troops and sent an aircraft carrier group and hundreds of warplanes into the gulf. Saddam quickly backed down and even decided to finally recognize Kuwait's sovereignty and borders in hopes of getting U.N. sanctions on his country lifted.

Bandar described the episode as one of the rare "bonding" occasions for him during the eight years of the Clinton administration, as the U.S. and Saudi governments worked in tandem to counter the new Saddam threat. Clinton made his sole visit to the kingdom to show U.S. support and hold his only face-to-face meeting with Fahd. For a brief moment, the two countries were comrades in arms as they had been during the Gulf War. The king awarded Clinton the kingdom's highest honor, the King Abdulaziz Medal, and the two leaders lavished high praise on the U.S.-Saudi special relationship. Later, the king let it be known that he was pleased Clinton had asked his advice on the peace process and that he had found Clinton a lot warmer than Bush, whom he described as "rather distant."[23]

But the episode ended by bringing into the open seriously conflicting views on gulf security. The Pentagon sought to revive its old plan, rejected three years earlier, for pre-positioning supplies throughout the Arab gulf states to counter future threats. Secretary of Defense William Perry made public in mid-October that the United States wanted to store enough war matériel, including tanks and aircraft, to equip an entire division. Equipment for one of the division's three brigades would be housed at King Khalid

Military City in Saudi Arabia. The plan would also require periodic joint training exercises with U.S. forces.[24] Perry presented the plan to Fahd personally and even had the nerve to ask the kingdom, at that point fighting bankruptcy, to foot most of the five-hundred-million to one-billion-dollar storage cost.

Once again, the House of Saud said no to the American gulf security plan. The Saudis did not want to escalate the American military presence in the kingdom and did not have the money to pay for it, anyway. Sultan reminded Perry that they were struggling to pay for the thirty billion dollars in arms on order already.[25] In the end, the Clinton administration pushed ahead with its gulf security plan without Saudi Arabia, dividing up equipment for the three brigades in Qatar, Kuwait, and the United Arab Emirates. Bahrain had already become the Persian Gulf base for the U.S. Navy's Fifth Fleet. But the proposed centerpiece of the plan, Saudi Arabia, was missing. It intended to limit its association with the United States in regional security matters to the Southern Watch operation over Iraq. This was now becoming more of a challenge because, in the wake of Saddam's military feint toward Kuwait, Clinton had decided the United States would enforce a ban on operations in southern Iraq not only by Iraqi aircraft but by its elite army units.

In his reflections on this 1994 mini-crisis over Iraq, Bandar was highly critical of Clinton. "We all decided we are not going to allow Saddam Hussein to jerk us around. He cannot decide when we mobilize, or when we don't, or when we bring troops," Bandar said.[26] But according to the prince, Clinton had failed to come up with any strategy to contain Saddam or deal with his tantrums. "We were waiting for America to come with this policy that has a strategic objective, where everybody knows where to play in it," he said. "That policy never came." He never acknowledged that the kingdom had wanted no part of the proposed U.S. containment strategy and had rejected the role Washington had asked it to play. For the prince, the denouement of the crisis was that U.S.-Saudi relations went on "autopilot," with each country "doing their own thing."

Bandar never offered any explanation for the Saudi rejection of the U.S. gulf security plan. He might well have cited domestic pressures, but like all Saudi royals he refused to wash the kingdom's political laundry in public. Yet the kingdom at the time was seething with religious discontent, and the main reason was the residual American military presence. Less than a month before Saddam's saber-rattling exercise on Kuwait's border, Wahhabi militants mounted a street protest in Buraydah, a stronghold of religious conservatism and the hometown of Sheikh Salman al-Audah, a leader of the Islamic Awakening. A series of gatherings outside his mosque came to be called—at least by the Wahhabi opposition—the Buraydah Uprising, a bit of hyperbole but no small matter in Saudi terms. It had been sparked by the arrest on September 9 of Sheikh Safar al-Hawali, another mover and shaker of the Awakening.

The Buraydah demonstrations went on for three days, and when al-Audah, too, was arrested, there were more street protests and an invasion of the Buraydah governor's house by the sheikh's partisans.[27] The kingdom had not witnessed demonstrations of this magnitude before, and they shocked the royal family into action. Already the fiery sermons of al-Audah and al-Hawali, criticizing the Saudi alliance with America, had been gaining an ever-wider audience. Even Saudi participation in the Middle East peace process was under attack. There was no local press coverage of the Buraydah Uprising, but foreign diplomats estimated that five hundred of al-Audah's followers had occupied the governor's mansion, while the opposition claimed that up to eight thousand had participated in the street protests and thirteen hundred had been arrested.[28]

Buraydah was a sign of the times. In the mid-1990s, the House of Saud found itself under serious religious assault both at home and abroad. Militant preachers were challenging in their weekly sermons not only its authority but that of the official Wahhabi establishment supporting it. A bitter religious and political war was under way between radical and official Wahhabi clerics. For the first time, there was a steady drumbeat of criticism in cassettes, bulletins, and broadcasts from Islamists based in London. Six radical scholars and clerics had set up the Committee for the Defense of Legitimate Rights (CDLR) in May 1993. Several of its members, led by Mohammed al-Masari, had fled to London, where the CDLR became a major thorn in the side of the al-Saud family, flooding the world's newsrooms, and later Internet sites, with news about its corruption, infighting, and intrigues. It published a monthly news bulletin, the *Monitor*, filled with similar stories and the latest scandals. The committee even called the House of Saud un-Islamic and therefore deserving to be overthrown. To the great annoyance of the Saudi royals, the British government refused to silence the CDLR's voice.

Yet another broadside against the House of Saud was building up from another quarter—Osama bin Laden, the wayward son of one of the king-dom's wealthiest families and strongest supporters of the al-Saud monarchy. The Bin Laden Company did billions of dollars in construction business with the government. The family's one black sheep, Osama, the Afghan war hero, had slipped out of the country in 1991 after the king rejected his offer to lead another jihad, against Saddam Hussein's army in Kuwait. He had taken up residence across the Red Sea in Sudan's capital, Khartoum. The Saudi government stripped him of his citizenship and froze his assets in April 1994, but this did nothing to halt his ever-more-radical pronounce-ments and activities. Osama championed the cause of the Awakening sheikhs after their arrest in September 1995. The following August, he sent an open letter to Fahd demanding an end to the American military presence in the kingdom. "Your kingdom is nothing but an American protectorate and you are under Washington's heel," he told the king.[29]

On November 13, 1995, the political agitation roiling the kingdom took a far more ominous turn. At eleven thirty in the morning, a powerful bomb went off in a parking lot outside the Saudi Arabia National Guard training center in Riyadh, where scores of U.S. military and civilian advisers were working. The blast killed five Americans and wounded thirty others, many of whom were eating lunch at a snack bar outside. The perpetrators were hitting a perfect symbol of the U.S.-Saudi alliance. The Americans were there as a result of a $5.6 billion program run by the U.S. Army Materiel Com-mand and Vinnell Corporation to modernize, train, and equip the national guard, commanded by Prince Abdullah, who would become king in 2005. Press reports noted that there were about five thousand U.S. military person-nel working in the kingdom, mostly in Dhahran or Riyadh, and that one thousand were employees of either Vinnell or its parent company, BDM In-ternational Inc., based in McLean, Virginia. The reports made clear that neither the companies nor the U.S. and Saudi governments welcomed the spotlight being placed on the American military presence.[30] This, of course, was precisely what the bombers had intended and achieved.

Two unknown groups, the Islamic Movement for Change and Tigers of the Gulf, took credit. The first had threatened in the spring of 1994 to attack U.S. military personnel unless all were withdrawn by June 28. Speculation spread that either Iraq or Iran was behind the bombing. In great secrecy, Saudi security agencies tracked down and arrested four Saudis who "con-fessed" to the plot. Announcing their arrest in April 1996, Saudi interior minister Prince Naif bin Abdulaziz also made public their confessions. They were summarily executed the following month, but not before Naif had rejected a formal U.S. government request that the FBI be allowed to interview them. This incident would prove to be the first of many sore points that would come to mar U.S.-Saudi cooperation in the war on terrorism.

What we know about the four terrorists stems entirely from their confessions, or more precisely the official Saudi version of them. They were apparently all hardened veterans of the Afghan jihad, but they gave no indication that they were part of or acting under orders from al-Qaeda. They said that they had been influenced by the writings of bin Laden but also those of CDLR leader al-Masari. What was far more surprising was their mention of a then-obscure Palestinian Jordanian cleric by the name of Abu Muhammed al-Maqdisi, who would later gain fame as the spiritual mentor of Abu Musab al-Zarqawi, the first leader of al-Qaeda fighting the U.S. occupation forces in Iraq.

U.S. intelligence officials and political analysts knew virtually nothing about al-Maqdisi. However, these four young Saudis had carefully read his book *Clear Evidence of the Infidel Nature of the Saudi State*. And they had been deeply influenced by his notion that even Arab rulers and regimes could be declared *kafir*, or "infidel," based on two considerations: failure to live up to Islamic sharia law and alliances with non-Islamic countries.[31] The four young terrorists said they had deliberately targeted the American military mission to the national guard to demonstrate their displeasure with the kingdom's reliance on the United States. Al-Maqdisi was having a tremendous impact on young militant Saudis by providing the religious justification and inspiration they sought for their twin jihads against the House of Saud and the United States. One of the four said he had visited the sheikh in Jordan "on many occasions."[32]*

The jihad against the House of Saud and its American ally was just warming up. Seven months later, on June 25, 1996, a massive truck bomb with an explosive force estimated at twenty thousand pounds of TNT equivalent went off alongside Khobar Towers, near Dhahran, which housed U.S. Air Force personnel involved in the Southern Watch program over Iraq. The explosion, larger than the one at the federal building in Oklahoma City,

* A decade later, a U.S. Army "atlas" of militant Islam concluded he was "the most influential living *jihadi* theorist."[33]

killed 19 Americans and wounded 372 others plus several hundred Saudis and third-country nationals.

The bombing led to an outpouring of criticism of U.S. intelligence for failing to recognize the terrorist threats facing the American military in the kingdom. In presenting his report on the bombing, House National Security Committee chairman Floyd Spence said that the intelligence available to the U.S. military was at that point "virtually devoid of specific knowledge of terrorist and dissident activity inside Saudi Arabia."[34] This seemed extraordinary given the bombing at the national guard training center less than a year before, not to mention the religious turmoil sweeping the kingdom. One reason, according to FBI director Louis Freeh, was the Saudi failure to share what they knew, such as the arrest of a Saudi Shiite carrying explosives across the Saudi-Jordanian border two months earlier. The Saudi had told Saudi authorities that he had also been involved in surveillance of Khobar Towers.[35] There had also been myriad U.S. complaints about the lack of Saudi response to requests for better security around the towers.

The bombing put an abrupt end to Bandar's complaint about U.S.-Saudi relations cruising along on autopilot. It marked the start of a decade-long battle over Saudi cooperation, or the lack thereof, in combating terrorism. This was to become a cancer eating away at the vaunted special relationship. The FBI and other U.S. security agencies complained bitterly, and ever more publicly, about the Saudi refusal to share information about the Khobar Towers bombing suspects. Even Freeh and Attorney General Janet Reno vented their anger in public. Bandar found himself in the middle of the crossfire between two old allies suddenly extremely wary of each other. One little-known terrorist group, Saudi Hezbollah, had taken credit for the bombing, but nobody was sure who they were or who might be behind them. The Saudis fairly quickly rounded up a large number of Saudi Shiites and eventually held about forty suspects. But they tenaciously refused to give the FBI access to them.

The reasons why provide important insights into the attitudes of both the Saudis and the Americans toward the looming war on terrorism that would become so all-consuming after 9/11. By November of 1996, there was considerable evidence of where the Saudi investigation was leading. The Saudis notified U.S. officials that month that they believed the bombing had been carried out with Iranian complicity. This still-tentative conclusion was based on information extracted from some of the Shiite suspects being held in

Saudi jails.[36] By the following April, the U.S. investigation had progressed to the point of identifying the Iranian handler of the Saudi terrorists—Brigadier Ahmad Sherifi, a senior official in Iran's Revolutionary Guard. Sherifi had been in contact after the bombing with the Saudi driver of the getaway car, Hani Abd Rahim al-Sayegh, who had fled to Canada, where he was arrested. But U.S. officials said they were still not sure about the precise nature of the Iranian role. Or maybe they simply didn't want to know.

The U.S. and Saudi governments each faced an awkward dilemma. If Iran were accused of masterminding the attack, the Clinton administration would come under enormous public pressure to retaliate. It already considered Iran the world's foremost sponsor of international terrorism. On the other hand, the Saudis were worried that any U.S. retaliation against Iran would provoke the Iranians into attacking the kingdom because of its close ties to Washington and its proximity to Iran. In addition, Crown Prince Abdullah had just launched a diplomatic opening to Tehran that included an exchange of visits with Iranian president Ali Akbar Rafsanjani.[37] So both Clinton and Abdullah had reason to avoid fingering Iran publicly. Meanwhile, Freeh, who had sent 150 FBI agents to Riyadh to investigate the bombing, was pressing the Saudis ever more pugnaciously to come clean with what they knew.

Bandar found himself caught in a very sticky wicket. He knew what Saudi security officials had discovered and concluded. But he didn't want to convey that information to the Clinton administration formally and officially. He later summed up the Saudi attitude by quoting a verse from the Koran: "Ask not about things which, if made plain to you, may cause you trouble."[38] So the prince had a number of "unofficial" meetings with Clinton's national security adviser, Anthony Lake, devoted to trying to convince the Clinton administration of the wisdom of this Islamic adage. The two would meet in downtown Washington's Bombay Palace Restaurant, where Bandar would drink martinis while Lake refrained to keep a clear head. Lake pressed Bandar time and again to be more forthcoming, while Bandar tried to explain why the Saudis could not: "He made it clear, at least indirectly, that the reason why they were not being forthcoming was that they were concerned that, if we discovered the Iranian hand in the death of Americans, we would then of necessity retaliate against Iran in some form," Lake recalled.[39]

Lake frankly admitted that he would indeed have recommended that the United States retaliate. And he realized Bandar feared that American retaliation would amount to putting "a stick in the hornet's nest while not destroying the nest" and so was keeping the Clinton administration just enough in the dark to avoid the Iranian bee sting. "Since we didn't know the nature of the [Iranian] involvement, we didn't know what the response would be. We weren't about to share with the Saudis any planning we were doing, for obvious reasons," he explained. As a result, Lake could not assure Bandar that the Iranians would not retaliate against Saudi Arabia. "It was a frustrating dance on both sides."[40]

Martin Indyk, who dealt with Saudi Arabia extensively as assistant secretary of state for Near Eastern affairs, found "the dance" to be pure vintage Bandar—coldly calculated to neutralize both the United States and Iran. While the Saudis wouldn't share their information with Washington, they did take it to Tehran to blackmail the Iranians, suggesting that if Iran did not cease its terrorism against the kingdom, the kingdom would give the Americans all the specifics about the bombing suspects they needed to justify retaliation. Denial of those specifics to Washington kept the United States from acting, while the threat of handing them over stopped Iranian terrorism. "It was a perfect Bandar formula."[41]

In *My FBI*, Freeh recounted his enormous frustration over his inability to gain access to the Saudi bombing suspects. The main culprit in his view was not the Saudis, but Clinton himself. Bandar had told Freeh that the only way the FBI was going to get that access was for Clinton himself to ask for it. The president finally got his chance when Crown Prince Abdullah visited Washington in September 1998. But Freeh maintained that Clinton never really pressed the issue. "Bill Clinton raised the subject only to tell the crown prince that he understood the Saudis' reluctance to cooperate and then he hit Abdullah up for a contribution to the Clinton Presidential Library."[42] After that, Freeh said, he went to former president George H. W. Bush and asked him to intercede on his behalf with Abdullah, and Bush did. Clinton heatedly denied Freeh's version of the Abdullah meeting and his judgment that Clinton had been a slacker in pursuing the Khobar Towers investigation. Clinton spokesman Jay Carson said that Freeh's account is just one of the "untruths in a book that's full of them." Daniel Benjamin, a Clinton counterterrorism official, said that Freeh was "factually wrong" and that the president had pushed Abdullah "quite hard" at their meeting.[43]

Wyche Fowler, Clinton's ambassador to the kingdom, provided yet another version of this tawdry episode. He said he had personally asked

Abdullah for U.S. access to the suspects three or four months before the crown prince's Washington visit. His answer had been "It will be done." But it hadn't gotten done before his arrival. So Fowler and Freeh had gone together to see Abdullah at Bandar's residence in McLean and been told again, "We're going to do this."[44] Whether Clinton had pressed the issue, Fowler certainly had.

The "access" for FBI agents, such as it was defined finally, happened a few months later and was limited to an indirect interrogation of the suspects. The agents watched through a one-way mirror as Saudi interrogators submitted their questions. But it was enough for Freeh. On his last day in office in June 2001, he announced the indictment of thirteen members of "pro-Iran Saudi Hezbollah" in a conspiracy to drive the United States out of the kingdom.[45] Freeh thanked the Saudis for "a genuine commitment to solving the case, despite the inevitable challenges, sensitivities and occasional setbacks that are inherent in complex international investigations."[46] The truth seems to have been that neither Clinton nor Abdullah had any appetite for a confrontation with Iran, each for his own reasons.

CHAPTER 8

Midlife Crisis

IN THE MID-1990S, Bandar went through a major midlife crisis. It coincided with the effective end of King Fahd's rule after a debilitating stroke in late November 1995. Bandar had been Fahd's personal messenger, confidant, and troubleshooter for more than twenty years. In the stroke of a heartbeat, he was no longer any of these. He was devastated. Furthermore, he was not close to Crown Prince Abdullah, who took over as de facto ruler. Abdullah immediately found himself in a power struggle with Bandar's father, Defense Minister Prince Sultan, who had had aspirations to become crown prince himself. This put Bandar in an extremely awkward position. He would have to overcome Abdullah's suspicions of his primary allegiance to his father. He would have to spend a lot of time in the royal court at the feet of the new ruler seeking to prove he could become Abdullah's personal messenger just as he had been Fahd's. Bandar withdrew from the Washington scene, spending more and more time either in Saudi Arabia lobbying for himself at the royal court or at his lavish mountainside retreat outside Aspen. He abandoned his duties as dean of the diplomatic corps. He hardly even went to his own embassy any longer. He handed in his resignation for the second time. He stopped seeing many of his old friends.

Bandar was still recovering from a third operation on his back, this one the most serious. The crash landing he had suffered in his U.S.-built F-5 in 1977 had left him with a chronic back problem that grew steadily worse. The prince had received erroneous medical advice in 1994 as to the cause and cure. Neurosurgeons had operated twice on several disks in his back, but the pain had not gone away. He had even had to use a cane to walk at times. Finally, during the third operation, in February 1995, they discovered that nerves between two vertebrae had become severely compressed, which explained why he had been losing sensation in his right leg. The nerves had turned blue, and he had been within six months of losing total usage of that leg. This time, the surgeons carved out more space in the bones to allow the nerves to pass between the vertebrae unimpeded.

The prince, who had a reputation as a party lover and more than occasional drinker, claimed he had become a born-again Muslim.[1] This was partly due, he said, to a death scare in his family. By that time, he had eight children ranging in age between twenty-three years and eighteen months, four boys and four girls. A car accident in March 1992 had involved two of his children, Noura, six, and Fahad, four, who were then in Jeddah with their mother celebrating the end of Ramadan. Bandar had remained behind in Washington. As the two children were leaving the family compound to visit Bandar's mother, a car rammed into theirs, killing their two nannies and the driver. One of the nannies managed to extract the two kids from the wreckage before she died, and a passerby rushed them to a nearby military hospital. Haifa came running out of the house and into the street, but by the time she reached the accident site her children were gone. "Somebody told her everybody in the car is dead," Bandar recollected.[2] Only when she got to the hospital did she discover that Noura and Fahad had survived without major injuries. Meanwhile, Bandar lived through the first agonizing hours of not knowing whether they were alive or dead until Haifa reached the hospital. Then he had to finish the king's business he was on before he could return to see them two days later. Afterward, the family went on a retreat to Aspen, where Bandar went through a kind of religious rebirth.

"You had the holy month. You had this beautiful area on the top of the mountains in Colorado, and you had these two kids that are not supposed to be alive. It does something to you. It really affected me dramatically ever since."[3]

As a result of the accident, the prince spent more time with his younger four children to make up for being an absent father for the first four. He also took to reading the Koran with them each day during Ramadan for an hour and a half.

Bandar had also fled Washington to avoid his much-disliked duties as dean of the diplomatic corps by virtue of his seniority among diplomats. He was away so often that the head of the State Department's protocol office, Molly Raiser, called him "the invisible dean." Even when in town, the prince often refused to carry out the dean's duties—attending diplomatic cocktail parties, national day celebrations, State of the Union speeches, and welcoming ceremonies for visiting dignitaries. He even stopped appearing at the Saudi National Day celebration at his embassy.

Hala Ranch, overlooking the Aspen airport on Star Mesa, became Bandar's retreat from Washington, and some hideaway it was.[4] Located in the foothills of the Rockies, the "ranch" resembled a kind of medieval fortress, with enough rooms to house probably one hundred family members. With its fifty-six thousand square feet of space, the main house rivaled the White House in size and had sixteen bathrooms. Dotted across the ninety-five-acre property were a horse barn, a corral, and a Swiss chalet–style "log cabin" the size of a small hotel, which Bandar had designed himself. Written into its guest book were the words "Some Log Cabin," scrawled by no less than former president George H. W. Bush. Inside stood a huge grizzly bear that Bandar had shot on a hunting trip in Alaska after being charged twice by the huge beast.*

The size of the house—and the water required to keep it going—had caused a major controversy among Aspen residents. Bandar was still dealing with a water dispute with one of his neighbors five years after work on the ranch had finished. One guitar-playing local by the name of Paul Anderson had written a saucy "Ode to the Prince" making fun of the diplomat and his humble hideaway—"a place to call my own, a haven and retreat / A humble little homestead, 55,000 square feet."[5] Bandar had won over Aspen by contributing several million dollars to local causes, and finally even Anderson succumbed after the prince invited him for tea one day. Bandar had hired a legion of servants and security personnel to run and protect the ranch. For a supposed hideaway from the world's affairs, it was incredibly well connected to everything that was going on by half a dozen

---

* When Bandar decided in 2006 to sell Hala Ranch, minus the log cabin and another guesthouse, he figured the property was worth $135 million, setting a U.S. record for a private home until the Beverly Hills estate of the late William Randolph Hearst went on sale for $165 million. In November 2007, the prince gave up the search for a buyer. But he did manage to sell off one of the more modest homes on the property that he had built for his daughter, Reema, for $36.5 million.

gigantic television screens featuring English and Arabic channels and kept going twenty-four hours a day.

Family, health, and a prolonged midlife crisis were three reasons for Bandar's increasingly prolonged absences from Washington, but there was another: pure and simple boredom with the Washington political circus after eighteen years. "We won the Cold War. We beat communism. We beat socialism. We beat Saddam Hussein. We have the peace process going. We won almost everything. You'd think we would be happy, relaxed, and having fun," Bandar recalled in February 1996. "The tragedy is we are not. Life is less exciting, boring. There are too many problems that are little problems."[6]

Bandar conceded that the transition from Bush to Clinton had been far more difficult than from Reagan to Bush because he had not known the current president and those around him nearly as well. He realized he had not gotten off to a great start with the new president. But he had "no complaints or disappointments" about the way he had been treated or the extent of access accorded him by the White House. He claimed he could still command near-instant entry when he was on urgent business. But he acknowledged that the days were over when he could just drop by the Oval Office unannounced and casually see the president even when he was attending to other affairs of state. There simply had been no bonding "by time or events" with Clinton. "There's nothing more bonding than going to war together," he remarked. "I did have a very special relationship with President Bush, Baker, Scowcroft, Cheney, and so on. I really did not expect to have as close a relationship or access with the new administration." He was quite aware that his standing now depended more on being the ambassador from the world's oil superpower than on any personal relationship with Clinton. "If I represented Timbuktu, nobody would say hello to me except at a cocktail party."[7]

Part of the problem as he saw it was that the times had changed. "It's a different world that is not black and white. There are a lot of gray areas." And just as there had been no really big events for the Saudis to cope with alongside the Americans, there were no new challenges any longer. Even the energizing battles with the powerful American Israel Public Affairs Committee and the Washington press corps were a thing of the past for him. There was nothing to get his adrenaline flowing any more.

His description of dealing with Clinton seemed to reflect his mental state, or perhaps his state of mind had come to color his view of the whole

U.S.-Saudi relationship. There was always motion but no clear direction, always events taking place but no real substance to them.[8] He would pass enjoyable evenings chatting with Clinton about world events or watching a movie with him at the White House. But he would never be able to put into words for King Fahd what he had learned because the president was so pleasantly wishy-washy. He never felt Clinton was anti-Saudi or anti-monarchy, but he wasn't sure where he stood on many issues. Dealing with Clinton was like dealing with the notoriously slippery Yasser Arafat. The Arabs had coined the phrase *"la'am"* after many frustrating discussions trying to pin the Palestine Liberation Organization leader down on his position in peace negotiations with Israel. *La'am* was the contraction of two Arabic words, *la*, meaning "no," and *naam*, meaning "yes." Arafat's replies were always *"la'am,"* both "yes" and "no" at the same time. You were never sure which it was. With Clinton it was the same.[9]

The one issue on which the prince felt he shared a common assessment with Clinton was that of energy and the importance of oil to the U.S.-Saudi relationship. After all, the kingdom was the world's largest producer and exporter, the United States its largest consumer and importer. Long before President George W. Bush would take note of the scourge of American "addiction" to oil in his State of the Union Address in January 2006, Bandar was saying the same thing. But he admitted his own country suffered from the same addiction. "To be honest with you, we are both addicts. We are addicted to what we get from oil; you're addicted to our oil."[10] For most of Clinton's time in office, oil prices were reasonably low, even plummeting to ten dollars a barrel in 1997. So the American "addiction" ran high, and Clinton's energy policy was limited to talk of conservation measures promoted mostly by Vice President Al Gore. Only toward the end of the Clinton administration did escalating oil prices become a political problem, which Clinton resolved by tapping the U.S. Strategic Petroleum Reserve.

Bandar's oil policy for the kingdom had just one tenet and goal: Saudi Arabia must remain the number-one provider of foreign oil to the United States.[11] Oil equaled access; oil meant political influence for the kingdom and for him personally. It also meant assuring U.S. security as the quid pro quo, shoring up the twin pillars of the relationship. If remaining number one required a subsidy to the American consumer, so be it. Bandar found himself more than once arguing with the Saudi oil minister, Ali al-Naimi, in front of the king over what the kingdom's policy toward the United States should be.

At Bandar's insistence, the kingdom had for years deliberately acted to undercut its competitors by selling oil to the United States at a discount of at least twenty to thirty cents a barrel, sometimes much more. At the 1.5 million barrels per day the United States was importing from Saudi Arabia, a minimum twenty-cent discount per barrel amounted to $300,000 daily, or some $109 million a year. At thirty cents, it was $163 million a year. The Saudis were spending hundreds of millions of dollars in discounted oil to assure their political clout in Washington and Bandar's access to the White House. One U.S. oil specialist concluded that Saudi Arabia was spending "approximately $350 million per year" to subsidize the American consumer.[12]

In the mid-1990s, Saudi Arabia suddenly found itself challenged by Venezuela as the leading foreign source of oil for the American market. Despite the Saudi oil discount, Venezuelan oil imports were growing steadily. The Saudi share fell from 24 percent in 1991 to 14 percent in 1997, while Venezuela's climbed to 17 percent that year. In addition, the price of oil fell to ten dollars a barrel, making Venezuelan oil more competitive because transportation costs were a lot lower than from Saudi Arabia. The Venezuela challenge caught the Saudi eye, and Bandar's first.

The visit of Bandar's father, Prince Sultan, to Washington in late February 1997 provoked Bandar into thinking about how the U.S.-Saudi oil dependency might be used to revitalize the lackluster relationship. Sultan's visit was not a success, with the media highlighting the lack of Saudi cooperation in the investigation of the Khobar Towers bombing. FBI director Louis Freeh publicly criticized the Saudis.[13] Sultan sought to reassure Freeh and Secretary of State Madeleine Albright that the Saudis would step up their cooperation, which he assured a skeptical Washington media corps was already "excellent." The military relationship was also problematic, because the Saudis had no money and were six to seven billion dollars in arrears on their payments for arms they had already committed to purchasing. Bandar said his father was concerned that the economic underpinnings of the U.S.-Saudi relationship were fast eroding. "There was nothing really on the table to discuss," said Nathaniel Kern, president of the Washington-based Foreign Reports and a sometime energy consultant to Bandar.[14]

Sultan's visit led to a series of private talks between Bandar and Peter Bijur, who in 1997 was chairman and chief executive of Texaco, the only U.S. company still allowed to operate in the kingdom, if only in the odd-shaped "neutral zone" between Saudi Arabia and Kuwait. Texaco and Saudi Aramco (formerly Aramco), the kingdom's gigantic state oil company, were also partners in a distribution company inside the United States that operated thirteen thousand Texaco gas stations on the East Coast. Bandar and Bijur discussed the possibility of the Saudis reopening their oil and gas fields, taken over by the government in the 1970s, to outside exploration by American firms. This would have constituted a major turnaround in Saudi oil policy and risked being highly controversial inside the kingdom.

So in the summer of 1997, Bandar tasked Kern with producing a study of the pros and cons of allowing foreign operators back into the world's largest energy reservoir. Kern listed a number of potential benefits.[15] Saudi Aramco could use the competition to improve its own performance, since foreign companies would set new benchmarks for costs and efficiencies of operations. The foreign investment, which was bound to run into the billions of dollars, would stimulate the entire Saudi economy and create a lot of new jobs. Countries like Iran, Algeria, and Venezuela were welcoming foreign investment in their oil sectors, and Saudi Arabia was losing out to them. Finally, Kern cited an important political benefit: It would be an excellent gesture by Crown Prince Abdullah, who had a reputation in the United States for being somewhat anti-American. The downside was the political exposure of the Saudi royal family to possibly considerable criticism from militant Islamists inside the kingdom and abroad and a barrage of charges that it was selling the kingdom out to America. The Kern study languished for a year.

Then, in August 1998, Bandar learned that Abdullah had decided to make his first trip as crown prince to Washington and wanted to make a splash. Bandar decided to take another look at the Kern study, since an invitation for U.S. companies to come back into Saudi Arabia would certainly catch Washington's attention. The report was sent back to Abdullah, and in two days his positive response came back. Kern wasn't surprised. "It fit the crown prince's style. He wanted to 'smash the icons' and put his stamp on the kingdom's new style of rule."[16]

On September 26, Bandar invited to his sprawling residence on Chain Bridge Road in McLean, Virginia, the chairmen, presidents, and CEOs of America's then leading seven oil companies—Exxon, Mobil, Chevron, Texaco, Phillips, Conoco, and Arco.* The choice of companies was full of

---

* Exxon and Mobil have since merged, as have Conoco and Phillips; Chevron bought Texaco, and BP took over Arco.

history: Starting in the early 1930s, Chevron, originally known as Standard Oil of California, had been the founding father of Aramco and had then brought in Texaco, Exxon, and Mobil to explore and develop the kingdom's vast oil resources. These energy giants were basically responsible for turning the desert kingdom into the world's largest oil producer. They were told that the reason for the meeting was to meet Crown Prince Abdullah, who had something important to tell them.

The historic meeting took place in the residence's exquisite Moroccan Room, so named because Bandar had brought over Moroccan tile and woodwork specialists to decorate the floor and walls. It began with a speech by Saudi foreign minister Prince Saud al-Faisal, who reviewed the long and important involvement of American companies in the kingdom's transformation. Then Abdullah spoke. Noting that American companies had been "the bedrock" of the U.S.-Saudi relationship for half a century, the crown prince announced that the kingdom wanted them involved again in forging a new strategic energy partnership. The government was ready to consider their proposals for investment in the Saudi energy sector. He left it unclear whether this meant both its oil and gas fields. Participants heard different things. One said Abdullah had asked them to submit "recommendations and suggestions" for the role their companies might play in developing both gas and oil fields. Bandar and his aides assured reporters that if all went well, it would be just a matter of time before American and other foreign companies were given access to the kingdom's vast oil reservoirs.[17] However, there was one Saudi official in the room who was even more surprised by the crown prince's offer than the American oilmen—oil minister al-Naimi. He had been left out of the loop on the whole plan. Abdullah had not bothered to tell him in advance because he knew his oil minister would oppose it. Indeed, he did and ferociously so.

Abdullah's offer was quite a coup for Bandar. He had convinced the crown prince to go way out on a political limb in a bid to breathe new life into the U.S.-Saudi relationship. Abdullah had a reputation for being a staunch Saudi nationalist and not particularly close to the United States. So if anyone could sell the idea at home of allowing American oil companies back into the kingdom, it was he. Bandar was making both the kingdom's oil and foreign policy in promoting the plan. What was more extraordinary was that he had convinced Abdullah to adopt it, since he was still early in the process of establishing a personal relationship with the crown prince.

Bandar maintained another lasting impression of Abdullah's trip to Washington that fall. Clinton had become embroiled in a sex scandal involving White House intern Monica Lewinsky. The unfolding tawdry saga turned out to be a major distraction even for Abdullah. Bandar said the crown prince had expected to talk with Clinton about "big issues" regarding war and peace in the Middle East during their White House meeting on September 25. Instead, Abdullah found himself commiserating with Clinton about his political predicament over the Lewinsky affair. In fact, they spent two thirds of their meeting talking about it. Abdullah could not understand how the leader of the world's only superpower could possibly be on the verge of political catastrophe simply because of an extramarital affair.[18]

BANDAR GOT HIS first chance to serve as Crown Prince Abdullah's personal envoy in 1997. It came about in a convoluted way involving Libya's quixotic leader, Muammar Gaddafi, and South Africa's highly respected president, Nelson Mandela. Gaddafi had been an international pariah for nearly a decade because of his regime's extensive involvement in terrorism. It was the prime suspect behind the bombing of Pan Am Flight 103 over Lockerbie, Scotland, in December 1988, which had killed all 259 people aboard as well as 11 on the ground. Libya was also being blamed for the bombing of UTA Flight 772 over Niger in September 1989.

The only respectable chief of state with even the slightest sympathy for Gaddafi happened to be Mandela. He had never forgotten Libya's support for his African National Congress during its long struggle to overthrow the white apartheid government in South Africa. The Libyan leader had embraced the cause and provided millions of dollars and training for ANC guerrillas. Mandela felt he owed him and wanted to see Gaddafi rehabilitated. He realized that to achieve this, he would have to convince the Libyan eccentric to turn over for trial the two Libyan intelligence agents suspected of masterminding the two plane bombings. But Mandela also realized he had to convince Washington and London to accept some sort of compromise. Since Saudi Arabia had connections in both capitals, Mandela turned to Abdullah for help, and the crown prince assigned Bandar to the task. The prince and Mandela began working like coconspirators to extricate Gaddafi from his predicament.

In July 1997, Mandela came to speak in England at the opening of the

Oxford Center for Islamic Studies, whose construction had been financed largely through a donation from King Fahd. Not by chance, he stayed at Bandar's Glympton estate, near Oxford. The two began plotting a deal that would convince Gaddafi to hand over the two terrorist suspects and Clinton and British prime minister Tony Blair to support the lifting of U.N. sanctions on Libya. Their tactics for achieving these goals initially infuriated both Washington and London.

On October 18, Mandela questioned the U.N. policy of isolating Gaddafi and announced that he intended to make a trip to Libya to see him on his way to a Commonwealth conference in Edinburgh. Six days later, he flew to Tunis and then went by road to Tripoli, where the Libyan leader greeted him outside the carefully preserved ruins of a U.S. air attack on his living quarters back in 1986. Gaddafi hailed the visit as "a devastating blow to America." For his part, Mandela reminded the world that while the United States had supported the South African white apartheid regime, the Libyan leader had backed the African nationalist cause. Mandela stopped in Tripoli again on his way home from Edinburgh to bestow upon Gaddafi South Africa's highest award, the Order of Good Hope. The South African leader also called upon the international community to agree to a trial for the two terrorist suspects in a neutral country in return for the lifting of U.N. sanctions. By that time, Gaddafi had publicly stated he would accept a trial taking place in the Hague under Scottish law and even before a Scottish jury. But nobody in the Clinton administration thought he was serious.

Mandela did, however, and he was able to move Blair to launch his own initiative to find a compromise. But even Blair was not having much success with Clinton. At that point, Mandela decided to make use of Clinton's state visit to South Africa in March 1998 to lobby him personally on an opening to Gaddafi. First, he awarded his American visitor the same Order of Good Hope he had presented to the Libyan leader, a gesture of equal esteem doubtless little appreciated by the president and his delegation. Then, during a meeting of the two leaders and their delegations in Cape Town, Mandela suddenly asked to see Clinton alone. Such a private meeting had not been scheduled, and Clinton's aides were not happy when Clinton agreed. Once the delegations had left the meeting room, Mandela sprang his trap. Who should walk in to join the two leaders but Prince Bandar, who had flown into Cape Town to seize the opportunity to talk to Clinton. Mandela and Bandar then teamed up to press Clinton to take Gaddafi up on his offer of a trial in the Hague under Scottish law and presided over by Scottish judges. Clinton's national security adviser, Samuel "Sandy" Berger, who distrusted Bandar thoroughly, was furious and leaked the story to the press immediately.[19]

Berger wasn't the only one upset by Bandar's underhanded tactics. Martin Indyk, the State Department official dealing with Libyan matters, was too. Clinton's aides were all deeply suspicious that the prince was doing little more than serving as Gaddafi's advocate. They even suspected Bandar had his own personal motives for trying to help him. They had been determined to keep Bandar from talking to Clinton about Libya. The fact that the prince had been obliged to fly all the way to Cape Town and use the Mandela-Clinton meeting to make his case for Gaddafi was for Indyk proof positive of "how difficult it was for Bandar to get in to see the president" on this issue.[20] His interference was deeply resented because they did not know what the prince was telling Gaddafi, and they feared he might be misrepresenting U.S. views. To deal with the "Bandar problem," they decided to ask U.N. secretary-general Kofi Annan to be an intermediary.[21]

Bandar didn't care what Berger or Indyk thought of him. He was on a mission for Crown Prince Abdullah, not Clinton, and he was determined to succeed. This required a lot of hand-holding to convince a deeply suspicious Gaddafi that he was not walking into a trap. Would U.N. sanctions really be lifted once he turned over the two intelligence agents? What else would he be asked to do? Would relations really get better with Washington? Would the United States lift its own sanctions on Libya? The prince made numerous trips to reassure the mercurial Libyan leader that he was doing the right thing, sitting around for hours waiting upon Gaddafi's notoriously fickle moods to see him, sometimes in a desert tent or wherever he happened to be in his meanderings around Libya.

In July 1998, U.S. officials announced they were going to call his bluff and take Gaddafi up on his proposal to turn over the two wanted Libyan agents for a trial in the Hague. The U.S. offer was on a take-it-or-leave-it basis, with no more negotiations.[22] But there were months more of discussions regarding the details of the trial, such as where the two Libyans would serve their sentences if convicted. And Gaddafi learned that in return the United States and Britain were only willing initially to "suspend" U.N. sanctions, not lift them altogether. Whatever Bandar had told the Libyan leader, his rehabilitation was clearly going to be a long process. Still, on April 5, 1999, Gaddafi gave up the two Libyans, and they were flown to the Netherlands for trial—under Scottish law and presided over by Scottish judges—at a heavily fortified former U.S. air base, Camp Zeist. One of the witnesses to their handover at the Tripoli airport was Bandar, there to celebrate his mission accomplished.

At that point, Bandar's task changed dramatically, and so did the U.S. attitude about his possible usefulness as an intermediary to Gaddafi. The Clinton administration wanted to take advantage of the Libyan leader's desire to come in from the international cold and convince him to also end his support for terrorism, join the battle against al-Qaeda, and even abandon his chemical weapons program. (At this point, U.S. intelligence was unaware that Libya also had a nuclear weapons program under way.) There was in addition the unresolved issue of Libyan compensation to the families of the Pan Am victims.

The Clinton administration opened up two secret channels to Gaddafi. One involved using the Palestine Liberation Organization's Mahmoud Abbas.* Indyk said they asked Abbas to verify whether Gaddafi was in fact expelling radical Palestinians as he said he would do. Both the British and the Americans had asked the Libyan strongman to take this step to show that he was truly ending his support for terrorism. But Abbas was being used for another purpose, according to Indyk: to verify that what Bandar was telling Washington about Gaddafi's good intentions was in fact true. "We weren't quite sure we could trust Bandar because of his relationship with Gaddafi."[23]

The other U.S. channel was so secret it went behind Prime Minister Blair's back as well, according to Indyk.[24] This channel involved talks between Gaddafi's top intelligence official, Musa Kusa, and a three-man delegation led by Indyk, who was then an assistant secretary at the State Department. The facilitator of these meetings turned out to be no less than Prince Bandar himself. And the venue was either his Glympton estate or his father's home above Lake Geneva. Despite his deep distrust of Bandar, Indyk relied on him to host these meetings, a development he later described as the natural outcome of the prince's role in facilitating at the same time the normalization of relations between the United States and Libya.[25]

---

* Abbas later became prime minister and then president of the Palestinian National Authority after Yasser Arafat's death in November 2004.

Indyk's account of his secret meetings with Kusa makes for fascinating reading. The first one took place in May 1999 in Prince Sultan's glitzy Lake Geneva residence, which Indyk remembers as being covered with gold fittings, mirrors, and television screens, a style he dubbed "Saudi modern." Bandar took Indyk and his two aides to the downstairs recreation room, introduced them to the three-man Libyan delegation, and then left them alone to talk. Indyk spelled out the deal the United States was prepared to strike: If Gaddafi would get out of "the terrorism business," provide compensation to the Pan Am families, and end his efforts to develop weapons of mass destruction, Washington would support the lifting of first U.N. and then U.S. sanctions. Kusa liked the proposal and even suggested Libya might join multilateral Middle East peace negotiations.[26]

Upon returning to Washington, Indyk ran into enormous skepticism from his colleagues at the State Department and the White House. Kusa's word on Libyan willingness to cooperate against al-Qaeda would have to be tested. So a second meeting took place, again in Sultan's residence outside Geneva, where Kusa provided bits of Libyan intelligence on al-Qaeda but was less convincing regarding the Libyan commitment to fighting terrorism. A third session was arranged in December 1999. This time, the location was Bandar's Glympton estate, which featured a British pub replica in the basement recreation room well stocked with single malt whiskey and Cuban cigars. By then, there was clear evidence Gaddafi was getting out of "the terrorism business," and the meeting went extremely well.[27] Eventually, the Libyan leader also settled on a $2.7 billion payout to the 270 Pan Am families.

Resolution of the Pan Am bombing dispute after eleven years was a major achievement for the Clinton administration. It had taken a large cast of international characters to accomplish it, and Bandar had certainly played a role, albeit a disputed one. But he had fulfilled his royal mission and proved his worth to his new boss, Crown Prince Abdullah. He had shown he could shift his allegiances and become Abdullah's messenger and troubleshooter just as he had been Fahd's. Less clear was whether the prince was any more appreciated, or trusted, by Clinton and his people. He certainly had rendered them a service by brokering secret talks between Libyan and U.S. officials. He had also helped convince Gaddafi to hand over the two Libyans. Clinton offered a perfunctory thanks to both Bandar and Mandela the day Gaddafi turned over the two suspects, but the president reserved his warmest praise for Secretary-General Annan, who had played a comparatively minor role in the prolonged dealings with the Libyan leader.[28]

ON DECEMBER 16, 1998, Clinton unleashed U.S. air might on Iraqi communication centers, Republican Guard headquarters, Saddam Hussein's presidential palaces in Baghdad, and suspected sites around the country for his chemical, biological, and nuclear programs. Giant B-52 bombers, F-117 Stealth aircraft, and F-15 fighters poured a rain of bombs on these and other targets for four days, while hundreds of Tomahawk missiles were launched from U.S. warships in the Persian Gulf. The operation, code-named Desert Fox, was in retaliation for Saddam's refusal to cooperate any longer with U.N. inspectors scouring the country for evidence of his weapons of mass destruction. For months, Saddam had played a cat-and-mouse game with the inspectors, blocking their visits and making it ever more difficult for them to operate.

Clinton's decision to let loose American air power on Iraq had been highly controversial. Russia, China, and France had opposed any military action in the U.N. Security Council, and only Britain joined in Desert Fox. America's Arab allies in the gulf were sharply divided too, and all were worried about the collateral damage that would be inflicted on Iraq's civilian population, already suffering from severe medical and food shortages due to U.N. sanctions. Secretary of Defense William Cohen worked hard to round up support for the operation during a trip to the area in early November. But he found little enthusiasm. The most negative response awaited him in Riyadh. Cohen was informed that "Saudi Arabia doesn't approve using its territories as a springboard for attacks on Iraq," an unnamed Saudi official told reporters.[29] Such a stand by the most pro-American gulf Arab leader was a clear indication of just how unpopular association with U.S. military activities in Iraq was becoming. Eventually, only Kuwait and Oman allowed their bases to be used for launching aircraft on attack missions, while the Saudis restricted their assistance to hosting U.S. and British refueling planes.

Desert Fox would prove to be a turning point in the Saudi attitude toward U.S. military activities inside the kingdom. Following the Khobar Towers bombing two years earlier, the Saudis had agreed to allow the U.S. Air Force aircraft and personnel involved in Operation Southern Watch's activities monitoring Iraq to move from the heavily populated Dhahran area to an isolated desert site outside al-Kharj, fifty miles southeast of Riyadh. The Prince Sultan Air Base, as the place was called, was huge—eighty square miles and with a three-mile-long airstrip. But it had gone largely unused even by the Saudi Royal Air Force. It seemed the ideal spot for keeping the forty-five hundred military personnel from the United States, Britain, and France involved in Southern Watch out of public view, for both political and security reasons. But Desert Fox highlighted that the American presence remained a political thorn in the side of the House of Saud even though it was far removed from public sight.

The question remained: Why hadn't the Saudis used the Khobar Towers bombing as an excuse to move the American military back "over the horizon"? At the time, Bandar himself had helped to convince Fahd and Abdullah to allow the United States the use of Prince Sultan Air Base as a fallback. Forcing the Americans to leave in response to the bombing would have meant handing al-Qaeda, Iran, or whoever was behind it a major propaganda victory. "You were scared to leave [because] people will say you cut and run. We were scared to tell you to leave [because] people will say, 'Hey, you are not grateful,'" the prince recollected.[30] So neither side had brought up the issue then. It was, in Bandar's thinking, another example of the "autopilot" paralysis in the U.S.-Saudi relationship at the time. Now the December 1998 operation showed that the Americans didn't need Saudi bases to deliver a punishing blow to Saddam's regime, and nobody could accuse Washington of bowing to terrorism.

Indyk remembered a different Bandar, one who was a super-hawk when it came to Saddam. "He was always pushing for the United States to bomb Iraq, much more than Paul Wolfowitz." He was referring to the neoconservative scholar and senior Pentagon official who would later press so hard for the U.S. invasion of Iraq in 2003. "He wanted us to knock off Saddam."[31] Indyk was convinced the prince had a personal grudge to settle with Saddam. When the State Department had taken away his security detail after Clinton came into office, Bandar had protested vociferously, arguing he needed it because Saddam had taken out a contract to have him killed. Also, Saddam had tried to assassinate his favorite U.S. president, George H. W. Bush, while he was visiting Kuwait after leaving office in April 1993. So the prince couldn't wait for the U.S. bombs to fall.

Indyk recalled Bandar's unannounced visit to his State Department office the night before Desert Fox was first scheduled to start, in early November

1998.[32] Bandar was not supposed to know that the first missiles and bombs were set to fly the next morning at nine, but he had found out from his CIA or Pentagon friends and wanted to celebrate. There was a good chance one of the American bombs or missiles would find and kill the Iraqi dictator. So he carried with him a two-hundred-dollar bottle of Johnnie Walker Blue Label whiskey to share with Indyk and his aides. As it turned out, the bombing was called off at the last minute because U.N. secretary-general Annan announced that Saddam had agreed to allow international inspectors back in. But Bandar had already informed Crown Prince Abdullah of the presumed precise day and time. When Indyk tried to contact the prince early that morning to explain the delay, he was nowhere to be found. Bandar had already left for Riyadh to present his excuses to Abdullah for providing him with the wrong information.

WHATEVER ITS DOUBTS, the Clinton administration time and again turned to Bandar for help. Such was the case in its frenzied effort to achieve a breakthrough in the stalled Middle East peace process as Clinton's time in office drew to a close. In early 2000, Clinton called Bandar to the White House, and the two discussed Clinton's ideas for a peace accord between Israel and Syria. There are conflicting versions as to whether Clinton or Bandar initiated the meeting and even when it was held.[33] But in any case, the prince suddenly became Clinton's personal messenger to Syrian president Hafez al-Assad. His mission was so secret that even Secretary of State Madeleine Albright was deliberately left out of the loop. Clinton wanted Bandar to convince Assad, a notoriously hard bargainer and skeptic regarding Israeli intentions, to come to a meeting with Israeli prime minister Ehud Barak in Geneva to strike a peace deal. Clinton thought he could coax Barak into agreeing to an Israeli withdrawal from the Syrian Golan Heights, occupied since the 1967 war, in return for Syria's normalization of relations with Israel.

The crux of the matter was getting the two enemies to agree on the demarcation of their common border along the Sea of Galilee and the Jordan River. Barak didn't want Syria to have access to its waters and insisted the borderline be set back from the edge several hundred meters. He was ready to leave the precise demarcation to a later time but agreed in principle to return to the 1967 border between the two countries. He also wanted Assad to put an end to the fighting in southern Lebanon, where Syrian-backed

Palestinian and Shiite guerrilla groups were harassing an Israeli-backed Lebanese faction. Assad, on the other hand, insisted on the border being demarcated as part of any deal. Clinton's tactic was to get bottom-line demands from both sides and then try to broker a compromise. The president had been carrying on his own conversations with both Assad and Barak, but neither would spell out his bottom-line position. In early January 2000, Clinton even sponsored a talkathon, held over thirteen days in Shepherdstown, West Virginia, between Barak and Syrian foreign minister Farouk al-Shara, but to no avail.

According to Dennis Ross, Clinton's point man on Middle East negotiations, Bandar's mission was flawed from the start by a "misunderstanding" on Bandar's part that Clinton was ready to squeeze Barak into making an offer that met all of Assad's demands. That had never been the U.S. intention; rather, it was to get both Assad and Barak to spell out their bottom lines, align them close enough to make a deal a near certainty, and then hold a summit to bridge the final gap and sign an agreement.[34]

Bandar went off to Damascus and spent three and a half hours sounding out Assad on his bottom line. He came back with a glowing report, according to Ross. Assad was ready to do a deal and ready to meet Barak one-on-one to accomplish this. He was raring to go and "get the deal done now, not play games."[35] There had to be agreement on the border demarcation, but the Syrian leader was ready to be flexible. The prince also reported that Assad, who was actually near death, appeared to be in surprisingly good physical and mental condition.

Ross was highly skeptical of Bandar's report, but the Americans and Israelis decided to press ahead anyway. After much pushing and prodding, Ross managed to convince Barak to spell out his bottom line for the border demarcation, or at least come close enough to make the U.S. negotiator think they could get a deal. But Clinton wanted to meet with the Syrian president alone first. At that point, Assad began having second thoughts, refusing even to take one of the president's phone calls and playing games about the date for their proposed meeting. First he said he would come to Geneva on March 18, though he had been told that was the day Clinton was leaving for a trip to India. Finally, he agreed to meet in Geneva on March 26, when Clinton would be on his way back from South Asia. Since Assad rarely went abroad even in perfect health, his intention to fly to Geneva in failing health seemed to herald a breakthrough.

Such expectations were quickly dashed. To the shock of Clinton and his aides, Assad stonewalled right from the start. He didn't even allow Clinton to finish his description of Barak's bottom line and summarily rejected the Israeli leader's offer to withdraw to a commonly agreed-on border based on the 1967 line, provided Israel could keep a narrow strip of shoreline. The summit was an unqualified disaster, a "high visibility failure," as Ross put it. He was reminded of Clinton's adage: "The people don't pay us to fail."[36] Bandar was equally stunned by the outcome but denied he had misread Assad's intentions and negotiating position during their three-and-a-half-hour talk, or misrepresented them later. He pleaded with Ross not to give up on Assad, to which the frustrated U.S. negotiator replied curtly, "The ball is in his court."[37] Later, the prince blamed Clinton for any "misunderstanding." He had written down what Clinton had asked him to convey to the Syrian leader and repeated it three times; he had not misrepresented Clinton's position either. Clinton simply had not fulfilled his promise to deliver Barak on an Israeli withdrawal to a clearly demarcated 1967 borderline.[38]

Ross was reluctant to put all the blame on Bandar. He had dealt with the Saudi long enough to expect "a spin" in his account of his talk with Assad. He had been skeptical regarding Bandar's description of what the Syrian leader had said, and he had been very suspicious of his account of Assad's physical condition. "You can have your doubts but still feel it ought to be tested," he said of the prince's account of his Assad meeting. Then there had been the look on the Syrian foreign minister's face when Assad had indicated no interest in a border agreement based on the 1967 line. Al-Shara had been "truly surprised," and this made Ross think that the Syrian leader had simply changed his calculation about the need for any agreement at that point.[39] Clinton never had a chance to renew his Syrian-Israeli initiative. On June 10, Assad died.

Clinton and his Middle East negotiators turned to Bandar yet again during their last two months in office. The reason was one last attempt to resolve the Israeli-Palestinian dispute. Though this failed too, the historic compromise they devised is still regarded as the probable basis for any agreement in the future. U.S. and Israeli negotiators together drew up plans for a Palestinian state that would be established on about 95 percent of the West Bank and all of the Gaza Strip, with a corridor linking the two. On the hot-button issue of Jerusalem, the Palestinian state would also be able to claim the holy city as its capital, as both its Palestinian neighborhoods and one of Islam's most sacred shrines, the Haram esh-Sharif, or Temple Mount, were to be included. Each side could thereby proclaim Jerusalem as its capital.

The plan required a swap of some land and the regroupment of Israeli settlers on some piece of West Bank territory the Palestinians would have to give up. The proposed Palestinian state would be allowed a police force but no army. The Palestinians would also have to restrict to the new Palestine state the right of return for hundreds of thousands of refugees who fled, or were forced out, during the 1948–49 war; they could not go back to their homes inside Israel. Finally, a U.S.-led international peacekeeping force would replace the Israel Defense Forces in the West Bank and the Gaza Strip to oversee implementation of the agreement and keep the peace.

The last-chance talks started December 19 at Bolling Air Force Base, outside Washington. Four days later at the White House, Clinton presented the outlines of the deal as described above. On December 29, less than three weeks before the Clinton administration's final day, the Israeli cabinet approved the plan with some reservations. Yasser Arafat put off answering but came to Washington to see Clinton on January 2. Bandar weighed in together with Egyptian ambassador Nabil Fahmy to get Arafat to accept the terms. The prince lectured the slippery PLO chairman on the need to say yes to the best deal the Palestinians would ever be offered. "If you take this deal, we will all throw our weight behind you. If you don't take this deal, do you think anybody will go to war for you?"[40] It was all to no avail, though, despite Clinton's offer to travel to Israel to meet with Barak and Arafat "for one last roll of the dice."[41] Arafat suddenly found himself too busy to make the appointment. Clinton left office with no deal, having provided an example of presidential engagement in the search for Middle East peace that his successor would be determined never to follow.

IN THE SPRING of 2001, Prince Sultan came to Washington for a visit. Bandar decided to arrange a special meeting for his father with Ross at the embassy residence in McLean, Virginia. The purpose: to explain to Sultan exactly where the negotiations with the Syrians and Palestinians stood as the newly elected Republican president, George W. Bush, was settling into office. Ross said he "laid it out for him" and was surprised by his reaction. "If we'd only known, we could have done much more to help."[42] What did Sultan mean by "if we'd only known"? Hadn't Bandar kept him informed on the state of play? Ross concluded that Bandar had chosen not to tell his own father what he had been doing or how close negotiations on both issues had come to a breakthrough. "I think a lot of what Bandar did he may have done pretty much on his own."[43]

Whether the prince was freelancing was a constant concern for Clinton's people. Did he speak for the king or only for himself? Was he accurately re-laying the views of those he claimed to represent when serving as an ap-pointed, or sometimes self-appointed, intermediary? At times, he was such a spinmeister they could not be sure. They were even less certain after King Fahd had his stroke in late 1995. Bandar had been extremely close to Fahd, almost his alter ego on issues involving the kingdom's relations with Wash-ington. Ross remembered sessions he attended with the king and Bandar where Fahd beamed with pride as he listened to the prince talking. "It was like a father's gaze on his son." By contrast, Abdullah and Bandar were dis-tant relatives. When Ross saw the two of them together on one of his peace-making visits to Saudi Arabia, he found their relationship "very formal."[44] Still, the crown prince and Bandar did share one family trait. They were both "outsiders." Abdullah did not belong to the politically dominant Su-dairi branch of the al-Saud family to which his rival peers—Fahd, Sultan, and Naif—all belonged. Abdullah had had to struggle against the Sudairi brothers to affirm his position as crown prince after Fahd's stroke. Bandar, on the other hand, was an outsider in the sense that his mother was a house-hold servant, and he had had to fight for recognition as a member of the House of Saud.[45]

But Bandar by virtue of his father, Prince Sultan, was still a Sudairi. So whether the prince had the confidence of Abdullah was far from clear. In any case, the Clintonites never trusted Bandar. This was reflected in Ross's summary judgment of the prince: There were times when Bandar was indis-pensable, others when he was "probably part con man," and still others when his role was useful "but not the one you would make it out to be."[46] Bruce Riedel, Clinton's Middle East national security adviser, said he had learned to "check, double-check, and triple-check" what Bandar told them, "particularly in the Abdullah era."[47]

CHAPTER 9

"You Go Your Way, I Go My Way"

IN THE WORDS OF PRINCE BANDAR, "It was too good to be true."[1] Bush the son in the White House. At the behest of Bush the father, the prince had coached George W. during the presidential campaign on the pitfalls of the Middle East, stressing the centrality of the still-festering Palestinian issue. If Bush listened politely but showed little interest, maybe it didn't matter. Or so Bandar thought at the time, because he was bringing in the same set of advisers who had surrounded his father. "My God, talk about a replay," said the prince, ticking off the names of old familiar friends—Vice President Dick Cheney, Secretary of State Colin Powell, and National Security Adviser Condoleezza Rice, whom he had known from the Reagan years. The prince raved about Paul Wolfowitz, the incoming deputy secretary of defense, a kindred spirit who would become a prime promoter of the Iraq invasion in 2003. Bandar described Wolfowitz as "more pro-Saudi than us," at least aside from the Israeli issue.[2]

Bandar felt he was so close to the key players in the incoming Bush administration that it was better initially to keep his distance. His reputation for being practically part of the Bush family was already well known, and he didn't want to draw any more media attention to it than necessary. "We hit the ground in very slow motion and very timid." But he had no concerns. He was convinced the Bush team was already well aware of Saudi Arabia's importance to the United States. Back in Riyadh, the al-Saud family was practically giddy at Bush's election, expecting, like Bandar, a replay of his father's policies and attitudes toward the Middle East.

Bandar said he sought to dampen expectations at the royal court, but it seems he didn't make clear for months just how determined the new Bush team was to avoid a repeat of Clinton's hands-on style of trying to manage the Israeli-Palestinian peace process. The prince admitted later, however, that he had been warned in very clear terms about the new hands-off policy of the White House.

"They were up-front. They were honest. They said, 'We cannot want peace in the Middle East more than the people in the Middle East. That's rule number one. Rule number two, if people are serious, call us. Come on over and give us a serious proposition from both sides. Then we will try and help you. If you are not serious, don't come. We're too busy . . . If you really need a shoulder to cry on, find your mother, or father, or a priest. Don't come here. We don't have shoulders to cry on.' "[3]

In essence, Bush and his advisers were telling the Saudis that everything Clinton had done to try to bring peace to the Middle East was now a model of what they intended not to do. The new White House mantra became "Anything but Clinton."[4] Camp David would be strictly for the president's rest and relaxation, not peace negotiations. This resolve was only strengthened after Clinton, on the morning of Bush's inauguration, called Secretary of State Powell to vent his frustration over the failure to clinch a deal between Israel and the Palestine Liberation Organization. His advice: "Don't you ever trust Yasser Arafat."[5]

Bandar claimed King Fahd and Crown Prince Abdullah failed to grasp the shifting White House attitude toward the Palestinian issue. But the prince himself was largely responsible for their misunderstanding, or perhaps illusions. It was his job to inform them, and nobody understood the new administration's "don't bother me" attitude better than Bandar. He had simply failed to deliver the bitter message he was hearing. "Everything Bush or Colin Powell or Condoleezza Rice told us they will or will not do, they stuck to it. It's just at that time we were not listening," Bandar recollected.[6] Instead, he kept counseling Riyadh to be patient and give Bush the son time. The new president was busy with domestic issues just as Clinton had been after he first came into office, and he had to consolidate his political base after a hotly contested presidential election whose outcome had depended on a Supreme Court decision.

The famed special relationship between the two countries began souring within a month of Bush taking office, and within nine months it would lie in total shambles. Its unraveling began on February 16, 2001, when the United States and Britain sent twenty-four warplanes to bomb Iraqi radar sites and military command centers, including some close to Baghdad. These were the first such attacks in two years outside the so-called no-fly zone covered by the Southern Watch program in southern Iraq. The attacks were in response to an increasingly aggressive Iraqi military that had begun firing surface-to-air missiles at U.S. and British warplanes. Saddam Hussein was testing the new Bush's resolve, and the president was intent on demonstrating he was determined to confront the Iraqi dictator. The aircraft flew from Kuwait and the USS *Harry S. Truman*, an aircraft carrier stationed in the Persian Gulf.[7] But reports emerged from the Pentagon that some had taken off from Saudi air bases, though these were, in fact, refueling planes, not attack aircraft.

The Saudis were furious. The unwritten rules for U.S. warplanes based in the kingdom was that they would not be used for attack operations over southern Iraq, much less further north outside the no-fly zone. The Saudis were above all deeply embarrassed by the spotlight again falling on the U.S. military presence in the kingdom. In the Arab world, the four-day operation was a public relations disaster. America's Arab allies in the region—Egypt, Jordan, and even Saudi Arabia—all condemned the attacks as illegal. So did Germany and France, which had refused to allow their aircraft assigned to Southern Watch to participate.[8] The U.S.-British action renewed calls for the lifting of U.N. sanctions, which were being blamed for food and medical shortages resulting in the deaths of thousands of Iraqi children.

The February raid provoked a crisis in Riyadh, particularly after a Pentagon spokesman disclosed under questioning in Congress that the United States had neither sought nor received Saudi permission to use aircraft stationed in the kingdom.[9] This "don't ask us, just do it" approach was precisely what Bandar had advised Pentagon officials to follow throughout the 1990s to avoid disputes. Bruce Riedel, the National Security Council official who advised both Clinton and Bush on Middle East matters, felt that Bandar took this somewhat cavalier attitude to avoid having to deal with the Saudi military himself to obtain permission. "In truth, you couldn't operate on that basis because Saudi commanders on the ground don't operate on that basis."[10]

This time, Bandar's advice got the Americans into real trouble. Crown Prince Abdullah suddenly began to ask why American aircraft were still in Saudi Arabia. He was not even sure there was an "Iraqi threat" any longer.[11] But the Saudis were paying one hundred million dollars annually to cover the local costs of stationing U.S., British, and French aircraft in the kingdom. All they were getting for their money was trouble. Abdullah reacted by imposing stiff new restrictions. U.S. refueling tankers would no longer be allowed to service American warplanes going to or coming back from Iraq. Attacking warplanes would not be permitted to fly through Saudi airspace even in transit from carriers or other countries to Iraq. This meant the U.S. Air Force could no longer store munitions in the kingdom that might be used by these warplanes.

"Most air force people would say the restrictions made the Saudi bases not worth the hassle," said one former Pentagon official responsible for Saudi affairs.[12] But it wasn't easy to move elsewhere at that point because the air bases being used by the United States and Britain in Kuwait and Bahrain were "saturated." And the United States still needed Saudi bases to sustain the Southern Watch operation. The basic problem was the absence now of a "strategic consensus" between Riyadh and Washington over how to deal with Iraq. The overall effect of the new Saudi restrictions was to oblige the U.S. Air Force to rebase eighteen to twenty strike aircraft elsewhere outside the kingdom.[13] The Saudis had begun their slow squeeze to kick the American military out, a process that would come to a conclusion after 9/11.

Relations between the two allies, and between Bush and Abdullah, continued to worsen. Uninformed by Bandar, or perhaps not wanting to believe that Bush intended no new peace initiative, Abdullah started writing to the president, pressing him to take action. The Saudis were getting desperate. Ariel Sharon, the Israeli super-hawk responsible for the massacre of Palestinians during the 1982 Lebanon war, had managed to spark a new Palestinian uprising, the second intifada, inside Israel. He did this by visiting the Temple Mount in September 2000 to emphasize Israeli claims to the disputed holy site. He then went on to win a landslide victory in February 2001 over sitting prime minister Ehud Barak. Sharon was intent on breaking the Palestinians' will to resist and showed not the slightest interest in peace negotiations.

Abdullah had a much stronger visceral attachment to the Palestinian cause than King Fahd and watched with increasing anger the Qatar-based

President Franklin Roosevelt and King Abdulaziz on Egypt's Great Bitter Lake, 1945.

President Dwight Eisenhower and a group of Muslim scholars at the White House, September 23, 1953.

Dharan Air Base, 1950.

Prince Bandar with President Jimmy Carter, December 5, 1979.

King Faisal.

Sheikh Ahmed Zaki
Yamani, former Saudi
oil minister.

Prince Bandar with
President Ronald
Reagan, May 20, 1986.

An American
serviceman walks
past a United
States AWACS
aircraft deployed to
Saudi Arabia during
the Gulf War,
August 20, 1990.

Prince Bandar
with President
George H. W. Bush,
February 22, 1990.

King Fahd.

Prince Bandar
with Secretary of
State James Baker
and President
George H. W.
Bush, July 8, 1991.

King Fahd Holy Koran Printing Complex in Medina.

Prince Sultan bin Abdulaziz,
Bandar's father.

Sheikh Saleh al-Sheikh,
minister of Islamic affairs,
2004.

Prince Bandar outside his house in Colorado, 1996.

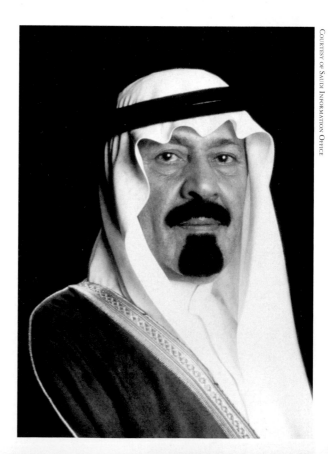

King Abdullah.

President Bill Clinton, Prince Bandar, and King Fahd.

Prince Naif, Saudi
interior minister,
February 5, 2002.

Prince Turki.

Prince Bandar with President George W. Bush at the Bush Ranch in Crawford, Texas, August 27, 2002.

Ali al-Naimi, Saudi oil minister.

satellite television network Al Jazeera's coverage of the Israeli army at work slowly grinding down the Palestinian resistance. Saudis across the kingdom had their eyes glued to TV screens watching the same scenes of the fighting repeated over and over again. The crown prince desperately wanted Bush to get Sharon to ease off, and he wanted Bush to meet with Arafat. This was just about the last thing the president intended after the Palestinian leader's stiffing of Clinton. As Bandar recounted, there was an accelerating process of disillusionment with Bush the son that was shared by Saudi royals and commoners alike. High hopes and expectations for the new president were giving way to anger and despair. Suddenly, the Saudis were asking, "What are our American friends doing to us? We're drifting and the region is boiling."[14]

Abdullah and other senior Saudi royals sent stronger and stronger signals to Washington of their growing angst. In mid-May, the crown prince let it be known he was canceling plans to visit the United States and turning down Bush's invitation to come watch the Kentucky Derby and stay at his family ranch in Crawford, Texas. The highlight of the visit was to have been a joint appearance by Abdullah and Bush at President Franklin Roosevelt's estate in Hyde Park, New York. There, they were to have reaffirmed the special relationship dating back to his meeting in 1945 with King Abdulaziz aboard the USS *Quincy* on Egypt's Great Bitter Lake. Other signals of Saudi discontent followed. A month later, Prince Sultan proposed the renewal of the Arab boycott on companies doing business with Israel "if the political situation [didn't] improve."[15] In mid-June, Bush the father called Abdullah to try to reassure the Saudi royals that his son really did have "his heart in the right place" and that he was "going to do the right thing" in the Middle East.[16]

But Abdullah saw no sign of this. In an interview with the *Financial Times* on June 25, the crown prince asked, "Don't they see what is happening to Palestinian children, women and the elderly—the humiliation, the hunger?" He warned that violence and terrorism were on the verge of exploding across the Middle East unless the United States took some action to revive the peace process.[17] At the end of June, Bush did send Powell to the Middle East to see Sharon and Arafat in an attempt to broker a cease-fire and a cooling-off period as a prelude to relaunching the peace process. Powell met with Abdullah, then in Paris, on his way back to Washington to try to reassure him that the administration was at least trying.

The crown prince remained unimpressed. The situation on the ground in the West Bank was steadily deteriorating. From Abdullah's viewpoint, it was also steadily deteriorating in Washington. In early August, Cheney openly encouraged Sharon to press on with his offensive to crush the Palestinian intifada by assassinating its leaders, stating that he saw "some justification in their trying to protect themselves by preempting."[18] Mounting Saudi frustration with Bush was aired by the kingdom's ambassador in London, Ghazi al-Qusaibi, who wrote a column in the Arab daily *Al-Hayat* in response. A diplomat-poet renowned at home for his sassy pen, the ambassador dissected "Little George's" many personal complexes toward "Big George" and mocked his inexperience in foreign affairs. Little George, he wrote, had become a menace to the entire world and deserved a special medal that he proposed be named "the Prize for Turning Friends into Enemies Without Effort."[19] Al-Qusaibi had been reprimanded by the kingdom's rulers for his poems in the past, but not this time.

On August 23, Israeli tanks and armored personnel carriers pushed into the heart of Hebron, on the West Bank, to protect the isolated community of four hundred Jews living in the city's center surrounded by a hostile Palestinian population. The incursion marked the deepest Israeli thrust into the West Bank to that point and resulted in the killing of two Palestinian men and the death of a sixty-five-year-old Palestinian woman waiting for an ambulance. It is not clear whether this was the woman who so moved Abdullah as he watched news coverage of the Israeli operation on television. But Bandar said the final straw for the crown prince was seeing an Israeli soldier that same day knock down a woman in a scuffle and then hold her on the ground by putting his foot on her head. Abdullah felt that was the ultimate insult to Arab pride, and "he went berserk."[20] This single incident was responsible for propelling the crown prince into a whirlwind of activity that would shortly produce the worst crisis in U.S.-Saudi relations since the 1973 oil boycott—even before the 9/11 disaster.

The next day, Bush held a press conference in Crawford, where he was on summer vacation. It had been called to announce the appointment of air force general Richard Myers as the next chairman of the Joint Chiefs of Staff. Bandar, who was at his home in Aspen, and Abdullah, who was in Riyadh, were both watching to see what the president would say about the Hebron incursion. The second question put to Bush by a reporter addressed that issue. The president was blunt. The Israeli incursion was basically the fault of Palestinian terrorists and particularly of Arafat, whom he blamed for all the violence. "I strongly urge Mr. Arafat to put 100 percent effort into solving the terrorist activity, into stopping the terrorist activity," he said. As for the Israelis, Bush said he "would hope" they showed restraint, but didn't demand it of them. This time Abdullah, in Bandar's words, "just went bananas."[21]

THE FIRST STEP the crown prince took was to order back home the Saudi army chief of staff, Salih Ali bin Muhayya, who had arrived in Washington on August 23 for annual consultations with Pentagon officials. Muhayya had come a few days early, hoping to visit his son, who was attending an American school. The Saudi general was told on the morning of August 25 to leave immediately. He didn't know what to tell his Pentagon hosts. No one had told him why he was being ordered home.[22] The same day, forty other Saudi officers who had boarded an aircraft in Riyadh on their way to join Muhayya were yanked off the plane and told their trip was being canceled. To Bandar, this was the first indication Abdullah was seriously upset, because "Saudis never screw around with military relationships with America unless they mean business."[23] The gesture went unreported in the U.S. media, and even Pentagon officials were left puzzling over what it meant. But Bandar called the White House to make clear that Muhayya's recall was in protest over Bush's comments and refusal to put any pressure on Sharon to stop his incursion into the West Bank. The prince said Abdullah's action caught Bush and his advisers off guard because their general, though erroneous, assumption had been that the Saudi leadership didn't care that much deep down about the Palestinian issue.

According to Bandar, both the White House and the Pentagon at that point should have been in a state of high alarm. The CIA and U.S. embassies across the Middle East were sending back reports warning that the mood was "getting ugly" in the streets and that attacks on U.S. facilities in Muslim countries could occur at any moment. The prince was convinced these reports were not reaching Bush, so the president was unaware how dangerous the situation was becoming for the United States and its Arab allies. Bandar was also still reluctant to conclude that Bush simply didn't care what happened to the Palestinians.

Abdullah ordered Bandar to lodge a diplomatic protest immediately with Bush and Powell over the Israeli incursion and mistreatment of Palestinian civilians. He told the prince that he had a lot more for him to relay to the U.S. president and that he was dispatching a courier overnight with his "talking points." Never mind that it was a lazy August weekend when most senior Bush officials were on vacation and out of town like the president. When the courier arrived the next morning with Abdullah's talking points, Bandar was shocked. He found they went on for twenty-five pages and at times were so menacing in tone that he asked the crown prince to reconsider. He argued that it was "not the right time" for a confrontation, but Abdullah insisted. So Bandar delivered the message to the two highest officials he could find still in Washington at the end of August, Powell and Condoleezza Rice.

"From Roosevelt to Clinton, we had more agreements than disagreements," Bandar opened in summarizing the message's gist. "But the disagreements we understood why. We never thought, never had any doubt, that America would protect its national interests in the region, and that Saudi Arabia's interest is part of America's national interest.

"However, now we believe there was a strategic decision by the United States that its national interest in the Middle East is 100 percent based on Sharon. Not even Israel. Sharon's policies. We really believed that this was not true. And everybody denied this to us for these last few months.

"Now we have discovered that actually this is not a slip of the tongue from the vice president. This is not [out of] anger [that] Arafat should be doing something. This is a strategic decision [taken] consciously. The administration sat down and decided that they have only one national interest that should be protected in the Middle East, and that is Sharon as a person, his policies.

"In that case, it changes the equation between our two countries. We respect America as a superpower. We respect America to make its decision as a sovereign nation, and we respectfully disagree with you. Starting from today, as they say, 'You're from Uruguay. I am from Uruguay. You go your way, I go my way.'*

"From now on, we will protect our national interests regardless of where America's interests lie in the region politically, militarily, and security-wise . . . We have to get busy rearranging our lives in the Middle East."[24]

Abdullah laid down the gauntlet. Either Bush needed to move immediately to put new life into the peace process and ease the Palestinian plight or

---

* Bandar's expression appears to come from a knock-knock joke that goes as follows: "Knock, knock. Who's there? Uruguay. Uruguay who? You go Uruguay, and I'll go mine."

Saudi Arabia would freeze its military, political, and security cooperation with the United States.

Bandar said he had never carried a message "more plain, more depressing, more painful" to the White House. He felt personally betrayed by Bush because he had been making excuses for him back home for the past six months, pleading with Abdullah to "just give them time." But the crown prince had been right, and he had been wrong. He was the one who had misread Bush, or at least refused to believe what he was hearing from the White House. He had to admit he had nothing to show for the three phone calls and three letters he had arranged between Abdullah and Bush, or for the two meetings between Powell and the crown prince over the past six months.

Abdullah sent yet another signal to Washington that he was deadly serious about his threat to freeze relations with Washington. At the end of August, he abruptly forced Prince Turki to resign as head of Saudi intelligence after serving in that post for a quarter of a century. Mystery has long surrounded the reason for his resignation and the timing of its announcement. The American-educated Turki was regarded in both Riyadh and Washington as decidedly "pro-American." He had been reappointed to his post only two months earlier. The crown prince had dispatched him in late spring to survey the Washington scene and gather information on Bush and his Middle East intentions. Turki seemed to have advised the same "wait and see" line as Bandar. However, Abdullah was becoming increasingly suspicious of what both of his top pro-American advisers, Bandar and Turki, were telling him. He had decided to dismiss Turki as a signal of his rejection of their advice and readiness to break away from the United States. This, at least, was the message conveyed explicitly to Bush's top Middle East expert, Bruce Riedel, who remarked, "Turki's removal was another sign that business was not going to be as usual anymore."[25] Later, another Saudi explanation for his dismissal emerged: Abdullah had examined expenditures by the Saudi General Intelligence Directorate under Turki and found too many deep black holes into which unexplained billions of dollars had been poured with few results to show for the investment.

How close did Saudi Arabia come to wielding its enormous oil power to pressure the White House? Bandar said he was concerned that Abdullah's threat of a Saudi break with the United States would be taken with the same grain of salt as King Faisal's warnings of a Saudi oil boycott prior to the 1973 Arab-Israeli war. Nixon had not listened then because he had assumed Saudi

Arabia could not do without the U.S. security blanket. Would Bush assume the same? Bandar feared he would. So, he said, in a series of what diplomats call unrecorded "non-meeting meetings" with senior Bush officials, Bandar included an oil threat among the steps Abdullah was prepared to take if Bush did not respond positively. The steps included ending the U.S. Air Force's use of Saudi air bases and freezing Saudi cooperation with the CIA and FBI. But there was more, according to Bandar. Saudi Arabia would call an emergency Arab summit and publicly declare it was putting its special relationship with the United States on ice and was prepared to cut Saudi oil production by one million barrels a day. In addition, Abdullah would call upon other Arab producers to match this amount for a total decrease of two million barrels.[26]

Freezing military, security, and political cooperation would be sufficient to deal a devastating blow to the special relationship. However, a cut in Arab oil production would go far beyond punishing the United States alone. A drop of two million barrels a day would double, possibly triple, world oil prices, which were then averaging in the mid-twenty dollars a barrel. All oil-importing countries would suffer, not just the United States. Had Abdullah really told Bandar to threaten Bush with such a measure? Certainly, Abdullah had come to the end of his tether with the president, as his message indicated, and freezing relations and ejecting the U.S. military were plausible threats. But his willingness to wield the Saudi oil weapon remains questionable for several reasons. First, in response to a question asked during a June 25 interview with the *Financial Times*, Abdullah stated, "Oil is a strategic commodity upon which the prosperity of the industrial as well as the developing countries depends. Our oil policy is a prudent one, seeking a logical balance between the interests of producers and consumers. It serves no purpose to speak about oil outside this framework."[27]

Riedel, who was dealing with the crisis, said he did not recall the threat of the Saudi oil weapon ever being made. "That's pretty dramatic news. I think I would remember that."[28] Bandar's oil-cut threat seems to have been another example of his freelancing, on this occasion to impress a reporter even if it meant misrepresenting the crown prince to accomplish his goal. Even if he didn't flex the kingdom's oil muscles, though, Abdullah finally seized the Bush administration's full attention. Bandar felt like he was staring at "a defining moment in our relations," one that would determine whether he still had a job worth holding.[29] The prince had thought it would take four or five days to get a reply from the White House. To his great surprise, the administration went into overdrive, and thirty-six hours later he had Bush's response in hand.

It was just two pages long and "very classic Texan" in its bluntness, as Bandar remembered it. Bush rejected the notion that the blood of a Palestinian child was any less dear to him than that of an Israeli one. "I believe innocent people's blood is the same—Palestinian, Israeli, Jewish, Christian, Muslim." Bush even directly addressed Abdullah's cry of pain over the mistreatment of the elderly Palestinian lady by the Israeli soldier, saying, "I don't accept the humiliation of people." He also rejected those who said, "When you kill a Palestinian, it's defense; when a Palestinian kills an Israeli, it's a terrorist act." He laid out what he thought both Arafat and Sharon had to do to get negotiations going, exhibiting a balance of blame and responsibility that had been so notably lacking in Saudi eyes at his Crawford press conference. Finally, Bush committed the United States for the first time in writing to seeing a Palestinian state established alongside Israel.[30]

Bandar was overwhelmed. He hadn't thought the young Bush had had it in him. He described the tone of his letter to Abdullah as "almost rhythmic" and "very flowery." He had never seen this Bush expressing such humane concerns. "We found this guy really has feelings and emotions. To him, it's not OK for a soldier to put his foot on a woman's head, regardless of whether she's Israeli or Arab." Even more important in his eyes, "the letter the president sent to Crown Prince Abdullah was groundbreaking in the sense that things in it had never been put in writing."[31] He doubted that Bush's stated commitment to an independent Palestinian state was the result of this sudden scrambling by his advisers to put together a response to Abdullah's threats. This had to be something they had been contemplating secretly for some months. But at that point, he was so delighted that he didn't mind having been kept out of the loop on the Bush administration's deliberations over its first policy statement on the Palestinian question.

Abdullah was equally moved and relieved. Maybe there was hope after all for Little George. He wanted his peers to know that, too. The first thing he did was to share the contents of his message to Bush and the president's reply with the leaders of Egypt, Syria, Jordan, Yemen, and Lebanon. Abdullah wanted to show that he could be tough with Washington and that he was by no means Bush's poodle, as British prime minister Tony Blair was viewed in the Arab world and elsewhere. He also intended to demonstrate that he could get results out of the White House and that he was willing to break with Saudi Arabia's protector to do so. He commanded Arafat, who was in Durban, South Africa, attending a conference, to come to Riyadh immediately. Abdullah made it clear to the PLO leader that he had "to fish or cut bait." He insisted that Arafat give Bush a commitment in writing, too, that he would take the steps asked of him to end the violence and get back to peace talks. The commitment became an attachment to Abdullah's reply to Bush's letter.[32]

Bandar delivered the crown prince's reply to the White House on Friday, September 7, asking that Bush make public his new pledge to work for a Palestinian state. At the same time, he offered reassurances that "America's national interests [would] be protected" in Saudi economic, military, security, and political policies. The Saudi threat of a freeze in relations was over. Bandar was able to report back to the crown prince that Bush's advisers were hard at work over that weekend of September 8–9 drafting a major Middle East policy speech and that the only remaining question was whether the president himself or Secretary of State Powell would deliver it. They decided on Powell. But the secretary was scheduled to leave Monday on a trip to Latin America and would not be back before Wednesday. So the plan was for him to give the historic speech shortly after he returned.

Bandar spent that weekend celebrating his close escape from the pending cataclysm in relations. On Saturday night, he attended a party hosted by Bruce Riedel, and most of the official Middle East policy community was there, including both the Saudi and Israeli ambassadors, as was CIA director George Tenet. Afterward, Bandar left with Tenet for an all-night schmooze that lasted through breakfast on Sunday morning. According to Riedel, the prince told Tenet that the crisis in U.S.-Saudi relations they had just weathered had been but the tip of an iceberg. The leading lights of the House of Saud had undertaken a sweeping reappraisal of the kingdom's ties to the United States, and the debate had gone on for months. A consensus had emerged in favor of a dramatic change in direction away from reliance on the Americans. In his message, Abdullah had been speaking not just for himself but for the entire family. The good news was that events of the past week had changed all that, and U.S.-Saudi relations were back on track.[33]

All the same, Bandar was still holding his breath fearing something would go wrong at the last moment, and with good reason. On Monday, September 10, the American side suddenly realized it had not briefed the Israelis on the momentous U.S. policy shift on the Palestinian question. According to

Bandar, Bush's top advisers were evenly divided as to what to do. Some feared that Sharon, if told, would "hit the roof" and go public before Powell delivered his speech, in a bid to derail it. Others were equally concerned that not forewarning the Israelis would upset them even more and make Powell's speech seem more dramatic than they intended. It seemed the prince was being kept fully informed of White House and State Department deliberations almost hour by hour. In the end, Sharon was informed the same day, Monday, and the Israeli cabinet did heatedly debate whether to blow the whistle but decided it did not want to "get on the wrong side" of the young Bush so early in his administration. So Sharon said nothing. Everything seemed set to go, and on the eve of 9/11 Bandar went to bed "the happiest man in town."[34]

CHAPTER 10

"Everybody Has a Price"

IN LATE NOVEMBER 2001, Prince Bandar was on retreat in his palatial
McLean residence on Chain Bridge Road celebrating Ramadan with his
family and occasionally one or two guests. Two *Washington Post* reporters
were invited to join him for *iftar*, the Muslim breaking of the dawn-to-dusk
fast. The two were preparing a series of articles about the impact on U.S.-
Saudi relations of the September 11 terrorist attacks.[1] Fifteen of the nineteen hijackers in the four passenger airliners used were Saudi citizens. The
shock and horror of this fact were still being digested in both countries.
Americans suddenly had a different view of the kingdom, one of a country
whose religion was creating fanatics filled with hatred for the United States
and bent on destroying it. The Saudi royal family and public were still living
in a state of denial, accusing Zionists of being responsible for the attacks, or
other Arabs using stolen Saudi passports. Nearly three months after the
even, even Bandar still believed that half of the hijackers identified as Saudi
nationals were not really Saudi.

Bandar and his guests sat at a small dining table in his exquisitely deco-
rated Moroccan Room. The prince's mood alternated between manic and
depressive. His world had clearly spun out of control. U.S.-Saudi relations
lay buried in the ashes of the Twin Towers in New York, where twenty-eight
hundred Americans had just died. Though on the edge of despair over the
new realities of his mission in Washington, the prince talked for eight

straight hours, at times philosophical, at others analytical, but always re-maining the principal actor in the unfolding U.S.-Saudi drama.

In Bandar's mind, 9/11 was pure Greek tragedy. Everyone in both Saudi and U.S. intelligence agencies had known something was about to happen, but nobody could prevent it. Bandar supported CIA director George Tenet in his contention that he had been ringing the alarm bell loudly and clearly within the administration. For almost two months before the attacks, Tenet had sounded like "a broken record," running around saying, "Guys, I can see it. I can feel it. It's coming. It's going to be preposterous. Let's look out."[2] U.S. and Saudi counterterrorism officials had done everything they could, but they couldn't quite put the dots together. Part of the problem for the Saudis was the lack of cooperation among U.S. security agencies—the CIA, the FBI, and the Immigration and Naturalization Service (INS). Still, the Americans had almost run some of the terrorists to ground, arriving less than four hours too late to intercept two of them.

If U.S. security agencies had failed by only four hours to disrupt the 9/11 plot, the Saudis had been off by years in understanding that Osama bin Laden, son of one of the richest construction magnates in the kingdom, was a menace to the world. Bandar said they had never taken him seriously. He had been just a "young misguided kid" with a big mouth and a lot of money. "Who cares? Not a threat to the system, not a threat to anyone." When he had started doing "a few bad things," like blowing up the U.S. embassies in Kenya and Tanzania in 1998, the Saudis had begun to take notice.[3] They had tried to convince the Taliban government in Afghanistan, which only Saudi Arabia, Pakistan, and the United Arab Emirates ever recognized, to turn him over. But the Taliban had refused.

The prince did not explain why the Saudis themselves had rejected taking him in 1996 when bin Laden's Sudanese hosts had offered to extradite him back home. "We never gave him the importance, or we never classified him as the danger that he turned out to be." Bandar attributed this partly to sheer complacency and partly to a fragmented Saudi security system that apparently mirrored the American one. Also like the Americans, the Saudis had underestimated the danger because they "didn't feel the threat inside the kingdom." Instead, the kingdom had been focused on Saudi dissidents in London, Washington, and elsewhere. While these Saudis were regarded by foreign governments as dissidents with a right to free speech, in Riyadh they were viewed as terrorists who had to be silenced. They were not the Jeffersonian democrats they pretended to be, but Wahhabi retrogrades offering "one man, one vote, one time."[4]

Bandar felt personally wounded when the U.S. media opened fire on Saudi Arabia in the wake of 9/11, portraying his homeland as a den of evil and a wellspring of Islamic extremism. The media outrage had only worsened when it was discovered that the White House had given permission for nine chartered planes to evacuate 160 people, mostly Saudis, including members of the bin Laden family, from the United States starting three days after the attacks.[5] All the positive feelings toward the kingdom that he felt he had succeeded in generating among Americans during two decades of hard diplomatic work had evaporated overnight. The tens of millions of dollars spent on fancy Washington public relations firms had gone for naught. Saudi Arabia had lost the goodwill of "Joe Six Pack," as he called the average American. The polls certainly confirmed this. Zogby International, a public opinion agency in Utica, New York, discovered in a December poll that 58 percent of Americans held an unfavorable view of the kingdom and only 22 percent believed it to be a good ally.[6]

Bandar felt Americans were refusing to see Saudi Arabia for what he believed it really was—a moderate Arab country with a half-century record as a faithful U.S. ally. He drew an analogy to the attitude of whites toward blacks as depicted by Ralph Ellison in *Invisible Man*, his classic study of racism in America. The prince kept returning to Ellison throughout the night. Americans were suffering from "the invisible man syndrome" when looking at Saudi Arabia. "If I can make you all feel guilty by remembering the invisible man story, I think you would take another look at us and see us in a different way than the first picture that comes to your mind. In other words, the reason you don't see me is not because I don't exist. You choose not to see me. What more can I say."[7]

The kingdom was not the closed and mysterious "secretive kingdom" constantly portrayed in the American media. In the first place, there were forty to fifty thousand Americans living in the kingdom right then, and hundreds of thousands who had spent years working there and then gone home with fond memories. They certainly appreciated what the "real" Saudi Arabia was all about. The same was true of the general Saudi attitude toward America. More than two hundred thousand Saudis had gone to American colleges and graduate schools, and many of them considered America their second home. In fact, some hundred thousand Saudis owned homes or apartments there.

Didn't Americans realize, Bandar wondered, that other than Great Britain, Saudi Arabia was the closest ally the United States had enjoyed anywhere in the world since World War II? The U.S.-Saudi alliance was not just by chance. The two countries were natural allies, each a superpower in its own right complementing the other. The United States was the world's greatest consumer of oil, and Saudi Arabia was its leading oil producer. The two countries were inextricably chained together by their common dependence on, or "addiction" to, petroleum. And it was American companies that had discovered that precious commodity and then built Saudi Arabia into the oil power it had become.

The U.S. media deliberately ignored all this positive history, he claimed. Whenever they bothered to examine the kingdom, which happened about once a decade, they painted a very damning picture, like Ellison's white Americans looking at blacks. The Saudi government was depicted as inherently unstable, the king awaiting the same fate as the shah of Iran at any moment. The kingdom was pictured as teeming with unhappy people afflicted by either an excess of wealth or unemployment and religious intolerance. And all Saudi youth were seen as worshipping bin Laden, whom they held to be the Muslim version of the Cuban revolutionary Che Guevara, who had died fighting in the mountains of Bolivia. "If it's true bin Laden is so charismatic and has such great followers," Bandar summed up, "why is he staying in Afghanistan in a cave? Come home and lead because you cannot stop the people. Look what happened in Iran."[8]

According to Bandar, the American media had it all wrong. The al-Saud family was not detached from society, nor was the king about to join the shah in the dustbin of history. The al-Sauds knew their people. They worked hard to keep their finger on the pulse of "downtown Riyadh." If the House of Saud had ruled for the better part of three hundred years, it was precisely because it had learned how to handle a profoundly conservative society and at what speed to move in bringing about change. Change had always come from the top, not the bottom, of that society. The al-Sauds had been the driving force for modernization, whether it was the introduction of television, schools, education for girls, or a modern welfare system. The family had lavished four hundred billion dollars on building the infrastructure of a modern state and nation. It had done this while at the same time managing to keep the loyalty of the Wahhabi religious establishment, which had opposed much of the change that had taken place. "It has not stayed in a leadership position from 1747 until now by being politically dumb. They know when to duck. They know when to move."[9]

The prince bristled at the American media depiction of the al-Sauds as both "repressive" and "corrupt." He cited as evidence of a general Saudi acceptance of royal rule the fact that nearly all Saudis who went abroad for higher education came back home and willingly so. There was no exile Saudi community anywhere in the world. They didn't want to live in Western or even other Muslim countries. There were Irish Americans, Italian Americans, and even Egyptian Americans, but there were no "Saudi Americans" because none wanted to stay in the United States. Nor was there any evidence of a groundswell of discontented Saudis inside the kingdom, as had happened in Iran prior to the shah's overthrow. In Bandar's eyes, the al-Sauds had to be doing something right, or at least right enough to avoid an Iranian-style popular uprising. "If the demonstrations we saw in 1977 and 1978 in Tehran take place in Saudi Arabia, we do not have one quarter of what the shah had as a security force to maintain law and order." He wanted to know why Americans were not asking themselves the reason there had been no mass demonstrations in Riyadh such as the world had seen in Tehran? Either the kingdom had twenty million "stupid people who are drugged," or "maybe they are satisfied more than people think."[10]

As for charges in the American media that the al-Saud family was hopelessly bogged down in corruption, Bandar had few apologies to make. He had amassed his own considerable fortune while serving as ambassador in Washington and maintained a lifestyle way beyond those of most of his princely peers. He had eight palaces, estates, ranches, and apartments in four countries; flew the world in his own custom-designed Airbus; kept a retinue of friends to accompany him; and employed a private security force that most senior Saudi princes could not afford. If he talked like an American redneck, he lived like a king. When asked about one or another estate, he would say it was a gift for his services to the king and kingdom. He unabashedly defended his controversial comment during a PBS *Frontline* interview in late September 2001 that the al-Sauds had probably siphoned off $50 billion for themselves over the years.[11] This might well have been a tender subject for the prince, since both he and his father, Prince Sultan, had become prime examples for Saudi dissidents and al-Qaeda of the rampant corruption in which the House of Saud was soaked. But the prince refused to recognize there was any problem. The kingdom had spent $350 billion to $400 billion in building a modern Saudi state and nation, and if $50 billion of that had been lost through corruption, "so what?" The Saudis had their own form of political patronage that was no worse or better than the American equivalent. "Take away certain words, and we do nothing differently." Both produced corruption, which was just part of human nature, dating back to Adam and Eve. "I can buy you. You can buy me. Everybody has a price. It depends how much."[12]

IN JANUARY 1996, a story appeared on the front page of the *Washington Post* explaining the internal workings of Saudi corruption. At that time, a lawsuit involving a former communications minister, Alawi Darweesh Kayyal, had become public knowledge and the talk of the kingdom. Kayyal had allegedly cheated his dying business partner out of $150 million the two had purportedly accumulated in bribes and commissions from foreign companies to secure government contracts. It was the first time any Saudi minister had been put through such a public ordeal and hauled before a court on corruption charges. The London-based Islamic opposition was at the time regularly lambasting the royal family for its various exploitative schemes. But U.S. and other Western diplomats stationed in the kingdom had also become extremely concerned that corruption had gotten out of hand and risked affecting the House of Saud's political stability. "The Saud family is not mending its ways," said one State Department official.[13] Bandar and his half brother General Khaled had been named in two lawsuits filed in U.S. courts. The story cited press and diplomatic reports that estimates of their commissions on the $30 billion al-Yamamah arms deal with Britain in the mid-1980s "begin in the hundreds of millions of dollars."*[14]

Royal corruption thrived on arms deals, land sales, and shell companies. Commissions were theoretically limited by Saudi law to 5 percent on non-military sales and barred on military sales. But according to Saudi and U.S. specialists quoted in the story, commissions on arms deals could run as high as 40 percent "of the notional contract value," though they were much lower on multibillion-dollar ones. The article went on to explain how Saudi shell

---

* Bandar was later accused of receiving $2 billion in payoffs from the al-Yamamah deal.

service companies were used to circumvent U.S. anticorruption laws by laundering bribes and commissions as "salaries" to one or another prince. Two cases in U.S. courts in the early 1990s involved Americans who alleged they had been fired from U.S. firms doing business in Saudi Arabia because they had blown the whistle on what they regarded as illegal commissions paid through such shell companies. They had named both Bandar and Khaled in their suits as two of the princes involved in these schemes. The lawsuits were eventually settled out of court and therefore the allegations were never adjudicated.

But the most widespread form of Saudi royal corruption involved the seizure of *emiri*, or "royal," lands for public or real estate projects. The government would register the land in the name of one or another prince, who would then sell it back to the government or to developers at a highly exorbitant price. The biggest such land deal of the 1980s, at the height of the oil boom, involved Riyadh's new international airport. It was touted at the time as the biggest and most modern anywhere in the world. The government had put the official cost at $3.5 billion, but diplomatic and other sources believed it was closer to $6 billion. Neither of these figures, however, included the cost to the government of purchasing ninety-four square miles of desert land for the project. U.S. government sources estimated the cost to be an astronomical $16 billion. The land had been registered in the names of a large group of princes, including Sultan, who in addition to being defense minister was also head of the Saudi civilian aviation authority. The *Post* story quoted a former State Department official as describing the land grab as "$16 billion in pure corruption."[15]

Bandar's defense of the $50 billion corruption figure, which he mentioned again during his outpouring that Ramadan night in November 2001, was twofold.[16] First, he argued that the kingdom hardly had a monopoly on the problem and that criticism from the United States was a case of the proverbial kettle calling the pot black. Look at media stories about the Pentagon paying $600 to U.S. companies for a single toilet seat, he said. Look at the national guard, which could not account for billions in spare parts. Look at the U.S. military budget: The Pentagon presented Congress with a budget request for, say, $100 billion, but senators and representatives insisted on their pet projects, which increased it to $140 billion to please one or another constituency. Wasn't this excess $40 billion in U.S. military expenditures just a form of corruption made legal by congressional approval?

Members of Congress regularly dipped into the U.S. government pork barrel to stay in office. Appropriation bills were loaded down with pork for constituents back home. Senators and House members all supported one another's pork projects, asked and did favors for one another. Where was the line between favors and corruption, anyway, in a political system dominated by special interest groups, lobbyists, and donors to presidential and congressional campaigns expecting returns on their investments?

Bandar wanted to know whether the favors asked of him by various U.S. presidents, senators, and representatives should be labeled acts of corruption or were just par for the American political course. On which side of the line did a donation to the charity or pet project of an American president, or his wife, fall? "Every library of any president I know of, Republican or Democrat, we contributed to. Now is that corruption? Is that payoffs? I don't know. Is it better when Coca-Cola or Lockheed contribute? I don't know."[17] It never seemed to occur to the prince that the behavior of a foreign diplomat in Washington should be any different from that of an American politician.

One practice Bandar was particularly proud of was lavishing attention on high-ranking American officials, mostly secretaries of state, presidents, and vice presidents, as they were leaving office at the end of an administration. This was carefully calculated to impress both those departing and those arriving. "If the reputation builds that the Saudis take care of friends when they leave office, you'd be surprised how much better friends you have who are just coming into office." So he would regularly dine the outgoing ones and invite them to go bird hunting on his estate in Glympton, England, or use his Hala Ranch, outside Aspen.* "I have never thought of all these things as corruption."[18]

He also invested in the Carlyle Group, in which Bush Sr. and former secretary of state James Baker—two of his closest American friends—just happened to be a partner or adviser. During most of the 1990s, Carlyle owned BDM International Inc., a defense contractor whose subsidiary, Vinnell Corporation, had trained and supported the Saudi national guard since 1975. The company was also responsible for managing the Saudi government's "offset program," under which U.S. companies doing business

---

* He gave his good friend Colin Powell a replica of his old beloved 1995 Jaguar a few weeks after he retired as secretary of state in November 2004.

with the Saudi military were supposed to invest 35 percent of earnings from every sale back into the Saudi economy. The prince would not say how much he sank into Carlyle, but wealthy Saudis around Prince Sultan, the defense minister, were encouraged to invest in Carlyle as a favor to the elder Bush.[19]

Bandar insisted his involvement was a favor not to Bush, but to himself. He had turned a handsome profit on his investment, and if he hadn't, he would have taken it out even though Bush and Baker were part of the company. "For Bandar bin Sultan to put money in Carlyle surely is not to buy his way to the Bushes or the Bakers, because I know them. They are my friends."[20] He couldn't be accused of bribing them because they were out of office when he became involved with Carlyle. To him, the engagement of Bush and Baker in Carlyle was pretty typical of the Washington scene; scores of former senators and representatives had gone to work for firms and industries that had once courted them in Congress for favorable legislation. This was Washington's famous revolving door between government and business at its best. "To us, that sounds logical," he remarked. "To you [in the media], it smells funny."[21]

BANDAR'S SECOND LINE of defense against accusations of massive royal corruption was that the American media misunderstood how the Saudi system of political and social patronage functioned. The al-Sauds had their own trickle-down theory of economics, combining noblesse oblige with religious and social obligation. It was true, Bandar admitted, that Saudi princes received royal allowances, but these handouts should not be exaggerated. Most were $1,000 per month or less.* The Saudi billionaire Prince Waleed bin Talal publicly called for the abolition of the royal allowances in November 2001, disclosing that his own family received $180,000 a year.[22] Bandar defended the practice, arguing that all rich royals felt obliged to dole out a lot of their wealth to scores, if not hundreds, of retainers and petitioners. He cited as one example his own driver, for whom he had bought homes for his two wives and paid for the whole fam-

---

* Estimates of the number of Saudi princes vary from six thousand to ten thousand. A U.S. Embassy study in the late 1990s found the allowances ranged from $100 to $200 a month for grandchildren to $4,000 to $5,000 for most princes.

ily to go on vacation in London. But he was also constantly handing out small amounts to supplicants who showed up at his gate—students, the needy, and the sick.

The al-Sauds, he pointed out, also looked after all Saudis through an extensive government-provided social welfare system. Unlike in the United States, there were relatively few poor people in the kingdom, and they had access to free health care, education, and other services. Bandar found the American attitude toward its own poor by contrast appalling. How could forty million people go uninsured in the richest nation in the world? How was it possible that nobody would help the guy sleeping on the street outside the Saudi embassy in Washington? Whose responsibility was he, anyway?

Had the Saudi oil bonanza corrupted the House of Saud to the point that Washington should be concerned? Bandar was ready to concede that the kingdom's enormous oil wealth had indeed exercised a corrosive influence on Saudi society. The U.S.-Saudi relationship hadn't escaped, either. "There are too many opportunities for too many people to get rich or make a lot of money on the side." There had been too many "tips" given and too many "favors" granted by both Saudis and Americans. The "incredible windfall" from the discovery of an ocean of oil beneath the desert had made it too hard to resist multiple temptations. Yes, there was too much money in the relationship. Both countries had become addicted to and corrupted by oil in different ways. "I think we have been corrupted by each other."[23]

Bandar argued, however, that there was a different cultural attitude in Saudi Arabia toward how to deal with corruption, one that seemed nicely exculpatory of royal family excesses. "To expose somebody who does something wrong in the government here [in America], the higher the better, and the more 'obligation' within your culture that their hides not be protected." By contrast, he claimed, the Saudi attitude was more forgiving and less demanding of exposure. He quoted a verse from the Koran: "Have mercy on the high and mighty people who have been humiliated." The Saudi high and mighty did fear public humiliation, and this helped to curb excessive corruption. But in his mind, there was a distinction to be made between acceptable and unacceptable corruption. It depended on whether one party was exploited or an injustice committed. The rich could afford to bribe one another, and thus it was a lesser sin. There was a difference between a bureaucrat asking a cabdriver earning three hundred dollars a month for a hundred-dollar bribe to get his license and a millionaire who shelled out one thousand dollars for one. The former was unacceptable, but the latter, "It's OK. It's not going to hurt him."[24]

BANDAR TALKED AS if lost in a stream of consciousness, jumping from one topic to another as he offered his guests juices, tea, and coffee but no alcohol. He described the phases he went through as Americans turned on Saudi Arabia with a vengeance. It didn't happen immediately. There was an initial phase of offering condolences, as when someone in the family dies and relatives and friends gather to grieve together. This lasted for about a week. Then came a second period consumed by a scramble to identify the nineteen known hijackers and a hunt for other terrorists possibly still at large. The reason President Bush and Vice President Dick Cheney were kept in separate locations for a long time after the attacks was that, according to Bandar, a spate of intelligence reports claimed that an al-Qaeda operative was on the loose armed with a "dirty bomb"—a device containing radioactive material that can be dispersed by setting off a conventional explosion to make much of an entire city unlivable. It was not clear whether this terrorist was headed for Saudi Arabia or the United States, so the manhunt was under way in both countries.* For the Saudis, it was a nightmare scenario. If such a bomb went off with the spotlight already on the fifteen Saudi hijackers, the presumption might well be that this terrorist, too, was Saudi. In fact, CIA, FBI, and Saudi officials shortly would be looking for a Saudi-born naturalized American, Adnan el-Shukrijumah, who they feared had obtained radioactive material at a Canadian university before entering the United States.

Elsewhere, CIA officials were tracking down reports that two Pakistani nuclear scientists had discussed with Osama bin Laden the use of such weapons and even shown him a cylinder filled with radioactive material. The Saudis were terrified that a dirty bomb might be used to close down one or more of their oil facilities or even to take over the Holy Mosque in Mecca. The CIA had told the Saudis that one of the two Pakistani scientists, whose family name was Khan, might be on the way to Saudi Arabia.† Saudi

---

* The *Washington Post* wrote about this hunt for a dirty bomber in a story published on December 4, 2000.[25] So, did CIA director George Tenet in his book *At the Center of the Storm*.[26]

† This was not the famous father of the Pakistani bomb, A. Q. Khan, who was later implicated in selling nuclear weapons technology to North Korea, Iran, and Libya.

officials took the threat seriously enough to make a study of how they would go about cleaning up the Holy Mosque if a dirty bomb was exploded on its premises.[27]

In the post-9/11 atmosphere, anything seemed possible. Bandar was living on pure adrenaline, with little sleep for weeks at a time and the ultimate catastrophe of a dirty bomb explosion looming in his mind. The stress became so great that the prince came to the verge of a mental breakdown and had to check in to Sibley Hospital for five days to recover, neither the first nor the last time he would be hospitalized.[28]

FOR BANDAR, THE most agonizing phase of the 9/11 fallout began about a month after the event, when the U.S. media turned with a vengeance on Saudi Arabia, and the prince realized he had a public relations disaster on his hands. The extent of the crisis came home to him when he began receiving letters from American veterans of the first Gulf War who were returning medals the Saudi government had doled out in appreciation of their service to the kingdom. One veteran wrote him, "I cannot wear a medal from people who are killing my people." That letter shook Bandar "more than ten senators attacking me on TV."[29] If the half million U.S. soldiers who had fought to defend Saudi Arabia and then liberate Kuwait felt the same way, then the kingdom was in real trouble. It was losing whatever popular support it had had in America.

Bandar's predicament was only made worse by statements of denial coming from senior Saudi officials. In late November, Saudi interior minister Prince Naif publicly took issue with the notion that nineteen individuals could possibly have acted alone to carry out the multiple attacks, saying, "I think they [Zionists] are behind these events."[30] Then, the Saudi billionaire Waleed bin Talal donated ten million dollars toward the relief efforts under way around the fallen Twin Towers, but suggested the terrorist attacks were the result of America's biased stand toward the Palestinian cause. His remarks caused New York mayor Rudy Giuliani to return the gift.

Bandar tried to combat the tide of furor rising against the Saudis by mounting a public relations campaign highlighting the value of Saudi-American cooperation throughout past decades. He hired Qorvis Communications on a two-hundred-thousand-dollar-a-month retainer to run a yearlong campaign to restore the Saudi reputation. The PR effort cost close to four million dollars.

It included full-page ads placed in newspapers in major U.S. cities expressing Saudi grief over 9/11 and reminding Americans of the two countries' close cooperation over almost six decades, dating back to the days of President Franklin Roosevelt. The purpose of the campaign, according to one Qorvis official, was to answer the question in the minds of millions of Americans regarding whether "Saudi Arabia is a friend or foe. A lot of people don't know." The newspaper ads stressed, "The People of Saudi Arabia: Allies Against Terrorism."[31]

Bandar was mortified when copies of these ads were returned to him with hostile comments attached. One reader wrote, "You hypocrites, you kill our people and you come and put an ad to pay your condolences!" The reader gave his address. So the prince had him tracked down and talked to him on and off for three days in an attempt to change his views. He also conducted his own personal PR campaign, appearing on numerous news and talk shows to answer questions. But he had a strong sense of futility, as if he were a fighter pilot engaged in a deadly air battle and "running out of airspace, airspeed, and ideas."[32] Bruce Riedel, Bush's Middle East expert, used the same analogy. "The space was too small for Bandar to operate in any longer."[33]

Part of the new Saudi "image" in America was that of a country refusing to cooperate with U.S. authorities in combating the rising menace of terrorism in the American homeland. The Saudis had balked at giving the FBI or CIA any information about the fifteen Saudi hijackers and denied requests to interview their families. Their embassy in Washington likewise offered no help to reporters, insisting that no Saudis could possibly have been responsible. Even in late November, Bandar was not ready to concede that all the fifteen identified by U.S. authorities as Saudis were in fact Saudis. Their passports might be Saudi, but this didn't mean they necessarily were.[34] The persistence of Saudi denial only served to fuel American outrage. The Saudis were also being castigated in the media for refusing to freeze the bank assets of private Saudi financers of al-Qaeda, a charge many U.S. government agencies were making privately to reporters. Even Saudi textbooks came under attack for their anti-Christian and anti-Jewish biases. To his enormous frustration, Bandar found himself fighting a propaganda war on half a dozen fronts simultaneously and losing on all of them.

The initial Saudi lack of cooperation did extensive damage to an already badly frayed relationship. Bush took the attitude that America's friends around the world were either with the nation or against it. There could be no partial cooperation. Bandar felt he was boxing with shadows in his quest to convince the U.S. media that the Saudis were indeed fully cooperating. Bush, Powell, and CIA chief George Tenet would publicly affirm that they were satisfied by the level of Saudi cooperation. The president even called Crown Prince Abdullah in late October to tell him that he was "very pleased" with the state of Saudi cooperation and that he "strongly disagreed" with media reports to the contrary.[35] But their aides would imply quite the opposite when talking to reporters. The prince found himself at a loss to cope with this official-unofficial dichotomy among administration spokespeople.

Bandar's frustration was all the greater because in instances when the Saudis did offer to help, they found a thoroughly disorganized and standoffish American partner. U.S. authorities were throwing out names of suspects and possible financers of terrorism and asking the Saudis to check every one. They wanted Riyadh to arrest or interrogate individuals on the slightest pretext and to close down their bank accounts. When the Saudis asked the FBI or CIA for evidence of their wrongdoing, they wouldn't divulge what they knew. The Americans would give the Saudis a suspect's telephone number, but they wouldn't share sensitive National Security Agency (NSA) transcripts of their electronic intercepts of his telephone conversations.

Sharing NSA intercepts turned into a major bone of contention. Just providing telephone numbers was a waste of time and energy in the Saudis' eyes. Often the phone numbers belonged to mobiles that were being used overseas, not from inside the kingdom. Sometimes the numbers were not Saudi ones at all. Saudi intelligence officials would check out CIA or FBI leads only to discover that the presumed "bad guys" were perfectly legitimate. They also discovered that various U.S. intelligence services had collected different bits of information that they were not sharing with one another, let alone with the Saudis. Finally, the NSA did agree to hand over some of their tapes for analysis. Bandar said Saudi intelligence discovered that the suspects would use code words taken from Saudi falconry—such as references to Saudi wild and domesticated birds to make a distinction between international and domestic flights while they debated which was better to target for attack. As a result of Saudi access to the NSA tapes, several suspects were tracked down and apprehended by either American or Saudi officials.[36]

Tracking down suspected financers of terrorism proved just as exasperating for the Saudis. The Americans wanted the Saudi government to freeze bank accounts of various suspects, but provided no justification. The Saudis would track transfers out of accounts in the kingdom to foreign banks, but if and when they went through New York, that was the end of the trail. Their routings onward suddenly became a "privacy issue." Bandar tried to explain to U.S. authorities that the Saudi government had privacy issues as well and could not just peer into bank accounts indiscriminately and without cause.

Ironically, probably the most important Saudi support for the United States in the weeks and months after 9/11 went largely unreported in the U.S. media. The Saudis had only themselves to blame because they never sought to publicize it. The day after the attacks, Abdullah summoned his oil minister, Ali al-Naimi, to discuss what the Saudis could do to quell fears of an oil shortage and price hike. Security of supply was foremost in the minds of all Western governments at that point. Abdullah decided Saudi Arabia would renege on its pre-9/11 commitment to the Organization of the Petroleum Exporting Countries to cut its oil production in order to bolster sagging prices. Instead, the kingdom would rush an extra nine million barrels to U.S. markets to ensure ample supplies. For the next two weeks, the Saudis shipped out five hundred thousand barrels daily using their own tankers.[37] The surge had a dramatic effect. The cost of crude, which had been twenty-eight dollars a barrel in late August, dropped to around twenty dollars within a couple of weeks. By mid-October, oil prices had declined to their lowest levels in two years.[38]

ON THAT NIGHT of Ramadan reflection in late 2001, Bandar was having serious doubts about whether the U.S.-Saudi relationship would ever be the same again. Perhaps he was just reflecting the angry mood back home among Saudi commoners and royals alike. In early November, Abdullah spoke for an entire nation when he blasted "the ferocious campaign" against the kingdom in America, which he claimed was nothing but an "expression of its hatred toward the Islamic system" and its religious practices.[39] If nothing else, 9/11 had abruptly brought to an end the "autopilot syndrome" from which, Bandar felt strongly, both Riyadh and Washington had been suffering for most of the previous decade, with neither side willing to ask any hard questions. For example, maybe it was time for the U.S. military to recognize it had overstayed its welcome. Bandar began thinking out loud during his long monologue about how to transform the American military presence into a smaller and less-visible footprint.[40] The message was clearly meant for the Bush administration, and the prince was using the *Washington Post* to convey it indirectly. Instead of U.S. warplanes being stationed on Saudi air bases, why not have frequent joint exercises—a week every three months, two weeks every six months, or two months every year? Anything was better than a permanent presence. The Americans were welcome in Kuwait. The U.S. and British aircraft could carry out the same missions from there, or Qatar, as they were from Saudi Arabia. Or why couldn't the United States just rely on the aircraft carriers they had stationed in the Persian Gulf? Weren't these floating air bases built precisely so that American power could be "over the horizon"?

Maybe the time had come to rethink the Southern Watch surveillance program over Iraq, too. Sooner or later, something bad was going to happen. An American aircraft was going to crash in southern Iraq. An American pilot was going to be captured. A U.S. air-launched missile was going to go astray and cause serious damage to the civilian Iraqi population. If an American pilot was captured, "do we go to war for that pilot?" he asked. "We've been lucky so far. Cut it and win. I think this administration can do it without being accused of running." The message could not have been clearer, and it was coming from the most pro-American resident of the House of Saud.[41]

U.S. and Saudi military officials had been at loggerheads once again over the American use of the Prince Sultan Air Base. This time the cause was the U.S. drive to topple the Taliban regime and uproot al-Qaeda in Afghanistan in retaliation for 9/11. In the wake of the 1996 Khobar Towers bombing, in which nineteen American servicemen had died, the U.S. Central Command had moved all its aircraft from Dhahran inland to Prince Sultan Air Base for greater protection. The Saudis had allowed the Pentagon to build a super-sophisticated Combined Air Operations Center there to cover warfare anywhere in the Persian Gulf region. Now, the Central Command wanted to use it to orchestrate its air and ground war against the Taliban.

The Pentagon had decided to follow Bandar's "don't ask, just do it" approach on such matters. On September 22, an unnamed Pentagon military briefer told reporters the United States was going to use Saudi Arabia as its command center for forthcoming Afghanistan operations and was sending a top air force commander, Lieutenant General Charles Wald, to take charge. The news came as a shock to the Saudis, who had indeed not been asked, been consulted, or agreed. "No government likes to learn from the press that its territory is to be used by a foreign power to conduct offensive military operations against a third country," noted Joseph McMillan, a former Pentagon officer in charge of its dealings with the kingdom.[42]

The Saudis found themselves in a serious bind. They were caught in the crosscurrents of the virulent anti-Saudi campaign under way in the United States and a Saudi backlash that had aroused nationalistic and religious fervor to new heights. Bandar disclosed that his government had taken a secret opinion poll in the wake of 9/11 and discovered that preachers in 6,000 in a sample of 11,200 mosques had initially come out in favor of the Taliban government and against the U.S. plan to overthrow it.[43] At the same time, the Saudi foreign minister, Prince Saud al-Faisal, was assuring Americans his government was ready to cooperate fully "not just to track down the criminals of the Sept. 11 attacks, but to exterminate the infrastructure that helps the terrorists."[44] Indeed, the Saudis withdrew diplomatic recognition of the Taliban government on September 25 and condemned its protection of bin Laden. And yet Saudi defense minister Prince Sultan was assuring his people that the kingdom would never allow "the presence in our country of a single soldier at war with Muslims or Arabs."[45] Faced with these conflicting signals, the Bush administration sent Secretary of Defense Donald Rumsfeld in early October to clarify Saudi intentions about American use of Prince Sultan Air Base. Bandar felt that the Americans made a mistake in asking the Saudis for permission instead of just going ahead quietly with their operations. "The Americans have this disease. They always ask questions, too many questions. Hence they might get the wrong answers."[46]

When the Americans asked, the Saudis started asking questions, too. How many people did the Pentagon want to send to man the command center? Why so many? What were their duties? The Pentagon then asked for an increase in the number of flights by U.S. warplanes over Saudi airspace. The Saudis objected and demanded a reduction; it wasn't the principle, but the large number. The Saudis finally agreed to an increase but with a caveat: If the flight was not time sensitive, the Americans should ask permission ahead of time.[47] Behind this game of twenty questions lay pent-up Saudi frustrations over the U.S. Air Force's misbehavior and misuse of its presence on the base. The Saudis felt they were being overbilled for the food they provided the four to five thousand Americans there. They had caught the Americans stealing electricity from the Saudi power grid and discovered that the air force was flying in people without obtaining visas for them, acting as if the base were American territory. These were small issues, but they had added up to one big irritation.[48]

The haggling led to bigger questions. The Saudis began asking themselves why the U.S. Air Force needed Prince Sultan Air Base, anyway. Wasn't it far more distant from targets in Afghanistan than the three U.S. aircraft carriers then assembling in the Gulf of Oman for the operation? Wouldn't planes flying out of Saudi bases require more aerial refueling? It didn't make sense logistically. In the end, the Saudis did agree that the Pentagon could use the command center but insisted that warplanes on attack missions fly from the carriers or other gulf countries. These were the same restrictions they had initially placed on U.S. and British aircraft flying missions for Southern Watch to distance themselves from that operation and avoid Arab criticism. Bandar said the Saudis simply did not regard Prince Sultan Air Base as crucial to the success of the U.S. air campaign or understand the military logic of flying aircraft from Saudi Arabia to Afghanistan.[49] The Saudis were starting to go their own way.

In truth, Bandar was also worried about the ugly mood of revenge sweeping the Bush administration and the American public in the wake of 9/11. Had the terrorists come from London, the United States probably would have attacked the British homeland, Bandar said, adding, "and I don't say that as a joke." America was so bent on revenge and immediate action that it had become a danger not only to its enemies but to its friends and even itself. "This country is really dangerous. Why? Because you're too big and you're too powerful." The prince felt the administration had to be handled very carefully, because in its rage it was ready to strike out in any direction, regardless of the consequences.[50]

Bandar had other beefs to air about American conduct and hegemony in the world. He was fed up with persistent U.S. government efforts to mold Saudi Arabia in the American image by trying to impose its values and culture. The Bush administration was already gearing up to make the export of democracy a signature element of its foreign policy, which would shortly become yet another bone of contention in U.S.-Saudi relations. Bandar argued that Saudi Arabia was profoundly different in its values and culture and that the United States had to accept and live with this. It was extremely conservative socially. Saudi parents accepted that their daughters should be educated, but they did not accept the idea of their going out on dates or appearing in public with unmarried men. It would be a long time before Saudi society came around to allowing Saudi women to drive.

Bandar argued that societies were like human beings. Just as heart and kidney transplant operations were extremely difficult to perform without the body rejecting the new organ, so, too, were "cultural transplants" of the type Americans were seeking to engineer in Saudi Arabia. Saudi society had to be prepared carefully for change with an "antirejection medicine" just like a patient awaiting a heart transplant. The royal family was hard at work preparing a bedouin society for sweeping changes and had accomplished much already, whether it was introducing television, computers, education for girls, or jobs for women. "We are progressive compared to the society we live in, and you come and attack us for having a policy that creates bin Ladens!" Didn't Americans realize that bin Laden also wanted to overthrow the House of Saud in order to return Saudi society to an eighteenth-century puritanical and backward form of Islam?[51]

Bandar felt his message was falling on deaf ears in America, and his task of explaining and defending Saudi Arabia before the American public had been made far more complicated by the new era of instant information and globalized communications. He felt CNN and C-SPAN had made his job impossible. Congressional attacks on the kingdom—a daily event in the aftermath of 9/11—were seen and heard not only by millions of Americans but by thousands of Saudis as well. He was bombarded daily by telephone calls from home asking why some senator, columnist, or U.S. official was slandering the kingdom. Before, he had been able to serve as a filter and censor for what got back to Riyadh, but that was no longer possible in the age of satellite television, computers, and cell phones. "They get it raw, and boy oh boy, does it make life more difficult and less fun."[52]

Bandar's world had spun out of control. He had lost his sea legs on the Washington ship. His modus operandi of secret diplomacy and special relations with America's political elite was suddenly useless in his struggle to turn the tide of anti-Saudi emotions washing across the United States. And there was nothing he could do, either, to stem the tide of anti-Americanism engulfing the kingdom or to stop Saudis from watching the unrelenting coverage of Israeli soldiers killing or beating Palestinian civilians, beamed into the kingdom by Al Jazeera. He was mystified as to why his own government, which in theory controlled the media, had not acted to block these broadcasts, which he felt were largely responsible for whipping up enmity toward America among Saudis and which were making his task of repairing the U.S.-Saudi relationship a nightmare.

On that emotion-filled Ramadan night, Bandar seemed at times even unsure of who he was as a person or what he represented. He felt culturally torn between two very different worlds and strangely detached from both. For whom did bicultural Saudis like him speak? He was not a "classic Saudi" in any sense. "We actually represent very little," he commented at one point. From time to time, he had to remind himself, "I do not represent the people of Saudi Arabia." Government policies, yes. The vox populi, certainly not.[53] Who was he, then?

Bandar thought of himself as some kind of Saudi-American hybrid or perhaps "Jekyll and Hyde." He was of the Saudi royalty but not wholly part of it because of his commoner mother. He preferred to think of himself as a "peasant royal." He had devoted half his life to a career of piloting warplanes and then applied those skills to the task of diplomacy. He used the language of a jet fighter pilot when he talked about handling one or another diplomatic crisis. His time in Washington had deeply affected him, and the American culture he so readily rejected for his own people, he embraced with enthusiasm for himself. He realized he was a creature of American politics, which he admitted he thrived on and reveled in. He loved the rough-and-tumble of political combat in Washington, just as he relished that of American football. He had been a dedicated Dallas Cowboys fan from the day he first laid eyes on its "magnificent" players—and "great-looking" cheerleaders—at the Dallas airport in 1970. He had painted his private Airbus in Cowboys colors. Even after becoming ambassador and living in Washington, where the Redskins were heroes, he had stuck with the Cowboys. Bandar loved thinking of himself as an "outside insider," whether it was the peasant royal, the fighter pilot diplomat, or the Cowboys fan in Washington.

But 9/11 had shattered this world. It had forced him to become the front-line defender in America of everything Saudi—politics, culture, and religion. He felt that those fifteen Saudi terrorists had hijacked not only four airliners but the entire U.S.-Saudi special relationship. They had forced upon him a mission impossible: He had to explain to America how the worst attack on the United States since Pearl Harbor had nothing to do with his country's defining religion, Wahhabism, castigated in the U.S. media as the prime breeder of terrorism and the most intolerant, anti-American creed in Islam.

CHAPTER 11

Wahhabi Islam at Home and Abroad

SHEIKH SALEH AL-SHEIKH is a likable Wahhabi holy man with an engaging smile encased in a full beard. He wears a white robe known as a *thobe* and covers his head with a red-and-white-checkered head scarf called a *shimagh*. In dress, there is little to distinguish him from most other Saudi males. But al-Sheikh is no ordinary Saudi. Since 1999, he has been Saudi Arabia's minister of Islamic affairs, overseeing the kingdom's fifty thousand mosques, its clerics and prayer callers. His ministry is also in charge of *dawah*, propagating Islam around the world. His cousin Sheikh Abdulaziz bin Abdullah al-Sheikh is the grand mufti, the kingdom's highest religious authority. Another relative is Justice Minister Abdullah bin Mohammed al-Sheikh. Western diplomats regard Saleh al-Sheikh as the leading progressive light of his family.

The al-Sheikhs are the aristocrats of the Wahhabi religious establishment because the male members are direct descendants of Mohammed bin Abd al-Wahhab, the eighteenth-century founder of Saudi Arabia's defining Islamic creed. Wahhabism provides the kingdom with its distinct character, and its religious precepts act as a very powerful glue holding the country's myriad tribes together. The al-Sheikhs and the al-Sauds are the kingdom's two most powerful families and rule together as a result of a religious and political compact struck back in 1747, which left the al-Sauds in charge of the state and the al-Sheikhs in charge of the mosque. This meant the al-Sheikhs deferred to the al-Sauds in political matters and vice versa when it came to religious and social affairs.

In practice, state and mosque in Saudi Arabia have at times treaded on each other's turf as the al-Sauds have sought to modernize the kingdom and the al-Sheikhs to maintain the Wahhabi straitjacket on Saudi society. In foreign policy, the two families have not always agreed, either, but the al-Sheikhs have bowed time and again to the al-Sauds, especially on the family's controversial alliance with the United States and its dependence on non-Muslim soldiers during the 1990–91 Gulf War to defend the Land of the Two Holy Mosques. But on one foreign policy issue, there has been little discord—the export of the Saudi puritanical interpretation of Islam around the world with the goal of making it the dominant school.

Until 9/11, Prince Bandar's diplomacy toward the United States had always sought to keep the religious side of the kingdom out of the American limelight. The Wahhabi establishment abhorred the probing eyes of the Western media, which in turn had precious little sympathy for it. The dislike, or even disdain, for Wahhabism among visiting Western reporters was largely due to the heavy-handed tactics of the Saudi religious police, the *mutawwa'in*, in enforcing the Wahhabi ultraconservative dress and social code on an increasingly restless society. Within official Wahhabi circles, the late grand mufti, Sheikh Abdulaziz bin Baz, was highly respected and his death at age ninety in 1999 much lamented. But among reporters, the blind sheikh was viewed as a Neanderthal because of his view that Planet Earth was pancake flat, a contention he was said to have abandoned only after Saudi astronaut Prince Sultan bin Salman flew around the globe in the U.S. space shuttle *Discovery* in 1985. Not surprising, then, that Saudi authorities were reluctant to subject the Wahhabi establishment to outside questioning. As a result, the House of Sheikh remained even more remote and secretive than the House of Saud, even as it was bringing its formidable soft power to bear on the U.S.-Saudi relationship and driving a wedge between the two partners.

Any Westerner visiting the kingdom cannot help being deeply impressed by its overwhelming religiosity. The al-Sheikhs may not rule, but they have fixed an indelible imprint on Saudi society. The Koran serves as the kingdom's constitution, and Islam is the law of the land. Public life still comes to a halt five times a day for prayers, a time-out strictly enforced by the five thousand *mutawwa'in* who make sure that stores close, shopping stops, and Saudis run to the nearest prayer room. The kingdom's senior princes constantly receive senior Wahhabi clerics at their courts to hear their views on the issues of the day. These princes also sponsor competitions for Koran recitals among Saudi youth that are as common and popular as spelling bees in America. The Koran is used in Saudi schools not only for religious instruction but to teach children to read and write Arabic.

For Wahhabi clerics, control of women's behavior in society is a fixation. Until recently, the clerics were responsible for girls' education. The clerics still dictate their social behavior based on the fanatic Wahhabi dedication to keeping women segregated outside the home, isolated from unmarried men, and hidden in public behind Taliban-like face veils. They have also prevailed to date in their struggle to keep Saudi women from driving, even though other Arab gulf states now allow them behind the wheel, even Wahhabi-ruled Qatar next door. Only in 2006 did Saudi women begin to get their own identity cards, separate from their husbands. Scholars and diplomats who have studied Saudi society in depth say the conservatism of Wahhabi clerics is nothing compared with that of the kingdom's tribal and clan leaders, whose autocratic tendencies are mirrored in the style of al-Saud rule.

After 9/11, the guardians of Wahhabism found themselves in an extremely difficult position. They had no intention of disowning their own religion. But they were hard-pressed to explain how it had managed to produce so many "deviants," as they decided to call the hundreds of Saudis joining the ranks of al-Qaeda to perform the sacred duty of jihad against invading Christian infidels. The main explanation that both the al-Sauds and the al-Sheikhs came up with was the pernicious impact of foreign Islamic groups, like the Egyptian Muslim Brotherhood, and false prophets of jihad, like Osama bin Laden. Prince Naif, the Saudi interior minister, was the most explicit in blaming this "deviancy" on the brotherhood. In November 2002, Naif declared that the brotherhood had done "great damage" to Saudi Arabia, despite the fact that it had found refuge in the kingdom whenever its members had been persecuted in their own countries. "All our problems come from the Muslim Brotherhood. We have given too much support to this group."[1] Naif was doubtless personally piqued because he had employed the brotherhood's late leader, Mamoun al-Hodeiby, as his adviser for several years during al-Hodeiby's exile in Saudi Arabia from 1980 to 1987.

Islamic Affairs Minister Saleh al-Sheikh offered much the same explanation from his remarkably plain office in downtown Riyadh, insisting that Wahhabism was not the wellspring of Islamic extremism it was made out to be in the American media. The minister, then forty-seven, objected strongly to the term "*Wahhabism*" and to Saudis being referred to as "Wahhabis."[2]

By that time, the latter term had become practically synonymous with "terrorists" in the media's lexicon and given a black name to the kingdom's founding religion around the world. Saleh preferred the generic term for Islamic fundamentalism, "Salafism."* According to him, no Saudi cleric worthy of this name had anything to do with preaching or promoting terrorism. In fact, the kingdom's religious hierarchy had strongly condemned 9/11 as un-Islamic and its perpetrators as criminals and religious deviants. "Acts of terrorism done in the last two years are related to some extreme Islamic movements, including the Muslim Brotherhood and Islamic Jihad," he said. "Salafism, the Saudi school of thought, was innocent of such acts."[3] These deviants had received both their theological and their military training outside the kingdom and were not true Saudi Salafis in any sense of the word.

Saleh argued that true Saudi Salafis could not possibly have participated in 9/11 or other terrorist activities, for the Saudi Salafi movement had already achieved its historical objectives—the reform of Islam and the founding of a modern, powerful state to protect the sect. So there was no need for genuine Salafis to rise up against the state, resort to terrorism, or even push for "reform," a word he found equally distasteful. He preferred to talk about "development," whether referring to the Saudi individual or to the Saudi state and nation. Saudi clerics strongly supported modernization so long as this was not synonymous with Westernization. Saudi Salafis in his view were not reactionaries seeking to restore the mores and times of the eighteenth century, as they were portrayed in the Western press.

The minister readily conceded there was plenty of room for improvement in Saudi society, but insisted the goal should not be to copy the West or its form of democracy, as President Bush seemed to be pushing the kingdom to do. Islamic democracy, he said, was "a little bit different sometimes from Western democracy," but the two were still compatible in their goals. Only the means were different, and these had to take account of the specific conditions of Saudi society and politics. There was nothing wrong with change, but it had to come according to Saudi speed limits, not American ones, to avoid "shocking some social forces inside the kingdom." With respect to the rights of women and especially their right to drive a car, the minister acknowledged that no religious prohibition stood against it, only "social

---

* The Wahhabis are also called Muwahiddin, or "unitarians," because they believe in the unity of God.

forces" opposing change, which would be "educated" slowly to accept it. Saleh pointed out that Saudi women were already driving when outside the kingdom with no problems, so why not eventually inside, too?[4]

The minister stressed the important role his family was playing in the kingdom's modernization as a result of its special relationship with the House of Saud and the al-Sheikhs involvement in all sectors of modern Saudi Arabia. Saleh insisted his extended family was not as large as most Westerners might think, numbering only some two thousand males. And far from all of them were clerics and religious scholars. In fact, most were doctors, engineers, lawyers, and teachers engaged in the process of modernization. He never made clear why there were so many fewer al-Sheikh than al-Saud family members, believed to number between eight and ten thousand.* After all, the genealogies of the two families both dated to the eighteenth century. Perhaps it was due to the numerous intermarriages over the centuries that had caused many al-Sheikh women to be absorbed into the al-Saud family. The mother of King Faisal (1964–1975), the most popular of recent Saudi rulers, had been an al-Sheikh, and he himself had been brought up in an al-Sheikh household.

Saleh provided the classic Wahhabi description of his family's role in governing the kingdom: "assisting the king and the crown prince but not leading." In his mind, the two families had separate but equally important tasks. "We are concerned first for the stability and power of the state. If the Saudi state is strong, then Islam itself will be strong within the kingdom." He took a swipe at Iran's Shiite theocracy, saying the al-Sheikhs were "against close-minded religious scholars who were imposed in some states" and prevented them, he claimed, from becoming modern nations.[5]

SALEH'S EFFORTS TO disassociate Wahhabism from Islamic extremism stood in sharp contrast to another widely held theory that came to the fore after 9/11, namely that the puritanical Saudi creed had blended with the Muslim Brotherhood's political militancy to create a potent new hybrid of "neo-Wahhabis." These Islamic militants were seen as the blowback from the Saudi policy of offering asylum to thousands of Egyptian, Syrian, and Jor-

---

* Estimates of the royal family's size vary widely, owing in part to disagreements over who has the right to be included as a prince or princess.

danian brethren since the mid-1950s. They had washed up on Saudi shores in waves to fill the ranks of the Saudi education, justice, and religious systems and cut their teeth on the decade-long jihad against the Soviets in Afghanistan, which had also drawn seven to ten thousand Saudi youth to the battlefield, or at least neighboring Pakistan. Another source of this new political activism had been the Islamic Awakening, led by homegrown militant preachers in Saudi Arabia like Sheikhs Salman al-Audah and Safar al-Hawali, who were at once socially conservative and politically radical. They had been in the forefront of petitions for a crackdown on corruption, an elected parliament, a constitutional monarchy, and jihad against foreign intrusion into the Muslim world. Many of these neo-Wahhabis were also *"takfiris,"* believers in the right of a Muslim religious scholar to declare another Muslim, or even a Muslim government, an apostate warranting elimination. They were out to challenge the traditional Wahhabi paradigm of the separation of state and mosque and the clergy's subservience to the king.

After the 1991 Gulf War, dozens of fiery Saudi sheikhs had proliferated across the kingdom, demanding political reform at home and jihad abroad. By the early 2000s, the kingdom was seething with theological debate— much of it conducted through cyberspace's chat rooms, blogs, and Web sites—that was radically changing the nature of Saudi political discourse on the ground. Little of this religious turmoil was understood or reported on in the Western media, partly because of its esoteric nature. Only after 9/11 did the reality of this new militancy come to be appreciated, as both establishment and nonofficial Saudi religious scholars came forth with radical positions in response to the U.S. military assaults first on the Taliban in Afghanistan and then on Saddam Hussein in Iraq.

Sheikh Nasir bin Hamid al-Fahd, a highly respected scholar tracing his ancestors back to the tribesmen who had fought alongside King Abdulaziz in the 1920s to create the present-day Saudi state, wrote a book titled *The Blasphemy of Those Who Help the Americans.* In May 2003, he issued a fatwa, or religious ruling, justifying the use of weapons of mass destruction "if the Muslims could defeat the infidels only by using these kinds of weapons."[6] The ruling, titled "Regarding the Use of Weapons of Mass Destruction Against Infidels," provided justification regarded by some scholars as precedent setting: "If a bomb was dropped on them [the Americans] that would annihilate ten million and burn their lands to the same extent that they burned the Muslim lands—this is permissible with no need to mention any other proof."[7] Al-Fahd did not stop there. "If the *Jihadists* decide that the infidels' evil would not stop except by surprising and attacking them with the weapons of mass destruction, it is possible to use it [WMD] even if it kills them all."[8]

Al-Fahd focused a lot of his writings on Muslim governments that had associated themselves with the United States in its military ventures in Kuwait, Afghanistan, and Iraq, claiming they had committed a grave sin and deserved to be overthrown. This was obviously a very delicate issue for the al-Saud family and helped explain why al-Fahd found himself thrown into prison before and after 9/11. But it was his defense of al-Qaeda terrorism that proved the final straw. He and two other like-minded clerics were arrested in May 2003 after they came out in support of the bombing of three compounds housing foreigners in Riyadh. He was released but then rearrested after he applauded a fourth compound bombing in November of that year. This time, he renounced many of his most fiery fatwas and denounced the latest al-Qaeda attack, which had killed seventeen people, the vast majority Muslims, including seven Saudis and nine children. "No sane person approves of such an act, let alone a Muslim or a student," he confessed on Saudi state television. "We disavow such acts in front of God."[9] The death toll had been tiny compared with what could be expected from a chemical or nuclear bomb, but al-Fahd was apparently moved to repentance by the death of Muslims and Saudis. Still, the government decided to silence him by keeping him in jail, where he still was in mid-2007. It also shut down his Web site.

On the other hand, the government took no action against twenty-six Saudi clerics who in November 2004 delivered an "open sermon" urging the Iraqi resistance onward in its sacred battle to end the American occupation. "Without a doubt, fighting the occupiers is a duty of [all] who [are] able," they said. It was a "defensive jihad" against "warriors of aggression," and divine law dictated "fighting them back so they leave humiliated and diminished." For Muslims to provide any kind of help or support to the U.S. military in its operations against other Muslims was strictly forbidden. They warned against sectarian warfare between Sunnis and Shiites, called for the unity of the country, and asked Muslims worldwide "to stand by their brothers in Iraq."[10] Among the signatories were leading university professors and Islamic scholars as well as Sheikhs al-Audah and al-Hawali. The sermon was distributed internationally on the former sheikh's Web site, Islam

Today. The government took no steps to interfere. Only the official religious establishment still remained dutifully mum on the American presence in Iraq.

Militant Wahhabi clerical voices were so common that the al-Saud leadership became very cautious about reining them in. It realized that Saudi society as a whole had become far more militant and that anti-Americanism was rampant. Bin Laden had become a folk hero for many Saudis, the untouchable Robin Hood standing up to the Sheriff of Washington. Saudi officials were shocked when a rare independent poll taken in 2003, with more than fifteen thousand Saudis participating, found that 49 percent applauded his fiery speeches, even though less than 5 percent viewed him as an acceptable replacement for the al-Sauds.[11] The poll's director, Nawaf Obaid, noted that few Saudis approved of bin Laden's terrorist methods and indiscriminate killing of innocent victims. But he quoted one of the poll's respondents to explain his popularity: "When we hear bin Laden railing against the West, pointing out the corruption and incompetence of the Arab governments and the suffering of the Palestinians, it is like being transported to a dream."[12]

Saudi Arabia's homegrown radical clerics were not alone in pushing the rising tide of Islamic militancy inside the kingdom. Some of the most influential preachers luring young Saudis onto the road of jihad were either Syrians or Palestinian Jordanians. One such sheikh was Abu Muhammed al-Maqdisi, whose treatise "Clear Evidence on the Infidel Nature of the Saudi State" had been widely distributed within the kingdom. Al-Maqdisi, a Jordanian of Palestinian origin, was a good example of foreign clerics extending their voices into the Saudi internal debate after 9/11. Their impact was enormous, as Saudi authorities found out in 2004 after interrogating 639 Saudi *jihadis* among the several thousand they had succeeded in rounding up by then. The most influential spiritual guide among them was not bin Laden but this foreign cleric. "Maqdisi is a very important figure. They listen to him," said one Saudi involved in a program to reeducate these prisoners.[13]

Another cleric from abroad who influenced the theological debate was the Syrian sheikh Mohammed Surur Zein al-Abidin, a former Muslim Brotherhood member who had gone to Saudi Arabia in 1965 to escape persecution at home. He ended up promoting his own brand of Salafi Islam. Surur became a stateless person, a kind of wandering Islamic evangelical no Arab government could tolerate for long. He spent eight years in Saudi

Arabia before leaving for Kuwait, then settled in London and finally in Amman, Jordan, where he was living in 2006 at the age of seventy-two.[14] According to some scholars and Saudi officials, Surur had the largest following of any cleric among religious-minded Saudis, even among officials within the ministries of education and Islamic affairs. Yet few outsiders had ever heard of him. According to one Saudi analyst, the main fear of Surur and his followers was a "secular takeover" of the kingdom by Western-educated Saudis. "Their aim is to prevent that by all means, and they see the United States pushing for that."[15]

Another of Surur's driving concerns was the independence of the clerical establishment from the government, both financially and politically. But he also opposed outright rebellion against Saudi rulers because he feared that would provoke chaos. Surur became the leader of a third school of Wahhabi thinking separate from the Saudi establishment and the *jihadis*. He was considered a *wasati*, or centrist, a growing trend in Saudi Wahhabi religious circles after 9/11. But any independent thinking was enough for the official Wahhabi leadership to view Surur and his followers as troublemakers. Interestingly, Surur told one Saudi scholar that he believed the kingdom's al-Sheikh clerics had influenced him as much as he had them, citing in particular the former grand mufti Mohammed ibn Ibrahim al-Sheikh, who had died in 1969.[16]

NOWHERE HAS THE partnership between the houses of al-Saud and al-Sheikh been more clearly evident than in their joint pursuit of exporting Wahhabism to make it the dominant faith among the world's 1.3 billion Muslims. Saudi Arabia is a missionary state, and the export of Islam, according to a U.S. diplomat in Riyadh, "is central to their view of what their world outlook is."[17] The projection of this Saudi soft power began under King Faisal in the 1960s, gained the financial wherewithal with the quadrupling of oil prices after the 1973 Arab-Israeli War, and took on a worldwide dimension under King Fahd. The king, noted for his youthful debauchery, had decided to seek his redemption by making Islam's propagation central to his foreign policy. It seems more than a little ironic that Fahd, the most pro-American of contemporary Saudi kings, was also responsible for the spread of an Islamic creed that after 9/11 became noted for its anti-Christian, anti-Jewish, and anti-American biases. Amazingly, this bipolar disorder in Saudi policy toward the United States did not come to the attention of U.S. policy makers or the American public before then.

In truth, the Saudi export of Wahhabi Islam did not seem to have much impact on the U.S.-Saudi relationship before 9/11 because Osama bin Laden appeared to be an isolated case of Saudi deviancy. In this respect, Bandar had succeeded admirably in his diplomacy aimed at keeping Wahhabism from becoming an irritant in the relationship. All this changed abruptly, however, with the discovery that the hijackers on 9/11 had been predominantly Saudi, and the later discovery that Saudis constituted the largest contingent of any nationality captured during the U.S. campaign to overthrow the Taliban in Afghanistan. According to Pentagon statistics, Saudis accounted for 137 of 759 prisoners detained in Guantánamo, Cuba, starting in January 2002.[18]

The effectiveness of the export effort was enhanced by an elaborate complex of interlocking government institutions, agencies, and charities established for the purpose by King Fahd, whose reign began in 1982 and lasted until 2005. He was faced with the challenge of a revolutionary Shiite theocracy in Iran that had ousted the shah in 1979 and set out to expand Iranian religious and political influence worldwide. Fahd was determined to meet the challenge, and so were his Wahhabi clerics, who regarded the Shia as heretics. The king issued a directive that "no limit be put on expenditures for the propagation of Islam" and in 1993 established the Islamic Affairs Ministry, one of whose responsibilities was the propagation of Islam abroad.[19] He also built the largest printing house for the publication of the Koran in the Muslim world and spent billions of dollars on upgrading the two holy sites in Mecca and Medina. To help finance his campaign, he set up a special off-the-books oil fund, most of which was spent on improving facilities to host the two million pilgrims visiting Mecca every year.

The government allocated as much as two hundred thousand barrels of oil a day to this fund, which generated $27 billion in revenues before being closed down in the early 2000s. The king boasted on his personal Web site that he had been responsible for establishing two hundred Islamic colleges, 210 Islamic centers, fifteen hundred mosques, and two thousand schools for Muslim children in non-Islamic countries. The Koran publishing plant, in Medina, built at the start of his reign at a cost of $130 million, had by 2000 distributed 138 million copies worldwide.[20] Fahd ordered that copies be handed out for free to every pilgrim coming to Mecca. It is difficult to determine just how much the king spent on his drive to export Islam, but David Aufhauser, a former Treasury Department general counsel, told a Senate committee in June 2004 that estimates went "north of $75 billion."[21]

To coordinate the government's campaign, Fahd in 1995 established the Supreme Council for Islamic Affairs under the tutelage of Prince Sultan, Bandar's father. Appointing the kingdom's longtime defense minister underlined the king's determination to curb the influence of the Muslim Brotherhood, which had opposed Saudi involvement in the first Gulf War. The council's membership included the ministers of justice, higher education, Islamic affairs, and foreign affairs as well as the head of the General Intelligence Directorate and the secretary-general of the Muslim World League. Its mission, according to Islamic Affairs Minister Saleh al-Sheikh, was to "coordinate the Islamic policies of the different ministries outside the kingdom."[22] Saleh's ministry served as the council's secretariat, which met on a weekly basis and became a kind of second Foreign Ministry for the kingdom. In the opinion of a U.S. embassy analyst in Riyadh, the Islamic Affairs Ministry pretty much "ran its own show" overseas, and the Saudi Foreign Ministry, trying after 9/11 to assert its authority, "found it very hard to get control" of its activities.[23]

The drab concrete-and-glass building of the Islamic Affairs Ministry, located in Riyadh's al-Malaz District, belied the ministry's central role in the kingdom, as did its relatively modest $530 million annual official budget, most of which went for the salaries of the kingdom's own fifty thousand mosque preachers. The government did not publish the ministry's actual budget or its expenditures on propagating Islam because, as one knowledgeable Saudi source put it, "there really isn't any set budget." He estimated the total Saudi expenditure on exporting Islam, including both the government and the royal family, at between $2 billion and $2.5 billion a year.[24] One measure of the ministry's authority in Saudi foreign policy was its legion of missionaries and clerics working abroad. In 2005, they numbered exactly 3,884, six times as many as the 650 Saudi diplomats assigned to the kingdom's seventy-seven embassies.[25] Ministry officials were also assigned to embassies to run their Office of the Islamic Call. Usually Wahhabi clerics, these officials were particularly influential in Africa and Asia, where they sometimes wielded as much power, and money, as the Saudi ambassador himself. They also acted as "political commissars," writing reports on the alleged misbehavior of embassy officials that could result in reprimands and even demotions.[26]

In addition to its army of missionaries, the Saudi government relied on various charities and Islamic international bodies to spread the call to Islam as well as humanitarian aid. By far the oldest and best known were the Muslim World League, the World Assembly of Muslim Youth, and the International Islamic Relief Organization, the latter operating in 120 countries on behalf of the league. All had their headquarters in the kingdom. Saudi financing and increasingly Saudi staff were essential to the operation of these three institutions, and they were often led by Saudis. There were more than 240 smaller Saudi charities, the vast majority involved in humanitarian work within the kingdom. Only nine worked abroad, and probably the most popular were those dedicated to helping the Palestinian cause or protecting Islamic holy sites in Jerusalem. By 2002, the Saudi government calculated overall official and private contributions to the Palestinians at $2.61 billion.[27] The motivation for these donations, however, was more to show Saudi political support and counter Iranian inroads into the Palestinian community than to promote the export of Wahhabi Islam.

The royal family had long taken the lead in showing support for the Palestinians, its leading princes competing with one another to show their personal commitment. Both King Fahd and Prince Naif, the powerful interior minister, had their own charities. Naif headed the Saudi Committee for Supporting al-Quds Intifada, which regularly sent money to families of Palestinians killed by the Israelis, regardless of whether they had belonged to the militant Islamic Resistance Movement (Hamas) or the more moderate Fatah faction. The al-Quds Committee had spent close to $200 million on thirty-one relief projects in the Gaza Strip and the West Bank as of late 2003. A single telethon held under Fahd's patronage in April 2002 raised $100 million.[28] Another leading royal, Prince Salman bin Abdulaziz, the governor of Riyadh Province, led still another charity aiding the same cause, the Popular Committee for Assisting the Palestinian Mujahideen. It provided $8.8 million between 2000 and 2003.[29] Pro-Israeli groups in the United States and Congress focused much of their ire on these groups after 9/11 because of their support for Hamas, which was on the U.S. government's list of "specially designated global terrorists." The FBI, too, targeted various charities in the United States suspected of helping Hamas, such as the Saudi-funded Muwafaq Foundation. Both this charity and its leader, Yassin al-Qadi, were put on the terrorist list shortly after 9/11.

The Saudi charity that became the worst bone of contention between the

U.S. and Saudi governments, however, was al-Haramain Islamic Foundation, named after the Two Holy Mosques and founded in 1988 in Karachi, Pakistan, with headquarters established in Riyadh three years later. Al-Haramain was used by Saudi authorities specifically to combat the influence of Muslim Brotherhood–run charities around the world in the wake of the first Gulf War. Its annual budget ran between forty and sixty million dollars. The charity supported the work of three thousand missionaries in fifty countries and paid for mosques, Korans, and even Saudi-approved veils for women. But it also built schools, dug wells, and ran orphanages. It had particularly close ties to the Islamic Affairs Ministry, as minister Saleh al-Sheikh was its official supervisor. But Saleh claimed he and his ministry had no direct responsibility for al-Haramain's day-to-day operations.[30] This, of course, was the problem with all Saudi charities working abroad—the lack of government supervision of and accountability for their activities. There was nothing equivalent to the accountability American charities have to demonstrate to the U.S. government, explaining their annual revenues, expenditures, and activities. After 9/11, one branch after another of al-Haramain around the world became formally "designated" by the U.S. Treasury Department as a terrorist group because of its financial or material support to al-Qaeda.

THE SAUDI CAMPAIGN to spread Wahhabi Islam reached deep inside the United States, and here Bandar's embassy became the chief facilitator. There was scant evidence that this worldly "Arab Gatsby" of the Washington social scene had much personal interest in promoting this effort. But the prince did nothing, either, to curb the activities of his Islamic Affairs Department, or Dawah Office, which grew by leaps and bounds. The main reason for his tolerance may well have been the Iranian challenge to Saudi influence within the Muslim community of America in the wake of Iran's 1979 Islamic Revolution. One of the first battlegrounds where the two Islamic rivals fought was the white limestone Islamic Mosque and Cultural Center on Massachusetts Avenue in downtown Washington, just a couple of miles away from the Saudi embassy. The mosque became heavily subsidized by Saudi contributions (five hundred thousand dollars annually plus the salary of its Saudi imam) after an Iranian takeover attempt in the early 1980s. Bandar eventually became the mosque's patron saint and board chairman. But the religious war between Shiite Iran and Wahhabi Saudi Arabia did not stop in Washington; it extended to the entire Muslim student community across America, where pitched theological battles broke out as well as struggles to control national groups like the Muslim Students' Association and the Islamic Society of North America.

By the mid-1980s, the Islamic Affairs Department at the Saudi embassy in Washington had mushroomed to forty clerics, scholars, and other employees, most of whom carried Saudi diplomat passports. The best known in the Islamic world was Jaafar Sheikh Idris, a Sudanese scholar close to Hassan al-Turabi, leader of Sudan's militant Islamists. The office had a budget of eight million dollars.[31] There were also thirty-one Saudi-financed missionaries at work across America.[32] King Fahd himself became directly involved. His personal Web site listed sixteen Islamic and cultural centers that he had helped build in California, Missouri, Michigan, Illinois, New Jersey, New York, Ohio, Virginia, and Maryland. The largest was the King Fahd Mosque in Culver City, outside Los Angeles, constructed with eight million dollars in donations from the king and his son Abdulaziz bin Fahd.[33] The Saudis also put millions into the Institute for Islamic and Arabic Sciences in America, founded in 1989 and located in Fairfax, Virginia, outside Washington. The institute was staffed by professors from Imam Mohammed ibn Saud Islamic University in Riyadh, one of the kingdom's main centers of Wahhabi instruction.

In the late 1980s, a few Saudi officials at the embassy in Washington began questioning the wisdom of investing so much government money and energy into spreading the Wahhabi doctrine inside America. One worried official warned a gung ho colleague, "You are feeding a crocodile that will come back and bite us." The concerned official became even more convinced it was money misspent after none of the Saudi-financed clerics and scholars in the United States came out in support of the United States and Saudi Arabia during the 1991 Gulf War. Many Saudi embassy staffers were asking, "Why in earth are we paying for these callers?" By the mid-1990s, the embassy had begun cutting its support for these missionaries, reducing the Islamic Affairs Department's budget from eight million to two million dollars.[34]

The impact of this Saudi missionary effort in the United States by the time of 9/11 was mixed. A 2000 survey of the Muslim community in America, estimated to number between six and seven million, found that only two million were even "associated" with a mosque. So a vast majority of

Muslims in America were either practicing their faith at home or not practicing at all. But the same survey also discovered that 70 percent of mosque leaders were Salafi fundamentalists and 21 percent were Wahhabi followers. One indicator of their combined growing influence was the percentage of mosques segregating women during prayer services; it had increased from half to two thirds of the total in six years.[35] Muslim scholars seemed sharply divided in their assessment of the extent of Wahhabi influence. According to Hamid Algar, a professor of Islamic studies at the University of California at Berkeley, Wahhabi followers were "relatively few in number" and after 9/11 became even fewer.[36] On the other hand, Khaled Abou El Fadl, author of *And God Knows the Soldiers*, was ringing the alarm bell. He had found in his travels around the United States and across the world that Wahhabi practices, particularly toward women, had become the "orthodox Islamic position." He believed that the Saudis had succeeded in taking over the entire Salafi fundamentalist movement, thus enabling them to spread Wahhabism worldwide.[37] A U.S. analyst working at the American embassy in Riyadh had a different view: He believed there was an inverse ratio between the impact of Wahhabi Islam and its geographic distance from the kingdom: "The closer to Saudi Arabia you are, the less impact it has. The further away, the more impact it has."[38] Indeed, none of Saudi Arabia's immediate neighbors are followers of the Wahhabi sect except Qatar, which has adopted a far more liberal interpretation of its doctrines, including allowing women to drive.

CHAPTER 12

The Hunt for Wahhabis
in America

THE 9/11 CATASTROPHE TOUCHED OFF a nationwide manhunt in America for al-Qaeda operatives, sleeper cells, nuclear dirty bombers, financers of terrorism, and Muslim charities fronting for the group and for the militant Palestinian Islamic Resistance Movement (Hamas). Because the hijackers were mostly Saudis, Saudi Arabia was immediately painted by the media as the wellspring of Islamic extremism and terrorist financing. The result was that Saudis of all rank, from royal princes and billionaires to students and tourists, were caught up in the U.S. government's dragnet. Even Bandar and his wife, Haifa, did not escape suspicion. Massive lawsuits by six hundred families of the 9/11 victims accused Saudi banks, charities, merchants, and businessmen of financing, or promoting in other ways, the calamity that had befallen the country. Both Prince Sultan, Bandar's father, and Prince Turki, the former head of Saudi intelligence and future ambassador to Washington, were named as defendants. (The U.S. District Court for the District of Columbia ruled in November 2003 that both were entitled to foreign sovereign immunity because of their official status.) The kingdom was portrayed as practically al-Qaeda's central bank after the discovery in March 2002 of the so-called Golden Chain list of what were alleged to be its supporters. Found in the office of the Benevolence International Foundation in Sarajevo, Bosnia, the list had been drawn up by Osama bin Laden and included twenty Saudi bankers, merchants, businessmen, and officials who had made major donations to the Afghan mujahideen's war against the Soviet Union during the 1980s. Because of this, bin Laden apparently looked upon them as prospective backers of his cause. Whether they had made donations to al-Qaeda was never clear. But the U.S. Justice Department used the Golden Chain as evidence in some of its own antiterrorism cases, thereby giving credibility to accusations that at least some of them had.

The anti-Saudi frenzy after 9/11 was fueled by the activities of multiple U.S. government agencies. While President Bush issued statements of faint praise for Saudi cooperation in his new "war on terrorism," the FBI, the CIA, and the Treasury Department launched investigations into groups, charities, and scores of individuals associated in some way with the kingdom. The intelligence community had already identified Saudi Arabia as "the primary source of money for al-Qaeda both before and after the September 11 attacks."[1] It didn't help the Saudi cause that in the immediate aftermath of 9/11, the manhunt for other suspected terrorists centered on Saudi-born Adnan el-Shukrijumah, who was feared to be in possession of a dirty bomb. His father, Gulshair el-Shukrijumah, was the Saudi-trained imam of a mosque in Florida and one of the thirty-one missionaries on the payroll of the Saudi Islamic Affairs Ministry working in the United States.

Nor did it help the Saudi cause that bin Laden family members had been among more than one hundred Saudis allowed by the Bush administration to leave the United States on special flights in the first few days after the 9/11 attacks. Another early departure, though on a regularly scheduled flight, had been Saleh al-Hussayen. His departure became enormously controversial because he had stayed at the same Marriott Residence Inn in Herndon, Virginia, as three of the hijackers of the American Airlines jet that crashed into the Pentagon.*

Al-Hussayen was no ordinary Saudi. A highly respected senior religious figure who would become the head of the Presidency of the Two Holy Mosques Affairs, with the rank of minister, he had been invited to undertake a lecture tour by two Saudi-supported groups, the Islamic Assembly of North America and the International Institute of Islamic Thought, located outside Washington. FBI agents had questioned both al-Hussayen and his wife at the hotel. There was no evidence he had met with the hijackers or

---

* His nephew, Sami Omar al-Hussayen, was a graduate student at the University of Idaho and the Web master for the Islamic Assembly of North America. In February 2003, the FBI arrested Sami on suspicion of providing material assistance to al-Qaeda and its affiliates. He was acquitted at his trial in June 2004 of all terrorist charges.

even knew they were staying there. But the coincidence was enough to set off media speculation that he had some connection to the hijackers and had been in the United States to promote Wahhabi fundamentalism.[2] In an interview in Riyadh in March 2004, al-Hussayen vented his rage at the press coverage of his trip. He denied he had even "touched" on religious issues in his lectures. He confirmed he and his wife had been questioned at length by the FBI, and he said they had been shown pictures of the hijackers to see whether they could identify any of them. They had not been able to do so and had been cleared to leave the country.[3]

Within months of 9/11, it was clear the FBI and the Treasury Department intended to force the closure of most Islamic charities, regardless of who or what they were associated with. One of the very first charities to be targeted was the Global Relief Foundation in Bridgeview, Illinois, outside Chicago, the second-largest Islamic charity in the United States. In 2001, it had raised $5.2 million from more than twenty thousand contributors, and it had a mailing list of 250,000 potential donors.[4] The charity ran aid programs in twenty-two countries, including such hot spots as Bosnia, Afghanistan, and Chechnya. In November of that year, FBI agents raided its offices without a warrant, seized all documents, and froze its $900,000 in assets. The same day, the group's office in Kosovo, Serbia's southern province, was also searched, on the suspicion that some of its members were "planning attacks against targets in the U.S.A. and Europe," according to a NATO statement.[5] Ten months later, the Treasury Department declared Global Relief a "specially designated global terrorist," a power given to it by the 1977 International Emergency Economic Powers Act and the USA Patriot Act, which Congress had passed six weeks after 9/11. By the time the charity was designated, it had already gone out of business because its assets had been frozen.

Global Relief was likely a Muslim Brotherhood operation. Two other charities the FBI targeted, the Benevolence International Foundation and al-Haramain, were definitely Saudi in origin and met the same fate as Global Relief. Al-Haramain in particular came to personify the troublesome commingling of the official Saudi drive to export Wahhabism and the kingdom's support for Islamic extremism, inadvertent or otherwise. The charity was directly under the supervision of Islamic Affairs Minister Saleh al-Sheikh and came the closest in the view of the 9/11 Commission to being the kingdom's "United Way" for private Saudi foreign assistance.[6] A special commission monograph on terrorist financing said its purpose was "to promote

Wahhabi Islam by funding religious education, mosques and humanitarian projects around the world." But the U.S. government by early 2003 had identified twenty al-Haramain offices, including its headquarters in Saudi Arabia, where its personnel "were aiding and abetting al-Qaeda and its affiliated terrorist groups."[7] After 9/11, a tug-of-war between U.S. and Saudi authorities ensued over the closure of one after another of its worldwide branches.* The CIA and FBI had been gathering intelligence on al-Haramain's operations since the bombings of the U.S. embassies in Kenya and Tanzania in 1998 and had sought Saudi government cooperation in their investigation to no avail. The commission concluded that the U.S. government had not pushed very hard for better cooperation before 9/11 and that "the Saudis were content to do little."[9]

Even after 9/11, the Bush administration was reluctant to press the Saudis too hard for fear of compromising Saudi help on other counterterrorism issues. Not until January 2002 did the U.S. government formally ask the Saudis to freeze the accounts of eight Saudi entities and individuals and join Washington in designating them as global terrorists. The list included al-Haramain offices in Bosnia and Somalia. The Saudis agreed two months later to take action and close them, the first of many to be targeted. But within a few months, the U.S. government discovered the two offices had reopened under different names. The Saudis claimed they had been unaware of it and kept asking for more information on the activities of their own charity.[10]

Only at the end of 2002—fifteen months after 9/11—did the U.S. government finally put together a strategy for dealing with Saudi Arabia on counterterrorism, which included handing over a "non-paper," an unofficial document, on what the CIA and FBI knew about al-Haramain activities. This detailed branches, individuals, and methods of transferring funds in support of terrorism and was delivered to the Saudis at the end of January 2003. It even included U.S. information about the role of al-Haramain's headquarters in Riyadh "in supporting terrorist organizations."[11] This seems to have triggered the first serious Saudi investigation of the charity, and by May the U.S. embassy in Riyadh was reporting that the Saudis were ready to close down ten other al-Haramain branches. But again, they took

---

* The 9/11 Commission's monograph on terrorist financing documented this struggle in great detail in one of its case studies.[8]

no immediate action. The 9/11 Commission's terrorist-financing study concluded the government had run into stiff resistance from the Islamic Affairs Ministry.[12]

Even the al-Qaeda bombing of three compounds in Riyadh that May, which killed thirty-five Americans and Saudis and injured two hundred others, did not lead immediately to Saudi action against the ten al-Haramain offices. Not until another compound bombing occurred in November 2003 were the Saudis finally jolted into taking action. The following month, the U.S. and Saudi governments acted together to designate Vazir, the charity in Bosnia that had replaced al-Haramain, as a terrorist group. Then in January 2004, al-Haramain offices in Indonesia, Kenya, Tanzania, and Pakistan were also designated. The same month, the Saudi government sacked Aqeel Abdulaziz al-Aqil, the founder and long-serving executive director of the charity's headquarters in Riyadh. Finally, the two governments jointly designated five other branches that June (Afghanistan, Albania, Bangladesh, Ethiopia, and the Netherlands), and the Saudis shuttered al-Haramain's Riyadh headquarters. But the Saudis refused to go along with the United States when, on June 2, 2004, it put al-Aqil on its terrorist list as "a suspected al-Qaeda supporter."[13]

Al-Aqil's dismissal marked a turning point—the first time the Saudi government admitted something had gone wrong even inside al-Haramain's headquarters in Riyadh. But the charity's supervisor, Islamic Affairs Minister al-Sheikh, still insisted that misconduct was being committed not by the charity as a whole but rather by "some individuals who belonged to this institution." He said his ministry had found no "major mistakes by the institution itself" and he pleaded for recognition of its reputation for good humanitarian works around the world.[14] Al-Aqil himself was clearly one of those "individuals." He had defied Crown Prince Abdullah's orders to close down al-Haramain activities in Somalia, including a home for orphans to which he had personally carried funds in defiance of royal orders. U.S. authorities believed he was also funneling money to a Somali fundamentalist group, al-Ittihad al-Islamiyya, which was another designated global terrorist group. In addition, there were suspicions that some charity funds had been embezzled and used for building villas on the French Riviera.[15] Treasury official Juan Zarate referred to these problems in a statement at the time of al-Aqil's designation as a global terrorist. The Saudi, he said, had sought "to evade Saudi controls on his finances" and under the cloak of charity "to benefit himself and al-Qaeda."[16]

The long saga of U.S. dealings with al-Haramain included its operations in the United States as well. American authorities took about as much time as the Saudis before acting to close it down, probably for lack of sufficient evidence of wrongdoing inside the United States. In February 2004, the Treasury Department finally froze the assets of its office in Ashland, Oregon, "pending investigation." But the charity was not formally designated a terrorist group until that September, fully three years after 9/11. Also designated was its Egyptian-born Saudi director, Soliman al-Buthe, who had long since left the country and taken up residence in Riyadh. The Treasury Department said its investigation had found direct links between the U.S. branch and Osama bin Laden, criminal violations of tax laws, and money laundering. Some of its funds had gone to rebel leaders in Chechnya "affiliated with the al-Qaeda network."[17] This was a reference to $150,000 the American branch had raised in 2000 and sent back in the form of traveler's and cashier's checks to al-Haramain headquarters in Riyadh. Al-Buthe had been the courier but had failed to declare the amount at the airport when he left the United States as required by U.S. law.

The charity's American lawyers said the money had gone to a Chechen refugee relief project approved by the Saudi and Russian governments. Al-Buthe himself said he had never met or raised money for bin Laden, even when the Saudi dissident had been fighting the Soviets in Afghanistan in the 1980s. He also noted that there had been no U.S. prohibition on fund-raising for Chechen refugees in 2000.[18] Al-Buthe never returned to the United States after his designation, but the Saudi government froze his bank account, and his name was on an international no-fly list, making it impossible for him to travel outside the kingdom. Still, he was given a high-level city government job in Riyadh and paid in cash to circumvent his frozen account. The Saudis were taking care of him.

THE U.S. GOVERNMENT's deep suspicion of official Saudi funding of terrorism led before long to an intensive investigation of the Saudi embassy and even Bandar himself. Without ever saying so publicly, the government was clearly determined to end the embassy's support for Wahhabi missionary work in America. In early 2003, the State Department began examining the status of all Saudis to whom it had issued diplomatic visas to see whether they were legitimate. It discovered that many Saudi religious scholars, clerics, and professors held diplomatic passports and decided to put an end to this privilege.

The first victim of this new policy was Fahad al-Thumairy, an Islamic Affairs Ministry official who had served in the Saudi consulate in Los Angeles since 1996. He was also a preacher at the King Fahd Mosque in nearby Culver City. Upon returning to Los Angeles on a flight from Frankfurt, Germany, on May 6, 2003, al-Thumairy was stopped at the airport and told he had to leave. Homeland Security officials first told reporters it was because the Saudi had no right to a diplomatic passport, but before long the media also discovered he might have had contacts with two of the 9/11 hijackers, Nawaf al-Hazmi and Khalid al-Mihdhar, after their arrival in the Los Angeles area. There was never any evidence al-Thumairy knew what they were plotting, but the simple fact that he had known them at the Culver City mosque was enough to paint him as practically a coconspirator.*

Soon after, the U.S. purge of Saudi "religious diplomats" continued with the expulsion of Jaafar Sheikh Idris, the leading light of the embassy's Islamic Affairs Department. He had been the director of the research center at the Institute for Islamic and Arabic Sciences in America, in Fairfax, Virginia, and was the founder of the American Open University in Herndon. In late November 2003, Idris left the country. When his departure became known in early December, the State Department finally disclosed its new policy of revoking diplomatic passports held by Saudi clerics. Idris was not a full-time embassy employee and therefore "no longer entitled to any diplomatic or official status in relation to the embassy," department spokesman Richard Boucher declared.[20] A Saudi embassy official stated that his government had adopted a new policy: "We are going to shut down the Islamic affairs section in every embassy." The embassy was also ending its sponsorship of the Institute of Islamic and Arabic Sciences in order "to keep embassies free of any task related to religious affairs."[21]

In late January 2004, sixteen staffers at the institute, most of them Saudi scholars and clerics, lost their diplomatic status and went home, along with several dozen others connected to the embassy, leaving only one or two Saudi diplomats to deal with religious affairs like the annual pilgrimage to Mecca.[22] Altogether, the purge affected about seventy individuals. The

---

* After a thorough investigation of its own, the 9/11 Commission concluded there was no evidence al-Thumairy had provided assistance to the two hijackers.[19]

embassy also suspended the distribution of the Koran. The same month, authorities in California arrested a Saudi-sponsored Somali missionary, Omar Abdi Mohammed, who had been on the Islamic Affairs Ministry payroll, with a monthly salary of $1,700 and a $6,000 housing stipend. He had run his own "charity" for Somalis back home and allegedly made false statements about receiving $326,000 from the Global Relief Foundation, which had been declared a terrorist group by the U.S. government.[23]

Bandar and his wife did not escape the probe of virtually all Saudi embassy activities. He and Haifa—the daughter of King Faisal, the most respected Saudi king in contemporary history—were treated as though they were suspected financers of terrorism. Treasury and FBI agents took possession of all embassy bank records in a search for possible criminal transactions. Bandar had agreed to cooperate to clear their names, though he might have evoked the embassy's sovereign immunity and diplomatic privileges. Such a probe of an embassy's finances, especially those of a close ally, was rare in U.S. diplomatic history.

American banks are supposed to file "suspicious activity reports," or SARs, with the Treasury Department's Office of the Comptroller of the Currency. Many banks had been negligent in this duty. In particular, Riggs National Bank in the nation's capital, Washington's oldest and best known, came under intense scrutiny. Riggs had handled Saudi embassy accounts for two decades. Treasury's investigators discovered the bank had failed to file a number of SARs during 2001 and into 2002, and among the "suspicious" transactions were some coming from Saudi accounts that involved tens of millions of dollars. The accounts were those of Bandar and Haifa.

What doubtless sparked Treasury's interest was the discovery that funds from one of Haifa's accounts had possibly ended up in the hands of the two hijackers in California. The two were suspected of having been in contact with a mysterious Saudi Civil Aviation employee, Omar al-Bayoumi, possibly a Saudi intelligence agent, and a Saudi student, Osama Bassnan. The media became aware of all this in November 2002 as the result of leaks from a special House-Senate Joint Intelligence Committee probe into possible official Saudi funding of the hijackers. Committee investigators were hot on the trail of a monthly check of thirty-five hundred dollars from Haifa's Riggs account that was suspected of having ended up in the hands of the two hijackers. The committee shortly afterward published a nine-hundred-page report that only further fed the anti-Saudi frenzy by leaving twenty-eight pages on possible Saudi financing classified, even though Bandar asked to have it made public.[24]

It took the Saudis some time to explain Haifa's checks, but in late December 2002 the Saudi embassy's legal adviser, Nancy Dutton, disclosed that a total of about $140,000 had been sent over a period of four years from the accounts of Bandar, Haifa, and the embassy medical office to a woman, Majeda Dweikat, who happened to be married to Bassnan, the Saudi student under suspicion. The family had been in "economic and medical need." The FBI had arrested and interrogated the couple, who were subsequently deported.[25]

Not until *The 9/11 Commission Report* appeared in July 2004 did the cloud of suspicion over Saudi funding of one or more of the hijackers dissipate, at least somewhat. Its separate monograph on terrorist financing said that there was no evidence that the two hijackers in question, al-Hazmi and al-Mihdhar, had received any money from either Bassnan or al-Bayoumi or that Princess Haifa had "provided any funds to the hijackers directly or indirectly."[26] There was evidence, however, that another Saudi student, Yazeed al-Salmi, had given al-Hazmi nineteen hundred dollars.[27] He, too, had been deported. The report exculpated the Saudi government and senior royals of funding al-Qaeda. But at the same time, it suggested that Saudi charities and wealthy donors might well have done so, describing Saudi Arabia as "fertile fund-raising ground" for the terrorist group.[28]

Bandar's woes were far from over. In January 2004, press reports began surfacing that as a result of Riggs's violations of the SAR requirements, U.S. authorities had imposed "unusually stringent controls" on its operations.[29] Among additional transactions that had drawn their attention were thirty-six million dollars in withdrawals from Haifa's account in 2001 and 2002.[30] By March, reports were circulating within the Washington press corps that the Saudi embassy was not paying its employees or outside contractors. The reason became clear the following month: Riggs had closed down all Saudi accounts, so Bandar could no longer pay his bills. It took several months of scrambling around to find another bank that would accept Saudi accounts, but in the end the London-based HSBC took them over.

As for Riggs, the probe spelled the beginning of the end. It was fined twenty-five million dollars for "numerous violations of the Bank Secrecy Act" and was sold in July 2004 to Pittsburgh's PNC Financial Services Group Inc. Its demise could not truthfully be ascribed solely to its Saudi connection. Riggs was already a failing bank suffering from mismanagement and poor leadership. But U.S. government suspicion of all Saudi activities inside the United States after 9/11 had sparked the federal probe that became the last straw in the downfall of this venerable Washington institution.

ANSWERS TO THE mystery surrounding the flow of so much money through Bandar's Riggs accounts began to emerge in mid-2007 as the result, ironically, of a thwarted British government investigation into alleged massive corruption stemming from the so-called al-Yamamah arms sale agreement with Saudi Arabia. Prime Minister Tony Blair had personally intervened in December 2006 to stop the probe, launched by the British government's Serious Fraud Office, after the Saudis had threatened to cancel another forty-billion-dollar deal involving the purchase from Britain of seventy-two Eurofighters. The Saudis had also threatened to pull their ambassador out of London and cut off intelligence sharing on terrorism.

The messenger King Abdullah dispatched to London with this stern warning was none other than Prince Bandar, who had negotiated the al-Yamamah deal directly with Prime Minister Margaret Thatcher in the summer of 1985. Al-Yamamah had turned out to be Britain's largest foreign arms sale ever, as other contracts had been added on over the next twenty years. The deal had led to the Saudi purchase of nearly 150 Tornado and Hawk warplanes and a vast array of service contracts valued at more than eighty-five billion dollars. To put that figure into perspective, the total value of all U.S. military sales to the kingdom between 1953 and 2003—including arms, maintenance, training contracts, and construction—had been about eighty-four billion dollars. Britain had surpassed the United States as the kingdom's number-one arms supplier, and the new Eurofighter contract promised to consolidate that lead.

In June 2007, the *Guardian* and the British Broadcasting Corporation (BBC) brought out the results of their own probes into al-Yamamah, alleging that BAE Systems, the plane manufacturer, had contrived to send secret payments to Bandar's Riggs accounts on a quarterly basis amounting to $240 million a year.[31] Altogether, Bandar would have received more than $2 billion. Some of this vast sum, the report claimed, had gone to buy and maintain the private, custom-built Airbus used by the prince to fly himself and his personal retinue around the world. The BBC alleged that the al-Yamamah contract had included secret annexes that had disguised these payments to Bandar under the rubric of "support services."

Whether these payments had been legal remained fuzzy in the BBC account since bribery of a foreign official had not been made an offense in Britain until 2001. Also, if both the British and Saudi governments, which had negotiated the deal, had agreed to a "support contract" benefiting Bandar, it was not clear the payments could be qualified as "illegal." The BBC program included an interview with David Caruso, a former Riggs employee, who alleged Bandar had taken some of the money for his own personal use. Part of the problem, he said, was that there was no distinction between royal family and official Saudi government accounts at Riggs.[32]

Bandar issued a statement saying that he was "dismayed and shocked" by the stories, which he said contained "an extremely serious allegation" and obliged him to speak out "to try and repair some of the damage done" to his reputation. He said he had been an authorized signatory on the Riggs account in the name of the Saudi Ministry of Defense and Aviation (MODA) and insisted that any money he had taken out was "exclusively for purposes approved by MODA." There had been no "improper secret commissions or back handers" paid. Audits by both the Defense Ministry and the Finance Ministry had never signaled any irregularities. "I required and obtained all requisite Saudi government authority to disburse any funds from Riggs accounts," Bandar asserted.[33]

What went unnoticed at the time was that Bandar had sought to provide a plausible explanation of al-Yamamah's "financial black holes" in the authorized biography of his life written by William Simpson, a British classmate at England's Royal Air Force College at Cranwell. The prince didn't dispute that funds had been siphoned off for other purposes and justified the practice on national security grounds. Both "sources close to Bandar" and the former head of Britain's Defence Export Sales Organisation, Tony Edwards, told Simpson that the Saudis had used al-Yamamah as "a backdoor method of covertly buying U.S. arms for the kingdom." The reason for this was allegedly to escape U.S. congressional oversight and opposition from the powerful American Israel Public Affairs Committee, which had strenuously opposed major aircraft sales to the kingdom in the 1970s and 1980s.[34]

Edwards claimed the Saudis had used al-Yamamah funds to pay for the

U.S. Peace Shield program, a multibillion-dollar command, control, and communications air defense system covering the entire kingdom and built by Hughes Aircraft Company and Boeing Company in the early 1990s;[35] in fact, records show it was a well-known program vetted in detail by Congress and paid for by the Saudis under the official U.S. Foreign Military Sale Program. But al-Yamamah proceeds may have been used to pay for U.S.-made Blackhawk helicopters built under license by the British firm Westland, and Bandar may have profited from that deal through a related service contract. This, at least, is what whistle-blower Thomas Dooley, a former Sikorsky Aircraft Corporation salesman, alleged in a 1991 lawsuit that was eventually settled out of court. Dooley, too, claimed that al-Yamamah had been used to circumvent Congress, and that Westland had signed a bogus contract for helicopter maintenance with a Saudi businessman who had passed most of the contract payments on to various sons of Prince Sultan, including Bandar.[36] Since the lawsuit was settled out of court, the truth of Dooley's allegations was never adjudicated.

Under the Arms Export Control Act, the Pentagon must inform Congress of all arms sales or service contracts valued at one million dollars or more to any foreign country, no matter whether the beneficiary is the U.S. government or a private American contractor. These reports are sent to both the Senate and the House of Representatives on a quarterly basis. If the value of the transaction is fourteen million dollars or more, the Pentagon has to inform Congress thirty days before any contract is signed. According to a knowledgeable congressional source, there was no way the Saudis could have sailed under the congressional radar screen to buy arms or services in the United States, particularly of the Peace Shield's magnitude. Maybe the Saudis had used al-Yamamah to buy arms from France or Germany, but "it sure as hell was not the way they did it with the Americans."[37]

Another, more likely explanation of the huge sums in Bandar's Riggs bank accounts starts with the realization that, under the al-Yamamah deal, the Saudis paid for the aircraft and services with oil, not cash. It was essentially an off-the-books operation bypassing the Saudi budgetary process. The amount of oil, in the hundreds of thousands of barrels, was fixed, but the price was not, leading to endless arguments. In times of low oil prices, the Saudis were hard put to meet the annual bill. In 1994, for example, when a barrel of oil brought around fifteen dollars, the Saudis could not even meet the government's own operating budget which had to be cut by 20 percent.

That year, they had to turn over five hundred thousand barrels a day to Britain to pay for the warplanes.[38] But in other years, oil prices were considerably higher, and before long the Defence Export Sales Organisation, which handled the oil sales, found itself with a surplus. Some of that surplus was "parked" in accounts at Riggs belonging to the Saudi Defense Ministry. Bandar, who had access to those accounts, could tap them to finance both embassy costs and some of his own personal ones, according to this explanation, which still leaves many unanswered questions.[39] Why would the Saudi embassy's costs be covered by the Saudi Defense Ministry rather than the Saudi Foreign Affairs Ministry? Why should the Defense Ministry be paying for Bandar's personal expenses? Was there really no difference between royal family and government expenditures?

Bandar, his family, and his close friends had been the target since 2004 of British media reports about the alleged corrupt practices stemming from al-Yamamah. A BBC report that year presented evidence that Prince Turki bin Nasser, whose son was married to Bandar's daughter Reema, had been a major beneficiary of a BAE Systems secret slush fund estimated at sixty million pounds, set up to provide various services for those senior Saudi royals involved in the deal and their families. Turki had been Saudi Royal Air Force chief, overseer of the al-Yamamah plane purchases, and a lifelong friend of Bandar's. The fund was used to pay for the family's hotels, limousines, air flights, exotic holidays, gift shopping, and security details.[40] In 2007 the *Sunday Times* alleged that BAE had also paid five hundred thousand dollars to cover the expenses of Princess Reema and Prince Faisal bin Turki's six-week-long Asia honeymoon in 1996, which included fourteen thousand dollars to take over a private club in Sydney, Australia, for one night so they could watch a Dallas Cowboys game live.[41] Like Bandar, Faisal was an avid Cowboys fan. BAE continued to deny all these allegations, but the reek of corruption oozing from al-Yamamah grew stronger and stronger, and Bandar's name was ever more frequently mentioned.

In June 2007, the U.S. Justice Department launched its own investigation into the allegations of BAE kickbacks to Bandar and others in possible violation of U.S. antibribery laws. In September that year, an unlikely lawsuit was filed in the U.S. District Court for the District of Columbia by the City of Harper Woods Employees' Retirement System in Michigan, which held BAE shares. The pension fund lawsuit alleged that the British firm had violated U.S. antibribery laws and engaged in activities damaging its business and reputation to the detriment of its shareholders. Basing its case largely on *Guardian*, BBC, and other press reports, the lawsuit alleged that BAE officials had breached their fiduciary duties by paying over two billion dollars in bribes and kickbacks to Bandar and making other improper payments to his family. (At the time of this writing, this lawsuit was still on going and therefore the allegations had yet to be adjudicated.)

THERE IS NO disputing the Saudis were slow to recognize any inspirational connection between Wahhabi Islam and al-Qaeda terrorists, including their own "deviants." After 9/11, they lived at first in a state of complete denial, and then for twenty months they circled their wagons in defense of kingdom and religion. Even bin Laden's open declaration of war against the House of Saud, broadcast on al Jazeera on February 11, 2003, failed to rouse the kingdom from its defensive, do-nothing mode. The al-Qaeda leader castigated Arab rulers and all Muslims offering any kind of assistance to the Americans in the region. He called upon true Muslims to rise up "in order to break free from the slavery of these tyrannical and apostate regimes" and "establish the rule of Allah on earth." Saudi Arabia was among those named as "ready for liberation."[42] Not until the bombings that May of three compounds in Riyadh housing foreigners did the Saudis begin to take the terrorism threat seriously. In the words of Robert Jordan, the U.S. ambassador to Saudi Arabia at the time, the May attacks, which killed thirty-five people, including nine Americans and nine suicide bombers, were the kingdom's Pearl Harbor.[43] One of the compounds hit belonged to the Vinnell Corporation, the U.S. company involved in training the Saudi Arabia National Guard under Crown Prince Abdullah's command. The bombers had targeted a perfect symbol of the U.S.-Saudi alliance.

Jordan was livid over the lack of adequate Saudi protection for the compounds. He had sent the Saudi interior minister, Prince Naif, three letters over the previous two weeks, the last just two days before the May 12 bombings, asking for more guards. "I obviously would have preferred a quicker response to our requests for additional security," he told NBC in a live broadcast from Riyadh two days later. There had been a plan to increase security, but the Saudis had "some way to go on that quite frankly."[44] Jordan's public criticism of the Saudi performance was the beginning of his end in the kingdom—yet another example of an American ambassador who fell victim to royal wrath. His public comments particularly angered Naif, whom Jordan was publicly blaming for the failure.

But his downfall was probably sealed by other remarks he was reported to have made at a private dinner party in early July 2003. According to the London Arabic daily *Al-Quds al-Arabi*, the ambassador had suggested it was time for Abdullah to replace the long-ailing Fahd as king and for the royal family to choose a younger prince than Sultan, Bandar's father, as the next heir apparent.[45] The same month, Jordan submitted his resignation after serving less than two years. He left in mid-October amid a flurry of unconvincing formal denials by both U.S. and Saudi officials that he had been expelled.[46]

One day after the May 12 attacks, a furious Abdullah vowed "to confront and destroy the threat posed by a deviant few and those who endorse or support them. With the help of God Almighty, we shall prevail."[47] The attack, according to CIA director George Tenet, had "brought the message home to the royal family in a way nothing else had."[48] He flew immediately to Riyadh to brief Abdullah on the agency's assessment of the dire al-Qaeda threat facing the family. His mission bore a strong resemblance to that of top U.S. Pentagon officials who had gone to see Fahd after Saddam's invasion of Kuwait in August 1990 with the aim of gaining the king's permission for American troops to enter the kingdom. Once again, Bandar was present acting as interpreter and had already pressed Tenet to "lay everything on the line" to convince Abdullah to join forces with Bush.[49]

Tenet's briefing was a terrifying account of what awaited the royal family. Al-Qaeda had decided to make the prime objective of its worldwide jihad the overthrow of the House of Saud. It was prepared to assassinate royal family members and hit key oil targets to paralyze the economy. The kingdom was in the same position as the United States prior to 9/11, only it was a lot worse because al-Qaeda operatives were all over the kingdom planning and plotting. Furthermore, some of them were using the kingdom as a base for planning attacks against the United States.[50] According to Tenet, his briefing energized Abdullah and the royal family into launching their own immediate war on terrorism.

In truth, Abdullah had little choice. Al-Qaeda had indeed launched its war against the House of Saud, and the compound bombings had been just the opening shots. The entire·kingdom was about to become an open battlefield. There would be shoot-outs in the streets of Riyadh and Jeddah, running gun battles with terrorists in cars, sieges of hideouts in desert villages, kidnappings and assassinations of Westerners, and attacks on government buildings in broad daylight. Some battles lasted for three days. The Saudis published a list of the twenty-six "Most Wanted" terrorists and proceeded to track them down one by one. When most had been caught or killed, they published another list of twenty-six names. They uncovered secret cells all over the kingdom involving several hundreds of al-Qaeda operatives. They even discovered that al-Qaeda had set up a number of desert training camps that somehow had gone undetected by Saudi security services.[51]

In November 2003, al-Qaeda operatives managed to set off another huge truck bomb at a fourth compound in Riyadh, this one housing mostly Arabs, which killed another 17 people and injured 120. By April 2004, the U.S. embassy had ordered all nonessential personnel to leave. The following month, terrorists infiltrated the Oasis Resort compound, a residential site for oil workers in Khobar, in eastern Saudi Arabia, and killed 22 people, including 19 foreigners, then managed to escape the Saudi siege of the site. Other terrorists kidnapped and killed three Americans working for U.S. companies, beheading one of them. A BBC cameraman was killed and another wounded.

The Khobar attack inspired Bandar to call for a "general mobilization for war" and the launching of a national jihad against all Wahhabi deviants in the kingdom. "War means war," he wrote in the Saudi newspaper *Al-Watan*. "It does not mean Boy Scout camp." The war would be brutal, he warned, but had to be pursued until all extremists were eliminated. He expressed concern that Saudis did not fully appreciate the seriousness of the situation or the possibility that the deviants might prevail. Bandar noted that there was a precedent in Saudi history for taking such an uncompromising stand—the battle of al-Sabla in 1929, where the kingdom's founding father, King Abdulaziz, had crushed Wahhabi zealots who were part of his army fighting to unify the country but were opposed to his alliance with the British and introduction of modern technology, namely the telephone. Citing the Koran, Bandar exhorted the royal family and all Saudis to "obey the honored directive of Allah and kill those who spread corruption in the land." The prince's war proclamation appeared a few days later as an op-ed in the *Washington Post*.[52]

In early December 2004, al-Qaeda brazenly attacked the U.S. Consulate in Jeddah, breaching the gates, occupying parts of the sprawling compound, and killing five locally employed staff and a Saudi guard, though no Americans. Later that month, they also bombed the Saudi Interior Ministry and a special forces training center. Some idea of the scope of this largely urban warfare emerged from the tally of casualties made public by Interior Minister Naif in July 2005: 91 foreigners and Saudi civilians killed and 510 wounded; 41 security force members killed and 218 wounded; 112 terrorists killed and 25 wounded.[53]

Many other signs signaled the new attitude in Riyadh after the May 12 bombings. Saudi authorities issued a ban on boxes for collecting donations at mosques and other public places, whose proceeds might be used to finance terrorist causes. They also introduced new banking regulations forbidding charities from transferring funds abroad. In February 2004, King Fahd issued a decree establishing a government-run Commission on Relief and Charity Work Abroad to administer and control all private Saudi activity. That June, the Saudis shut down al-Haramain's headquarters in Riyadh.

U.S.-Saudi cooperation began taking on substance, too. The Saudis agreed to establish a Joint U.S.-Saudi Task Force on Terrorism and a Financial Intelligence Unit to work with similar groups in other countries tracking suspected terrorist financing. Saudis whose names appeared on both the U.N. and U.S. lists of global terrorists had their bank accounts frozen and sometimes their passports lifted. The 9/11 Commission reported that "more than 40" Saudis suspected of links to terrorism saw their accounts closed down.[54] The FBI was allowed to open an office in Riyadh, and the National Security Agency began making available to Saudi security agencies real-time electronic intelligence on the movements of suspected terrorists. After two years of steady complaints about the lack of Saudi cooperation, FBI and other U.S. government officials by mid-2004 were telling Congress of definite signs of progress in working with the Saudis.[55]

Some U.S. officials, particularly at the Treasury Department, continued to express frustration. The Saudis had refused to treat the Muslim World League, the Islamic International Relief Organization (IIRO), and the World Assembly of Muslim Youth like other charities even though the three had their headquarters in the kingdom. The rationale offered was that these groups were "international" and could not be subjected to Saudi fiat. They also argued that foreign-based Saudi charities, such as al-Muntada al-Islami, operating out of London, could not be regulated, nor could transactions between different branches of Saudi charities outside the kingdom. Using as an example the IIRO, Treasury official Daniel Glaser chided the Saudis before Congress in November 2005, saying that they "must take care not only of what happened in IIRO Riyadh, but they must also be concerned with what transpires in every other IIRO office around the world." Organizations so closely associated with Saudi Arabia were "de facto Saudi responsibility" and had to become a focus of Saudi foreign policy.[56]

Less understandable was why the Saudi government had not succeeded by late 2007 in launching its promised Commission on Relief and Charity Work Abroad. Its creation had been announced in February 2004 and publicly promenaded in Washington that June as certain proof of Saudi cooperation in the war on terrorist financing. Stuart Levey, the Treasury Department's undersecretary for terrorism and financial intelligence, cited this commission as a perfect example of the "real lag time between what they [said] they were going to do and what they [did]."[57] Also as of late 2007, the Saudis still had not prosecuted any Saudi formally designated by the United States and the United Nations as a global terrorist. The most they had done was to freeze some bank accounts. Finally, a common complaint of U.S. authorities was that the Saudi government was not taking sufficient action to monitor and prevent individual Saudis from serving as donors and even couriers of funds. Levey complained to Congress that the Saudi government was doing little to locate and stop "those deep pocket [Saudi] donors . . . still funding terrorism abroad." Private Saudi funds were still going to terrorist groups in Iraq, Southeast Asia, and "other places where there are terrorists."[58]

PERHAPS THE MOST innovative action the Saudis undertook in their war on terrorism inside the kingdom was a campaign to rein in Wahhabi zealots by combating the ideology inspiring them. It took on the dimensions of a national detoxification program as the government sought to cleanse the nation's mind and soul of neo-Wahhabism, that highly toxic mixture of Wahhabi fundamentalism and Muslim Brotherhood political activism. The official clergy began speaking out on Saudi TV and radio in condemnation of al-Qaeda's perversion of Islam to justify terrorism. They resorted to theological arguments and Koranic verses to combat bin Laden's justification for jihad, branding his followers as dangerous "deviants" who had discredited the true meaning of Wahhabism. They fought to take back their religion from the spiritual gurus of Islamic terrorists. At the same time, the Islamic Affairs Ministry purged radical preachers from the mosques, imprisoning some and sending others to reeducation schools. At the end of May 2003, the ministry announced it had sacked forty-four mosque preachers, 160 imams, and 149 prayer callers. Another 1,357 of them had been suspended from their duties and ordered to undergo religious retraining, and 900 more were suspended over the next ten months.[59] The number of dismissals and suspensions was impressive, but still only a tiny fraction of the eighty thousand imams and preachers at the kingdom's fifty thousand mosques.

Before long, the Saudi hearts-and-minds campaign turned to the *jihadis* themselves, the real holy warriors. The Interior and Islamic Affairs ministries devised a program based on what Egypt had done with one of its extremist groups, Gamaat Islamiya, whose leaders had been convinced to renounce terrorism after exhaustive theological debates carried on inside prison. Interior Ministry officials tracked down hundreds of Saudi *jihadis* or would-be *jihadis*, partly by tapping into extremist Web sites, and engaged them in theological debate. They discovered that cyberspace had become a virtual battlefield and the main one in their struggle to combat al-Qaeda ideology. The two ministries set up a counseling committee with twenty-two full-time members, helped by one hundred clerics and thirty psychiatrists. Through their interviews with 639 prisoners, they already knew Saudis were being influenced as much by foreign Islamic scholars, like the Palestinian Jordanian Sheikh Abu Muhammed al-Maqdisi, as by bin Laden.[60]

Three clerics involved with the reeducation program said they had succeeded in establishing a dialogue through Web sites with 800 al-Qaeda sympathizers and believed that as of May 2006 they had changed the minds of about 250. Most of their clients for reeducation, though, were Saudis being held in jail. The program there required them to take part in sessions on theology, where they underwent a kind of reverse brainwashing, often at the hands of ex-radical clerics like Sheikh Salman al-Audah and Sheikh Safar al-Hawali. Both these leaders of the militant Islamic Awakening movement, after recanting many of their own extremist views, had agreed to help in the reeducation program, which involved a grueling process: Almost daily, sometimes for months, three clerics and a psychiatrist engaged just one prisoner at a time until he saw the error of his ways. Each was obliged to pass a theological exam before he could be released. By November 2007, Saudi authorities were claiming the campaign a major success: Fifteen hundred youths out of thirty-two hundred arrested and offered counseling had repented.[61] Graduates were released back into society and helped to find jobs, housing, and in some cases even wives. Saudi authorities claimed that none of those released had reverted to terrorism, but they kept them under close surveillance.[62]

Yet the overall impact of this reeducation campaign remained unclear even to Saudi authorities. Lieutenant General Mansour al-Turki, spokesman for the Interior Ministry, conceded in 2006 that the government was having great difficulty in staunching al-Qaeda's appeal among Saudi youth. They were subjected daily to television, radio, and Internet accounts of the resistance to the U.S. occupation in Iraq and the Palestinian intifada in Israel. A host of militant clerics, foreign and Saudi, were perpetually urging the youth to go fight the Western infidel invasion of the Muslim world. Hundreds of Saudis were making their way to Iraq to join the resistance. As long as these conditions prevailed, the call to jihad would always find new recruits.[63] One of the clerics involved in the government's program, Sheikh Abdul Mohsen al-Obeikan, compared the challenge of combating neo-Wahhabism in the kingdom to the war on drugs in the United States: As soon as one terrorist cell or group was eliminated, another popped up.[64] Prince Naif admitted in mid-2007 that the campaign continued to face an uphill struggle and chastised the Wahhabi establishment for its lukewarm commitment. "We need greater efforts from religious scholars, sheikhs, thinkers and people working in educational institutions," but "unfortunately these efforts have not yet been seen."[65]

Beyond the kingdom's borders, efforts against religious extremism were tempered by the kingdom's missionary zeal and the ever-worsening rivalry with Shiite Iran. Islamic Affairs minister Saleh al-Sheikh claimed his ministry was checking the scholarly credentials of the thousands of Saudi-financed missionaries working abroad and firing those who were without a higher theological degree.[66] It had also stopped funding Pakistan's madrassas, religious schools that had become hotbeds of extremism and jihad recruiting centers. But there was no renouncing of the kingdom's central mission—*dawah*, spreading the call to Wahhabi Islam worldwide. The astute British ambassador in Riyadh in 2004, Sherard Cowper-Coles, put it this way: "For Saudi Arabia to stop *dawah* would be a negation of itself. It would be like Bush telling the evangelical Christians to stop missionary work abroad."[67] So long as the kingdom's *dawah* mission continues to produce neo-Wahhabi militants, however, the massive soft power of the Saudi state will pose a serious challenge to redefining the U.S.-Saudi relationship.

CHAPTER 13

"Just Say No"

PRINCE BANDAR'S "AMERICA FIRST" POLICY disintegrated in stages following the attacks of 9/11. While Americans addressed the question "Saudi Arabia: Friend or Foe?" Saudis found themselves asking the same question of America, not fathoming how the kingdom, one of the United States' closest and oldest Arab allies, could possibly be described, as it was in July 2002 by a Pentagon adviser, as "the kernel of evil, the prime mover, the most dangerous opponent" Washington faced in the Middle East.[1] The Saudis, for their part, adopted a new motto toward incessant White House, Pentagon, and State Department demands for help. In the words of one of King Abdullah's advisers, "We just say no."

The underpinnings of the special relationship were knocked out one by one by the Saudis, starting with the U.S. military presence in the kingdom. Bandar was the bearer of the bad news, conveying the message that Saudi rulers believed the U.S. military had "overstayed its welcome" and that new forms of cooperation needed to be devised that were less conspicuous. Nothing would be done precipitously to force the United States out, in order to avoid the impression that the Saudis were responding to Osama bin Laden's diatribes against the American presence. But the Americans had promised to leave as soon as the job was done at the start of the first Gulf War, and the Saudi leadership wanted the U.S. Air Force to stop using Prince Sultan Air Base, which it had occupied since leaving Dhahran as a result of the 1996 Khobar Towers bombing. Abdullah had led the faction within the royal family arguing that the kingdom would be safer without a U.S. military presence, and he had at least one ally in Congress, Senator Carl Levin, a Democrat from Michigan and the chairman of the Armed Services Committee. "We need a base in that region, but it seems to me we should find a place that is more hospitable . . . I don't think they want us to stay there."[2]

The Pentagon was dismayed, however. In mid-2001, it had completed building the Combined Air Operations Center at the base to manage operations over Iraq, Afghanistan, or anywhere else in the Persian Gulf region— "the most sophisticated air command post" anywhere in the world and "the key to how the Air Force operates today," in the words of one Pentagon reporter who visited the site.[3] The heavily guarded, squat building contained computers gathering electronic intelligence from satellites, U-2 spy planes, and Predator reconnaissance aircraft that was used to provide targeting information for U.S. pilots. The base also housed F-15 fighter jets, EA-6B Prowler airborne electronic jammers, KC-135 aerial refueling tankers, and AWACS command-and-control aircraft. The operations center had coordinated the air war for the U.S. campaign to overthrow Afghanistan's Taliban regime in the fall of 2001 and was slated to do the same for the invasion of Iraq to overthrow Saddam Hussein, which was already in the offing.

Abdullah, however, was dead set against it. After a testy meeting with Bush at his ranch in Crawford, Texas, in August 2002, the crown prince said through his spokesman and Bandar's deputy, Adel al-Jubeir, "There is no country in the world that supports it. There is no legal basis for it. There is no international sanction for it. There is no coalition for it."[4] Vice President Cheney had just made a speech justifying military action against Saddam, and al-Jubeir made the rounds of TV newscasts with a point-by-point rebuttal of Cheney's speech. The Saudi spokesman called his effort "preempting an attack against Iraq."[5] Abdullah himself had warned Cheney before meeting with Bush to stop spreading rumors that Abdullah was privately in favor of a war to oust Saddam. "No. The answer is no. I said 'No' in Saudi Arabia. I say 'No' now and I will say 'No' tomorrow," he bluntly told Cheney.[6]

One Saudi royal, however, was very much in favor of the war: Prince Bandar. And he was the one spreading the rumors of Saudi backing for U.S. military action to topple the Iraqi dictator even as he was delivering Abdullah's message that the air force should evacuate Prince Sultan Air Base. He bore a personal grudge against Saddam for his duplicity leading up to the first Gulf

War, when the Iraqi dictator had assured the prince he had no intention of invading Kuwait. Saddam had made a fool of Bandar and even used him to deliver his false reassurance to Prime Minister Margaret Thatcher of Great Britain and President George H. W. Bush. Bandar had confidently delivered these assurances only a few days before Iraqi troops had crossed the border on their two-day blitzkrieg to swallow up the neighboring country. The prince also believed Saddam had put out a contract to have him assassinated.

Bandar had been a prime promoter of a mid-1990s covert operation to kill Saddam in a palace coup using disaffected Iraqi military officers. The Saudis were supporting the opposition Iraqi National Accord (INA), which was led by Ayad Allawi, who was allegedly in contact with these dissident officers. Allawi was a former Baath Party official and a secular Shiite who had fallen out with Saddam, fled Iraq, and tried to organize an opposition from London during the 1990s. He was almost assassinated there for his efforts. Allawi became the great hope of the intelligence services of Saudi Arabia, the United States, and Jordan, who were working together to promote Allawi's palace coup. But Saddam's highly effective security people infiltrated the plot and in June 1996 arrested and executed more than one hundred INA officers. Bandar was frustrated by the INA's failures, but even more so by what he considered to be President Clinton's dithering over what to do about Saddam. As soon as George W. Bush came into office, the prince began pushing him to be more decisive. Bandar told the new U.S. president, who invited him to Crawford at the end of August 2002, after Abdullah's visit, that Clinton's policy of containment was bankrupt and that there should be no compromise with Saddam. He also advised Bush not to believe the public comments of Arab leaders who said they opposed military action against the Iraqi dictator.[7]

From August 2002 until the outbreak of war in March 2003, Bandar served as a de facto member of the U.S. neoconservatives' "war party." He argued that since Bush was determined to take action, there was nothing the Saudis could do to prevent it. The question for him was "What can I do to maximize my national interest?" In any case, he believed Saudi and U.S. interests were identical in the case of Saddam; both countries wanted to get rid of him.[8] As early as January 11, 2003, Cheney, the administration's leading hawk, and Secretary of Defense Donald Rumsfeld called Bandar in to brief him on the secret war plan and assure him that Saddam would be overthrown, in fact alerting him to Bush's decision to go to war even before

Secretary of State Colin Powell.[9] But Bandar did more than press Bush for action. In the months leading up to the war's outbreak, he lobbied the U.S. media on behalf of the administration. He even sought to convince reporters of the heatedly contested proposition that Saddam was linked to al-Qaeda and backing its terrorist campaign, encouraging the allegation that became one of the main rationales the Bush administration put forth to convince the American public of the need to go to war; he even used ambiguous U.S. intelligence information to bolster his argument.[10]

Even the CIA didn't believe there was a connection between Saddam and al-Qaeda. In its final report on this issue before the war, published in late January 2003, the agency concluded that there were three "areas of concern" regarding Iraq as a safe haven for terrorists. But CIA analysts "could not translate this data into a relationship where these two entities had ever moved beyond seeking ways to take advantage of each other."[11] Bin Laden operatives were using a camp in northeastern Iraq run by Kurdish Islamists under the Jordanian al-Qaeda leader Abu Musab al-Zarqawi, but the site was in an area beyond the Iraqi government's control, along the Iranian border in Kurdistan. Meanwhile, the CIA had also found "absolutely no linkage between Saddam and 9/11."[12]

But the CIA's assessment did not stop the Bush neocons, or Bandar, from pressing Saddam's terrorist connections in their argument for war, and Bandar's argument for joining the bandwagon finally prevailed at the royal court, at least partly. There would be no public backing of Bush's war to take out Saddam, and U.S. fighter planes would not be allowed to fly from Saudi Arabia. But the Saudis did make available their airports at Arrar and Tabuk, near the Iraqi border, for U.S. Special Forces teams to operate inside Iraq. They also permitted the Pentagon to use the Combined Air Operations Center at Prince Sultan Air Base to coordinate the massive air campaign, involving two thousand planes and forty-six thousand missions, during the brief war to oust Saddam in March and April 2003.[13] The U.S. military presence inside the kingdom doubled to ten thousand personnel during the Iraqi campaign.

As soon as the war was over, however, the Americans were sent packing. Rumsfeld made the announcement of the U.S. departure three weeks after Saddam's overthrow while visiting the air base on a postwar tour of the region to assess the new regional security situation. Prince Sultan, the Saudi defense minister, said there was "no need for [U.S. forces] to remain" while pretending it was the Americans themselves who had decided to leave, not the Saudis who had asked them to.[14]

Actually, the Pentagon had begun making plans to leave well in advance. U.S. war planners had never been sure the Saudis would allow access to Prince Sultan Air Base after the restrictions put on the American military during the campaign to overthrow the Taliban government in the fall of 2001. At that time, the Pentagon had started installing the infrastructure for an alternative command post at the French-built al-Udeid Air Base in Qatar as a backup to Prince Sultan Air Base, and a year before the Iraq war it had quietly built a tent city there that was housing two thousand Americans.[15] Unlike the Saudis, the Qataris welcomed the U.S. military with open arms and placed no restrictions on the "rules of engagement" for U.S. warplanes operating from there. By the end of the summer of 2003, the Pentagon had closed down the operations center in Saudi Arabia, and the last Americans had left the air base.

The Saudis also sent the major American oil companies packing in the wake of the Iraq war. This was a huge defeat for Bandar's personal policy of making oil the key bonding agent in the relationship. He had been the prime promoter of the plan to bring U.S. oil companies back into the kingdom. In September 1998, Abdullah asked unbelieving oil executives assembled in Bandar's sprawling residence outside Washington to submit proposals for the development of the kingdom's energy sector. Bandar and his aides were telling reporters Saudi Arabia hoped to attract up to one hundred billion dollars in new investments over all, and the "gas initiative" being announced by Abdullah was just the start. That initiative alone was expected to involve twenty billion dollars, since the Saudis wanted the companies to invest in power and desalinization plants and an expansion of the kingdom's petrochemical industry as well. Abdullah had wanted to make a splash and "smash the icons," and so he had on his first visit to Washington as the kingdom's de facto ruler.

It took time for the gas initiative to take shape. The Saudis also invited companies from Europe and elsewhere to make proposals. In June 2001, they finally announced the winners: To nobody's surprise, the Americans came out at the top of the list. The U.S. giant Exxon Mobil was chosen to lead two of three core ventures, each a consortium of companies exploring and developing gas fields around the kingdom and building related energy and power projects. Four other American firms—Phillips, Marathon,

Conoco, and Occidental—were offered a piece of the action, and so were Royal Dutch/Shell, BP, and France's TotalFinaElf. The big surprise was that Chevron, the historic founder of Aramco, had been left out. But the Americans had clearly been given priority, and the Exxon Mobil investment alone was put at twenty billion dollars. A Bandar aide explained, "If Exxon Mobil has a major investment in the Saudi oil industry, then they'll want to redeem it by pumping Saudi oil even when global demand may be soft." More important, he said, by creating a new American economic stake it "will insure that our relationship with the United States will be solid for the next 50 years."[16] Exxon Mobil was so certain it was back in business that it immediately took over seven floors in al-Faisaliah, Riyadh's most fashionable glass-and-marble skyscraper.

But Bandar's grand design for reviving the U.S.-Saudi partnership went up in smoke, victim to too grandiose a vision, stiff opposition from the state oil company, Saudi Aramco, and finally 9/11. The three core ventures proved extremely complicated, involving as they did not just gas exploration but the building of power, desalinization, and petrochemical plants. Negotiations dragged on for two years with no resolution of the financial issues, centered ostensibly on differing rates of return on huge investments. In fact, the biggest obstacle was the determined opposition of Saudi Aramco's officialdom and in particular Saudi oil minister Ali al-Naimi. In a clear example of the new power that nonroyal technocrats were amassing inside the kingdom, and of their ability to thwart the will of its al-Saud rulers, they conducted a bureaucratic stalling operation to keep the big western international oil companies out, despite Abdullah's decision to put Foreign Minister Saud al-Faisal in charge of the negotiations to assure their success.

Al-Naimi, who had spent his whole life working for Saudi Aramco, ultimately took over the negotiations and began introducing conditions that would assure their failure. The oil companies would be allowed to explore for gas only and not for the oil Bandar and his aides had indicated would be the next step. And they could not have access to Saudi Aramco's Strategic Reserve Area, where they knew they would find enough gas to make the venture profitable. When Exxon Mobil suggested it sought a 15 to 18 percent return on a sixteen-billion-dollar investment in one core venture and a five-billion-dollar investment in another, al-Naimi made clear he thought 8 to 10 percent was quite enough. The struggle became personal, with Exxon Mobil chairman Lee Raymond and al-Naimi often at loggerheads and shouting at each other in meetings. Raymond complained in a letter to King Fahd about the oil minister's hard-line negotiating tactics. Foreign Minister Saud tried to mediate between the two, even interrupting a medical trip to Los Angeles in March 2002 to diffuse one of the many crises in the negotiations. Deadlines came and went with no agreement. The oil companies did their best to unseat al-Naimi by spreading rumors that he would not be reappointed when his term expired in May 2003, hoping to get a better deal from his successor.[17] Throughout the torturous negotiating process, it was never clear whether Abdullah was backing al-Naimi's tough tactics, but the crown prince did nothing to rein him in.

By the spring of 2003, the fallout from 9/11 had so poisoned the U.S.-Saudi relationship that both sides were questioning whether the other was friend or foe. The atmosphere was hardly conducive to the royal family's announcing it was allowing America's giant oil companies to put their hands on the kingdom's crown jewels. The signal that Abdullah, de facto king because of Fahd's advanced illness, had unalterably changed his mind came on April 30. To the considerable shock of the oil companies, al-Naimi was reconfirmed as oil minister in a long-awaited cabinet reshuffle. They had expected him to be removed not only because of his hard line in the negotiations but because he had already served two four-year stints as minister. Yet not only was al-Naimi reappointed, but this mild-mannered Saudi commoner was made sole negotiator with the oil companies. On May 20, he met for a last time with Exxon Mobil's Raymond and with Philip Watts, chairman of Royal Dutch/Shell, the leader of the third core venture. The oil minister gave them a final take-it-or-leave-it proposal with a deadline of June 4. There would be no access given to the Strategic Reserve Area to help assure higher returns. When no answer came, he let them know the very next day that the negotiations were over.

So what had the Bush administration done to help American oil companies regain a toehold in the world's most coveted oil fields? Were not the House of Bush and the House of Saud linked in a secret relationship based on mutual oil interests and close personal ties between the two families? This had become general popular mythology in America after 9/11.[18] But in the case of the biggest gas, and potentially oil, deal early in the twenty-first century, it had turned out to be just that—mythology. So far, no evidence has come to light that either Bush the father or Bush the son weighed in to pressure the Saudis to help America's Big Oil. A senior Saudi Oil Ministry

official involved in the talks said he could recall no U.S. government intervention on behalf of the companies.[19] Instead, Foreign Minister Saud,
whose own commitment and reputation were on the line, had led the effort
to salvage the negotiations. President Bush was preoccupied elsewhere. During the last six months of the negotiations, he had become totally engrossed
in promoting his war against Saddam Hussein.

If anything, Bush may have been the decisive factor in convincing Abdullah to slam the door shut on the American companies. Bush had gone to the
Egyptian Red Sea resort of Sharm al-Sheikh for a summit on June 3 with
four Arab leaders, including Abdullah, in a bid to relaunch the Middle East
peace process and obtain their support for the U.S. war on terrorism. Bush's
trip was seen as his first major effort after two and a half years in office to
respond to Arab pressure, particularly from the Saudis, to become engaged
in the so-called road map for solving the Israeli-Palestinian issue on the basis of an independent Palestinian state. Bush had committed to this after
9/11, but had done nothing to make it happen. So the Sharm al-Sheikh summit was big news. The following day, another meeting took place in Aqaba,
Jordan, where Prime Minister Ariel Sharon and the new Palestinian prime
minister, Mahmoud Abbas, met for the first time to talk peace.

But all did not go well in Sharm al-Sheikh. The Saudi crown prince
balked when Bush tried to get him to sign on to a joint statement supporting
the normalization of ties with Israel. In the middle of the fray was Prince
Bandar. He had delivered the Saudi message back in Washington that there
could be no normalization until agreement was reached on the Palestinian
issue. The summit's start was delayed for two hours while the participants
wrangled over what to do. The Arab press called it a "24-hour crisis" between Bush and Abdullah that almost provoked the crown prince into going
home early.[20] Finally, no joint statement was possible. The four Arab leaders
issued their own, while Abdullah made no public pronouncements before,
during, or after the meeting and flew home that night "in a fury."[21] The next
day, al-Naimi sent his letter to the oil companies telling them to go home.

The Saudis subsequently made it abundantly clear that they had every in-
tention of working with other partners than the Americans. They invited
fifty international oil companies to submit new bids for just gas exploration.
In November 2003, they entered into a three-way partnership with Royal
Dutch/Shell and TotalFinaElf to explore for gas in the south of the desolate
Rub' al-Khali (empty quarter). The following January, they announced the

winners of the new competition for gas exploration and production in the northern part of the region. The results came as a shock and marked unequivocally the end of hopes for a new special relationship between U.S. oil companies and the kingdom. The main winners—Russia's Lukoil, China's Sinopec, Italy's ENI, and Spain's Repsol YPF—were all newcomers to Saudi Arabia, and most surprising was the entry of Russia and China into an oil patch long dominated by U.S. firms. Exxon Mobil had not even participated in the new round of bidding, but Chevron/Texaco had and still lost out. In March 2004, Saudi Aramco finally formed three partnerships, keeping a 20 percent interest for itself in each. Lukoil president Vagit Alekperov was jubilant at the signing ceremony. "For the first time in the history of bilateral relations the doors to Saudi Arabia have been opened to the Russian petroleum business community."[22]

THE SAUDI "JUST say no" attitude to Bush's Washington did not stop with the U.S. military and the oil companies. It extended even more emphatically to Bush himself as he sought to hoist the banner of democracy over the Middle East, starting with Iraq. Bush was just as determined to export democracy to the Arab world as the Saudis were to export Wahhabi Islam. His campaign laid bare one more glaring contradiction in the strategic objectives of the two former allies, highlighting particularly how far apart they were in their world missions and ideologies.

In a speech at the National Endowment for Democracy in Washington in November 2003, Bush declared that the United States was ending sixty years of Western nations "excusing and accommodating the lack of freedom in the Middle East." He announced a new U.S. policy he called "a forward strategy of freedom," and his description of what made for successful societies was the antithesis of Saudi Arabia. Bush hailed those cultures that allowed for healthy civic institutions, political parties, labor unions, and an independent media; punished official corruption; recognized the rights of women; and guaranteed religious freedom. The kingdom did not permit any of those bodies to function; royal corruption was common; freedom of religion (other than for Wahhabi Islam) was nonexistent; and the rights of women were limited. Bush said he was determined to do something about the "freedom deficit" in the Arab world and urged the royal family to show "true leadership" by giving Saudis a greater voice in government.[23]

Bush's "freedom speech" represented a fundamental shift in what had been a U.S. policy of ignoring the state of Saudi internal politics, an attitude that dated back to the start of the special relationship in 1945. All U.S. administrations, except that of President Kennedy, had carefully avoided criticizing the lack of freedoms inside the kingdom. (Kennedy had pushed for an end to slavery.) Prior to the first Gulf War, when the huge American troop presence had forced both sides to begin dealing with their conflicting cultures, the tens of thousands of Americans who had worked and lived in the kingdom over the years had been told to hold their noses, adjust to the Wahhabi-imposed lifestyle and the Saud-dictated lack of American-style freedoms, or leave.[24] Now Bush was changing the terms of the U.S.-Saudi compact. For the first time, an American president was insisting publicly on democratic reforms inside Saudi Arabia.

Bush kept up a steady drumbeat on behalf of his newfound democracy-export "mission." In his State of the Union Address in January 2004, he linked the need for greater freedom in the Middle East to success in his war on terrorism and thus to America's national security. "As long as the Middle East remains a place of tyranny and despair and anger, it will continue to produce men and movements that threaten the safety of America and our friends," he said. His "forward strategy of freedom," he added, was meant to be a challenge to those opposing reform in the region and a warning that he would demand "a higher standard from our friends."[25] When word leaked out the following month that the Bush administration was preparing a Greater Middle East Initiative, which it hoped the G-8 summit at Sea Island, on the Georgia coast, would endorse in June, America's two most important "friends" in the Arab world, Saudi Arabia and Egypt, went into high gear to block it.

Egyptian president Hosni Mubarak flew to Riyadh to see Crown Prince Abdullah and coordinate a counteroffensive. Mubarak declared himself ready to "forcefully reject" what he called "the ready-for-use prescriptions proposed abroad under the cover of what are called reforms and attempts to impose them on the region."[26] In a joint statement after their meeting on February 24, the two Arab leaders joined hands in denouncing the Bush initiative and counterattacked by calling for a speedy end to the U.S. occupation of Iraq. In early March, the entire Saudi cabinet condemned Bush's initiative. Choosing its words carefully, the Saudi leadership said that Arab states would take their own "path of development, modernization and reform" in keeping with their "Arab identity," and it carefully avoided any use of the term "democracy."[27] What particularly alarmed the Saudis and Egyptians was that U.S. officials, in explaining Bush's initiative, claimed that the model was the 1975 Helsinki Accords, which had promoted human rights and political change inside the Soviet Union. "The results on the Soviet Union we all know," said the Princeton-educated Saudi foreign minister, Prince Saud. "It was broken up. It suffered economic deprivations, its people the unhappiest people for at least two decades . . . We really don't see much lure in the Helsinki Accords."[28]

Not only did the House of Saud resoundingly reject Bush's initiative, but it began a crackdown on Saudi agitation for more democracy that had heretofore been mostly confined to an onslaught of petitions sent to Abdullah. In mid-March 2004, Saudi security forces rounded up eleven well-known academics, reform activists, and lawyers who had just submitted a request to the government to form an independent human rights organization. Most of them had been signatories of a petition sent to Abdullah the previous December calling for a constitutional monarchy, and they had continued to press for elections and other reforms. The arrests marked the end of what some Saudi reformers had dubbed their "Riyadh Spring" after the 1968 Prague Spring reform period in Czechoslovakia. Its death knell was rung so that Washington could hear it loud and clear.

Four days after the reformers' arrests, Secretary of State Colin Powell arrived for a visit to the kingdom. He could hardly avoid the issue of reform or the arrests. Indeed, at a press conference during his visit Powell said he had had "a very long discussion" with Abdullah about Bush's new "forward strategy of freedom" in the Middle East. Quickly, however, he appeared to back off. At the awkward joint appearance with Saudi foreign minister Saud, Powell said he had reassured Abdullah that Bush agreed that "reform has to come from within the region, it can't be imposed from outside." And the United States also agreed that each nation had to proceed at its own speed. He had expressed U.S. "concern" over the arrests of the eleven reformers, he said, but he downplayed their significance. Four had already been released, and just "procedural and legal issues" remained to be resolved before the others would be too.[29]

Hard-nosed interior minister Prince Naif, who was spearheading the crackdown, was insisting that the detainees renounce all political activities as a condition for release. Saud, embarrassed by the timing of the arrests, still had to defend Naif's action. The eleven reformers had sought to sow discord within Saudi society while national unity was essential in the face of the terrorist threat. They had also added the names of some Saudis to their petitions under false pretenses.[30] Four of the remaining seven still in detention eventually signed a statement forswearing any further political activity. The final three were sentenced to six to nine years in prison after a secret trial in May 2005.*

AWAY FROM THE limelight, another drama was unfolding in the same Saudi crackdown on reform, this time in the Red Sea port of Jeddah. There, the U.S. consul general, Gina Abercrombie-Winstanley, had been reaching out to the reformers in unique ways. Her unusual style of diplomacy was the talk of the city, and she even gained kingdom-wide attention after the Saudi media picked up the story of her confrontation with two Wahhabi religious policemen from the Haya'a, the Commission for the Promotion of Virtue and Prevention of Vice, while on a visit to Riyadh. They had tried to bar her from entering a restaurant for not wearing the abaya, or black cloak, that all Saudi women are obliged to don in public. She had identified herself as an American diplomat and thus exempt from wearing an abaya. In response, one of the policemen had spit on his hand and wiped the sole of his foot to show how little he respected her diplomatic status. She could not go into the restaurant, period. When the owner of the restaurant had tried to help her, the two *mutawwa'in* had ordered that it be shut down. Abercrombie-Winstanley had reported the incident to the Interior Ministry and eventually received an apology.[31]

The forthright consul general engaged in several nonconventional diplomatic ways to reach out to Saudi reformers. She went online to answer questions about U.S. policies, tapping into the popular Saudi Internet site Al-Saha to exchange views with America's detractors. She took to attending the *majlis*, or "private salon," of Saudi reformers. Accused by Wahhabi clerics of encouraging Saudi women to throw away the hijab, or face veil, she wanted to make it clear she had done no such thing. So she posted a clarification

---

* One of Abdullah's first acts upon becoming king after Fahd's death in August of that year was to grant the last three reformers an amnesty. But in February 2007, ten others were arrested, this time on charges of collecting funds for suspected terrorists.

on Al-Saha stating, "I'm not for the hijab or against the hijab. I do believe that women should have a choice whether to cover, and I respect the choices made by women one way or another."[32] She did confirm, however, that she had twice attended the *majlis* of Mohammed Said Tayeb, a human rights activist and one of the eleven reformers arrested in March 2004.

Abercrombie-Winstanley's participation in Saudi discussion groups and Internet chat programs before long caught the attention of Saudi security officials. After one of her visits to Tayeb's *majlis*, King Fahd's own son, Abdulaziz bin Fahd, dropped by to counter her presence and message, making clear to the fifty or so people gathered there that the government thought it was "inappropriate" for an American diplomat to be attending Tayeb's salon. Abdulaziz told them to stop listening to her because she was about to return home, which wasn't true.

The king's son wasn't the only one trying to put distance between the consul general and Saudi reformers. Prince Naif also warned Tayeb to stop inviting her to his home. At a meeting with a dozen reformers on March 22, Naif denounced them as "agents of America" and warned that the government was "not weak" and that the United States would not protect them. The al-Sauds had come to power "by the sword" and they were not afraid to use it in order to stay there.[33] He reiterated that one reason for arresting the eleven reformers had been to put a stop to their contacts with American diplomats. Abdulaziz and Naif had delivered the al-Saud family message for all Saudis to hear: America's promotion of democracy in Saudi Arabia would not be tolerated.

CHAPTER 14

The Search for New Allies

EIGHT DAYS AFTER 9/11, SAUDI oil minister Ali al-Naimi was in Shanghai attending the World Petroleum Congress and talking about Saudi Arabia's desire to build a "strategic relationship and partnership" with China "at all levels."[1] Al-Naimi had already visited China five times before, first in 1992 when he was Saudi Aramco's president. Crown Prince Abdullah had also visited, in 1998, but it was Prince Bandar who had opened the door to dealing with China back in the mid-1980s, when the kingdom had conducted secret negotiations for China's medium-range, nuclear-capable CSS-2 missiles. The prince had developed through that experience a deep appreciation for Chinese hospitality and respect for the government's ability to conduct secret diplomacy. The Saudis' purchase of these missiles had come as a shock to Washington because of the enormity of the Saudi deception. The Chinese had worked perfectly with the Saudis to carry out the shipment of the missiles into the kingdom without the CIA's discovering their presence until it was too late. At that point, Saudi Arabia did not even have diplomatic relations with China because of the kingdom's deep aversion to communism and alignment with Washington in the Cold War. But China had proved its friendship by providing missiles the United States would not provide to protect the kingdom from Iranian threats during the Iran-Iraq War. Then in 1990, the Saudis had agreed to establish diplomatic relations in return for Chinese support at the United Nations for war resolutions against Saddam Hussein.

Within two years, al-Naimi had begun exploring what the two countries had most in common: oil. Asia, led by China and India, was fast becoming the world's leading new consumer of oil, with overall demand there expected to grow from twenty million barrels a day in 2000 to thirty to thirty-five million in 2020—more than one third of worldwide consumption. Saudi Arabia wanted to be the foremost provider and quickly began reorienting its markets away from Europe and the United States; the share of Saudi oil exports going to Asia increased from 10 percent to 60 percent during the 1990s. Al-Naimi also disclosed in Shanghai that during the past decade he had been busy negotiating to invest in China's refining sector, with the aim of securing an important market share for Saudi oil there.[2]

Clearly Saudi Arabia had begun looking for new strategic partners well before 9/11 to assure both its security and markets for its oil. There was a new Saudi attitude developing toward Washington. Whereas Bandar thought of the U.S.-Saudi relationship as a "Catholic marriage"—one lasting forever with perhaps occasional dalliances—Foreign Minister Saud al-Faisal suggested a strikingly different analogy: "It's a Muslim marriage, not a Catholic marriage." The Muslim man is allowed to take up to four wives so long as he treats them all equally well. According to Saud, Saudi Arabia was not seeking divorce from the United States; it was just seeking marriage with other countries.[3]

China rapidly began to emerge as Saudi Arabia's second wife, with the prospect of displacing the United States as its favorite, at least in matters relating to oil. The two had a lot more in common. Both were authoritarian and secretive, and both were desperately seeking to control the modernization of their backward societies without losing central control. They also held a common disdain for U.S. efforts to promote democracy, human rights, and civil society. At the same time, they enjoyed the same potential complementary relationship as had the United States and the kingdom—oil in exchange for security. The biggest and most welcome difference from the Saudi perspective was that China eagerly sought Saudi oil; the United States by contrast had come to look upon all oil imports, particularly from the Arab Middle East, as a national security risk and actively sought to redress its "addiction," as President Bush termed it in his 2006 State of the Union Address.

Abdullah wasted little time in making known his interest. The first trip he took abroad after becoming king was to China, in January 2006, and oil was at the center of his discussions there. By then, China had displaced Japan as the world's second-largest consumer of oil after the United States. The two sides laid plans for a $3.5 billion refinery in Quongang, Fujian Province, to handle high-sulfur Saudi oil; signed an agreement on energy cooperation; and discussed the provision of Saudi crude to fill a new Chinese 100-million-barrel strategic reserve. The kingdom had become China's top supplier of crude oil by 2002, and it remained number one in 2006, providing nearly 470,000 barrels a day.[4] The Chinese were talking to Pakistan about the building of a pipeline across that country from the port of Gwadar, on the Arabian Sea, to facilitate an ever-greater volume. China's unquenchable thirst for oil not only guaranteed the Saudis a major new market for decades to come; it also meant that the price of oil was likely to remain at fifty dollars a barrel or higher, which would keep Saudi coffers full for decades.

In April 2006, Chinese president Hu Jintao returned Abdullah's visit on his way back from the United States. There, his meeting with Bush had been marred by diplomatic faux pas such as the playing of the wrong national anthem (Taiwan's rather than mainland China's) and a heckler who had hassled Hu at his press conference. Bush and Hu hadn't reached any agreements, either. No such incidents marred the Chinese leader's visit to the kingdom. When Hu addressed the Saudi Consultative Council on April 23, he made a point of reminding the Saudis that China's relationship to the kingdom went back a lot further than that of the United States. More than two thousand years ago, the ancient Silk Road had linked China to the Arabian Peninsula. He quoted an old Chinese proverb that seemed to reflect his view of the shifting balance of power between China and the United States: "Regarding history as a mirror, we can understand what will be rising and what will be falling."[5]

In contrast to Bush's incessant calls for confrontation with the "axis of evil" countries (Iran, North Korea, and Iraq) and joining the "war on terrorism," Hu emphasized the need for dialogue, peace, and harmony among nations. Nations shouldn't be invading one another (as the United States had done in Iraq), and they should all oppose "the use of force, or threatening each other with force at random." They also had a right to choose their own social and political systems, and each should respect the choice of the other. Repeatedly, Hu spelled out a Chinese foreign policy that appeared to diametrically oppose that of the Bush administration. The United States, of course, was never mentioned by name.

The one issue left wrapped in secrecy was cooperation between the two countries on security matters. The official Saudi media said the two sides had signed a "contract on defense systems" but gave no details.[6] Speculation centered, of course, on the fate of the fifty to sixty Chinese medium-range missiles from the 1980s deal, which were badly in need of modernization, if not replacement, if they were to have any credibility as a deterrent to Iran's missiles and nuclear ambitions. The Chinese CSS-2s had never been armed with nuclear weapons, but they were capable of carrying them. Richard L. Russell, a National Defense University security analyst, noted in the summer of 2001 that these aging missiles "would serve as ideal delivery systems for Saudi nuclear weapons," suggesting that the Saudis might well seek to develop a nuclear capability in secret, just as they had done so successfully in obtaining the missiles in the first place. Russell admitted there was no "smoking-gun evidence" that the Saudis were doing this. But he said there was "strong circumstantial evidence" they were "at least leaning toward—if not already working on—a nuclear-deterrent option." But that assessment, he said, was based on the work of another scholar who claimed he had obtained "private information" in the United States to substantiate it.[7]

Another theory about Saudi Arabia's nuclear intentions held that China and Pakistan together would establish a nuclear umbrella over the kingdom to protect it from would-be enemies like Iran. The Chinese would update or replace its old missiles, and the Pakistanis would make nuclear warheads available on a standby basis. The warheads wouldn't be kept inside Saudi Arabia, but they could be quickly transferred if Iran ever threatened to use such weapons, if or when it developed any.[8] Under this scheme, the Saudis could continue to deny they had nuclear weapons or even intended to develop their own capacity to build them. Another variation on this same theory was that Pakistan would make available a nuclear-armed missile brigade if ever the Saudis called for help.[9]

Foreign Minister Saud insisted in 2004 that the kingdom had a standing policy of not seeking to develop any weapons of mass destruction (WMD) and would keep pursuing its efforts to make the whole Middle East a nuclear-free zone, which meant demanding that Israel give up its nuclear force. "An atomic weapon is dangerous whether in the hands of an Iranian or an Israeli," he said. Even if Iran was becoming a nuclear power, Saudi Arabia had taken a decision not to enter this race. "We think it is stupidity incarnate because these weapons will not give security. All they will do is add to the insecurity of a country, because now it will be afraid of somebody attacking it with WMD," he said. Saud insisted that there was "absolutely no truth" to reports that Saudi Arabia had opted for nuclear weapons.[10]

Yet the history of Saudi foreign policy has been to meet forcefully whatever challenge Iran presented to the kingdom, whether religious, political, or military in nature. After the 1979 Iranian revolution, the Saudis vastly expanded their efforts to export Wahhabi Islam in order to counter Iranian Shiite religious influence. When Iran threatened to attack Saudi Arabia with Scud missiles because of its support for Saddam Hussein during the Iran-Iraq War in the 1980s, the Saudis bought far-more-powerful Chinese missiles. The Saudis remain extremely sensitive to both the Persian Shiite challenge to their leadership of the Islamic world and the military threat emanating from Tehran. The Saudi view of the "Persian danger" was expressed in an unusually frank article that appeared in October 2003 in *Asharq Alawsat*, a London-based newspaper owned by Prince Faisal bin Salman, son of Riyadh's governor. The editor, Abd al-Rahman al-Rashid, dismissed the notion that Iran had any intention of ever attacking Israel or the United States with a nuclear weapon. The real target would be Iran's immediate neighbors. "The Iranian nuclear danger threatens us in the first place before it frightens the Israelis or the Americans."[11]

The Saudi turn to Muslim Pakistan to bolster its security in the post-9/11 era of U.S.-Saudi alienation would hardly be surprising. Saudi Arabia's security and defense relationship with Pakistan dates back to the 1970s, when the Pakistanis helped the Saudis develop and maintain their infant air force, even providing pilots. They also sent two divisions—about sixteen thousand troops—as well as air force units to the kingdom in the early 1980s to help defend its oil fields in the Eastern Province and its border with Yemen. In return, the Saudis for years provided Pakistan with oil at a discounted price. They also paid most of the one-billion-dollar cost for Pakistan's purchase from the United States of forty F-16 fighter bombers in the early 1980s.[12] Throughout the decade-long war against the Soviet Union in Afghanistan, the two countries cooperated closely in their assistance to the Afghan mujahideen. Then at the start of the first Gulf War, Pakistan rushed a contingent of ten thousand troops to help defend Saudi territory.

Despite Foreign Minister Saud's disclaimers of Saudi interest in a nuclear deterrent, there were multiple indications starting in the late 1990s that Saudi-Pakistani cooperation was being extended to the nuclear field. The

Saudi defense minister, Prince Sultan, stirred much of the speculation about Saudi-Pakistani nuclear cooperation in May 1999 by visiting Pakistan's uranium enrichment facility at Kahuta and its missile factory at Ghauri. His visit was publicly announced, and it was the first time the Pakistanis had allowed any foreign visitor into these sites. Sultan also met with A. Q. Khan, the Pakistani scientist credited with designing that country's first nuclear weapon and later with selling the technology to North Korea, Libya, and Iran. Then Khan visited Riyadh in November 1999. If Pakistan helped Iran, the main rival of Saudi Arabia in the Persian Gulf, surely it could and would do the same for Pakistan's closest Arab ally.

Those tracking Saudi nuclear intentions also point to the 1994 allegations of Mohammed al-Khilewi, one of the rare Saudi diplomats ever to have defected to seek asylum in the United States. He went public with what he said was information contained in documents he had taken from the Saudi U.N. mission in New York. Khilewi claimed the documents showed the Saudi government had provided five billion dollars to help Saddam Hussein develop a nuclear capacity. He also asserted that Pakistan had committed itself to the kingdom's defense if Saudi Arabia was ever threatened with a nuclear attack.[13] His claims were never corroborated. But he was not the only one fanning smoke about Saudi nuclear ambitions.

After a visit by Abdullah to Islamabad in November 2003, the Israeli Defense Forces' senior intelligence officer, Major General Aharon Zeevi Farkash, claimed the crown prince had gone there to acquire nuclear warheads that could be placed on the Saudis' Chinese missiles. The State Department said it had no information to substantiate the general's "bold assertions" and sought to void them of credibility by noting that similar stories had been around for a decade.[14] But there had been reports in September of that year that Saudi policy makers were debating options in light of what they believed were Iran's efforts to build a nuclear bomb. Among the twenty-nine participants at a three-day symposium titled "Saudi Arabia, Britain and the Wider World," organized by the Oxford Center for Islamic Studies, had been six Saudis, including Prince Turki al-Faisal the former Saudi intelligence chief and then ambassador to London. The participants had discussed three options: one, mirroring the Iranian effort to build a nuclear bomb; two, seeking an alliance with an existing nuclear power that would provide this deterrent; and three, pressing for an agreement on making the Middle East a nuclear-free zone.[15] The preponderant evidence to date suggests the Saudis have chosen option two, and that Pakistan has become the kingdom's nuclear protector with China's help.

THE SAUDI SEARCH for new allies inevitably led to Moscow as well. Though the Soviet Union had been the first country to recognize the new Saudi kingdom in 1932, its communist diplomats had been frozen out, and relations had not been restored until 1990. After that, remarkably little happened to improve their long-distant relations. Saudi support for Muslim rebels in the breakaway Chechnya republic continued throughout the 1990s to sour a relationship in search of a meeting point. Russia's involvement in building a nuclear reactor in Iran posed another obstacle. But the fundamental challenge was that Russia and Saudi Arabia found themselves to be competitors, rather than allies, in the post–Cold War era. They were both huge energy giants vying for markets abroad. Russia was counting on growing oil and gas exports to restore its clout in global affairs. In the last quarter of 2002, Russia managed to edge out the kingdom as the world's largest oil producer (7.97 million barrels a day versus 7.86 million).[16] Russia was a new challenge to Saudi dominance of the global oil market. The Russians even played on U.S. fears of reliance on Middle East oil to present themselves as an alternative, and more secure, source of supply. The two countries thus warmed up to each other slowly.

The war in Iraq and the failure of Abdullah's U.S.-oriented gas initiative finally brought them together. Saddam was ousted in March 2003, and American oil companies were locked out of Saudi Arabia in June. The same month as Saddam's downfall, Saudi oil minister al-Naimi was in Moscow inviting Russian energy companies to come invest in the gas initiative. He was also there to coordinate oil production with the Russians to offset any shortfall in supply because of the Iraq war. After that, the exchange of visits by high-level officials picked up noticeably, and in September Abdullah became the first Saudi king or crown prince ever to travel to Moscow.

Abdullah's three-day visit held more symbolism than substance. The Saudi political commentator Abdulaziz Sager wrote that for seventy years it had been the U.S.-Saudi relationship that had occupied center stage, and the time had come for a change. Since Saudi Arabia and the United States were at serious odds, "it was only a matter of time before Saudi policymakers began looking for friends elsewhere." Russia was a natural choice because the two countries together accounted for 64 percent of the world's known oil reserves, so "cooperation between the two countries [held] the key to oil prices and world economic growth."[17] The Russian press also took note of Saudi Arabia's faltering relationship with Washington and opined that this "could lead to a monstrous leap forward for Moscow" in the Saudi energy sector.[18] As the first result of this budding Russian-Saudi relationship, the Russian private oil company Lukoil was chosen in January 2004 to replace Exxon Mobil and other U.S. oil companies in the opening of the Saudi energy sector to outsiders.

Three years later, Russian president Vladimir Putin formally opened the door to the House of Saud for Russia. The scene setter for his visit was a blistering attack on the United States that he made at a security conference in Munich on his way to Riyadh. Russia had had enough of a "unipolar world" dominated by America that had resulted in "new human tragedies," local and regional conflicts, and "an almost uncontained hyper use of force" in international relations. The United States had "overstepped its national borders in every way" and sought to impose its economic, cultural, political, and educational policies on other nations. "Who is happy about this?"[19] For Putin, this unbridled American use of force was causing countries to develop weapons of mass destruction to protect themselves. He didn't mention Iran by name, but it was clear he was blaming the United States for the Iranian pursuit of a nuclear capability. Nor did he mention Iraq by name when he condemned countries for "airily participating in military operations" that were difficult to consider legitimate and resulted in the death of hundreds of thousands of civilians. There was a crying need for a new world order based on multiple centers of power, and these were emerging as nations like Brazil, Russia, India, and China converted their growing economic power into political clout.[20]

Two days later, Putin arrived in Riyadh seeking to dispel the notion that the two countries were energy rivals and offering Saudi Arabia an alternative to its traditional reliance on the United States. The steady growth in the world demand for energy meant that they were "not competitors but allies, not competitors but partners."[21] The embodiment of this was Luksar, the joint venture between Saudi Aramco and Lukoil in the development of Saudi gas fields. Lukoil planned to invest two billion dollars in the venture and announced just in time for Putin's visit the discovery of its first oil and gas deposit. Before leaving, the Russian leader offered to help Saudi Arabia develop nuclear energy and to begin a military relationship with the purchase of 150 Russian T-90 battle tanks.*

The Saudis were delighted by Putin's courtship. Abdullah called the Russian leader "a statesman, a man of peace, a man of justice" and formally extended Saudi Arabia's "hand of friendship to Russia." The crown prince presented Putin with the kingdom's highest honor, the King Abdulaziz Medal, bestowed on only two other foreign leaders, France's Jacques Chirac and China's Hu Jintao.[22] Foreign Minister Saud declared there were "no barriers" to nuclear cooperation with Russia or to the Saudi purchase of Russian arms. "Russia is a country with nuclear experience and cooperating with it in this field is similar to cooperating in other areas."[23] An editorial in the *Arab News*, Jeddah's English-language daily, said that Putin's visit highlighted the kingdom's "shift eastward" away from an almost exclusive reliance on ties with the United States and Europe. "There is no doubt as to the popularity of diversification away from economic links with the West. There is deep public resentment that the US, with its despised regional involvements and policies, should still be Saudi Arabia's principal economic partner." Russia, on the other hand, had always supported the Palestinian cause and opposed the U.S. invasion of Iraq. "Despite the Cold War and the decades of communism, the Russians are seen as friends by ordinary Arabs."[24]

PRINCE BANDAR, THE most pro-American of the Saudi royals, served as a weather vane of the changing Saudi attitude toward Washington. The year 2003 started on a personal high note with the downfall in March of his old enemy, Saddam. But it was all downhill from there on. Within three months, all the policies he had promoted over twenty-five years to bond the two countries lay in ashes. During 2004, the relationship worsened. The fall presidential campaign brought accusations from the Democratic challenger, Senator John Kerry, that Bandar and the Saudis were intent on manipulating oil prices to help Bush get reelected. It didn't seem to matter that prices were

---

* By late 2007, Moscow was close to signing a contract with Riyadh for the sale of up to four billion dollars in arms, including not only the 150 tanks but one hundred attack and transport helicopters, twenty mobile air defense missile systems, and a large number of armored personnel carriers.

actually more than forty dollars a barrel and at an all-time record. The Democrats were intent on exploiting Bush's alleged close oil ties to the Saudis. "I want an America that relies on its own ingenuity and innovation, not the Saudi royal family," railed Kerry from the campaign trail.[25] Florida senator Bob Graham, another Democratic hopeful, charged in a book released just before that year's 9/11 commemoration ceremonies that the Bush administration had engaged in a cover-up of ties between the Saudi government and the hijackers. Graham called for Saudi Arabia to be held publicly accountable and for the twenty-eight pages about the Saudi role in the attacks redacted from *The 9/11 Commission Report* to be made public. "It was as if the President's loyalty lay more with Saudi Arabia than with America's safety."[26] Almost until Election Day, ads appeared in major newspapers seeking to tar Bush with his Saudi connections. A Democratic group, the Media Fund, spent $6.5 million on ads across the country highlighting the Bush-Saudi theme.[27] Bandar spent the entire fall answering these accusations, but not from Washington. He had decided to seek shelter back home in Saudi Arabia from the withering barrage of Democratic accusations against the kingdom.

In a sense, Bandar never really came back, not that he was spending much time in Washington by the fall of 2004. He had become a rare visitor to his own embassy on New Hampshire Avenue, across from the Watergate complex in downtown Washington. When his advisers urged him to speak out or do something to defend the kingdom, his standard refrain was "Why should I care?" He relied more and more on his Texas-educated aide Adel al-Jubeir, who spoke American English with the same flare and agility, to defend the kingdom. The young, energetic deputy replaced Bandar as the main Saudi talking head on TV and radio shows and the chief briefer of the Washington press corps. The prince, meanwhile, was spending more and more time back home patching up his shaky relationship with Crown Prince Abdullah and lobbying day and night for a new assignment at his court.

CHAPTER 15

End of the "Special Relationship"

FOR PRINCE BANDAR, NO DIPLOMATIC task would prove more daunting than bridging the yawning gap between President George W. Bush and Crown Prince Abdullah. These two world leaders were truly an odd couple—Bush a born-again WASP graduate from Ivy League Yale University and Harvard Business School and Abdullah an austere, blunt-spoken bedouin tribal chief with little formal education but enormous desert savvy. Both were deeply religious, but God and Allah did not bring them any closer together. This was because their agendas were so markedly different. Abdullah was obsessed with the Palestinian problem, and he wanted Bush to meet Palestine Liberation Organization (PLO) chairman Yasser Arafat to get the peace process going again. Bush refused to meet with Arafat under any conditions; indeed, he wanted him removed and backed Israeli prime minister Ariel Sharon, whom he lauded as a "man of peace," in his campaign to crush the Palestinian uprising and oust Arafat. While Palestine was Abdullah's obsession, Iraq was Bush's, and he wanted Saudi help for the pending U.S. invasion to unseat Saddam Hussein, which Abdullah opposed categorically.

For a brief period after 9/11, it appeared there was some hope for reviving the peace process. In November 2001, Secretary of State Colin Powell gave a speech at the University of Louisville in Kentucky in which for the first time a U.S. administration came out in support of an independent Palestinian state. Powell's words were historic: "We have a vision of a region where two states, Israel and Palestine, live side by side within secure and recognized borders." The secretary of state, who was Bandar's closest friend in this Bush administration, solemnly promised, "We will stay engaged," conceding that the peace process had "always needed active American engagement for there to be progress."[1]

When there was no follow-up to Powell's speech, Bandar began pressing the Saudi case for White House action in personal meetings with Bush and members of the Washington press corps. By late January 2002, he was telling reporters that Abdullah had become exceedingly frustrated. Bush was all "vision and no action." The United States could not walk away from its responsibilities in the Middle East, because the Israelis and the Palestinians, if left to their own devices, would never make peace. Bush had to get involved. Who else could do it? The prince said he realized Arafat had let down the international community by rejecting Clinton's peace plan, but the United States didn't have the right to quit, because "more people will die."[2]

Abdullah stepped up the pressure on Bush to engage. In February, he startled the world by putting forth during an interview with *New York Times* columnist Thomas L. Friedman a proposal that promised Arab recognition of Israel and the normalization of relations with the Jewish state if Israel agreed to withdraw to its borders before the 1967 Arab-Israeli War.[3] The Saudis had never before extended the olive branch to Israel in such explicit terms, and Abdullah's initiative became even bigger news when a month later, at its summit in Beirut, the Arab League adopted his proposal as the official pan-Arab position. To the deep disappointment of Abdullah, neither Washington nor Tel Aviv showed any interest in pursuing the Arab overture. Indeed, in retaliation for the bombing on March 27 of a restaurant in Netanya that had killed thirty Israelis, Sharon unleashed the Israeli army on the PLO's entire West Bank infrastructure, putting Arafat himself under siege in his headquarters in Ramallah.

In early April 2002, Bandar presented to the American public the Saudi case for immediate U.S. action to salvage the peace process, arguing in an op-ed column in the *Washington Post* that the upsurge of violence in Israel made pursuit of Abdullah's peace plan all the more urgent.[4] In response, Bush sent Powell on another mission impossible to Israel in mid-April, which only confirmed Bush in his basic instinct to do nothing. White House interest in expending the president's political capital on Middle East peacemaking had been minimal at the start of Powell's trip and was "nonexistent" by the end.[5]

Abdullah and Bush were thus at loggerheads before their star-crossed meeting on April 25 in Crawford, Texas, their first encounter ever. Bandar only made things worse by once again wielding the oil weapon on his own initiative as he had done in August 2001, but this time allowing it to become public, to the enormous embarrassment of Abdullah. The morning of the meeting, a story appeared on the front page of the *New York Times* that suggested the royal family was considering using the oil weapon if that was what it would take to get Bush to change his pro-Sharon policies. The unnamed "person close to the crown prince" went on to warn of a pending "strategic debacle" for the United States in terms that bore the unmistakable language of Prince Bandar. The situation had become so serious in Israel that it was a "mistake to think that our people will not do what is necessary to survive."[6] Bush later said Abdullah had made it clear that Saudi Arabia would not use oil as a weapon, and so did Saudi officials briefing reporters on the meeting afterward.[7] Once again, Bandar had badly miscalculated.

The five-hour meeting between Bush and Abdullah came close to being a personal debacle. The two talked past each other, Bush about the dangers of Saddam Hussein's regime and the need for Arab nations to join his war on terrorism, Abdullah about the need for U.S. intervention to save Arafat. The crown prince presented an eight-point plan aimed mostly at ending Sharon's invasion of the West Bank and solving the Palestinian crisis based on Abdullah's own peace plan. In a bid to arouse Bush's sympathies, the crown prince had brought pictures and a videotape illustrating Palestinian suffering at the hands of the Israelis. Bush did not seem familiar with Abdullah's peace plan or much interested in the Palestinian issue at all. Abdullah, on the other hand, demanded action and at one point threatened a walkout that may have been preplanned to convince Bush to pressure Sharon into lifting his siege of Arafat's office building, which at that point had been reduced to a pile of rubble.

Powell later described the Bush-Abdullah encounter as an "ugly scene," and during a break to allow tempers to cool off, he accosted Bandar, asking him, "What the hell did you do? How did you let it get to this?" Powell and Bandar then got into a shouting match loud enough for Bush to hear and come out to investigate.[8] Bush salvaged the situation by taking Abdullah on a drive around his ranch and engaging in small talk, afterward insisting that all had gone well and that he had established a "strong personal bond" with Abdullah. He also demanded that Israel finish its withdrawal from the West

Bank, despite the fact that none had yet begun. Nonetheless, no joint press conference or joint statement followed their meeting, and Abdullah's spokesman referred to unspecified "grave consequences" if Bush continued his do-nothing policy toward Israel and the peace process.[9]*

WHAT HAD BEEN orchestrated as an intimate get-together at the president's ranch had morphed into an embarrassing illustration of how far the House of Bush and the House of Saud had drifted apart, their interests starkly different, at some points even diametrically opposed. The growing distance between the two was highlighted once again when Abdullah dispatched Bandar to see Bush in Crawford that August to press the Saudi argument against an American invasion of Iraq and for the revival of the peace process. Their meeting was memorialized in a picture of the two that went round the world: the prince sitting on the edge of a couch looking down on the president as the two chatted apparently amiably. The informal setting and their seeming intimacy belied the reality of sharp differences. Bush was determined to uphold U.S. justifications for waging a war on Iraq, mainly because Saddam was "a menace to world peace" who had to go. Vice President Dick Cheney had just made the case publicly for preemptive action and had predicted confidently at a national convention of the Veterans of Foreign Wars, "After liberation, the streets in Basra and Baghdad are sure to erupt in joy." Abdullah's objective, on the other hand, was "pre-empting an attack against Iraq" to allow time for U.N. inspectors to find Saddam's weapons of mass destruction.[10]

The U.S. invasion of Iraq in March 2003 was a cataclysmic event for the whole Middle East, particularly Saudi Arabia. The Saudis had wanted to topple Saddam in a way that preserved minority Sunni rule in Iraq. This could only be accomplished through a palace coup or some other way, such as a military uprising, that would leave the Sunni-led Iraqi army in control. The Bush administration had been unable to foment the former and had opted to forgo the latter. The Saudis watched in horror as the American invasion created first a breakdown in law and order and then a complete

---

* Sharon continued to grind down Palestinian security forces, and Arafat remained under siege in his Ramallah headquarters until he died in November 2004 of a mysterious illness.

power vacuum, only made worse when the Coalition Provisional Authority leader, Paul Bremer, ordered the dissolution of the Iraqi army, the only functioning Iraqi national institution that remained. The step assured the end of Sunni rule in Baghdad, one of the historic "power towns" and seats of Sunni caliphs throughout Islamic history.[11] Worse yet from the Saudi perspective, the Americans installed a Shiite leadership through elections the Bush administration championed as part of its "forward strategy of freedom." The Saudis, who saw themselves as the Sunni Islamic world's religious center, viewed the Shiite rise to power as one of the most serious challenges to their prestige and influence in contemporary times.

Bandar later told associates that Bremer's decision to dissolve the Iraqi army marked the end of his support for the U.S. invasion, though he continued to support it publicly in America until the end of 2003.* The prince's role in promoting the U.S. invasion was never understood back home, and as it became increasingly unpopular, he was not anxious to highlight just how much he had argued for such a course of action. Starting in November 2002, he had pressed Bush to get serious about regime change in Iraq and promised Saudi support for U.S. military action. For Bandar, this would have served to rebond the two nations as the first Gulf War had done and make Saudi Arabia yet again a major ally of the United States.[12] He had been instrumental in convincing Abdullah to provide at least logistical support for the invading U.S. forces.

One of the foremost Saudi opponents of the U.S. invasion had been Prince Turki al-Faisal, the former intelligence chief, who had become ambassador to London in 2002. Apparently seeking a second opinion about Bush's war intentions, Abdullah had sent Turki to Washington that January to assess the situation. Turki had told reporters that the idea that the United States could solve its problem through the use of military might in Iraq was wrongheaded and downright dangerous. "A military invasion with U.S. soldiers is not going to be welcome, not by the Iraqi people, not by other people in the region. The people who will suffer are going to be the Iraqis," he had said. "I can't tell you how concerned everybody is and not only in the kingdom. We are the ones who have to live with the consequences."[13] Turki

---

* Bandar, in a speech to Houston businessmen in December 2003, praised Bush repeatedly for removing "a great evil from the world" and said that everyone should be grateful to him for getting rid of Saddam.

had continued to press the favored Saudi solution—a military coup encouraged by guarantees of U.S. air support to Iraqi army officers willing to take the risk. But he had conceded the lack of support for this at the White House.

As events turned out, the U.S. invasion created just the kind of instability and insecurity for Iraq's neighbors that Turki and his brother, Foreign Minister Saud, had so feared. The Saudis first pressed for as short an American occupation as possible. Then they reversed course when it became clear that Iraq risked falling apart and their archrival, Iran, was pouring money, arms, and men into Iraq to help consolidate Shiite rule. As opposition to the U.S. occupation turned into a full-scale insurgency and the al-Qaeda-induced sectarian struggle became ever more acute, the Saudi concern turned into alarm at the increasing fragmentation of Iraqi society and the entire nation. After more than two years of watching in silence the steady deterioration of conditions there, Abdullah finally decided to go public and to send a different messenger to voice his anxieties.

In September 2005, Foreign Minister Saud arrived in Washington to deliver the Saudi message. A Princeton graduate with thirty years of experience in dealing with the U.S. media, Saud was normally extremely restrained and diplomatic in his choice of words, but not this time. He convoked a press conference at the Saudi embassy and bluntly announced he had come to warn the Bush administration that Iraq was on the road to disintegration, threatening the entire region with catastrophe. "There is no dynamic now pulling the nation together. All the dynamics are pulling the country apart." The main worry of all of Iraq's neighbors was that separate Kurdish, Shiite, and Sunni states were emerging out of the American-induced chaos and that this was certain to bring other countries into the conflict.[14] In New York the same night, Saud spelled out more precisely the main Saudi fear: If the sectarian violence continues, he warned, "Iraq is finished forever. It will be dismembered. It will be not only dismembered, it will cause so many conflicts in the region that it will bring the whole region into turmoil." He predicted that the Iranians would come in from the south, the Turks from the north, and that "the Arabs," a reference to Saudi Arabia, Jordan, and Syria, would "definitely be dragged into the conflict" in response. He ended by noting the supreme irony of the American military intervention's having been fought to keep Iran out of Iraq. "Now we are handing the whole country over to Iran without reason."[15] Two days earlier, he had admonished the Bush administration in more colorful language for "handing over Iraq on a golden platter" to Iran.[16]

The question before the Saudi royal family was how to respond to both the Iranian challenge and Iraqi Sunni pleas for help. The Saudis felt obligated to assist their fellow Arab Sunnis; they were in the minority, only 12 to 15 percent of the total Iraqi population. And they were facing persecution from Shiite militias and death squads seeking revenge for decades of mistreatment at the hands of Saddam's Sunni-dominated regime. Arab Sunni tribes were spread across western Iraq and even across the Saudi border. The Shammar tribe, for example, extended into northern and central Saudi Arabia and even took its name from Jabal Shammar there. Like the founder of modern-day Saudi Arabia, King Abdulaziz, Abdullah had married into the Shammar tribe, so he was extremely sensitive to its sufferings in Iraq. As the conflict worsened, the Saudis found themselves coming under mounting pressure from Sunni tribal leaders asking for help in their struggle with "the Persians," as the Saudis referred to the Iranians. Also, a chorus of voices from the Sunni leaders of Egypt, Jordan, and other Arab countries called upon the Saudis to provide weapons and financial support for Iraq's beleaguered Sunnis.[17]

Providing such assistance posed an enormous dilemma for the Saudis. The insurgency fighting the U.S. occupation was a Sunni operation led by former Saddam supporters, with some seventy-seven thousand fighters who commanded widespread support among all Iraqi Sunnis and presented the most serious threat to Iraq's new Shiite rulers. At least, that was the Saudi estimate of the insurgency's force.[18] But the terrorist group al-Qaeda in Iraq (sometimes referred to as al-Qaeda in Mesopotamia) was also largely a Sunni operation, and the Saudis were locked in battle with its supporters inside the kingdom. More than five hundred Saudi youth had heeded the call to jihad and gone off to fight the American invaders, or "the Persians." Some had returned home and become part of al-Qaeda's struggle to overthrow the House of Saud. So if the Saudis gave out money and arms to imploring Sunni tribal leaders showing up in Riyadh, they could not be sure for what purpose and whose cause they would be used. They were also under enormous pressure from Washington not to make the situation for U.S. occupying forces any worse by providing aid to the insurgency.

Yet the Saudis felt they could not just stand by and watch Iran steadily consolidate its influence. Saudi intelligence agencies believed the al-Quds force, a special section of Iran's Revolutionary Guard, was busy training various Shiite militias and had infiltrated all levels of the Iraqi police, army, and government; they also believed it was arming Shiite death squads responsible for killing scores of Sunni tribal leaders, academics, and former army officers. The Iranian plan for penetrating Iraq, they claimed, also included the use of its clerics and charities to promote Shiism among its Sunni population. According to the Saudi assessment, the net result was that Iran was on the way to creating a state within a state and on the verge of fulfilling one of the Iranian revolution's most cherished objectives—its export to an Arab country.[19]

The U.S. invasion of Iraq had effectively transformed America's historic role as a guarantor of the kingdom's security into the exact opposite. The occupation was becoming a main source of Saudi insecurity by turning Iraq into an incubator of *jihadis* for al-Qaeda as much interested in overthrowing the House of Saud as in driving out the infidel American invaders. At the same time, Bush's call for regime change in Iran, backed up by a seventy-five-million-dollar democracy-promotion program there, only served to stimulate Iranian efforts to obtain a nuclear weapon, which presented yet another challenge to the Saudis. They had a second nightmare haunting them now, namely that Iran was on its way to becoming a nuclear power and that the United States would bomb its facilities in a bid to stop this from happening.

The third recurring nightmare in the recesses of the Saudis' minds was that the United States might become a direct threat to the kingdom itself. CIA and other U.S. assessments of the House of Saud almost inevitably raise the question of its long-term viability and whether it is a strategic ally or a "strategic problem." The latter was the term used by General John Abizaid, commander of U.S. forces in the Middle East in the mid-2000s. While Iraq and Afghanistan were America's two immediate concerns, Saudi Arabia and Pakistan were the "two broader strategic problems" the United States would have to deal with in the future because of the threat from Islamic extremists.[20] A similar assessment came at that time from highly respected CIA analyst Paul Pillar. In a study titled "The Middle East to 2020," he warned that the United States should not be surprised to see one or more "revolutionary changes," and he named Saudi Arabia as one country where such an event might occur, provoking a traumatic upheaval in its relations with Washington and likely determining the fate of the entire Middle East. Pillar also predicted that the chief proliferators of weapons of mass destruction, including nuclear weapons, could well become moderate states such as Saudi Arabia and Egypt rather than "rogue" regimes such as those in Libya and Syria. In his estimation, the rogues would likely forgo their nuclear ambitions, as Libya had done, to regain their respectability and standing in the world community, while the moderates would "seek ways to ensure their security without heavy reliance on the United States."[21]

Saudi jitters focused on possible American military action to prevent just such a radical change or proliferation. There had long been a Saudi paranoia about U.S. military intervention to assure the flow of oil from the kingdom's vast reservoirs, and London press reports in early 2004 served to justify that concern. A document released from Britain's National Archives showed that British intelligence had been convinced President Richard Nixon was seriously considering a takeover of oil fields in Saudi Arabia, Kuwait, and the United Arab Emirates in the wake of the 1973 Arab oil boycott.

The document, dated December 12, 1973, described this military action as "the possibility uppermost in American thinking" if Arab producers became carried away with "the success of the oil weapon."[22] Even if this didn't happen, according to the British assessment, "the US government might consider that it could not tolerate a situation in which the US and its allies were in effect at the mercy of a small group of unreasonable countries."[23] Nixon's secretary of defense, James Schlesinger, had issued warnings along these lines to the British ambassador to Washington at the time, Lord Cromer, who had told his government that "it was no longer obvious . . . that the United States could not use force."[24] Schlesinger had not been the only one talking about this in the fall of 1973. Press reports from this time show that U.S. Secretary of State Henry Kissinger had issued a similar veiled warning to the Saudis in an effort to pressure them into lifting the oil embargo. If it continued "unreasonably and indefinitely," he had said, the United States would consider "countermeasures."[25] In response, then Saudi oil minister Sheikh Ahmed Zaki Yamani had threatened to blow up Saudi oil fields if the United States took military action.[26]

Disclosure of the British intelligence report immediately set off a debate among Saudis about U.S. intentions toward the kingdom in the future. Mai Yamani, daughter of Sheikh Yamani, wrote, "Many Saudis, who believe America invaded Iraq to secure access to its oil, say they cannot exclude the possibility that their country will be next."[27] Little wonder, then, that in the mid-2000s the Saudis were in crisis about whether they could count on the United States for their security any longer. America, it seemed, had become an agent of instability, unpredictability, and insecurity for the whole region.

SOMETHING ELSE WAS fundamentally changing in the U.S.-Saudi equation as well. The Saudis were losing control of the world oil market and prices. Even had they wanted to, the Saudis could no longer assure the United States a sufficient supply at moderate prices. By early 2004, a debate over Saudi preeminence in the world oil market had become red-hot as a result of claims made by a Texas energy guru, Matthew Simmons, that Saudi Arabia was running out of oil and hiding its decline behind phony statistics. Simmons was a strong believer in peak oil, a theory that basically held that the entire world was running out of black gold. At a conference in Washington in February, Simmons laid out his thesis that the Saudi "oil miracle" had turned into a mirage and that the kingdom's claim to have 260 billion barrels, by far the world's largest reservoir, was highly questionable. The Saudi cash cow for more than fifty years had been the giant Ghawar oil field in the Eastern Province, dubbed by Simmons as "the King of all Kings," the world's largest and the source of more than half of all Saudi production. Basing his challenge on the 1975 Saudi estimate of Ghawar's reserves, 60 billion barrels, Simmons claimed the reservoir there had to be close to exhaustion. The same was true, he argued, of the kingdom's two other giant oil fields. Simmons further alleged that the Saudis had mismanaged the exploitation of their fields over the years and had only managed to keep them producing through a massive injection of water, which had damaged them.[28]

Simmons's other major claim was that Saudi prospects for finding sufficient quantities of new oil to keep pumping at present-day rates were highly questionable. "The entire world assumes Saudi Arabia can carry everyone's energy needs on its back cheaply," he said. "If this turns out to not work, there is no Plan B." The worst problem, according to Simmons, was that the Saudis refused to allow outside inspection of their estimates and reservoirs, so the world really didn't know whether it was facing "a giant oil energy crisis."[29]

No one had ever challenged the Saudis' oil statistics in such detail before. In response two months later, Saudi oil minister Ali al-Naimi offered a clear and simple message: Simmons was dead wrong, and Saudi Arabia, a reliable supplier of oil to the world even in times of turmoil, would continue to be so. Yes, it was true new discoveries in the kingdom would probably be smaller and more costly to exploit, but Saudi Arabia wasn't running out of oil, and neither was the world; in fact, his country was sufficiently confident of its reserves that it could easily increase its maximum production capacity from 10.5 million barrels a day to 12 or 15 million and maintain its output at that level for fifty years or more.[30]

That spring, the role of oil in the U.S.-Saudi relationship was in the headlines for another reason—the allegation in Bob Woodward's book *Plan of Attack* that Bandar had told Bush, during the run-up to the Iraq invasion, that the Saudis would make up any shortfall from the loss of Iraqi oil to the world market. Woodward also quoted the prince as saying the Saudis hoped to "fine tune oil prices over 10 months to prime the economy" before the presidential election in November of that year.[31] Woodward was even more specific during an interview on CBS's *60 Minutes*, where he described it as "the Saudi pledge" and opined that the Saudis could produce an extra two million barrels a day over the summer to force oil prices down dramatically by Election Day.[32]

This provoked a storm of controversy, and Senator Charles Schumer, a Democrat from New York, issued a statement calling upon Bush to take "immediate action to safeguard the integrity of the American electoral process by deporting Prince Bandar and canceling his diplomatic visa."[33] And yet the oil market that the world had known, and that the Saudis had almost single-handedly dominated for decades, was no longer theirs to control. The limits of Saudi power became evident on May 21, 2004, when al-Naimi, upon arriving in Amsterdam to attend an emergency Organization of the Petroleum Exporting Countries (OPEC) meeting, urged the group of thirteen oil producers to increase production "by more than two million barrels a day." Saudi Arabia, he disclosed, would immediately begin offering its customers 600,000 more barrels.[34] Oil prices had just topped forty dollars a barrel, seen as a barrier not to be exceeded. Two days later, U.S. energy secretary Spencer Abraham flew into Amsterdam to press al-Naimi for an even greater Saudi production increase to curb spiraling oil prices. After their meeting, a greatly relieved Abraham announced that Saudi Arabia alone would pump the two million barrels more a day that al-Naimi had urged all thirteen OPEC members to produce collectively.[35] This was the exact figure Woodward claimed Bandar had promised Bush to help him get reelected.

Abraham quoted the Saudi oil minister as saying the Saudis were ready to pump up to their full capacity of 10.5 million barrels a day to bring prices back to OPEC's agreed-upon price range of twenty-two to twenty-eight dollars a barrel.

Such a statement from the Saudi minister would normally have had the same effect on the world oil market as Alan Greenspan's comments had had on Wall Street during his long tenure as Federal Reserve chairman. Both men were regarded as oracles in their respective worlds. But speculators, oil traders, and producers were not listening to al-Naimi that day, nor would they heed his voice in the years to come as prices continued to rise. The Saudis made one last attempt to nudge them down before the U.S. presidential election. As Election Day approached and oil broke the fifty-dollars-a-barrel mark, al-Naimi announced the kingdom was expanding its production capacity to eleven million barrels per day, and Adel al-Jubeir, Bandar's top aide, declared prices had become "clearly way too high" and should be between twenty-two and twenty-eight dollars.[36] Their statements proved to be of no avail.

FACTORS WAY BEYOND Saudi control were dictating oil prices. The biggest long-term change was that demand from China was soaring, accounting for 40 percent of the total world increase in demand since 2000 and more explosive by far than the steady increase in the United States. Chronic instability in Iraq had dropped its exports, once 2.5 million barrels a day, to less than half of that. Exports from Venezuela and Nigeria were also dropping, owing to internal political turmoil. In the United States, no new oil refineries had been built for thirty years, and bottlenecks in existing ones remained unresolved. OPEC's ability to dictate prices was also being undermined by the trend of more and more oil being sold by independent traders on the open market and by speculators in oil futures on the New York Mercantile Exchange. Above all these logistical and marketplace considerations, Saudi analysts had begun talking about a "security premium" of ten to fifteen dollars a barrel or more, stemming from al-Qaeda threats to attack oil facilities in Saudi Arabia and other Arab gulf nations. But there was one purely Saudi factor in the new world oil equation that was contributing to the kingdom's loss of clout: Most of its much-vaunted spare export capacity of two million barrels a day consisted of oil with heavy sulfur content, which many U.S. and other refineries were not adapted to handle. As a result, there were not a lot of takers for the additional oil the Saudis had to offer.

Al-Naimi kept trying to force prices down. He announced in late November 2004 that the kingdom was now making plans to increase its production capacity even further, to 12.5 million barrels a day. A month later he declared that the official estimate of its known oil reserves, then set at 261 billion barrels and already by far the world's largest, would jump to 461 billion in a few years.[37] But oil traders and speculators still weren't listening. Al-Naimi blamed the loss of Saudi influence principally on the "fear factor" over the security and quantity of supplies, noting that this was unlike anything the world had seen during the two previous price surges, in 1973–74 and 1979–80, when in his view political decisions by governments had been the decisive cause.[38]

IN THIS TENSE atmosphere of ever-escalating oil prices, Bush and Abdullah met again in Crawford, Texas, on April 25, 2005. After their stormy encounter the same month and day three years before, both sides were anxious to project a new image and a new day in the U.S.-Saudi relationship. They chose an unusual way to do so. Bush waited to greet the crown prince outside the door of his ranch and, when he arrived, kissed him on both cheeks in Arab style. Bush then proceeded to take Abdullah's hand and guide him down the stone footpath to the ranch's office building, where they would meet. On the way, Bush pointed out a bed of bluebonnets and explained to Abdullah that they were the Texas state flower. The picture of the two men walking literally hand in hand in a public display of friendship became the subject of endless comment, and often derision, on every radio and television talk show in America and beyond. The *New York Times* was moved to run an entire story a week later devoted to explaining "Why Arab Men Hold Hands." The answer: "Holding hands is the warmest expression of affection between [Arab] men" and "a sign of solidarity and kinship."[39]

The focus of their meeting was oil. Reporters duly noted that the price had reached $55 a barrel and the cost for a gallon of gasoline in the United States was averaging $2.42 per gallon nationwide, compared with $1.41 when the two leaders had met three years ago. Abdullah came well prepared. He laid out Saudi plans to invest $50 billion in the long-term development of the kingdom's oil fields to increase production to up to 12.5 million barrels a day by 2010 and even higher, to 15 million barrels, in the following decade. U.S. secretary of state Condoleezza Rice and Bush's national security adviser, Stephen Hadley, were full of praise for the Saudi effort and for the "very positive, very strong personal relationship" that had emerged from their meeting, a tour of the ranch, and a long lunch. The two had agreed on a way to relaunch the two nations' troubled relationship, by establishing a permanent joint committee to be cochaired by Rice and Saud al-Faisal, the Saudi foreign minister, to deal with a wide range of "strategic issues."

So, what about the price of oil? That was what reporters wanted to know. What were the Saudis going to do to help curb skyrocketing gasoline prices? Hadley was optimistic. "Obviously," he said, "when Saudi Arabia increased production by that much it can't help but have a positive downward effect on prices."[40] It would calm the volatility of the market and assure the world that the necessary supply of oil to fuel the global economy would be forthcoming. But Hadley had to admit the Saudi plan was unlikely to do anything to lower prices in the short or even medium run. Abdullah's spokesman, Bandar aide Adel al-Jubeir, was more specific. It didn't matter if Saudi Arabia sent another million or two million barrels a day to the United States, he said. There were not enough refineries to process it.[41] In other words, high gasoline prices were not the Saudis' fault any longer, but that of America and its lack of refinery capacity. The kingdom could do little to solve that problem, though it was planning to build more refinery plants at home, al-Jubeir said, suggesting that maybe the United States should do the same. The Saudis knew the Bush administration was faced with a classic NIMBY—"not in my back yard"—problem in getting permission from any community across America to build a new refinery.

Like nothing before, the Crawford meeting made clear that the U.S.-Saudi relationship had entered a new era when it came to oil. It showed just what the Saudis would and couldn't do to relieve America's energy problems, which was limited. Even in the long run, the Saudi plan wouldn't be sufficient to meet world demand, according to the U.S. Department of Energy. It had long been projecting that the Saudis would have to produce twenty million barrels a day if future needs were to be met. "It's what they can produce and a realistic assessment given worldwide demand," said the department's long-range forecaster Dan Butler.[42] But the maximum production increase al-Naimi had mentioned was just fifteen million barrels a day.

The consequences of these new oil realities for Bandar personally were considerable. He could no longer credibly offer to help solve the White House's energy problems. Even his dictum that Saudi Arabia had to remain at the top of the list of foreign oil suppliers to America was no longer possible to adhere to. The share of Saudi oil in overall U.S. imports had already begun fading in 2003, with Canada, Venezuela, and Mexico all providing more or about the same. At the end of 2002, Saudi Aramco had ceased giving its old American partners the special discounts they had enjoyed for thirty years, which had helped the kingdom to remain America's foremost provider.[43]* As the place of Saudi oil in the American market decreased, so did Bandar's influence in Washington. As the Saudi leverage over oil prices slipped, so did the prince's magic at the White House.

In early 2005, Bandar decided he had had enough, even if it meant disobeying his king, who had often insisted he stay in Washington because of his unparalleled access to the White House. By then, he had dealt, over twenty-seven years, with five U.S. presidents, ten secretaries of state, eleven national security advisers, sixteen sessions of Congress, an obstreperous American media, and hundreds of greedy politicians. The first hint of his decision to leave, no matter the consequences at the royal court, came in March. Haifa informed the Mosaic Foundation, a Washington-based charity run by Arab ambassadors' wives, that they would have to find another board chairwoman because she was leaving. After that, Bandar just voted with his feet by staying away from Washington. King Fahd was too sick to deal with his defiance, and Crown Prince Abdullah seemed uncertain what to do with the headstrong prince.

The prince's final departure from Washington was carried out in a manner befitting his love for stealth and intrigue. At the end of June 2005, the Washington rumor mill was seized with reports that he was resigning, but the Saudi embassy put out a statement denying this, saying he was merely on vacation and would return in late August. Given his stature and long tenure in Washington, the reports raised enormous interest and speculation. Almost a month later, on July 20, the official Saudi Press Agency announced that Bandar had indeed submitted his resignation to the king "due to personal

---

* By 2006, Canada had become a far more important source of foreign oil than Saudi Arabia, which averaged 1.4 million barrels a day that year compared with Canada's 2.3 million. Mexico provided 1.7 million, and Saudi Arabia was vying for third place with Venezuela, which also accounted for 1.4 million barrels.

reasons" and that it had been accepted with high praise for his outstanding services to the kingdom.[44] At that point, Fahd, who had provided Bandar with all his power and standing in Washington, was only eleven days away from dying. The White House also heaped praise on Bandar, calling him a "close, steadfast friend" and "tireless advocate for close ties, warm relations and mutual understanding" between the two countries. "In troubled times, U.S. presidents past and present have relied upon Ambassador Bandar's advice. In good times, they have enjoyed his wit, charm and humor."[45]

Behind all these official Saudi and U.S. kudos lay the long history of Bandar's struggle to get out of Washington. The prince had submitted his resignation on at least two earlier occasions and had lobbied as far back as 1987 for the creation of a job as national security adviser to the king or to become head of the General Intelligence Directorate. Both Fahd and Abdullah had turned him down, even after Prince Turki's abrupt departure as intelligence chief in August 2001. By the mid-1990s, though tired of his ambassadorial post, he was staying on to please Fahd.

Bandar never said a formal good-bye to Washington. After inviting hundreds of friends, colleagues, and working acquaintances to his farewell party in September, he abruptly canceled it. He did find time, however, to drop by the White House to bid Bush a final farewell on September 8. A month later, Bandar finally succeeded in securing the job he had long coveted: national security adviser to the king. But there was no National Security Council, no backup support, not even an office where he could sit. He would have to create everything from scratch.

CHAPTER 16

The New "Strategic Dialogue"

THE NEW "STRATEGIC DIALOGUE" ESTABLISHED to replace the sixty-year-old "special relationship" as the official U.S.-Saudi mantra came about in stages. In mid-September 2005, Prince Turki al-Faisal was sent to replace Bandar, his brother-in-law. Turki was the youngest son of King Faisal, who ruled from 1964 to 1975 and was probably the most popular monarch in the history of modern-day Saudi Arabia. Turki thus boasted a far more prestigious pedigree than Bandar within the House of Saud, where the al-Faisal branch occupied a special room. Turki's older brother, Saud al-Faisal, had been foreign minister since 1975 and still held that position in early 2008. Another brother, Khaled, was the governor of Mecca, the most prestigious of the provincial governates. Turki himself had served as head of the General Intelligence Directorate for twenty-four years.

As Saudi Arabia's chief spymaster, Turki had overseen the Saudi end of the joint U.S.-Saudi covert operation to help the Afghan mujahideen in their decade-long struggle against the Soviets in Afghanistan during the 1980s. He had met Osama bin Laden, the al-Qaeda leader, five times during and after that war. These contacts would earn him the suspicion of America's neocons and make him a defendant in the one-trillion-dollar lawsuit filed by families of the 9/11 victims against various Saudi banks, entities, and individuals accused of aiding this master terrorist. Turki remembered bin Laden from his earlier days mostly as a "very shy person, very self-effacing, extremely sparse in his words and generally a do-gooder."[1] By the late 1990s, it was a totally different matter. King Fahd had sent Turki twice to negotiations with the Taliban government for his surrender to Saudi authorities, but to no avail. The 9/11 Commission found no evidence that Turki, or any other Saudi official, had helped the hijackers, and the case against him in American courts was dismissed.

Turki's upbringing was as rooted in the American experience as Bandar's, but it was quite different in nature. While Bandar attended various U.S. pilot training schools, Turki frequented its elite academic institutions. At age fourteen, he was sent to Lawrenceville School in New Jersey to prepare for Princeton University, where his older brother Saud had graduated in 1965. But Turki was kicked out of Princeton after the first term. He had failed his engineering courses and misbehaved.* He transferred to Georgetown University in Washington and switched to political science and international relations. But he didn't last long there, either. When the 1967 Arab-Israeli War broke out, he was so upset by the Arab defeat and U.S. support for Israel that he dropped out and went home. He returned later to "pursue" an undergraduate degree, as his official embassy biography put it, since he never officially graduated from Georgetown, either. But he ended up a member of the 1968 class together with Bill Clinton, though the two were scarcely more than passing acquaintances.†

By temperament, Turki was the polar opposite of Bandar—contemplative, bookish, cautious, and far less prone than his brother-in-law to risk taking or seeking confrontation as an answer to the world's problems. Above all, they had quite different notions of diplomacy. Without once mentioning Bandar by name, Turki spelled out those differences in a talk he gave to Georgetown students in July 2006. In effect, he said Bandar belonged to an old-fashioned school of diplomacy, dating from a time when the movers and shakers of the world were absolute monarchs and imposing statesmen like Metternich, Bismarck, and more recently Henry Kissinger. A handful of luminaries played "political chess," determining the fate of nation-states, making and unmaking alliances to gain political advantage, and deciding issues of war and peace.[2] It was an indirect critique of Bandar's notion of a

---

* When he returned to speak at Princeton as Saudi ambassador to Washington in December 2006, he joked about how he had spent some of his "misspent youth" there.
† Turki said during an interview with the author in January 2008 that he retained vague memories of Clinton having passed on to him some course notes prior to taking an exam.

special relationship that had been largely confined to Saudi kings and U.S. presidents, with him acting the part of Metternich or Kissinger. Turki argued that with the advent of the information age, "the old rules no longer apply." The Internet, satellite television, and information technology in general had empowered simple "individuals," and non-state actors like terrorists, as never before and made secret diplomacy conducted by national leaders and their emissaries obsolete. A new age of diplomacy had dawned "in a world in which national borders are blurred, hierarchies have been flattened and ambiguity about our allies is heightened."[3] For a spook, Turki proved amazingly outspoken, and this would eventually get him into trouble in Washington.

Turki saw himself as the implementer of the new style of diplomacy toward the United States, and it fell to him to launch the so-called strategic dialogue with Washington. There were two parts to the new approach, the first aimed at broadening the base of government-to-government contacts and institutionalizing them. The second part involved launching a public diplomacy campaign, whose goal was to reach what Bandar had once called "Joe Six Pack," the average American with views of the kingdom radically changed by 9/11.

The term "strategic dialogue" did not emerge publicly until the first meeting of the special committee President Bush and then Crown Prince Abdullah had created, to be headed by the two countries' foreign ministers. It was held in Riyadh in November 2005 in an atmosphere described by the *Washington Post* as marked by "skepticism still deep on both sides" even four years after the 9/11 attacks.[4] The outcome was an agreement to set up six working groups to deal with the multiple problems that had arisen in the relationship, everything from counterterrorism to visas for Saudi students and businessmen wanting to come to the United States. One of the key objectives was to "institutionalize relationships across government departments in both countries to ensure that issues [were] dealt with effectively."[5] But another was extremely revealing of the state of the relationship: to educate each other "about certain aspects of our respective societies and systems" and "ease some of the respective concerns we may have had about each other."[6] In other words, the two governments, not to mention ordinary Saudis and Americans, still harbored some deep misgivings about each other—quite a formal, and very public, admission of the lingering malaise.

A senior Saudi official provided some interesting historical background on what he thought had gone awry in the relationship even before 9/11. While never mentioning Bandar, it was clear that in his mind the prince bore part of the responsibility. Back in 1974, he said, the two governments had established a Joint Commission on Economic Cooperation, which had served extremely well as the umbrella for most American programs in the kingdom; it had launched multiple nation-building projects and in the process spawned myriad ties between ministries and departments of the two governments. But in the mid-1980s, the nature of the relationship had begun changing. President Reagan had taken to bypassing normal diplomatic channels to deal directly with King Fahd. The entire relationship had become "centered in the White House–to–Fahd channel."[7] Bandar, who had become ambassador in 1983, had of course been their go-between and chief translator of their conversations both oral and written. From that time on, the ambitious prince had made sure he remained the indispensable intermediary for every U.S. president's dealings with the king or crown prince and had pushed aside anyone who had interfered, including the U.S. ambassador in Riyadh.

As a result of Bandar's style of diplomacy, according to this Saudi official's analysis, none of the upper levels at the State Department or the National Security Council had really known what was going on in the relationship, or bothered to develop contacts with their Saudi counterparts. Even the secretary of state had often been left "clueless." Over time, there had been fewer and fewer American officials with any experience in dealing with the kingdom. The same had been true for Saudi officials dealing with the U.S. government. "We didn't know whom to call any longer."[8] Thus, the prime goal of the new strategic dialogue was to rebuild this hollowed-out relationship from the ground up. It was necessary to train a new generation of U.S. and Saudi officials with some knowledge of the relationship, the official said. "We've got to build more links and bridges in all areas, so if one bridge falls down, you still have other bridges." Above all, the relationship had to be refounded "on institutions rather than personalities."[9] What had made matters even worse, of course, were Bandar's ever-longer absences from Washington starting in the mid-1990s. Even the prince had had to admit that the kingdom's relationship with the most powerful nation on earth had been left on "autopilot" for an entire decade.

Yet Bandar could not leave Washington alone. After leaving, he set about building himself a new base of operations back in Riyadh. He had convinced King Abdullah to allow him to establish a National Security Council (NSC) modeled, in theory, on that of the U.S. government. Actually, in theory, it was to be even more powerful. The new Saudi council was supposed to oversee all the kingdom's intelligence agencies, and it was empowered to declare a national emergency and even war. The body was to review all "internal and external situations having a direct bearing on national security."[10] Abdullah was NSC chairman, Crown Prince Sultan his deputy, and Bandar the council's secretary general, put in charge of establishing the body, recruiting its personnel, and, of course, acting as the king's national security adviser. As such, he would continue to be the king's messenger. This also assured he would return to Washington, and frequently as it turned out.

The result was an increasingly tense competition between Bandar and Turki for access to the White House. But it was about more than access; it was also about the content of the message to be delivered there. The two princes, both longtime practitioners of Saudi realpolitik, had quite different notions of what the Bush administration should do regarding the Palestinian issue, Iran, Syria, Lebanon, and Iraq. Understanding their differences also required reading Saudi tea leaves and listening to the rumor mill in Washington and Riyadh, but their conflicting messages became serious enough that White House officials began asking in the fall of 2006, "Who speaks for the king?"[11]

Lebanon first brought the feud to the fore. On July 12, 2006, Israel launched a massive air war against Hezbollah, the Lebanese Shiite party, in retaliation for its incursion into Israel and capture of two Israeli soldiers. Israeli warplanes swooped down to attack not only Hezbollah sites but Lebanese roads, bridges, and power plants and Beirut's international airport. Two days later, an unnamed Saudi "official source" issued a remarkable statement through the Saudi Press Agency. The Saudi official called the Hezbollah incursion an "irresponsible act" that had created a "gravely dangerous situation exposing all Arab countries and their achievements to destruction."[12] For the normally soft-speaking Saudi government, this was incredibly strong language and highly unusual. The Saudi statement went on to say that Hezbollah's action could not be considered "legitimate resistance" but was rather a "miscalculated adventure" by what was basically a rogue Lebanese group acting without consulting the Lebanese government or other Arab countries. Within hours, Bush issued his own statement, welcoming the Saudi statement warmly. White

House press secretary Tony Snow could hardly conceal his delight, declaring that the Saudi statement showed that moderate Arab states now understood that Hezbollah was not a "legitimate government entity" but a threat to the entire Lebanese people.[13]*

Ten days later, the Saudi position changed dramatically into a fiery condemnation of Israel and demands for an immediate cease-fire. On July 23, Abdullah sent Foreign Minister Saud to Washington to implore Bush to pressure Israel into ending its destruction of Lebanon. There was no more criticism of Hezbollah for the rest of the Israeli operation, which continued until August 14. Hezbollah, defiant to the end and still sending its missiles deep into Israel, emerged a pan-Arab hero for its steadfast resistance to the Israeli air, sea, and ground attacks. In the Saudi Red Sea port of Jeddah, merchants that October were selling three-foot-long rockets for Ramadan fireworks celebrations that they dubbed Hezbollahs. In this atmosphere, the initial Saudi statement condemning Hezbollah stood out as a public embarrassment. A Saudi official later said that it had not come from the Foreign Ministry and that he suspected Bandar had been the instigator.[14]

Throughout the fall of 2006, Bandar was a frequent visitor to the White House as plans were being laid for the formation of an alliance of "moderate" Arab states—namely Saudi Arabia, Egypt, and Jordan—backed by both Israel and the United States. The central U.S. aim was to counter Iran and its expanding influence across the Arab and Muslim worlds. In mid-September, Bandar met secretly with Israeli prime minister Ehud Olmert in Amman, Jordan, an encounter that served to fuel speculation that the Saudis and the Israelis, with Washington's full encouragement, were beginning to deal with each other and make such an alliance possible. The prince promised Olmert that Saudi Arabia would deliver other Arab gulf states for a meeting with Israeli officials if Israel would accept the Saudi-led Arab League's 2002 peace plan as a basis for peace negotiations. The Saudis had never agreed to negotiate directly with Israel, so Bandar's pledge was a major shift. No wonder Olmert began saying in the fall of 2006 that there were positive aspects to the Arab peace plan.[15] But Bandar's offer was another example of his freelancing, for according to a European diplomat based in Riyadh, he did not have Abdullah's authorization to make it.[16]

* The U.S. government had already designated Hezbollah a terrorist organization in 1997.

Whether to deal with both Iran and Syria through confrontation or engagement became a central issue for the Saudis, who felt enormous pressure to counter Hezbollah's new popularity, which had the effect of also heightening the standing of its principal supporters. Abdullah was furious with Syrian leader Bashar al-Assad after he called Arab leaders who had criticized Hezbollah and not stood by its struggle with Israel "half men."[17] The king showed his pique over Assad's comment by meeting in October 2006 quite publicly with the leader of the Syrian opposition movement, former vice president Abdul Halim Khaddam, while rejecting all of Assad's efforts at reconciliation. The king also suspected Assad was responsible for the assassination in February 2005 of Lebanese prime minister Rafik Hariri, who had been the main conduit for Saudi money and influence in Lebanon for two decades and had become strongly anti-Syrian. The Saudis wanted his murderers, assumed to be Syrian agents, found and put on trial and were supporting American and French efforts in the U.N. Security Council to do just that.

In November 2006, Bandar was in Washington several times discussing the Bush administration's plan for a comprehensive new Middle East strategy. The prince was taking just as hard a line as Bush's neoconservative deputy national security adviser, Elliott Abrams, and Vice President Dick Cheney.[18] They wanted to fund pro-democracy groups in Syria and Iran in a bid to promote regime change as part of their grand design for a "New Middle East." Bandar assured them the kingdom would support this hard-line policy, and according to some reports, he committed Saudi money to help carry out covert operations against Hezbollah, Syria, and Iran.[19] He also backed the Bush administration plan to bolster the moderate Palestine Liberation Organization (PLO) leader Mahmoud Abbas in his struggle with Hamas, the militant faction that had unexpectedly won Palestinian parliamentary elections early that year.

In January 2007, Secretary of State Condoleezza Rice formally presented the administration's new policy in testimony before Congress, describing a "new strategic alignment" throughout the Middle East that took account of a fundamental divide between what she called "reformers and responsible leaders" and "extremists of every sect and ethnicity."[20] Among the former, she mentioned Israel, Turkey, and the "GCC+2," meaning Saudi Arabia and the five other Arab states in the Gulf Cooperation Council plus Egypt and Jordan—all Sunni Arab regimes. In addition, she praised the "young democracies" of Lebanon and the PLO, at least that wing of the movement under Abbas's leadership. The United States was holding "unprecedented consultation" with these reformers and responsible leaders to coordinate policy toward the extremists, she said, signaling out by name Iran, Syria, Hezbollah, and Hamas. The most important U.S. goal was to empower "democratic and other responsible leaders across the region." Most of America's allies, of course, were in the "other" category, such as the autocratic leaders in Egypt and the monarchs in Saudi Arabia, Jordan, and the Arab gulf states. The administration asked Congress to appropriate seventy-five million dollars to promote democracy and the opposition in Iran and another five million dollars for the same purposes in Syria, and it pledged one billion dollars in military and economic assistance to strengthen the pro-American government of Prime Minister Fouad Siniora in Lebanon against Hezbollah.

RICE'S MANICHAEAN OUTLOOK on the Middle East seemed to dovetail nicely with the increasingly general Sunni Arab view of the emerging struggle with an ascendant Shiite Iran and its allies. Indeed, King Abdullah II of Jordan and Egyptian President Hosni Mubarak had warned of a "Shiite crescent" stretching from Iran into Iraq, Syria, and Lebanon and threatening to overturn the long-standing balance of power between the Arab world's two main Islamic sects.[21] The problem came with differing views on how to deal with this challenge, through confrontation or engagement.

Within the Saudi royal family, there were also differing views. Bandar, a fighter pilot and a strong supporter of Saddam's overthrow, was by instinct ready for confrontation and a show of force in dealing with one's enemies. Turki, on the other hand, was openly advocating a different approach. In a series of speeches during the fall of 2006, Turki argued that Iran wasn't the most important challenge facing the United States in the Middle East at all; instead, it was the Palestinian-Israeli issue, and the Bush administration should expend its energies on reviving the peace process. And it should stop trying to deal with Iraq, Iran, Lebanon, and Palestine as isolated problems and realize they were all interlinked.[22] Turki cited in particular the Bush administration policy of trying to isolate Iran. The Saudis' experience, he said, had been that "talking with the Iranians is better than not talking to them." As for Iran's nuclear ambitions, Saudi Arabia believed it was vital to talk with Tehran "frequently and frankly." The kingdom had tried to isolate Iran and had even suspended diplomatic relations with it for a time during the 1980s, only to see the situation grow worse. "I think for the United States not to talk to Iran is a mistake," he said.[23]

The White House didn't like what Turki was saying publicly and found it sharply in contradiction to Bandar's message, which it preferred to believe reflected King Abdullah's real views. So Bush's aides made it difficult for the new Saudi ambassador to get appointments to see the president. Meanwhile, Bandar continued coming to Washington, flying in without telling Turki and staying at the posh Hay-Adams Hotel, overlooking Lafayette Park in front of the White House. He was two minutes away by foot from the Oval Office.* Bandar kept insisting he was the king's real messenger, and the fact that he came straight from Riyadh and the royal court seemed to lend credence to his claim. U.S. officials began asking other Saudis who came to the White House, National Security Council, and State Department for consultations whether they were "with Bandar or with Turki."[24]

Turki's position in Washington became increasingly untenable, but not only because of Bandar's frequent visits to the White House. He found that he was unable to finance his embassy and public diplomacy program. He believed a vital part of his mission was rebuilding the kingdom's bridges to the American people. During his short time in Washington, the prince traveled far and wide across the United States to give speeches, attend conferences, and meet Americans from all walks of life. He visited twenty-five states in a little more than a year. But he soon faced a major obstacle in carrying out his public diplomacy, namely a lack of money.

Among the many mysteries of Saudi diplomacy, none was less understandable to Saudi watchers than the running of the kingdom's embassy in Washington, arguably the most important posting for a Saudi diplomat anywhere in the world. The main embassy, on New Hampshire Avenue next to Washington cultural icon the John F. Kennedy Center for the Performing Arts, counted eighty-seven full-time accredited diplomats in 2003. Despite its enormous size, Bandar had reduced it pretty much to a one-person operation that he ran from his McLean residence or wherever he happened to be at the time—Aspen, his Glympton estate, Marrakech or Rabat in Morocco, Riyadh or Jeddah in Saudi Arabia, or on his Airbus somewhere in between.

---

* On one occasion in the fall of 2006, Turki only learned of Bandar's presence in Washington because he went to the Hay-Adams for lunch and ran into him there.

The prince's personal costs were considerable. He kept a massive security detail that followed him wherever he went, usually consisting of two or three escort cars filled with heavily armed men. He kept a bevy of personal servants at his beck and call, and he had his own custom-tailored Airbus on standby day and night to fly him around the world. It was an expensive operation, and the cost exceeded one hundred million dollars a year.[25] Toward the end of Bandar's tenure in Washington, Abdullah ordered a cutback in spending on all the kingdom's diplomatic activities abroad, which included reduced expenditures at its Washington embassy. Bandar refused, however, to make any cutbacks. Instead, he started using his own funds to make up the difference.

When Turki took over as ambassador in September 2005, he found the cost of running the embassy to be far in excess of its official budget. He immediately made the decision not to use any of his personal funds to make up the difference as Bandar had done.[26] Turki adopted an ambassadorial style far less regal and costly. He eliminated Bandar's massive security detail and used mostly commercial airlines instead of a private plane to fly around the United States. But these savings still were not sufficient to cover embassy costs, particularly his public diplomacy campaign. His pleas to the royal court for additional funds, however, were rejected. As a result, Turki and the embassy began running up bills they couldn't pay, and the sum soon reached into the millions of dollars.

By December 2006, the embassy's principal public relations firm, Qorvis Communications, was owed more than $10 million, and numerous contractors and service providers were out hundreds of thousands of dollars.[27] The personal embarrassment to Turki had to be enormous. Here he was representing the world's richest oil producer, with $77.5 billion in surplus oil earnings in 2006, and he could not pay his embassy's bills. The only public explanation he offered was that many of the unpaid bills belonged to the Foreign Ministry in Riyadh and not the embassy in Washington. Firms like Qorvis had contracted directly with the ministry for their services.[28]

In mid-October 2006, Turki informed Abdullah that he wanted to resign after only thirteen months in Washington. Abdullah at first refused. Though officially ambassador since the previous September, the prince had not really taken up his duties in Washington until January 2006, thus effectively serving only ten months. News that he was resigning became public on December 12, the day after he informed Secretary of State Rice that he was leaving.[29] His departure immediately provoked a storm of speculation about whether it reflected dissension within the royal family or a personal animosity between Turki and the king.

In fact, Turki's relationship with Abdullah had long been somewhat shaky, although the al-Faisal branch of the royal family was widely regarded as his natural ally. This assumption was based on the idea that they faced a common competitor for power—the dominant Sudairi branch, led by seven brothers who included the late King Fahd, Defense Minister Prince Sultan, and Interior Minister Prince Naif. But the personal chemistry between Turki and Abdullah was not always good; for example, they had had a falling-out at the time of Fahd's stroke in 1995. As head of Saudi intelligence, Turki had regularly provided Fahd with briefings, but Abdullah, who had become de facto ruler upon Fahd's stroke, hadn't wanted to be briefed by Turki.[30] Then in August 2001, Abdullah had fired Turki from his job as intelligence chief.

Turki was hard put to explain his decision to resign. He said he was exhausted and needed to spend more time with his family. He insisted he was leaving for personal, not political, reasons. He said that he had only agreed to a two-year stay in Washington, anyway. But something was clearly wrong. He was leaving nine months before the two years were up. There had been no announcement from the royal court that he was resigning, only from the *Washington Post*, which had broken the news. This was the third time in his life that Turki had abruptly quit what he was doing—having done so first as a student at Georgetown University in 1967 and then as chief of Saudi intelligence in 2001.

To the end, Turki refused to admit that policy differences between himself and Bandar had played any part in his resignation. At a meeting with several visitors in early February 2007, just days before he left Washington for good, he seemed totally relaxed and indifferent to the controversy surrounding his departure, and he kept to his schedule of speeches and appointments to the last day. He seemed relieved to be going and said he looked forward to taking over leadership of the King Faisal Center for Research and Islamic Studies, his family's foundation in Riyadh. Only after his departure did he indirectly concede there might have been differences of opinion between himself and Bandar; in an interview with a London-based Arab newspaper, Turki was asked directly whether he and Bandar had disagreed over how to handle Iran. His viewpoint, he insisted, was identical to that of his brother, Foreign Minister Saud, who had said many times that "any military action against Iran is against Saudi interests." This, he insisted, was the kingdom's official position. "There is no other stance adopted by Prince Bandar bin Sultan, Prince Turki al-Faisal or anyone else," he snapped.[31] But Turki never made clear whether he thought Abdullah favored confrontation or engagement.

In the view of one Saudi official close to the king, Abdullah had come to embrace both lines at once. He believed that the Saudis should continue to dialogue with Tehran (Turki's line), but that the Americans should keep up the pressure to isolate Iran internationally until it made concessions on its pursuit of nuclear weapons and backed off in Iraq (Bandar's line). The Iranians saw U.S. strength ebbing away in endless wars in Iraq and Afghanistan. Thus, any show of American weakness would only encourage Iran to push harder in Iraq, press on with its nuclear program, and become even more aggressive toward its Arab neighbors. The Saudis needed the threat of U.S. military action as leverage in their own efforts to persuade the Iranians to change course. But an actual attack on Iran's nuclear facilities would be, as Turki and his brother Saud kept warning, a "catastrophe" for the whole region.[32]

TURKI'S WASHOUT IN Washington took place in late 2006. Bandar's final debacle came the following spring.

After Rice outlined before Congress the Bush administration's vision of the "New Middle East," she decided to devote her remaining time in office to making a breakthrough in the moribund Middle East peace process. By March 2007, she was preparing for her fourth trip to the region to relaunch peace talks between Israel and the Palestinians and win the acceptance of Arab moderates for the opening of a dialogue with Israel. Israeli prime minister Olmert had confounded his critics by suggesting he would accept negotiations based on "some parts in the Saudi peace initiative" and intended to pursue direct contacts with Arab moderates.[33] At the same time, the Bush administration was seeking to strengthen PLO leader Abbas politically and militarily, partly by training a new police force directly under his command and partly by pushing for direct talks between Olmert and Abbas, while Israel worked to keep Hamas isolated in the Gaza Strip.

With Saudi backing, Rice hoped her new peace strategy might produce a breakthrough, but she had badly misread Saudi intentions thanks to Bandar's misleading assurances. Abdullah had something else at the top of his

agenda, namely putting an end to escalating fighting in Gaza between supporters of Abbas and Hamas. In late January, he summoned their leaders to
Mecca, where he pressed them to bury their swords and make a go of their
shaky coalition government. He locked the opposing delegations up in a
palace overlooking Islam's holiest of holies, the Kabaa, and kept them there
until they announced a deal on February 8. In the end, they patched together
a new unity government, and Abbas, under enormous Saudi pressure,
agreed to allow Hamas to lead it. But the Saudis only succeeded in convincing Hamas to "respect" past PLO agreements with Israel. This fell far short
of U.S. and European demands that it explicitly recognize Israel's right to
existence. Hamas felt triumphant and even claimed the Saudis had also
promised one billion dollars in aid to the new coalition government—a
claim it later had to deny. Still, Hamas had clearly come out on top at
Mecca, and the Saudis were now committed to implementing what they
called "the Holy Mecca Agreement."

The Bush administration was caught flat-footed, and Rice was non-
plussed. Just as she was about to return to the Middle East to press for the
opening of talks between Olmert and Abbas, the Saudis had engineered a
new Palestinian coalition government led by Hamas, which neither the Israelis nor the Americans would deal with. As a result, Rice's trip in late
March was a total bust. The best she could obtain was an agreement that
Olmert would hold biweekly talks with Abbas alone, but the Israeli prime
minister refused to discuss what Rice was calling a "political horizon" outlining a future Palestinian state.[34] Bandar at first tried to downplay the importance of the Mecca agreement, suggesting in his conversations with U.S.
and European diplomats in Riyadh that Abdullah did not really back it. Foreign Minister Saud, however, was telling the same diplomats that the king
did indeed support the Mecca agreement because Palestinian unity was vital
if peace talks were to succeed and Iran were to be prevented from strength-
ening its influence over Hamas.[35]

Bandar's credibility with the Bush administration continued to come into
question all through the spring of 2007 as evidence mounted that the king
was charting a separate course. In March, Abdullah rebuffed U.S. efforts to
keep Iran isolated by meeting with President Mahmoud Ahmadinejad in
Riyadh, even though Bush officials had asked him specifically not to. Then
at the opening of an Arab League summit in Riyadh on March 28, the king
denounced the American presence in Iraq as "an illegal foreign occupation,"

a term he had never used before. (Other translations of his speech used the term "illegitimate.") Abdullah also ended his boycott of Syrian leader Assad, meeting with him for two hours during the summit. As the summit began, the *Washington Post* disclosed that Abdullah had also canceled plans to come to Washington for a gala dinner at the White House on April 17.[36] The bearer of this bad news was none other than Bandar, who lamely told Bush administration officials that the king had a "scheduling problem."

Four days later, the same newspaper was questioning in an editorial why the Bush administration had ever described Saudi Arabia as "moderate." Abdullah had no intention of helping the Bush administration isolate Iran and Syria, stabilize Iraq, or settle the Israeli-Palestinian conflict on U.S.-Israeli terms. It was clear, the newspaper said, that Saudi Arabia saw these issues quite differently. Abdullah was far more interested in detaching Hamas from Iran's influence than in pressing it to negotiate with Israel. His meeting with Assad showed he was not going to play Washington's game of isolating and punishing him for Syrian "troublemaking" in Lebanon and Iraq. The Bush administration's partnerships with "Arab autocracies" like Saudi Arabia had resulted in mixed results at best and were "cancerous in the longer run." Rice should realize that Middle East dictators were neither moderate nor good allies.[37]

Bandar's personal efforts to redeem Saudi Arabia's standing in Washington lay in shambles and had led instead to more misunderstandings, bad feelings, and doubts. There was a strong feeling in Washington that the prince had seriously misrepresented Abdullah's views and intentions. It seemed, as the former U.S. ambassador to Israel Martin Indyk put it, that "the Bush administration had been listening to the wrong Saudi."[38] The prince's reaction was predictable. He disappeared for two months. After checking into Sibley Hospital in leafy northwest Washington for a medical checkup, he retreated first to Hala Ranch in Aspen and then to a health spa in California to deal with his various health problems. In early June 2007, he left for Morocco, where the king was vacationing, presumably to account for his actions in Washington. Bandar did not return on official business for the rest of the year.

IN MAY 2007, fighting between the Lebanese army and a group of Islamic fundamentalists broke out in the Nahr el-Bared Palestinian refugee camp, outside Tripoli in northern Lebanon. As the conflict dragged on, it became known that the Islamists were led by a Palestinian Islamic fanatic, Shaker al-Absi, who wanted to establish his own Islamic state inside Lebanon. He had attracted about 250 radical Palestinian and foreign fighters, and among these were 42 Saudis, according to the chief Palestinian spokesman in Lebanon.[39] In Iraq, U.S. and Iraqi officials disclosed in July that nearly half of the 135 foreigners in U.S. detention were Saudi *jihadis* and that the majority of suicide bombers were Saudis.[40] The "justice minister" of a self-proclaimed Islamic State of Iraq was a Saudi, Abu Sulaiman al-Utaibi. Iraqi officials disclosed that 160 Saudis in Iraqi detention involved in terrorist acts had been tried and sentenced and that hundreds of others awaited judgment.[41]

Numerous other examples of Saudi Wahhabi involvement in the activities of militant Islamists around the world had already come to light. In Bosnia, Muslim religious authorities complained about a group of foreign Wahhabi extremists in the north of the country who had fought on the Muslim side during the civil war there in the mid-1990s, married local women, and stayed on to spread their message. The Saudi government had built the King Fahd Mosque in Sarajevo, the Bosnian capital, after the war, the country's largest. In Somalia, the Islamic Courts Union tried to establish an Islamic state. Its leaders were heavily influenced by Wahhabi Islamic beliefs. When they were chased out of the Somali capital of Mogadishu by U.S.-backed Ethiopian troops in early 2007, a number of their leaders took refuge in Saudi Arabia. In Nigeria, five hundred fighters from a Wahhabi-influenced group attacked a police station in the northern city of Kano in April of that year to avenge the murder of the group's Wahhabi-trained preacher. In post-Soviet Central Asia, the authoritarian rulers continued to blame Wahhabis for inciting opposition to their regimes, and Russian authorities decried their leadership role in the bloody rebellion in Chechnya.

The reach of Saudi soft power around the world remained impressive, even if local authorities sometimes exaggerated the influence of local Wahhabi zealots. After spending billions of dollars and more than four decades on proselytizing, the Saudi government had generated considerable political clout through its export of Wahhabi Islam. Saudi soft power seemed likely to remain a major challenge to the United States, particularly if Islamic extremism as personified by al-Qaeda persisted as the root cause of the threat to American interests at home and abroad. At the end of the Bush administration, the U.S. war on terrorism focused increasingly on Pakistan, where local and foreign Islamic militants, including Osama bin Laden, were using the lawless provinces along the Afghan border as worldwide operation centers. Pakistan's ten thousand madrassas, or private religious schools, had come to be viewed as the source of religious extremism there, and they had been financed in part by Saudi Arabia until U.S. pressure was brought to bear after 9/11.*

At the same time, it was not clear at the end of the Bush administration what could repair the battered U.S.-Saudi relationship. The Saudis had lost their ability to force the world price of oil down, and the importance of Saudi oil to the United States was in decline. Whether the additional production capacity the Saudis hoped to gain from investing fifty billion dollars would restore their clout in influencing oil prices remained to be seen. Saudi oil minister Ali al-Naimi proclaimed in mid-2007 that he saw no reason for the kingdom to expand its production beyond the 12.5 million barrels per day already planned for 2009,[42] though the Paris-based International Energy Agency questioned whether this level would be sufficient to meet world demand or lower prices, which topped the once-unthinkable one hundred dollars a barrel in early 2008.[43]

Other areas of the relationship were stagnating. U.S. military sales were continuing but mostly to sustain old programs like the modernization of the Saudi national guard, while there were no deals announced for new warplanes, tanks, or ships. In the fall of 2007, the administration unveiled plans for $20 billion in new sales to the six GCC states, but by the end of the year it had notified Congress of only $1.4 billion for Saudi Arabia, even after overcoming opposition from pro-Israeli congressional members opposed to the transfer of satellite-guided bombs to the kingdom.[44] Meanwhile, the Saudis had signed an agreement with Britain's BAE Systems for the purchase of the most advanced European fighter aircraft, the Typhoon, in a deal expected to total $40 billion and assure that Britain, not the United States, would remain the key provider to the Saudi Royal Air Force for years to come.

The best hope for U.S. plane sales had lain with the civilian state airline, Saudia, which was considering Boeing's new 787 Dreamliner, at a cost of $160 million per aircraft. But in November 2007, the airline instead ordered

---

* Between 2002 and 2007, the U.S. Agency of International Development invested $256 million in reforming Pakistan's educational system to combat extremist teaching in its madrassas.

twenty-two European made Airbus A320s at $78 million each, while the Royal Saudi Air Force followed shortly afterward with an order for three Airbus A330 refueling tankers.* U.S.-Saudi military cooperation continued, with eight joint exercises held during 2007, but the Pentagon had lost its preeminent standing in the kingdom, and the Saudis were conspicuously absent from its list of "major non-NATO allies," which included other so-called moderate Arab countries like Egypt, Jordan, Kuwait, and Bahrain.

In mid-2007, both U.S. and Saudi officials were searching for ways to give new life and meaning to an old alliance. Both were citing the increasing number of Saudi students going to American schools again, with the total back up near fifteen thousand in 2007 after dropping to almost none in the wake of 9/11. The aim was to create a new generation of U.S.-educated Saudis who could help reestablish ties between the two countries. However, there was no such number of American students heading for Saudi schools, though plans to open twelve new institutions, including the King Abdullah University of Science and Technology in association with the University of California at Berkeley, Stanford University, and the University of Texas, raised Saudi hopes of attracting a large number.

The one area where the relationship between the two governments had grown noticeably closer was their common war against al-Qaeda. Still the Saudi government could not stop the outward-bound flow of young *jihadis* headed for Iraq, Lebanon, and elsewhere, and the United States would never make the crucial difference in the success, or failure, of the Saudi battle against al-Qaeda inside the kingdom. The United States did suggest ways to increase security at Saudi oil facilities, and in 2007 the Saudis responded by creating a special thirty-five-thousand-man force to protect them with American help. While these new forms of U.S.-Saudi security cooperation were important, they were hardly sufficient to replace the kind of overall protection America had once assured the kingdom. In its war against al-Qaeda and its own Wahhabi extremists, the House of Saud would have to stand or fall on its own.

King Abdullah seemed determined to redefine the relationship on Saudi terms and make the kingdom far more independent of Washington in both

---

* In November 2007, the Saudi billionaire Prince Waleed bin Talal became the first private individual to purchase the Airbus A380 Superjumbo, spending over $300 million to outfit the plane for his personal use.

appearance and substance. After sixty-five years, Saudi Arabia was breaking away from its dependency on the United States. The king's threat to Bush in August 2001 to take the kingdom "its own way" was coming to pass, his willingness to "just say no" to Washington's endless requests for help ever more evident and public. The decision of the two princes in the House of Saud most sympathetic to America to give up on Washington seemed emblematic of the deep malaise still persisting in the U.S.-Saudi relationship. Abdullah had turned to someone else for advice on America—Ghazi al-Qusaibi, his outspoken labor minister. He was perhaps best known as a popular poet with a biting tongue who had publicly belittled Bush as a bumbling ignoramus about the Middle East complicated by an inferiority complex toward his father.

Just what relations between the United States and a more independent Saudi Arabia might look like in the future remained murky. There might be a new "strategic dialogue" under way, but the two countries still had not defined common strategic interests or how to pursue them together. If they both agreed that Iraq should remain a unified country, they had a serious disagreement over Shiite rule there as well as whether democracy offered the best answer for keeping the country together. If they both opposed the expansion of Iranian influence, they disagreed on whether the formation of a moderate Arab Sunni bloc, openly backed by Israel and the United States, was the best way to contain Iran. If they both abhorred the idea of Iran becoming a nuclear power, they disagreed on whether U.S. military might should be wielded to prevent it. If they agreed on an independent Palestinian state alongside Israel, they were miles apart on whether Hamas should be integrated or isolated. Above all, they disagreed on whether American-style democracy was the answer to the rejuvenation of the Arab Middle East.

Prince Turki fired off another salvo against U.S. democracy-promotion efforts while attending the annual conference of the Jordanian-sponsored Arab Reform Initiative in Amman in April 2007. He focused on what this policy had brought to Iraq. "Democracy turned to a hateful sectarianism, justice turned to oppression, the rule of law ended up being the rule of the militias and human rights became death warrants." No wonder, said Turki, that Bush's call to democracy had few takers any longer among Arab rulers. It was perceived as "an invitation to abolish Arab identity and dismantle its components."[45]

Summing up the unsettled state of U.S.-Saudi affairs in mid-2007, a senior Saudi official remarked, "We have gained our independence. You have lost your piggy bank."[46] His point was that from the Saudi perspective, the relationship was healthier because the kingdom had become less dependent on America for its security and less subservient to its Middle East policies. On the other hand, he noted, America was also far less dependent on Saudi oil, with its share down to about 7 percent of total U.S. consumption. Also, the United States had little to fear from a Saudi oil boycott threat because such a step would now inflict serious injury on the kingdom's own investments. In 2007, over half of Saudi oil exports to America—890,000 barrels out of 1.4 million barrels a day—went to supply four refineries and eighteen thousand gas stations in the southern and eastern United States that were partially owned by Saudi Aramco.[47] When it came to wielding the oil weapon against America, the kingdom had pretty much neutralized itself.

IN LATE OCTOBER 2007, King Abdullah began a tour of European capitals, stopping first in London, where no Saudi monarch had set foot for twenty years. The historic visit did not go well. On the eve of his arrival, Abdullah infuriated the media by chiding the British government for allegedly having ignored Saudi warnings that terrorists were planning the July London subway attacks, which had resulted in the deaths of fifty-two commuters. Then, a day after his arrival in London on October 30, the Saudi-owned Al Arabiya television channel aired the first installment in a five-part series on Abdullah's life and reign, highlighting his achievements and importance in Saudi history. The series had taken fifteen months to produce and included first-ever interviews with members of the king's family, even several of his wives, and a number of world leaders. For months prior to its airing, Al Arabiya had invested enormous amounts of time and money in promoting the series, the first of its kind in royal history.

But as the king and his entourage watched the opening segment in London, they realized with mounting irritation that Prince Bandar had been given an inordinate amount of screen time. More than ten minutes of the one-hour program were devoted to Bandar as he touted his own role in convincing President Bush to call for the creation of a Palestinian state in 2001 and in persuading Libyan leader Muammar Gaddafi to hand over the two intelligence agents behind the 1988 bombing of Pan Am Flight 103. Abdullah was so furious he demanded the cancellation of the rest of the series and ordered Bandar to leave the official delegation for the rest of his European tour.[48]

That Bandar had fallen precipitously from the good graces of Abdullah seemed further confirmed when Bush made his first visit to the kingdom in mid-January 2008. Despite his long expertise in dealing with the White House and his position as national security adviser, Bandar did not participate in any of the meetings during the two-day visit. Whether he had declined or been told to stay away was not clear, as Saudi officials offered both versions. His absence, however, set off speculation that, what with his alleged involvement in the BAE arms scandal, Bandar had become a serious liability that Abdullah no longer wished to bear. Whether the prince, with all his resources and charms, could ever redeem his standing with this king remained questionable, but he could still hope for redemption once the heir to the Saudi throne, his father, succeeded Abdullah.

Acknowledgments

I am deeply grateful to the Woodrow Wilson International Center for Scholars in Washington, D.C., for its unstinting support throughout the writing and editing of this book. The center, where I was initially a fellow and am now a senior scholar, provided a wonderfully stimulating atmosphere amid scholars, policy makers, and journalists from around the world. Under the highly capable leadership of Lee Hamilton and his deputy, Michael Van Dusen, the center has managed to maintain a neutral political posture in a city marked by ideologically warring think tanks. For journalists, this quality of the place makes it particularly appealing.

The center also offered extensive services in the form of access to libraries and bright student research assistants. As regards the latter, I wish to thank Fareez Ahmed, Hossam Mansour, Brittany Clark, and Caitlin Wesaw for their immense help in tracking down obscure historical documents and pinning down data, dates, events, and endless background details. The center's own library staff, led by the resourceful Janet Spikes, was equally indefatigable in its assistance throughout my research for this book.

Nor could this book have been written without the support of the *Washington Post*, whose editors saw fit to send me as their correspondent to the Middle East. I wish to thank in particular two *Post* colleagues, Ronald Koven and Robert G. Kaiser, with whom I was privileged to work separately in writing two series on Saudi Arabia, the first at the very beginning of my career there and the second toward the end.

Over the years, many Saudis have offered me their gracious hospitality and endless hours of conversation that helped me greatly to understand better the intricacies of their society and government. Among them, I would like to thank in the first place the three Saudi ambassadors to Washington whom I have come to know through numerous interviews and private discussions—Prince Bandar bin Sultan, Prince Turki al-Faisal, and Adel al-Jubeir. Other Saudis who have been of enormous help in my quest to fathom the kingdom are Nawaf Obaid, Jamal Khashoggi, Hassan Yassin, Talaat Wafa, Awadh al-Badi, Abdulaziz Fahad, Khaled al-Maeena, Suleiman Nimer, and Abdullah Alshamari.

Among American specialists in Saudi affairs who have been particularly generous over the years in sharing their wisdom about the kingdom and the U.S.-Saudi relationship are David Long, James Akins, Chas. Freeman, Richard Murphy, Walter Cutler, Nicholas Veliotes, Frederick Dutton, Nancy Dutton, Ray Close, and James Placke. A number of British diplomats and specialists in Saudi affairs were also of enormous assistance in this regard, most notably Sherard Cowper-Coles.

Finally and most importantly, I wish to thank my editor, George Gibson, whose prodigious memory for repetitions, sharp pencil in line editing, and insightful suggestions for improvements in the manuscript were invaluable and much appreciated. And without the help of John "Ike" Williams, I would never have found such a top-notch editor.

Notes

Prologue

1. Interview with Prince Bandar, Nov. 30, 2001.

2. Ibid.

3. Helene Cooper, "Saudis Say They Might Back Sunnis if U.S. Leaves Iraq," *New York Times*, Dec. 13, 2006, and Nawaf Obaid, "Stepping into Iraq: Saudi Arabia Will Protect Sunnis if the U.S. Leaves," *Washington Post*, Nov. 29, 2006.

4. Ali al-Naimi, "Statement by Saudi Oil Minister al-Naimi," Amsterdam, May 21, 2004. PR Newswire, Amsterdam, May 21, 2004.

Chapter 1. Oil, Arms, and Allah

1. The account provided here of the tank controversy is based on the following newspaper articles: Elie Abel, "George Requests Inquiry on Tanks for Saudi Arabia," *New York Times*, Feb. 18, 1956; Abel, "U.S. Lifts Its Ban on Mideast Arms; Frees Arab Tanks," *New York Times*, Feb 19, 1956; "No Arms to Saudi Arabia," *Christian Science Monitor*, Feb. 18, 1956; Chalmers Roberts, "Saudi Envoy Warns U.S. on Tank Ban," *Washington Post Times Herald*, Feb 18, 1956.

2. Under Secretary Herbert Hoover Jr., State Department, "Memorandum for the Record," Feb. 21, 1956, Library of Congress Declassified Documents, declassified Aug. 31, 1981. The document outlines the sequence of events on February 17–18 regarding the tank shipment and U.S. policy considerations.

3. David Long, *The United States and Saudi Arabia: Ambivalent Allies*, 117; V. H.

Oppenheim, "Why Oil Prices Go Up. The Past: We Push Them," *Foreign Policy*, No. 25 (Winter 1976–77), 34–35.

4. "Letter from Franklin D. Roosevelt to Lend-Lease Administrator Edward Stettinius," Feb. 18, 1943, *Foreign Relations of the United States, Diplomatic Papers, 1943*, 859.

5. John Thompson, "U.S. Mission Talks Oil and War in Arabia," *Chicago Daily Tribune*, December 16, 1943.

6. Ibid.

7. J. H. Carmical, "Oil Plans in East Veiled in Secrecy," *New York Times*, Feb. 13, 1944; Henry E. Rose, "Arabian Oil," *Wall Street Journal*, Feb. 10, 1944; Ernest Lindley, "Arabian Pipeline," *Washington Post*, March 15, 1944.

8. "Lend Lease Plane Trails Arab King," *New York Times*, March 9, 1944; "U.S. Delivers Guns to Arabia on Lend-Lease," *Chicago Daily Tribune*, March 9, 1944.

9. "The Secretary of War (Stimson) to the Secretary of State," Oct. 27, 1944, *Foreign Relations of the United States, Diplomatic Papers, 1944*, 748.

10. Ibid., 750–51.

11. See Rachel Bronson, *Thicker than Oil*, 36–42; Bronson, interview with Saudi-US Relations Information Service, March 17, 2005.

12. "Arabian Pipeline Defended by Knox," *New York Times*, March 10, 1944.

13. James E. Webb, acting secretary to the president, "Assistant Secretary McGhee's Conversations with King Ibn Saud and Visit to Liberia," transmittal memorandum, May 9, 1950, *The Papers of Harry S. Truman*, declassified Oct. 4, 1978. State Department.

14. Ibid.

15. Ibid.

16. "Ibn Saud Signs U.S. Pact," *New York Times*, February 22, 1951.

17. "Saudi Arabia.—Agreement on American Use of Dhahran Air Base—U.S. Arms Supplies," *Kessing's Contemporary Archives*, July 21–28, 1951, 11609.

18. "Saudi Arabia.—King Saud's Visit to the U.S.A.—Discussions with President Eisenhower," *Kessing's Contemporary Archives*, March 23–30, 1955, 15450.

19. "More U.S. Arms Go to Saudi Arabia," *New York Times*, May 17, 1956; Associated Press, "U.S. Arms Sent to Saudi Arabia," *Washington Post Times Herald*, May 17, 1956.

20. "F-86F in Foreign Service," Joe Baugher's home page, http://home.att.net/~jbaugher1/p86_12.html. See also Robert F. Dorr, *F-86 Sabre: History of the Sabre and F-J Fury*, Motor Books International Publishers, 1993, 88–89.

21. E. W. Kenworthy, "Saudi Arabia to End Pact on U.S. Base at Dhahran," *New York Times*, March 17, 1961; "Saud Blames U.S. for Rift on Base," *New York Times*, April 16, 1961; *Foreign Relations of the United States, 1961–63*, 51–53.

22. "Saud Blames U.S. for Rift on Base."

23. "Memorandum from the Department of State Executive Secretary (Battle) to the President's Special Assistant (Dungan)," March 21, 1961, *Foreign Relations of the United States, 1961–63*, 51–53.

24. Ibid.

25. Ibid.

26. David B. Ottaway and Robert G. Kaiser, "Saudis May Seek U.S. Exit," *Washington Post*, January 18, 2002.

27. Muslim World League, *Resolutions and Recommendations of Islamic Conference*, May 18–20, 1962.

28. "OIC in Brief," Organization of the Islamic Conference, www.oic.org/english/main/oic_in_brief.htm.

29. Dilip Hiro, *Holy Wars*, 137–39.

30. *The Papers of Dwight David Eisenhower*, 2096–2097.

31. See, for example, Robert Baer, *See No Evil*; Rashid Khalidi, *The Iron Cage*; Robert Dreyfuss, *Devil's Game*; Robert Dreyfuss, "Cold War, Holy Warrior," *Mother Jones*, January/February 2006; Ian Johnson, "A Mosque for ex-Nazis Became Center of Radical Islam," *Wall Street Journal*, July 12, 2005.

32. The National Security Archive in Washington used declassified documents from the 1950s to illustrate in considerable detail how the U.S. government tried to manipulate intrinsic Saudi Islamic hatred of communism to promote its own Cold War public diplomacy in the region. For example, the State Department used Radio Jeddah to broadcast religious programs into the Soviet Union. See Joyce Battle, ed., "U.S. Propaganda in the Middle East—the Early Cold War," National Security Archive, December 13, 2002.

33. The White House log for September 23, 1953, described Ramadan as "Delegate of the Muslim Brothers." See *Dwight D. Eisenhower, Papers as President, 1953–1961, Appointment Books*, "Wednesday, September 23, 1953."

34. Joyce Battle, ed., "U.S. Propaganda in the Middle East—the Early Cold War."

35. See Joe Alex Morris Jr., "French Offer Stymies Big Saudi Arabian Arms Deal," *Los Angeles Times*, June 11, 1965; Morris, "British Grab Saudi Defense Deal from U.S.," Dec. 13, 1965; William McGaffin, "Officials Reticent on Sales of U.S. Arms to Mideast," *Washington Post Times Herald*, June 17, 1965; "Saudis Get Offer of Western Arms," *New York Times*, Nov. 17, 1965; John W. Finney, "Americans Lose Competition as Indecision Is Ended," *New York Times*, Dec. 14, 1965.

36. Finney, "Saudis Are Urged to Buy U.S. Arms," *New York Times*, May 30, 1965; "U.S. Offering to Sell $100 Million in Weapons to Arabia," *Washington Post Times Herald*, May 31, 1965.

37. Fouad al-Farsy, *Saudi Arabia*, 53.

38. Mordechai Abir, *Saudi Arabia in the Oil Era*, 127.

39. Michael Getler, "Saudis Seeking 24 to 30 Phantom Jets," *Washington Post*, June 5, 1973.

40. State Department, "Proposed Presidential Message to King Faisal," action memorandum, Oct. 12, 1973, declassified Dec. 31, 1981; "Message to the King from the Secretary," State Department cable 203672 to U.S. Embassy, Saudi Arabia, October 14, 1973,

declassified Nov. 8, 2000; William Burr, ed., *The October War and U.S. Policy*, documents 28 and 29A, National Security Archive, October 7, 2003.

41. "Oil Flow to U.S. Halted by Saudis," *New York Times*, October 21, 1973.

42. "Letter from President Roosevelt to King Ibn Saud, April 5, 1945," MidEastWeb, www.mideastweb.org/roosevelt.htm.

43. Nawaf E. Obaid. "Improving US Intelligence Analysis on the Saudi Arabian Decision Making Process," John F. Kennedy School of Government, Harvard University, May 1, 1998, 16.

44. John C. West, Daily Diary, John C. West Papers, "March 5, 1979." West was U.S. ambassador to Saudi Arabia from 1977 to 1981. He learned of King Faisal's offer in a conversation with Prince Turki al-Faisal, the Saudi intelligence chief.

45. Ottaway. "US Offered Arabian Oil for Share of Market," *Los Angeles Times*, Oct. 3, 1972.

46. Ottaway and Ronald Koven, "Saudis Tie Oil to U.S. Policy on Israel," *Washington Post Times Herald*, April 19, 1973.

47. Koven and Ottaway, "U.S. Oil Nightmare: Worldwide Shortage," *Washington Post Times Herald*, June 17, 1973.

48. Ibid.

Chapter 2. Making of the Messenger

1. Interview with Prince Bandar, March 28, 1996.

2. Ibid.

3. Ibid.

4. Ibid.

5. Ibid.

6. Ibid.

7. Ibid.

8. Ibid.

9. Ibid.

10. Interview with Prince Bandar, Nov. 30, 2001.

11. Interview with Prince Bandar, March 28, 1996.

12. Ibid.

13. Interview with Prince Bandar, Nov. 30, 2001.

14. Ibid.

15. Interview with Prince Bandar, March 28, 1996.

16. Ibid.

17. State Department, "Saudi Regional Role," briefing paper, May 1977, Box 36, Staff Offices Counsel, Lipshutz's Files, Middle East: Saudi Arabia 10/77–6/78, [CF O/A 712] Jimmy Carter Library.

18. U.S. Defense Department, Security Assistance Agency Administration and Management Business Operations, "Fiscal Year Series," Sept. 30, 2005.

19. Ibid.

20. For an excellent history, see Richard F. Grimmett, "Executive-Legislative Consultation on U.S. Arms Sales."

21. "Memorandum: F-15s to Saudi Arabia—A Threat to Peace."

22. "A Study of the American Jewish Lobby." Summer 1977 (?), Jimmy Carter Library, Box 35, Chief of Staff Jordan, Iran, 4/80.

23. Daily Diary, John C. West Papers, "Sunday, April 23, 1978."

24. Letter from John C. West to Prince Fahd bin Abdul Aziz, June 6, 1978, John C. West Papers.

25. West, Daily Diary, "Wednesday, April 19, 1978."

26. Interview with Prince Bandar, March 28, 1996.

27. Ibid.

28. Ibid.

29. Ibid.

30. Ibid.

31. Ibid.

32. Ibid.

33. Interview with Prince Bandar, Nov. 30, 2001.

34. Interview with Prince Bandar, March 28, 1996.

35. Ibid.

36. West, Daily Diary, "Thursday, May 4, 1978."

37. Ibid.

38. William Claiborne, "Holocaust Book Is Tool in Arms Lobbying," *Washington Post*, April 22, 1978.

39. George C. Wilson, "Study Backs Saudis' Need for F-15s," *Washington Post*, April 29, 1978; Don Oberdorfer, "Begin Appeals to American Morality in Week Long Search for Support," *Washington Post*, May 7, 1978; Richard Harwood and Ward Sinclair, "Lobbying for Warplane Brings Saudis out of Isolation," *Washington Post*, May 7, 1978; Nick Ludington, "An AP News Special," Associated Press, May 8, 1978; "Representing the Arab Point of View," *National Journal*, May 13, 1978; "Jewish Lobby Loses a Big One," *Time*, May 29, 1978.

40. West, Daily Diary, "Monday, May 15, 1978."

41. Robert G. Kaiser, "Jet Deal: 'Gang That Couldn't Shoot Straight' Wins One," *Washington Post*, May 18, 1978.

42. Ibid.

43. West, Daily Diary, "Friday, May 5, 1978."

Chapter 3. Return of the Messenger

1. Interview with Prince Bandar, March 28, 1996.

2. Ibid.

3. John C. West, Daily Diary, John C. West Papers, "Wednesday, April 19, 1978."

4. "Memorandum. To: HRH Bandar bin Sultan, Major, Royal Saudi Air Force. From: David E. Long, Professorial Lecturer, SAIS," May 30, 1979, Box 10, John C. West Papers.

5. "Memorandum for: Dean Robert Osgood, the Johns Hopkins University, School of Advanced International Studies. From: David E. Long," May 18, 1979, Box 10, John C. West Papers.

6. "Letter from George R. Packard, Dean, School of Advanced International Studies, the Johns Hopkins University to His Royal Highness Sultan Bin Abdul Aziz," June 19, 1980, Box 10, John C. West Papers.

7. West, Daily Diary, "Monday, Sept. 15, 1980."

8. Ibid., "Saturday, Sept. 13, 1980."

9. West, annotation, April 9, 1998, attached to "Letter from George R. Packard," June 19, 1980, Box 10, John C. West Papers.

10. "Letter from Zbigniew Brzezinski to John C. West," Oct. 7, 1980, Box 10, John C. West Papers.

11. Interview by telephone with David E. Long, Jan. 3, 2007.

12. Jimmy Carter, "Energy and National Goals," July 15, 1979, *Public Papers of the Presidents of the United States. Jimmy Carter*, vol. 2, 1979, 1235–1241.

13. Interview with Prince Bandar, March 28, 1996.

14. West, Daily Diary, "Wednesday, May 30, 1979."

15. Ibid., "Friday, June 1, 1978."

16. "Letter from President Jimmy Carter to HRH Prince Fahd ibn Abd al-Aziz Saud," June 6, 1979, Box 10, John C. West Papers.

17. "John C. West letter to President Carter," July 6, 1979, Box 10, John C. West Papers.

18. Ibid.

19. West, Daily Diary, "Friday, December 14, 1979."

20. Ibid., "Tuesday, Dec. 4, 1979."

21. Ibid., "Wednesday, Dec. 5, 1978."

22. Ibid., "Friday, December 14, 1979."

23. Ibid., "Wednesday, March 19, 1980."

24. Ibid., "Wednesday, April 2, 1980."

25. Ibid., "Friday, April 11, 1980."

26. "The President's Schedule-Wednesday-April 9, 1980," Jimmy Carter Library, Presidential Diary Office, Box PP-77, Diary File, April 1 through April 11, 1980.

27. West, Daily Diary, "Friday, April 11, 1980."

28. West, handwritten note, June 8, 1998, attached to "Draft. Letter to Crown Prince Fahd from President Carter," April 3, 1980, Box 10, John C. West Papers.

29. Ibid.

30. Carter, "The State of the Union," Jan. 23, 1980, *Public Papers of the Presidents of the United States: Jimmy Carter*, vol. 1, 1980–81, 194–202.

31. West called his study *The Six Crises*, the title of President Richard Nixon's book about the challenges he had faced in his political career. West noted that the seventh crisis, Watergate, "had done him in. The question, therefore, was could Saudi Arabia absorb another crisis, and what we could do to prevent it." West, Daily Diary, "Tuesday, March 11, 1980."

32. Ibid., "Thursday, March 13, 1980."

33. Ibid., "Sunday, Sept. 28, 1980."

34. Ibid., "Saturday, Oct. 4, 1980."

35. Ibid., "Sunday, Sept. 28, 1980."

36. Ibid.

37. Ibid., "Tuesday, Sept. 30, 1980."

38. Ibid., "Monday, Oct. 13, 1980."

39. "Letter from John West to President Carter," Sept. 16, 1980, Box 10, John C. West Papers.

40. West, Daily Diary, "Monday, Oct. 13, 1980."

Chapter 4. *"You Came a Long Way"*

1. Interview with Prince Bandar, March 28, 1996.

2. Ibid.

3. Nicholas Laham, *Selling AWACS to Saudi Arabia*, 90.

4. Richard F. Grimmett, *Executive-Legislative Consultation on U.S. Arms Sales*, 33–35.

5. Ronald Reagan, *An American Life*, 410.

6. See Steven Emerson, *The American House of Saud*; Grimmett, *Executive-Legislative Consultation on U.S. Arms Sales*.

7. Grimmett, ibid.

8. In a letter October 28, 1981, to George and Lolie Eccles, Reagan said, "I'm sitting here waiting out the long afternoon 'til 5 p.m. when the Senate votes on the AWACS sale to Saudi Arabia. At the moment, the count looks about even. One undecided senator told me he was praying for guidance. I told him if he got a busy signal it was me in there ahead of him with my own prayers." Ronald Reagan, *A Life in Letters*, 686.

9. John M. Goshko, "Senate Backs Reagan on AWACS Sale; Vote of 52 to 48 Is Major Victory," *Washington Post*, Oct. 29, 1981.

10. Paul Taylor, " 'Israeli Lobby' Voices Concern on U.S. Shift," *Washington Post*, Oct. 30, 1981.

11. Reagan, *An American Life*, 415.

12. See, for example, Jim Adams, "Saudi Prince Lobbies for AWACS Sale," Associated Press, Sept. 16, 1981; The Ear, *Washington Post*, Oct. 23, 1981; Donald M. Rothberg, "Some Took the High Road and Some Took the Low Road," Associated Press, Oct. 28, 1981; Lee Lescaze, "President, Hill Allies Make 'a Nice Save,' " *Washington Post*, Oct. 30, 1981.

13. Melinda Beck with John J. Lindsay, "Trying to Patch the AWACS Deal," *Newsweek*, Oct. 5, 1981.

14. Francis X. Clines and Bernard Weinraub, Briefing, *New York Times*, Oct. 31, 1981.

15. Adams, "Saudi Prince, Reagan, Senators Discussing AWACS Compromise," Associated Press, Sept. 25, 1981; Juan J. Walte, United Press International, Sept. 25, 1981.

16. Grimmett, *Executive-Legislative Consultation on U.S. Arms Sales*, 22.

17. Scott Armstrong, " 'Saudis AWACS Just the Beginning of New Strategy," *Washington Post*, Nov. 1, 1981.

18. Ibid.

19. U.S. Defense Department, Security Assistance Agency, Administration and Management Business Operations, "Fiscal Year Series," Sept. 30, 2005.

20. John C. West, Daily Diary, John C. West Papers, "Saturday, Oct. 4, 1980."

21. Interview with Prince Bandar, Nov. 30, 2001.

22. David B. Ottaway, "Saudi King Seeks Islamic Law Review," *Washington Post*, June 16, 1983.

23. "402 Die in Mecca as Iranians Riot," *Facts on File World News Digest*, Aug. 7, 1987 (New York: Infobase Publishing).

24. Dr. Muhammad Taqi-ud-Din al-Hilali and Dr. Muhammad, Muhsin Khan, *Interpretation of the Meaning of the Noble Qur'an* (Riyadh: Darussalam, 1996).

25. The concept of "soft power" as used here was first propounded by Harvard University professor Joseph Nye. He coined the term in reference to a nation's ability to influence others through culture or ideology. See Joseph S. Nye Jr., *Soft Power: The Means to Success in World Politics* (Cambridge, MA: Perseus Books Group, 2004).

26. Interview with Prince Bandar, March 28, 1996.

27. Ibid.

28. Ibid.

29. Interview with and memorandum from Alexander Haig Jr., March 5, 2007.

30. George Shultz, *Turmoil and Triumph*, 82.

31. Reagan, *Public Papers of the Presidents of the United States, 1986*, 797–799.

32. Reagan, *The Reagan Diaries*, 183.

33. Interview with Prince Bandar, March 28, 1996.

34. Ibid.

35. See Steve Coll, *Ghost Wars*; Rachel Bronson, *Thicker than Oil*.

36. Interview with Prince Bandar, March 4, 1996.

37. Ibid.

38. Interview with Prince Bandar, Nov. 30, 2001.

39. Interview with Prince Bandar, March 28, 1996.

40. Interview with Prince Bandar, Nov. 30, 2001.

41. "Book: Casey Went 'Off the Books' to Gain Ends," United Press International, Sept. 27, 1987. UPI quoted from Woodward excerpts that appeared in the *Washington Post* that day. See also Bob Woodward, *Veil*, 398.

42. The fourth person was William Simpson, author of *The Prince* (99–101). Simpson, however, does not make clear which year the election took place.

43. See Ottaway and Robert G. Kaiser, "Saudis May Seek U.S. Exit," *Washington Post*, Jan. 18, 2002; Kaiser and Ottaway, "Saudi Leader's Anger Revealed Shaky Ties," *Washington Post*, Feb. 10, 2002; Kaiser and Ottaway, "Oil for Security Fueled Close Ties," *Washington Post*, Feb. 11, 2002; Ottaway and Kaiser, "After Sept. 11, Severe Tests Loom for Relationship," *Washington Post*, Feb. 12, 2002.

44. Interview with Maxwell Rabb, Jan. 4, 2002.

45. Interview with William Wilson, Jan. 4, 2002.

46. Interview with Robert McFarlane, Jan. 4, 2002.

47. Woodward, *Veil*, 395–98.

48. Bill Moyers, "Target America," *Frontline*, PBS, Oct. 4, 2001.

49. "Spotlight: Bandar Survives Casey Book, but Saudi Arms Battle Looms," *Mideast Markets*, Oct. 12, 1987.

50. Reagan, *The Reagan Diaries*, 201.

51. Interview with Prince Bandar, March 28, 1996.

Chapter 5. *"Trust but Verify"*

1. Interview with Prince Bandar, March 4, 1996.

2. Ibid.

3. Ibid.

4. Ibid.

5. Ibid.

6. David B. Ottaway, "Saudi Lobby Losing Strength," *Washington Post*, May 10, 1986.

7. Ottaway, "Saudis Use Bush Visit to Signal Displeasure," *Washington Post*, April 21, 1986.

8. The Saudi production increase has been interpreted by some historians as part of a secret U.S.-Saudi plan to accelerate the economic collapse of the Soviet Union. The

Soviet Politburo had sent a letter to Fahd in early 1986 complaining about the collapse in prices that had cut the Soviets' own oil export earnings dramatically. Historian Peter Schweizer interpreted the Saudi action as an integral part of what he called Reagan's "secret strategy" to bankrupt the Soviet Union, though he conceded he had no idea what caused the Saudis to increase production in the first place. In any case, in the spring of 1986, both Vice President George H. W. Bush and Soviet leader Mikhail Gorbachev were pressuring the Saudis to cut production in order to push oil prices back up. See Peter Schweizer, *Victory*, 242–63.

9. Ottaway, "Bush, Saudi King Fahd Discuss Oil," *Washington Post*, April 6, 1986.

10. Ibid.

11. Interview with Prince Bandar, March 4, 1996.

12. Ibid.

13. Ibid.

14. Khaled bin Sultan and Patrick Seale, *Desert Warrior*, 137–42.

15. Ottaway, "Saudi Hid Acquisition of Missiles," *Washington Post*, March 29, 1988.

16. John M. Goshko and Don Oberdorfer, "Chinese Sell Saudis Missiles Capable of Covering Mideast," *Washington Post*, March 18, 1988.

17. Sergei Shargorodsky, "Deny Israel Considering Attack on Saudi Arabia over Missiles," Associated Press, March 25, 1988.

18. Interview with Prince Bandar, March 4, 1996.

19. Ibid.

20. Lionel Barber, "Reagan Warns Israel Against Pre-Emptive Saudi Missile Strike," *Financial Times*, March 26, 1988.

21. George C. Wilson and Ottaway, "Saudi-Israeli Tensions Worry U.S.," *Washington Post*, March 25, 1988.

22. Ibid.

23. E-mail exchange with and comments from Colin Powell, March 1, 2007.

24. Interview with Hume Horan, Dec. 10, 2001.

25. Ottaway, "Saudis Ask U.S. to Recall Envoy," *Washington Post*, April 1, 1988.

26. Interview with Horan, Dec. 10, 2001.

27. Ibid.

28. Interview with Prince Bandar, Nov. 30, 2001.

29. Interview with Nicholas Veliotes, Feb. 7, 2007.

30. Ibid.

31. Tad Szulc, "A Swedish Middleman Works the Middle East," *Los Angeles Times*, Dec. 25, 1988.

32. Norman Kempster, "U.S. to Talk with PLO as Arafat Meets Terms," *Los Angeles Times*, Dec. 15, 1988.

33. Samantha Sparks, "Angola: Saudi Aid to Rebels May be 'Brother' of Irangate Scandal," IPS-Inter Press Service, July 1, 1987.

34. Ibid.

35. Interview with Prince Bandar, March 4, 1996.

36. Ibid.

37. Horan believed the Chinese had paid Bandar $200 million in commissions on the Saudi purchase of the missiles. If so, the amount was probably less than 10 percent. The Saudis have never disclosed how much they paid, but estimates have ranged as high as $3.5 billion, including the cost for constructing two launching sites and various maintenance services and training contracts. Bandar himself told one European diplomat that he was handsomely rewarded for the deal by the king, who had made it possible for him to purchase the picturesque "village" of Glympton outside Oxford, England—a two-thousand-acre country estate with a Georgian mansion and twenty-one stone cottages valued at slightly less than $180 million. Interview with a European diplomat formerly stationed in Riyadh, June 27, 2006.

38. Steve Coll, *Ghost Wars*.

39. Ibid, 81–82.

40. Interview with Prince Bandar, March 28, 1996.

41. Woodrow Wilson International Center for Scholars, *Cold War International History Project Bulletin*, Issue 14/15, Winter 2003–Spring 2004, 143–92. This section has excerpts from Soviet Politburo meetings and exchanges between Gorbachev and Afghan leader Najibullah and Gorbachev and President Ronald Reagan.

42. Ibid, 166–67.

43. Interview with Prince Bandar, March 4, 1996.

Chapter 6. *"Going All the Way"*

1. Interview with Prince Bandar, March 4, 1996.

2. Ibid.

3. Ibid.

4. Interview with Prince Bandar, Nov. 30, 2001.

5. Interview with Prince Bandar, March 4, 1996.

6. Ibid.

7. George Bush and Brent Scowcroft, *A World Transformed*, 328.

8. Ibid, 325.

9. Ibid.

10. Interview with Prince Bandar, March 4, 1996.

11. Ibid.

12. Ibid.

13. Khaled bin Sultan and Patrick Seale, *Desert Warrior*, 317.

14. Interview with Prince Bandar, March 4, 1996.

15. Ibid.

16. Interview with Chas. Freeman Jr. by Charles Stuart Kennedy, April 14, 1995, Association for Diplomatic Studies and Training, Arlington, VA.

17. Interview with Prince Bandar, March 4, 1996.

18. Ibid.

19. Ibid. and interview with Freeman by Kennedy, April 14, 1995.

20. Interview with Prince Bandar, March 4, 1996.

21. Ibid.

22. Interview with Freeman by Kennedy, April 14, 1995.

23. Ibid.

24. Interview with Prince Bandar, March 4, 1996.

25. Ibid.

26. Interview with Prince Bandar, March 28, 1996.

27. Colin Powell, *My American Journey*, 242.

28. Ibid., 465.

29. Ibid.

30. Ibid., 474.

31. Ibid.

32. Interview with Prince Bandar, March 4, 1996.

33. Ibid.

34. Ibid.

35. John Judis, "On the Homefront: The Gulf War's Strangest Bedfellows," *Washington Post*, June 23, 1991.

36. David Makovsky, "Saudi Arabia Misled U.S. Jewish Leaders," *Jerusalem Post*, July 8, 1991.

37. Interview with Stephen Solarz, March 21, 2007.

38. Bin Sultan and Seale, *Desert Warrior*, 11–12.

39. Interview with Prince Bandar, March 4, 1996.

40. Molly Moore, "Iraq Said to Have Supply of Biological Weapons," *Washington Post*, Sept. 29, 1990; Michael R. Gordon, "CIA Fears Iraq Could Deploy Biological Arms by Early 1991," *New York Times*, Sept. 29, 1990.

41. Interview with Prince Bandar, March 4, 1996.

42. James A. Baker III, *The Politics of Diplomacy*, 359.

43. Bin Sultan and Seale, *Desert Warrior*, 348.

44. Interview with Prince Bandar, March 4, 1996.

45. Ibid.

46. Baker, *The Politics of Diplomacy*, 453.

47. Ibid.

48. Ibid.

49. Dennis Ross, *The Missing Peace*, 74–75.

50. Margaret Garrard Warner, "Pipeline to Riyadh: The Go-Between," *Newsweek*, Dec. 9, 1991.

51. Ibid.

52. Baker, *The Politics of Diplomacy*, 460.

53. Thomas Friedman, "First Full Meeting," *New York Times*, Oct. 31, 1991.

54. Abdulaziz H. al-Fahad, "From Exclusivism to Accommodation: Doctrinal and Legal Evolution of Wahhabism," *New York University Law Review* 79 (2004): 518–19.

55. The twelve "necessary" reforms are reprinted in R. Hrair Dekmejian, "The Rise of Political Islamism in Saudi Arabia," *Middle East Journal* 48, no. 4 (Autumn 1994): 630–31. See also "Conservative Moslems Urge Reform," *Facts on File World News Digest*, June 20, 1991.

56. Ibid.

57. International Crisis Group, "Saudi Arabia Backgrounder: Who Are the Islamists?," Report No. 31, Sept. 21, 2004.

58. Interview with Freeman by Kennedy, April 14, 1995.

59. Powell, *My American Journey*, 52.

60. Ibid., 535; Bob Woodward, *The Commanders*.

61. Bush and Scowcroft, *A World Transformed*, 489.

62. Ibid., 490.

63. Bin Sultan and Seale, *Desert Warrior*, 418–19.

64. Interview with Freeman by Kennedy, April 14, 1995.

65. Ibid.

66. Ibid.

67. Federation of American Scientists, "Arms Sales Monitoring Project, Saudi Arabia, http://fas.org/asmp/profiles/Saudi_Arabia.htm; interview with Freeman by Kennedy, April 14, 1995.

68. David Hirst, "Arabs See Sowing of Turmoil's Seeds," *Guardian*, Aug. 26, 1992.

69. John Lancaster, " 'No-Fly Zone' in Iraq Is Set, Scowcroft Says," *Washington Post*, Aug. 20, 1992.

70. Martin Walker, "Arab Doubts Delay Allied Moves on Iraqi Air Exclusion Zone," *Guardian*, Aug. 25, 1992.

71. Interview with Freeman, March 20, 2007.

72. Ibid.

73. Interview with Freeman by Kennedy, April 14, 1995.

74. Ibid.

75. Ibid.

76. U.S. Defense Department, Security Assistance Agency, Administration and Management Business Operations, "Fiscal Year Series," Sept. 30, 2003.

77. Interview with Freeman, March 20, 2007.

78. Interview with Freeman by Kennedy, April 14, 1995.

79. Ibid.

80. Ibid.

81. Bush and Scowcroft, *A World Transformed*, 489.

Chapter 7. Strategic Asset or Strategic Liability

1. Interview with Prince Bandar, Nov. 30, 2001.

2. Elsa Walsh, "The Prince," *New Yorker*, March 24, 2003.

3. David B. Ottaway, "Saudis Use Bush Visit to Signal Displeasure," *Washington Post*, April 21, 1986.

4. Interview with Prince Bandar, March 28, 1996.

5. Ibid.

6. Ibid.

7. Ibid.

8. Interview with Martin Indyk, April 20, 2007.

9. Ibid.

10. Interview with Anthony Lake, Oct. 18, 2006.

11. Interview with Prince Bandar, Feb. 2, 1996.

12. William Safire, On Language, "Jericho, Trumpets, Walls, Etc.," *New York Times*, Oct. 3, 1993.

13. Stephen Engelberg, "U.S.-Saudi Deals in 90s Shifting away from Cash Toward Credit," *New York Times*, Aug. 23, 1993.

14. John Lancaster and John Mintz, "Strapped Saudis Seek to Stretch Out Payments for U.S. Arms," *Washington Post*, Jan. 7, 1994.

15. Fred Barnes, "Saudi Doody; Presidential Export Advocacy; White House Watch," *New Republic*, March 14, 1994.

16. Interview with Indyk, April 20, 2007.

17. Interview with Prince Bandar, March 28, 1996.

18. "Announcement by President Clinton on Sale of Aircraft to Saudi Arabia," White House briefing transcript, Federal News Service, Feb. 16, 1994.

19. Ibid.

20. Elaine Sciolino, "Clinton Friend, in New Job, Keeps His Power," *New York Times*, Sept. 15, 1997.

21. Michael Collins, "Saudi Prince Pushes G-7 on Yemen," United Press International, July 8, 1994.

22. "Clinton Reassures Bandar," United Press International, July 9, 1994.

23. Sciolino and Eric Schmitt, "Saudi Arabia, Its Purse Thinner, Learns How to Say 'No' to U.S.," *New York Times*, Nov. 4, 1994.

24. Michael R. Gordon, "US Plans to Keep Planes and Tanks in the Gulf Area," *New York Times*, Oct. 14, 1994.

25. Sciolino and Schmitt, "Saudi Arabia, Its Purse Thinner."

26. Interview with Prince Bandar, Nov. 30, 2001.

27. Joshua Teitelbaum, *Holier than Thou*, 57–58.

28. Ibid.

29. Abdel Bari Atwan, *The Secret History of al Qaeda*, 168.

30. Dana Priest and John Mintz, "Attack Puts Spotlight on American Presence," *Washington Post*, Nov. 14, 1995.

31. "Four Arrested in Connection with the 1995 Riyadh Bombing Make Statements," BBC, April 23, 1996.

32. Ibid.

33. William McCants, ed., *Militant Ideology Atlas, Executive Report*, Combating Terrorism Center, West Point, NY, November 2006.

34. Statement of Chairman Floyd Spence on the report of the bombing of Khobar Towers, Aug. 14, 1996, and "The Khobar Towers Bombing Incident," staff report, U.S. House of Representatives, National Security Committee, Aug. 14, 1996.

35. Louis J. Freeh, *My FBI*, 10.

36. R. Jeffrey Smith, "Saudis Hold 40 Suspects in GI Quarters Bombing," *Washington Post*, Nov. 1, 1996.

37. David B. Ottaway and Brian Duffy, "Iranian Aide Linked to Bombing Suspect," *Washington Post*, April 13, 1997.

38. Interview with Prince Bandar, Nov. 30, 2001.

39. Interview with Lake, Oct. 18, 2006.

40. Ibid.

41. Interview with Indyk, April 20, 2007.

42. Freeh, *My FBI*, 25.

43. Howard Kurtz, "Ex-FBI Chief Puts Clinton Critique in Print," *Washington Post*, Oct. 7, 2005.

44. Interview with Wyche Fowler, April 16, 2007.

45. Federal Bureau of Investigation, press release, Washington, DC, June 21, 2001.

46. Ibid.

Chapter 8. Midlife Crisis

1. Interview with Prince Bandar, Feb. 2, 1996.

2. Ibid.

3. Ibid.

4. David B. Ottaway, "Been There, Done That," *Washington Post*, July 21, 1996.

5. Paul Anderson, "Ode to the Prince." Anderson gave the author a copy of the lyrics in March 1996.

6. Interview with Prince Bandar, Feb. 2, 1996.

7. Ibid.

8. Ibid.

9. Interview with Prince Bandar, Nov. 30, 2001.

10. Ibid.

11. Ibid.

12. Edward Morse, executive director, Hess Energy Trading, remarks before the Washington Institute for Near East Policy, March 30, 2000, reprinted in Washington Institute for Near East Policy, *Policy Watch*, April 5, 2000.

13. Elaine Sciolino, "At Lunch with the Saudis, FBI Director Complains," *New York Times*, March 1, 1997.

14. Interview with Nathaniel Kern, Nov. 27, 2001.

15. Ibid.

16. Ibid.

17. Ottaway, "Saudis Talk with 7 U.S. Oil Firms," *Washington Post*, Sept. 30, 1998.

18. Interview with Prince Bandar, Nov. 30, 2001.

19. Lynne Duke, "How South Africa Finessed Visit," *Washington Post*, March 29, 1998.

20. Interview with Martin Indyk, April 20, 2007.

21. Interview with a senior State Department official, Nov. 11, 1998.

22. Thomas Lippman, "Plan to Move Pan Am Trial Is Weighed," *Washington Post*, July 22, 1998.

23. Aaron Lobel and John Haas, transcript of interview with Martin Indyk, America Abroad Media, Oct. 27, 2006.

24. Ibid.

25. Interview with Indyk.

26. Lobel and Haas.

27. Ibid.

28. William J. Clinton, *Public Papers of the Presidents of the United States*, 502.

29. "Cohen Told That Saudi Arabia Is Off Limits for Any Attack on Iraq," Associated Press, Nov. 3, 1998.

30. Interview with Prince Bandar, Nov. 30, 2001.

31. Interview with Indyk.

32. Ibid.

33. See Dennis Ross, *The Missing Peace*, 568; Elsa Walsh, "The Prince," *New Yorker*, March 24, 2003. Ross, Clinton's chief Middle East peace negotiator, wrote that Bandar initiated the meeting. He said later in an interview on April 29, 2007, that it took place in late January 2000. Bandar told Walsh that Clinton asked to see him in March 2000.

34. Ross, *The Missing Peace*, 568–69.

35. Ibid.

36. Ibid., 587.

37. Walsh, "The Prince."

38. Interview with Ross, April 29, 2007.

39. Walsh, "The Prince."

40. Ross, *The Missing Peace*, 756.

41. Ibid.

42. Interview with Ross.

43. Ibid.

44. Ibid.

45. Interview with an aide to Prince Bandar, Feb. 26, 2007.

46. Interview with Ross.

47. Interview with Bruce Riedel, May 15, 2007.

Chapter 9. *"You Go Your Way, I Go My Way"*

1. Interview with Prince Bandar, Nov. 30, 2001. (All references in this chapter to interviews with the prince come from this one.)

2. Ibid.

3. bid.

4. Interview with Martin Indyk, April 20, 2007.

5. Interview with Bruce Riedel, May 15, 2007.

6. Interview with Prince Bandar.

7. James Dao with Steve Lee Meyers, "Bush Approves Attacks Beyond 'No Fly' Zone—First in 2 Years," *New York Times*, Feb. 17, 2001.

8. Anton La Guardia and Toby Helm, "Germans Attack Bombing as Rift on Iraq Deepens," *Daily Telegraph,* Feb. 20, 2001; "A Message from the Past for Baghdad," *Economist*, Feb. 24, 2001.

9. Rear Admiral Craig Quigley, "Special Defense Department Briefing: The Bombing of Iraq," Federal News Service, Feb. 16, 2001.

10. Interview with Riedel.

11. Ibid.

12. Interview with a former Pentagon official responsible for Middle East operations, Jan. 1, 2002.

13. Ibid.

14. Interview with Prince Bandar.

15. "Saudi Arabia to Other Arab Countries: Consider Renewal of Boycott," Globes Online, June 18, 2001.

16. Jane Perlez, "Bush Senior, on His Son's Behalf, Reassures Saudi Leader," *New York Times*, July 15, 2001.

17. Roula Khalaf, "Regal Reformer," *Financial Times*, June 25, 2001.

18. Dick Cheney, interview with Fox News, Aug. 3, 2001.

19. Ghazi al-Qusaibi, "Dubya Against the World," *Al-Hayat*, Aug. 9, 2001, reprinted in English by the Middle East Media Research Institute, Special Dispatch Series, no. 256, Aug. 15, 2001.

20. Interview with Prince Bandar.

21. Ibid.

22. Ibid.

23. Ibid.

24. Ibid.

25. Interview with Riedel.

26. Interview with Prince Bandar.

27. "Crown Prince Abdullah Urges Balanced U.S. Role in Middle East," transcript of Crown Prince Abdullah's interview with the *Financial Times*, GulfWire, June 25, 2001.

28. Interview with Riedel.

29. Interview with Prince Bandar.

30. Ibid.

31. Ibid.

32. Ibid.

33. Interview with Riedel.

34. Interview with Prince Bandar.

Chapter 10. *"Everybody Has a Price"*

1. The two reporters were myself and Robert G. Kaiser, at that time associate editor of the *Washington Post*.

2. Interview with Prince Bandar, Nov. 30, 2001. (All references in this chapter to interviews with the prince come from this one.)

3. Ibid.

4. Ibid.

5. *The 9/11 Commission Report* later absolved U.S. authorities for allowing the planes to leave. It said all the flights left between September 14 and 24, after U.S. airspace was reopened and not before, as had initially been reported. See *The 9/11 Commission Report*, 557.

6. Bob Deans, "Saudis Launch PR Effort in America," Cox News Service, April 26, 2002.

7. Interview with Prince Bandar.

8. Ibid.

9. Ibid.

10. Ibid.

11. "Interview: Bandar bin Sultan," *Frontline*, PBS, Oct. 7, 2001, http://www.pbs
.org/wgbh/pages/frontline/shows/terrorism/interviews/bandar.html. The interview was
conducted in late September 2001 and later posted on the PBS Web site.

12. Interview with Prince Bandar.

13. David B. Ottaway, "Saudi Court Case Raises Question of Wide Corruption by
Leadership," *Washington Post*, Jan. 2, 1996.

14. Ibid.

15. Ibid.

16. Interview with Prince Bandar.

17. Ibid.

18. Ibid.

19. Kaiser, "Enormous Wealth Spilled into American Coffers," *Washington Post*, Feb.
11, 2002.

20. Interview with Prince Bandar.

21. Ibid.

22. Douglas Jehl, "A Saudi Prince with an Unconventional Idea: Elections," *New
York Times*, Nov. 28, 2001.

23. Interview with Prince Bandar.

24. Ibid.

25. Bob Woodward, Kaiser, and Ottaway, "U.S. Fears Bin Laden Made Nuclear
Strides," *Washington Post*, Dec. 4, 2001.

26. George Tenet, *At the Center of the Storm*, 262–69.

27. Interview with a U.S. intelligence official, Dec. 2, 2001.

28. Interview with Prince Bandar.

29. Ibid.

30. Interview with Prince Naif bin Abdulaziz in *Ain-al-Yaqeen*, Nov. 29, 2001, translated by the Middle East Media Research Institute, Special Dispatch Series, no. 446, Dec.
3, 2002.

31. Deans, "Saudis Launch PR Effort in America."

32. Interview with Prince Bandar.

33. Interview with Bruce Riedel, May 15, 2007.

34. Interview with Prince Bandar.

35. Dana Milbank, "President Thanks Saudis for Anti-Terrorism Aid," *Washington
Post*, Oct. 26, 2001.

36. Interview with Prince Bandar.

37. Ottaway and Kaiser, "After Sept. 11, Severe Test Looms for Relationship," *Washington Post*, Feb. 12, 2002.

38. U.S. Department of Energy, "Annual Oil Market Chronology, 2000s."

39. Karen DeYoung, "Saudis Seethe over Media Reports on Anti-Terror Effort,"
Washington Post, Nov. 6, 2001.

40. Interview with Prince Bandar.

41. Ibid.

42. Joseph McMillan, "U.S.-Saudi Relations: Rebuilding the Strategic Consensus," Institute for National Strategic Studies, National Defense University, Washington, D.C., November 2001.

43. Interview with Prince Bandar.

44. Howard Schneider, "Ending Doubts, Saudis to Allow U.S. to Use Base," *Washington Post*, Sept. 28, 2001.

45. "Saudi Arabia Says No," CBS News, Sept. 30, 2001.

46. Interview with Prince Bandar.

47. Ibid.

48. Interview with a former senior Pentagon official responsible for Saudi Arabia, Jan. 1, 2002.

49. Interview with Prince Bandar.

50. Ibid.

51. Ibid.

52. Ibid.

53. Ibid.

Chapter 11. Wahhabi Islam at Home and Abroad

1. Interview with Prince Naif bin Abdulaziz in *al-Siyasa*, reprinted in *Ain-al-Yaqeen*, Nov. 29, 2002, and in Middle East Media Research Institute, Special Dispatch Series, no. 446, Dec. 3, 2002.

2. Interview with Sheikh Saleh al-Sheikh, March 17, 2004.

3. Ibid.

4. Ibid.

5. Ibid.

6. See Madawi al-Rasheed, *Contesting the Saudi State*, 140–49; "Islamist Websites and Their Hosts, Part II: Clerics," Middle East Media Research Institute, Special Report, no. 35, Nov. 11, 2004; Reuven Paz, "The First Islamist Fatwah on the Use of Weapons of Mass Destruction," Global Research in International Affairs Center, Prism Special Dispatches 1, no. 1 (May 2003).

7. Ibid.

8. For the original ruling in Arabic, see http://www.muslm.net/vb/showthread.php?p=1356353.

9. "Saudi Cleric al-Fahad Disavows Previous Fatwas, Statements on Saudi TV," BBC Monitoring International Reports, Nov. 23, 2003.

10. "The Fatwa of the 26 Clerics, Open Sermon to the Militant Iraqi People," *Frontline*, PBS, Feb. 8, 2005. The Fatwa was issued on Nov. 5, 2004, and later posted on the PBS Web site.

11. Nawaf Obaid, "Yes to bin Laden Rhetoric; No to al-Qaeda Violence," *International Herald Tribune*, June 28, 2004.

12. Ibid.

13. David B. Ottaway, "Saudi Effort Draws on Radical Clerics to Combat Lure of al-Qaeda," *Washington Post*, May 7, 2006.

14. Nibras Kazimi, "Zarqawi's Anti-Shia Legacy: Original or Borrowed." Footnote 5. Published in *Current Trends in Islamic Ideology*, vol. 4, 53–72 (Washington, DC: Hudson Institute, 2006).

15. Interview with Jamal Khashoggi, media adviser to Ambassador Prince Turki al-Faisal, March 3, 2004.

16. Al-Rasheed, *Contesting the Saudi State*, 74.

17. Interview with a U.S. embassy official in Riyadh, March 15, 2004.

18. "List of Individuals Detained by the Department of Defense at Guantanamo Bay Cuba from January 2002 Through May 15, 2006," http://www.defenselink.mil/news/May2006/d20060515%20List.pdf.

19. Ottaway, "U.S. Eyes Money Trails of Saudi-Backed Charities," *Washington Post*, Aug. 19, 2004.

20. Ibid.

21. Ibid.

22. Interview with Sheikh Saleh al-Sheikh.

23. Interview with a U.S. embassy official in Riyadh, March 15, 2004.

24. Ottaway, "U.S. Eyes Money Trails of Saudi-Backed Charities."

25. Ibid.

26. Interview with a Saudi security official in Riyadh, March 15, 2004.

27. "Saudi Arabia: Terrorist Financing Issues," Congressional Research Service, Library of Congress, February 8, 2006, 9–10.

28. Ibid., 11–12.

29. Ibid., 10.

30. Ottaway, "U.S. Eyes Money Trails of Saudi-Backed Charities."

31. Interview with a Saudi official, June 10, 2004.

32. Ottaway, "U.S. Eyes Money Trails of Saudi-Backed Charities."

33. Ibid.

34. Interview with a Saudi official, June 10, 2004.

35. Ottaway, "U.S. Eyes Money Trails of Saudi-Backed Charities."

36. Telephone interview with Hamid Algar, July 1, 2004.

37. Telephone interview with Khaled Abou El Fadl, March 4, 2004.

38. Interview with a U.S. embassy official in Riyadh, March 15, 2004.

Chapter 12. The Hunt for Wahhabis in America

1. National Commission on Terrorist Attacks upon the United States, *Monograph on Terrorist Financing*, 8.

2. Susan Schmidt, "Spreading Saudi Fundamentalism in U.S., Network of Wahhabi Mosques, Schools, Web Sites Probed by FBI," *Washington Post*, Oct. 2, 2003.

3. Interview with Saleh al-Hussayen, March 13, 2004.

4. David B. Ottaway, "Groups, U.S. Battle over 'Global Terrorist' Label," *Washington Post*, Nov. 14, 2004.

5. Ibid.

6. *The 9/11 Commission Report*, 114.

7. *Monograph on Terrorist Financing*, 12.

8. Ibid., 114–28.

9. Ibid., 116.

10. Ibid., 188–220.

11. Ibid., 121.

12. Ibid., 123.

13. "Additional al-Haramain Branches, Former Leader Designated by Treasury as Al Qaeda Supporters," U.S. Treasury Department, Office of Public Affairs, June 2, 2004, http://www.treas.gov/press/releases/js1703.htm.

14. Interview with Sheikh Saleh al-Sheikh, March 17, 2004.

15. Interview with a U.S. embassy official in Riyadh, March 15, 2004.

16. "Remarks of Treasury DAS Juan Zarate on Joint U.S. and Saudi Action in the Financial War on Terrorism," U.S. Treasury Department, Office of Public Affairs, June 2, 2004, http://www.treas.gov/press/releases/js1705.htm.

17. "U.S.-Based Branch of Al Haramain Foundation Linked to Terror; Treasury Designates U.S. Branch, Director," U.S. Treasury Department, Office of Public Affairs, Sept. 9, 2004, http://www.treas.gov/press/releases/js1895.htm.

18. E-mail interview with Soliman al-Buthe, Sept. 15, 2004.

19. *The 9/11 Commission Report*, 217.

20. Richard Boucher, daily press briefing, State Department, Dec. 8, 2003.

21. Schmidt and Caryle Murphy, "U.S. Revokes Visa of Cleric at Saudi Embassy," *Washington Post*, Dec. 7, 2003.

22. Murphy and Schmidt, "U.S. Revokes Visas of 16 at Islamic Institute," *Washington Post*, Jan. 29, 2004.

23. Ottaway, "U.S. Eyes Money Trails of Saudi-Backed Charities," *Washington Post*, Aug. 19, 2004.

24. *9/11 Report: Joint Congressional Inquiry*, U.S. House of Representatives, Permanent Select Committee on Intelligence, and U.S. Senate, Select Committee on Intelligence, July 24, 2003.

25. Charlie Brennan, "A Prince to Aspen," *Rocky Mountain News*, Dec. 28, 2002.

26. *Monograph on Terrorist Financing*, 138.

27. Ibid., 139.

28. Ibid., 171.

29. Glenn R. Simpson, "U.S. Regulators Scrutinize Many Bank Transactions Not Properly Recorded," *Wall Street Journal*, Jan. 14, 2004.

30. Kathleen Day and Terrence O'Hara, "Riggs May Be Fined over Bank Secrecy Act," *Washington Post*, April 2, 2004.

31. David Leigh and Rob Evans, "BAE Accused of Secretly Paying Pounds 1bn to Saudi Prince," *Guardian*, June 7, 2007; "Saudi Prince 'Received Arms Cash,'" BBC News, June 7, 2007.

32. Ibid.

33. "Saudi Prince Issues Statement, Denies BAE Payoff," BBC Worldwide Monitoring, June 12, 2007; "This Is an Extremely Serious Allegation," *Guardian*, June 8, 2007.

34. William Simpson, *The Prince*, 148–49.

35. Ibid., 148.

36. Larry Black, "Westland Faces Bribery Claim over Saudi Order," *Independent*, Oct. 8, 1991; Rosie Waterhouse, "Corruption Alleged over Helicopters Deal," *Independent*, April 18, 1992.

37. Interview with a congressional source dealing with U.S. arms sales to Saudi Arabia, June 15, 2007.

38. "Saudis' Arms Cut Threatens British Contracts," Press Association, Feb. 1, 1994.

39. Interview with a congressional source.

40. "BBC Lifts the Lid on Secret BAE Slush Fund," BBC News, Oct. 5, 2004.

41. David Leppard, "Arms Firm Paid $600,000 for Saudi Royal's Honeymoon," *Sunday Times,* June 17, 2007.

42. "Transcript of Osama bin Laden Tape Broadcast on al-Jazeera," Associated Press, Feb. 11, 2003, http://dc.indymedia.org/newswire/display/50812.

43. Scott Macleod, "The Enemy Within," *Time International*, May 26, 2003.

44. NBC News, *Today*, May 14, 2003.

45. "The U.S. Ambassador in Riyadh Drops 'Two Bombs' About the Crown Prince and the Throne," Financial Times Information, Global News Wire, July 9, 2003.

46. "US, Saudi Arabia Deny Reports Envoy Was Expelled," Agence France-Presse, Sept. 26, 2003.

47. Crown Prince Abdullah, "Address to the Nation," May 13, 2003. See http://saudiembassy.net/ReportLink/Report_Extremism_Oct03.pdf.

48. George Tenet, *At the Center of the Storm*, 247.

49. Ibid., 249.

50. Ibid., 248–49.

51. "Saudis Discover al-Qaeda Training Camps," Associated Press, Jan. 15, 2004.

52. Prince Bandar bin Sultan, "We Will Lose Our War Against Terror Unless . . . ," *Al-Watan*, June 1, 2004, translated under the title "Saudi Ambassador to Washington: We Must Declare War on Terrorists," Middle East Media Research Institute, special dispatch, no. 725, June 3, 2004, republished as an op-ed piece in the *Washington Post*, June 6, 2004.

53. "Top al-Qaeda Militant Killed," Reuters, July 4, 2005.

54. *Monograph on Terrorist Financing*, 127.

55. Ibid.

56. Testimony of Daniel Glaser, deputy assistant secretary, U.S. Treasury Department, Office of Terrorist Financing and Financial Crimes, before the U.S. Senate Committee on the Judiciary, Nov. 8, 2005.

57. "The Terrorist Finance Tracking Program," hearing before the U.S. House of Representatives Subcommittee on Oversight and Investigations, Financial Services Committee, July 11, 2006.

58. Testimony of Stuart Levey before the U.S. Senate Banking, Housing and Urban Affairs Committee, Federal News Service, April 4, 2006.

59. "Saudi Arabia Fired 200 Muslim Preachers," *Al-Bawaba*, May 29, 2003; "Saudis Suspend 900 Imams for 'Negligence,'" Agence France-Presse, March 17, 2004.

60. Ottaway, "Saudi Effort Draws on Radical Clerics to Combat Lure of al-Qaeda," *Washington Post*, May 7, 2006.

61. "Saudi Daily Says over 1,500 'Extremists' Freed After Repenting," BBC Monitoring Middle East, Nov. 26, 2007.

62. Ottaway, "Saudi Effort Draws on Radical Clerics." See also Terrence Henry, "Get out of Jihad Free," *Atlantic*, June 2007; Christopher Boucek, "Extremist Reeducation and Rehabilitation in Saudi Arabia," Jamestown Foundation, *Terrorism Monitor* 5, no. 16 (Aug. 16, 2007).

63. Ottaway, "Saudi Effort Draws on Radical Clerics."

64. Ibid.

65. Raid Qusti, "Two Religious Courts to Try Terror Suspects," *Arab News*, June 18, 2007.

66. Interview with Sheikh Saleh al-Sheikh, March 17, 2004.

67. Interview with Sherard Cowper-Coles, March 22, 2004.

Chapter 13. *"Just Say No"*

1. Thomas E. Ricks, "Briefing Depicted Saudis as Enemies," *Washington Post*, Aug. 6, 2002; Laurent Murawiec, "Taking Saudi out of Arabia," Defense Policy Board, July 10, 2002. See http://www.unitedstatesaction.com/taking_saudi_out_of_arabia.htm.

2. David B. Ottaway and Robert G. Kaiser, "Saudis May Seek U.S. Exit," *Washington Post*, Jan. 18, 2002.

3. Ricks, "American Way of War in Saudi Desert," *Washington Post*, Jan. 7, 2003.

4. Bill Sammon, "Saudis Want Inspections, Not Iraq Attack," *Washington Times*, Aug. 28, 2002.

5. Ibid.

6. Dana Milbank and Glenn Kessler, "Bush Moves to Ease Tensions with Saudis," *Washington Post*, Aug. 28, 2002.

7. Elsa Walsh, "The Prince," *New Yorker*, March 24, 2003.

8. Ibid.

9. Bob Woodward, *Plan of Attack*, 264–66.

10. Bandar met in mid-March 2003 with reporters from the *Washington Post*, the *New York Times*, the *Wall Street Journal*, and *Time*. Information was provided to the author by *Post* colleagues and a Bandar aide.

11. George Tenet, *At the Center of the Storm*, 350.

12. Ibid., 341.

13. Rowan Scarborough, "U.S. to Pull Forces from Saudi Arabia," *Washington Times*, April 30, 2003.

14. Ibid.

15. Bradley Graham and Ricks, "Contingency Plan Shifts Saudi Base to Qatar," *Washington Post*, April 6, 2002.

16. Ottaway, "Viewing Oil as a Bonding Agent," *Washington Post*, Feb. 12, 2002.

17. Ibid. For accounts of the negotiation's breakdown, see also the following: "Saudi Gas Opening Slams Shut," *Energy Compass*, June 5, 2003; Omar Hasan, "ExxonMobil Evaluating Letter from Saudi Oil Minister on Gas Project," Agence France-Presse, June 5, 2003; "Landmark Saudi Gas Deal 'Scrapped,'" BBC News, June 5, 2003; "Talks over Saudi Mega-Gas Deals Coming to a Close," *Al-Bawaba*, Jan. 23, 2003; "Saudi Arabia: Saudi Oil Minister to Go?," Economist Intelligence Unit, EIU Business Middle East, Feb. 1, 2003; "Exxon, Shell Bosses Prepare for Saudi Talks," *International Oil Daily*, June 20, 2002; "Saudi Arabia: Rise and Fall of Saudi Arabia's Great Gas Initiative," *Middle East Economic Digest*, June 27, 2003.

18. See, for example, Craig Unger, *House of Bush, House of Saud*; Robert Bryce, *Cronies: Oil, the Bushes, and the Rise of Texas, America's Superstate*.

19. Interview with senior Oil Ministry official in Riyadh, Feb. 6, 2008.

20. Abd-al-Latif al-Minawi, "Saudi Sources: Normalization with Israel Caused 24-Hour Crisis with US," *Asharq Alawsat*," reprinted in English by Financial Times Information, Global News Wire, June 5, 2003.

21. "Saudi Arabia: Rise and Fall of Saudi Arabia's Great Gas Initiative," *Middle East Economic Digest*.

22. "Saudi Arabia Signs Gas Exploration Deals with Sinopec, Lukoil, Repsol, ENI," AFX News Limited, March 7, 2004.

23. George W. Bush, remarks at the twentieth anniversary of the National Endowment for Democracy, United States Chamber of Commerce, Washington, DC, Nov. 6, 2003, http://whitehouse.gov/news/releases/2003/11/20031106-2.html.

24. Thomas Lippman, "Seventy Years of US Tolerance of Saudi Human Rights Abuses," testimony before the U.S. House of Representatives Subcommittee on International Organizations, Human Rights and Oversight, June 14, 2007.

25. Bush, State of the Union Address, White House, Jan. 20, 2004, http://www.whitehouse.gov/news/releases/2004/01/20040120-7.html.

26. Hassen Zenati, "Mubarak Takes Reins of Revolt Against Bush Mideast Initiative," Agence France-Presse, Feb. 26, 2004.

27. "No Reforms Under Foreign Pressure," *Arab News*, Feb. 25, 2004.

28. "Kingdom Warns US Against Imposing Reforms," *Arab News*, Feb. 20, 2004.

29. "Press Briefing by Secretary of State Colin L. Powell and Saudi Arabia Foreign Minister Prince Saud al-Faisal," U.S. State Department, Office of the Spokesman, Kuwait City, Kuwait, March 20, 2004.

30. Ibid.

31. Ottaway, "U.S.-Saudi Relations Show Signs of Stress," *Washington Post*, April 21, 2004.

32. Copy of e-mail statement by Consul General Gina Abercrombie-Winstanley to http://alsaha.net, Al-Saha, March 20, 2004.

33. Ottaway, "U.S.-Saudi Relations Show Signs of Stress."

Chapter 14. The Search for New Allies

1. Ali al-Naimi, "The Asian Outlook and Saudi Arabia's Oil Policy," World Petroleum Congress, Shanghai, China, Sept. 29, 2001.

2. Ibid.

3. Interview with Saud al-Faisal, March 17, 2004.

4. "China to Shift Crude Oil Imports Sources in 2007," Global Insight, Jan. 10, 2007; "Angola Tops China's List of Oil Suppliers in March," Platts Oilgram News, May 1, 2007.

5. "Chinese Leader Stresses Global Harmony in Speech to Saudi Advisory Body-Text," New China News Agency, Riyadh, April 23, 2006; BBC Worldwide Monitoring, April 24, 2006.

6. "Chinese President Concludes Visit to Saudi," Agence France-Presse, April 24, 2006.

7. Richard L. Russell, "A Saudi Nuclear Option?," *Survival* 43, no.2 (Summer 2001): 73.

8. Simon Henderson, "PolicyWatch #1095: Chinese-Saudi Cooperation: Oil but ALSO Missiles," Washington Institute for Near East Policy, April 21, 2006.

9. Interview with Chas. Freeman, Nov. 10, 2003.

10. Interview with Saud al-Faisal.

11. Abd al-Rahman al-Rashid, "Iran: Neighbors Fearful of Tehran's Drive to Acquire Nuclear Weapons," Asharq Alawsat, Oct. 8, 2003, reprinted in English by Financial Times Information's Global News Wire and BBC Monitoring International Reports, Oct. 8, 2003.

12. "U.S.-Pakistani F-16 Sale Goes into Effect," *Facts on File World News Digest*, Dec. 4, 1981; Mary Anne Weaver, "Military Men for Rent: World's No. 2 Tries Harder," *Christian Science Monitor*, Oct. 3, 1983.

13. Steve Coll and John Mintz, "Saudi Aid to Iraqi A-Bomb Effort Alleged," *Washington Post*, July 25, 1994; "Saudi Arabia Special Weapons," Global Security, Feb. 11, 2004, http://www.globalsecurity.org/wmd/world/saudi.

14. David R. Sands, "Israeli General Says Saudis Seek to Buy Pakistani Nukes," *Washington Times*, Nov. 23, 2003.

15. Ewen MacAskill and Ian Traynor, "Saudis Consider Nuclear Bomb," *Guardian*, Sept. 18, 2003; Henderson, "PolicyWatch #793: Toward a Saudi Nuclear Option: The Saudi-Pakistani Summit," Washington Institute for Near East Policy, Oct. 16, 2003.

16. Malcolm Moore, "Russia Becomes the Biggest Oil Producer," *Daily Telegraph*, Jan. 10, 2003.

17. Abdulaziz Sager, "Abdullah's Visit Signals New Saudi-Russian Era," *Arab News*, Sept. 3, 2003.

18. Delphine Thouvenot, "Saudi Crown Prince Makes Historic Visit to Russia, Focuses on Energy," Agence France-Presse, Sept. 2, 2003.

19. Vladimir Putin, speech at the forty-third Munich Conference on Security Policy, Feb. 10, 2007.

20. Ibid.

21. "Russia Is Saudi Partner on Energy Market," TASS News Agency, Feb. 12, 2007.

22. "Saudi King Holds Talks with Russian President, Says Relations 'Stronger,'" BBC Worldwide Monitoring, Feb. 12, 2007; "Putin Offers Saudi Arabia Nuclear Energy Cooperation from Russia," AFX International Focus, Feb. 12, 2007.

23. "Saudi Says 'No Barriers to Nuclear Cooperation with Russia,'" BBC Worldwide Monitoring, Feb. 15, 2007.

24. "Putin's Visit," *Arab News*, Feb. 13, 2007.

25. Oliver Knox, "Bush, Kerry Dueling over Saudi Arabia," Agence France-Presse, Aug. 12, 2004.

26. Tamara Lytle, "Graham Books Accuses Bush of Saudi Cover-up," *Orlando Sentinel*, Sept. 8, 2004.

27. "Saudis Concerned over Effort to Tie White House to Royal Family," *Frontrunner*, Oct. 5, 2004.

Chapter 15. End of the *"Special Relationship"*

1. Colin Powell, remarks at the McConnell Center for Political Leadership, University of Louisville, Kentucky, Nov. 19, 2001.

2. Interview with Prince Bandar, Jan. 30, 2002.

3. Thomas L. Friedman, "An Intriguing Signal from the Saudi Crown Prince," *New York Times*, Feb. 17, 2002.

4. Bandar bin Sultan, "Why Israel Must Stop the Terror," *Washington Post*, April 5, 2002.

5. Karen DeYoung, *Soldier*, 383.

6. Patrick E. Tyler, "Saudis Have Frank Message for Bush," *New York Times*, April 25, 2002.

7. James Gerstenzang, "Saudi Leader Warns Bush," *Los Angeles Times*, April 26, 2002.

8. DeYoung, *Soldier*, 386.

9. Gerstenzang, "Saudi Leader Warns Bush."

10. Bill Sammon, "Saudis Want Inspections, Not Iraq Attack," *Washington Times*, Aug. 28, 2002.

11. Vali Nasr, *The Shia Revival*, 21.

12. Bob Woodward, *Plan of Attack*, 229–30.

13. Interview with Prince Turki by editors and reporters at the *Washington Post*, Jan. 31, 2002.

14. Joel Brinkley, "Saudi Warns U.S. Iraq May Face Disintegration," *New York Times*, Sept. 23, 2005.

15. Saud al-Faisal, "The Fight Against Extremism and the Search for Peace," Council on Foreign Relations, Sept. 23, 2005.

16. Saud al-Faisal, "Saudi Arabia and the International Oil Market," James A. Baker III Institute for Public Policy, Rice University, Sept. 21, 2005.

17. Nawaf Obaid, "Stepping into Iraq," *Washington Post*, Nov. 29, 2006.

18. Obaid, "Fragmented Iraq: Implications for Saudi National Security."

19. Ibid.

20. "Saudi Arabia, Pakistan Emerging as Broad 'Strategic Problems' for US: Abizaid," Agence France-Presse, Jan. 29, 2004.

21. Paul Pillar, "The Middle East to 2020," paper presented for discussion at the annual Commonwealth Conference: Focus on 2020, Dec. 8–9, 2003, http://www.dni.gov/nic/NIC_2020_2003_12_08_intro.html.

22. "British Spy Chiefs Feared US Invasion of Saudi Arabia, Kuwait in 1973," Agence France-Presse, Jan. 1, 2004.

23. Ibid.

24. Lizette Alvarez, "Britain Says U.S. Planned to Seize Oil in '73 Crisis," *New York Times*, Jan. 2, 2004; Owen Bowcott, "UK Feared Americans Would Invade Gulf During 1973 Oil Crisis," *Guardian*, Jan. 1, 2004.

25. Robert C. Toth, "U.S. May Retaliate if Arabs Continue Boycott—Kissinger," *Los Angeles Times*, Nov. 22, 1973.

26. Reuters, "Saudi Arabia Warns U.S. Against Oil Countermoves," *New York Times*, Nov. 23, 1973.

27. Mai Yamani, "American Invasion Plan Stirs Fierce Saudi Debate: Echoes of 1973," *International Herald Tribune*, Jan. 9, 2004.

28. Matthew Simmons, "The Saudi Arabian Oil Miracle," PowerPoint presentation, Center for Strategic and International Studies Conference, Washington, DC, Feb. 24, 2004.

29. Ibid.

30. Ali al-Naimi, "The Global Energy Market and the U.S.-Saudi Petroleum Relations," Center for Strategic and International Studies Conference, Washington, DC, April 27, 2004.

31. Woodward, *Plan of Attack*, 324.

32. "Saudi Envoy Promised Bush a Drop in Oil Prices Ahead of Election," Bloomberg News, April 19, 2004.

33. "Sen. Schumer: Boot Saudi Ambassador from U.S. for Plotting to Fix Presidential Election," States News Service, April 19, 2004.

34. "Statement by Saudi Oil Minister al-Naimi," PRNewswire, Amsterdam, May 21, 2004; Bruce Stanley, "U.S. Energy Chief: Saudi Arabia Ready to Boost Crude Production," Associated Press, May 24, 2004.

35. Kate Dorian et al., "Crude Bearish as Naimi Calls for Extra 2-mil b/d," Platts Oilgram Price Report, May 24, 2004.

36. "Saudi Official Says Oil Price 'Clearly Way Too High,'" AFX News Limited, Sept. 29, 2004.

37. "Saudis Have Big Plans to Increase Oil Reserves," Canwest News Service, Dec. 28, 2004.

38. Jane Wardell, "Saudi Arabian Oil Minister Says Fear Factor Adding $10 to $15 to Oil Price," Associated Press, Nov. 29, 2004.

39. Hassan M. Fattah, "Why Arab Men Hold Hands," *New York Times*, May 1, 2005.

40. "Bush Administration Welcomes Saudi Energy Plan" and "U.S., Saudi Arabia Vow to Forge New, Strengthened Partnership," States News Service, April 25, 2005.

41. Ibid.

42. Interview with Dan Butler, Energy Department forecaster, Feb. 26, 2003.

43. "Securing U.S. Energy in a Changing World," Middle East Policy Council Forum, Russell Senate Office Building, Washington, DC, Sept. 17, 2004, http://www.mepc.org/forums_chcs/37.asp.

44. Saudi Press Agency, July 20, 2005, reprinted in *Ain-al-Yaqeen*, July 29, 2005.

45. "President's Statement on Saudi Arabian Ambassador Bandar," White House, Office of the Press Secretary, July 20, 2005.

Chapter 16. The New "Strategic Dialogue"

1. "Transcript of Interview with Prince Turki al-Faisal in the New York Times Magazine," August 28, 2005, Royal Embassy of Saudi Arabia, Washington, DC, http://www.saudiembassy.net/2005News/Statements/StateDetail.asp?cIndex=546.

2. "Transcript of Prince Turki al-Faisal's Address at Georgetown," July 24, 2006, Royal Embassy of Saudi Arabia, Washington, DC, http://www.saudiembassy.net/2006News/Statements/SpeechDetail.asp?cIndex=633.

3. Ibid.

4. Robin Wright, "U.S., Saudi Arabia Inaugurate New 'Strategic Dialogue,'" *Washington Post*, Nov. 13, 2005.

5. Sean McCormack, "U.S.-Saudi Strategic Dialogue," press statement, State Department, May 18, 2006.

6. Ibid.

7. Interview with a senior Saudi official, July 17, 2006.

8. Ibid.

9. Ibid.

10. NSC Given Wide Powers," *Arab News*, Oct. 19, 2005.

11. This information was provided by two Saudi officials involved in discussions at the White House in November 2006.

12. Saudi Press Agency, July 14, 2006; reprinted by Saudi-US Relations Information Service, July 18, 2006.

13. Tony Snow, Presss Briefing, White House Press Office, July 14, 2006, http://whitehouse.gov/news/releases/2006/07/20060714-4.html.

14. Interview with a Saudi official, June 12, 2007.

15. "Ehud Olmert's Sde Boker Address," *Jerusalem Post*, Nov. 27, 2006.

16. Interview with a senior European diplomat, March 16, 2007.

17. "Speech of President Bashar al-Assad at Journalists Union 4th Conference," Syrian Arab News Agency, Aug. 15, 2006.

18. Interview with a Saudi official, Nov. 9, 2006.

19. Seymour M. Hersh, "The Redirection," *New Yorker*, March 5, 2007.

20. Condoleezza Rice, "The New Way Forward in Iraq," U.S. Senate, Foreign Relations Committee, Jan. 11, 2007; "Hearing of the Senate Foreign Relations Committee; Subject: The Administration's Plan for Iraq," Federal News Service, Jan. 11, 2007.

21. Wright and Peter Baker, "Iraq, Jordan See Threat to Election from Iran," *Washington Post*, Dec. 8, 2004.

22. "Prince Turki Remarks at the 2006 Middle Eastern Studies Association Conference in Boston, Massachusetts on November 18, 2006," Royal Embassy of Saudi Arabia, Washington, DC, htte://www.saudiembassy.net/2006News/Statements/SpeechDetail.asp?cIndex=660.

23. "Transcript of Prince Turki al-Faisal Remarks to the Center for Strategic and International Studies in Washington, D.C.," Oct. 4, 2006, Royal Embassy of Saudi Arabia, http://www.saudiembassy.net/2006News/Statements/SpeechDetail.asp?cIndex =644.

24. This information comes from Saudi officials and Americans close to both Turki and Bandar who asked that they not be identified by name.

25. This figure was provided by a Saudi official who was uncertain whether it included both Bandar's embassy and personal expenses.

26. This information was provided by Saudi officials and Americans close to Prince Turki.

27. Wright, "Royal Intrigue, Unpaid Bills Preceded Saudi Ambassador's Exit," *Washington Post*, Dec. 23, 2006.

28. Fadilah al-Jaffal, "Former Saudi Ambassador in Washington Says He Will Devote His Time to Research and Studies Center," *Al-Hayat*, Feb. 11, 2007, reprinted in English under the title "Former Envoy to USA Comments on Ties, Iran, Iraq Issues," BBC Worldwide Monitoring, Feb. 12, 2007.

29. Wright, "Saudi Ambassador Abruptly Resigns, Leaves Washington," *Washington Post*, Dec. 12, 2006.

30. This piece of royal al-Saud family history is based on information from three sources interviewed during research for this book in 2006 and 2007.

31. Mohammed Ali Saleh, "Prince Turki Talks to Asharq Alawsat," *Asharq Alawsat*, Feb. 18, 2007.

32. Interview with a senior Saudi official, July 18, 2007.

33. "Ehud Olmert's Sde Boker Address."

34. Glenn Kessler, "Olmert, Abbas Agree to Hold Biweekly Talks," *Washington Post*, March 28, 2007.

35. Interview with a senior European diplomat, March 16, 2007.

36. Jim Hoagland, "Bush's Royal Troubles," *Washington Post*, March 28, 2007.

37. "The Limits of Bad Policy," *Washington Post*, April 1, 2007.

38. Martin Indyk, "The Honeymoon's Over for Bush and the Saudis," *Washington Post*, April 29, 2007.

39. *Gulf Times*, July 3, 2007; Nicholas Tohme, "Lebanese Troops Bombard Islamists," Middle East Online, July 9, 2007.

40. Ned Parker, "The Conflict in Iraq: Saudi Role in Insurgency," *Los Angeles Times*, July 15, 2007; "Many Detainees in Iraq Are Saudi," Associated Press, July 16, 2007.

41. "Iraq Detains Hundreds of Saudi Militants: Security Aide," Agence France-Presse, July 15, 2007.

42. Kate Dorian et al., "Saudis Hold to 12.5 million b/d Capacity Plan," Platts Oilgram Price Report, May 3, 2007.

43. "OPEC Production Cuts Have Created Tight Market Conditions, Pushing Oil Prices Toward New Highs," Economist Intelligence Unit, Country Monitor Select, July 9, 2007.

44. Christopher M. Blanchard and Richard F. Grimmett, "The Gulf Security Dialogue and Related Arms Sale Proposals," Congressional Research Service, Jan. 14, 2008.

45. Turki al-Faisal, "Setbacks in the Reform Process and How to Revive the Momentum," Arab Reform Initiative Annual Conference, Amman, Jordan, April 18–19, 2007.

46. Interview with a senior Saudi official, July 17, 2007.

47. Starting in 2003, Saudi Aramco was in a joint venture with Royal Dutch/Shell called Motiva Enterprises, which owned four refineries and 18,279 gas stations. See "Foreign Direct Investment in U.S. Energy 2003," U.S. Department of Energy, Energy Information Administration, http://tonto.eia.doe.gov/ftproot/financial/fdi2003.pdf.

48. Information provided to the author in January 2008 by a Saudi official who worked on the Al Arabiya production.

Selected Bibliography

Abir, Mordechai. *Saudi Arabia in the Oil Era: Regime and Elites, Conflict and Collaboration*. Boulder, Co: Westview Press, 1988.

Al-Farsy, Fouad. *Saudi Arabia: A Case Study in Development*. London: Kegan Paul International, 1986.

Al-Rasheed, Madawi. *Contesting the Saudi State: Islamic Voices from a New Generation*. Cambridge, UK: Cambridge University Press, 2007.

Albright, Madeleine. *Madame Secretary: A Memoir*. New York: Miramax Books, 2003.

Allen, Charles. *God's Terrorists: The Wahhabi Cult and the Hidden Roots of Modern Jihad*. Cambridge, MA: Da Capo Press, 2006.

Alsanea, Rajaa. *Girls of Riyadh*. New York: Penguin Press, 2007.

American Israel Public Affairs Committee. "Memorandum: F-15s to Saudi Arabia—A Threat to Peace." Washington, DC. No date.

Atwan, Abdel Bari. *The Secret History of al Qaeda*. Berkeley, CA: University of California Press, 2006.

Baer, Robert. *See No Evil: The True Story of a Ground Soldier in the CIA's War on Terrorism*. New York: Three Rivers Press, 2002.

———. *Sleeping with the Devil: How Washington Sold Our Soul for Saudi Crude*. New York: Crown Publishers, 2003.

Baker, James A., III. *The Politics of Diplomacy: Revolution, War and Peace, 1989–1992*. New York: G.P. Putnam's Sons, 1995.

Battle, Joyce, ed. *U.S. Propaganda in the Middle East—the Early Cold War*. Electronic Briefing Book No. 78. National Security Archive, George Washington University, Dec. 13, 2002.

Bin Sultan, Khaled, and Patrick Seale. *Desert Warrior: A Personal View of the Gulf War by the Joint Forces Commander*. New York: HarperCollins, 1995.

Bradley, John R. *Saudi Arabia Exposed: Inside a Kingdom in Crisis*. New York: Palgrave Macmillan, 2005.

Brisard, Jean-Charles, and Guillaume Dasquié. *Ben Laden: La Vérité Interdite*. Paris: Éditions Denoël, 2001.

Bronson, Rachel. *Thicker than Oil: America's Uneasy Partnership with Saudi Arabia*. New York: Oxford University Press, 2006.

Bryce, Robert. *Cronies: Oil, the Bushes, and the Rise of Texas, America's Superstate*. New York: Public Affairs, 2004.

Burr, J. Millard, and Robert O. Collins. *Alms for Jihad: Charity and Terrorism in the Islamic World*. Cambridge, UK: Cambridge University Press, 2006.

Burr, William, ed. *The October War and U.S. Policy*. Electronic Briefing Book No. 98. National Security Archive, George Washington University, Oct. 7, 2003.

Bush, Barbara. *Reflections: Life After the White House*. New York: Scribner, 2003.

Bush, George, and Brent Scowcroft. *A World Transformed*. New York: Alfred A. Knopf, 1998.

Cambridge Energy Research Associates Inc. "The U.S.-Saudi Relationship: Still Special, but Changing." Cambridge, MA, August 2007.

Carter, Jimmy. *Public Papers of the Presidents of the United States: Jimmy Carter*. Vol. 2, 1978. Washington, DC: U.S. Government Printing Office, 1979.

———. *Public Papers of the Presidents of the United States, Jimmy Carter*. Vol. 2, 1979. Washington, DC: U.S. Government Printing Office, 1980.

———. *Public Papers of the Presidents of the United States, Jimmy Carter*. Vol. 1, 1980–81. Washington, DC: U.S. Government Printing Office. 1981.

Clinton, Bill. *My Life*. New York: Alfred A. Knopf, 2004.

Clinton, William J. *Public Papers of the Presidents of the United States: William J. Clinton*. Vol. 1, 1999. Washington, DC: U.S. Government Printing Office, 2000.

Coll, Steve. *The Bin Ladens: An Arabian Family in the American Century*. New York: Penguin Books, 2008.

———. *Ghost Wars: The Secret History of the CIA, Afghanistan, and Bin Laden, from the Soviet Invasion to September 10, 2001*. New York: Penguin Books, 2004.

Congressional Research Service. *Saudi Arabia: Current Issues and U.S. Relations*. CRS Report for Congress, August 2, 2006. Library of Congress.

———. *Saudi Arabia: Terrorist Financing Issues*. CRS Report for Congress February 8, 2006. Library of Congress.

Crile, George. *Charlie Wilson's War: The Extraordinary Story of How the Wildest Man in Congress and a Rogue CIA Agent Changed the History of Our Times*. New York: Grove Press, 2003.

DeYoung, Karen. *Soldier: The Life of Colin Powell*. New York: Alfred A. Knopf, 2006.

Delong-Bas, Natana J. *Wahhabi Islam: From Revival and Reform to Global Jihad*. New York: Oxford University Press, 2004.

Denard, Cheryl. *Civil Democratic Islam: Partners, Resources, and Strategies*. Santa Monica, CA: Rand Corporation, 2003.

Dreyfuss, Robert. *Devil's Game: How the United States Helped Unleash Fundamentalist Islam*. New York: Henry Holt and Company, 2005.

Ehrenfeld, Rachel. *Funding Evil: How Terrorism Is Financed—and How to Stop It*. Chicago: Bonus Books, 2003.

Eisenhower, Dwight D. *Papers as President, 1953–1961, Appointment Books*. Dwight D. Eisenhower Library, Abilene, KS.

———. *The Papers of Dwight David Eisenhower*. Vol. 16, *The Presidency: The Middle Way*. Baltimore: Johns Hopkins University Press, 1996.

———. *Dwight D. Eisenhower, Records as President, 1953–1961*. White House Central Files, Official File, Box 737, OF 144-B4, Islamic and Moslem Religion.

El Fadl, Khaled M. Abou. *And God Knows the Soldiers: The Authoritative and Authoritarian in Islamic Discourses*. Lanham, MD: University Press of America, 2001.

Elbel, Robert E. *China's Energy Future: The Middle Kingdom Seeks Its Place in the Sun*. Washington, DC: Center for Strategic and International Studies, 2005.

Emerson, Steven. *The American House of Saud: The Secret Petrodollar Connection*. New York: Franklin Watts, 1985.

Erlich, Haggai. *Saudi Arabia and Ethiopia: Islam, Christianity and Politics Entwined*. Boulder, CO: Lynne Rienner Publishers, 2007.

Foreign Relations of the United States, Diplomatic Papers, 1943. Vol. 4, *The Near East and Africa*. Washington, DC: U.S. Government Printing Office, 1964.

Foreign Relations of the United States, 1955–1957. Vol. 8, *South Asia*. Washington, DC: U.S. Government Printing Office, 1987.

Foreign Relations of the United States, Diplomatic Papers, 1944. Vol. 5, *The Near East, South Asia and Africa*. Washington, DC: U.S. Government Printing Office, 1965.

Foreign Relations of the United States, 1961–63. Vol. 17, *The Near East 1961–1962*. Washington, DC: U.S. Government Printing Office, 1994.

Freeh, Louis J. *My FBI: Bringing Down the Mafia, Investigating Bill Clinton, and Fighting the War on Terror*. New York: St. Martin's Griffin, 2005.

Gold, Dore. *Hatred's Kingdom: How Saudi Arabia Supports the New Global Terrorism*. Washington, DC: Regnery Publishing, 2003.

Grimmett, Richard F. *Executive-Legislative Consultation on U.S. Arms Sales*." U.S. House of Representatives, Foreign Affairs Committee. Washington, DC: U.S. Government Printing Office, 1982.

Haig, Alexander M., Jr. *Caveat: Realism, Reagan, and Foreign Policy*. New York: Macmillan, 1984.

Henderson, Simon. *After King Fahd: Succession in Saudi Arabia.* Washington, DC: Washington Institute for Near East Policy, 1994.

Hiro, Dilip. *Holy Wars: The Rise of Islamic Fundamentalism.* New York: Routledge, 1989.

International Crisis Group. *Saudi Arabia Backgrounder: Who Are the Islamists?* Report No. 31, Sept. 21, 2004.

Kechichian, Joseph A. *Succession in Saudi Arabia.* New York: Palgrave Macmillan, 2001.

Khalidi, Rashid. *The Iron Cage: The Story of the Palestinian Struggle for Statehood.* Boston: Beacon Press, 2006.

Kissinger, Henry. *Years of Renewal.* New York: Simon and Schuster, 1999.

Laham, Nicholas. *Selling AWACS to Saudi Arabia.* Westport, CT: Praeger, 2002.

Lippman, Thomas W. *Inside the Mirage: America's Fragile Partnership with Saudi Arabia.* Boulder, CO: Westview Press, 2004.

"List of Individuals Detained by the Department of Defense at Guantanamo Bay Cuba from January 2002 Through May 15, 2006." http://www.defenselink.mil/news/May2006/d20060515%20List.pdf.

Long, David. E. *The Kingdom of Saudi Arabia.* Gainesville, FL: University Press of Florida, 1997.

———. *The United States and Saudi Arabia: Ambivalent Allies.* Boulder, CO: Westview Press, 1985.

MacArthur, John R. *Second Front: Censorship and Propaganda in the Gulf War.* New York: Hill and Wang, 1992.

Maley, William, ed. *Fundamentalism Reborn? Afghanistan and the Taliban.* New York: New York University Press, 1998.

Marshall, Paul, ed. *Radical Islam's Rules: The Worldwide Spread of Extreme Sharia Law.* Lanham, MD: Rowman and Littlefield Publishing Group, 2005.

McMillan, Joseph. "U.S.-Saudi Relations: Rebuilding the Strategic Consensus." Post 9/11 Critical Issues Series, no. 186. Institute for National Strategic Studies, National Defense University, November 2001.

Muslim World League. *Resolutions and Recommendations of Islamic Conference.* May 18–20, 1962. Vol. I. Singapore: Tak Seng Press, November 1963.

Nasr, Vali. *The Shia Revival.* New York: W.W. Norton and Company, 2006.

National Commission on Terrorist Attacks upon the United States. *Monograph on Terrorist Financing.* Staff Report to the Commission, 2004, http://www.9-11commission.gov/staff_statements/911_TerrFin_monograph.pdf.

———. *The 9/11 Commission Report: Final Report of the National Commission on Terrorist Attacks upon the United States.* Washington, DC: Government Printing Office, 2004.

Obaid, Nawaf E. "Fragmented Iraq: Implications for Saudi National Security." Saudi National Security Assessment Project, Riyadh, Saudi Arabia, March 15, 2006.

————. "Improving US Intelligence Analysis on the Saudi Arabian Decision-Making Process." John F. Kennedy School of Government, Harvard University, May 1, 1998.

————. *The Oil Kingdom at 100: Petroleum Policymaking in Saudi Arabia.* Washington, DC: Washington Institute for Near East Policy, 2000.

Pillar, Paul. "The Middle East to 2020." Commonwealth Conference: Focus on 2020, December 8–9, 2003.

Posner, Gerald. *Secrets of the Kingdom: The Inside Story of the Saudi-U.S. Connection.* New York: Random House, 2005.

————. *Why America Slept: The Failure to Prevent 9/11.* New York: Random House, 2003.

Powell, Colin L. *My American Journey.* New York: Random House, 1995.

Rabasa, Angel M., et al. *The Muslim World After 9/11.* Santa Monica, CA: Rand Corporation, 2004.

Reagan, Ronald. *Reagan: A Life in Letters.* Edited by Kiran K. Skinner, Annalise Anderson, and Martin Anderson, New York: Free Press, 2003.

————. *The Reagan Diaries.* Edited by Douglas Brinkley. New York: HarperCollins, 2007.

————. *An American Life: The Autobiography.* New York: Simon & Schuster, 1990.

Ross, Dennis. *The Missing Peace: The Inside Story of the Fight for Middle East Peace.* New York: Farrar, Straus and Giroux, 2004.

————. *Statecraft: And How to Restore America's Standing in the World.* New York: Farrar, Straus and Giroux, 2007.

Sardar, Ziauddin. *What Do Muslims Believe? The Roots and Realities of Modern Islam.* New York: Walker and Company, 2007.

Schweizer, Peter. *Victory: The Reagan Administration's Secret Strategy That Hastened the Collapse of the Soviet Union.* New York: Atlantic Monthly Press, 1994.

Shultz, George P. *Turmoil and Triumph: My Years as Secretary of State.* New York: Charles Scribner's Sons, 1993.

Sheehan, Edward R. F. *The Arabs, Israelis and Kissinger.* New York: Thomas Y. Crowell Company, 1976.

Simpson, William. *The Prince: The Secret Story of the World's Most Intriguing Royal.* New York: HarperCollins, 2006.

Suskind, Ron. *The One Percent Doctrine: Deep Inside America's Pursuit of Its Enemies Since 9/11.* New York: Simon and Schuster, 2006.

Teitelbaum, Joshua. *Holier than Thou: Saudi Arabia's Islamic Opposition.* Washington, DC: Washington Institute for Near East Policy, 2000.

Tenet, George. *At the Center of the Storm: My Years at the CIA.* New York: HarperCollins, 2007.

Tertzakian, Peter. *A Thousand Barrels a Second: The Coming Oil Break Point and the Challenges Facing an Energy Dependent World.* New York: McGraw-Hill, 2006.

Trofimov, Yaroslav. *The Siege of Mecca: The Forgotten Uprising in Islam's Holiest Shrine and the Birth of al Qaeda*. New York: Doubleday, 2007.

Truman, Harry S. *The Papers of Harry S. Truman*. Confidential File. Harry S. Truman Library and Museum, Independence, MO.

U.S. Defense Department. Security Assistance Agency. Deputy for Operations and Administration Business Operations. *Fiscal Year Series as of September 30, 2003* and *Fiscal Year Series as of September 30, 2005*.

U.S Department of Energy. Energy Information Administration. "Annual Oil Market Chronology, 2000s." 2001.

Unger, Craig. *House of Bush, House of Saud: The Secret Relationship Between the World's Two Most Powerful Dynasties*. New York: Scribner, 2004.

United States Government Accountability Office. *Information on U.S. Agencies' Efforts to Address Islamic Extremism*. GAO Report to Congressional Requesters, September 2005.

Vitalis, Robert. *America's Kingdom: Mythmaking on the Saudi Oil Frontier*. Palo Alto, CA: Stanford University Press, 2007.

"The War in Afghanistan, 1979–1989." *Cold War International History Project Bulletin*, Woodrow Wilson International Center for Scholars, no. 14/15 (Winter 2003–Spring 2004). 139–192.

Warde, Ibrahim. *The Prince of Fear: The Truth Behind the Financial War on Terror*. Berkeley, CA: University of California Press, 2007.

West, John C. Daily Diary. South Carolina Political Collections, University of South Carolina, Columbia, SC.

———. The Papers of John C. West. South Carolina Political Collections, University of South Carolina, Columbia, SC.

Woodward, Bob. *Plan of Attack*. New York: Simon and Schuster, 2004.

———. *Veil: The Secret Wars of the CIA, 1981–87*. New York: Simon and Schuster, 1987.

———. *The Commanders*. New York: Simon and Schuster, 1991.

Index

A Note on the Author

David B. Ottaway worked for the *Washington Post* from 1971 to 2006, as assistant foreign editor, Africa bureau chief, Cairo bureau chief, national security correspondent, and investigative/special projects reporter. He is the author of several books, including *Chained Together: Mandela, De Klerk, and the Struggle to Remake South Africa*. He is currently a senior scholar at the Woodrow Wilson International Center for Scholars and lives in Washington, D.C.